SWIMMING AGAINST THE CURRENT IN CONTEMPORARY PHILOSOPHY

**STUDIES IN PHILOSOPHY
AND THE HISTORY OF PHILOSOPHY**

General Editor: Jude P. Dougherty

Studies in Philosophy
and the History of Philosophy   Volume 20

Swimming Against the Current in Contemporary Philosophy
Occasional Essays and Papers

by Henry B. Veatch

THE CATHOLIC UNIVERSITY OF AMERICA PRESS
Washington, D.C.

Copyright © 1990
The Catholic University of America Press

All rights reserved

Printed in the United States of America

Library of Congress Cataloging-in-Publication Data
Veatch, Henry Babcock.
  Swimming against the current in contemporary philosophy : occasional essays and papers / by Henry B. Veatch.
  p. cm.—(Studies in philosophy and the history of philosophy ; v. 20)
  Bibliography: p.
  Includes index.
  1. Philosophy, Modern—20th century. 2. Ethics, Modern—20th century. 3. Humanities—History—20th century. 4. Natural law—History—20th century. I. Title. II. Series.
B21.S78 vol. 20
[B804]
100 s—dc 19
[149]   88-18940
ISBN 978-0-8132-3076-4

To Father Armand Maurer, C.S.B., and Father Joseph Owens, C.Ss.R., of the Pontifical Institute of Mediaeval Studies, Toronto—old friends who have never scrupled to suffer at least one old fool gladly!

Contents

Acknowledgments   ix

Introduction: On Trying to Be an Aristotelian or a Thomist in Today's World   1

PART I. QUIETING VARIOUS OF THE ALARMS AND EXCURSIONS IN RECENT PHILOSOPHY

1. Can Philosophy Ever Be a Thing for Hoosiers?   23
2. Folly and Sense in Present-Day Philosophy   43
3. Is Quine a Metaphysician?   57
4. Richard Rorty's Would-Be Deconstruction of Analytic Philosophy   80

PART II. WHAT PRICE ETHICS IN THE EYES OF MODERN MORAL PHILOSOPHERS?

5. Telos and Teleology in Aristotelian Ethics   99
6. Variations, Good and Bad, on the Theme of Right Reason in Ethics   117
7. Language and Ethics: "What's Hecuba to Him, or He to Hecuba?"   141
8. In Appreciation and Refutation of Alan Gewirth's Principle of Generic Consistency   158
9. Ethical Egoism, New Style: Should Its Trademark Be Libertarian or Aristotelian?   173

PART III. A CONCLUDING MISCELLANY, RANGING FROM A DEFENSE OF THE HUMANITIES TO A DEFENSE OF NATURAL LAW

10. The What and the Why of the Humanities   201

viii   CONTENTS

11. Why Need a General Be Human? 219
12. The Poor, Hapless Humanities 237
13. Natural Law: Dead or Alive? 254
14. Can John Finnis Bring Off a Revival of Natural Law? 279
15. Natural Law and the "Is"–"Ought" Question: Queries to Finnis and Grisez 293
16. A Poor Benighted Philosopher Looks at the Issue of Judicial Activism 312

Select Bibliography 331
Index 335

Acknowledgments

I should like most gratefully to acknowledge the kindness of the several publishers, editors, and journals, listed below, who so kindly granted me permission to reprint in this book the following previously published essays and papers:

"Can Philosophy Ever Be a Thing for Hoosiers?" *The Georgetown Symposium on Ethics,* ed. by Rocco Porreco. Lanham, MD: University Press of America, 1984, 1–17.

"Folly and Sense in Present-Day Philosophy." Presidential Address. *Proceedings of the American Catholic Philosophical Association* 14 (1980), 1–14.

"Is Quine a Metaphysician?" *The Review of Metaphysics* 31, 3 (March, 1978), 406–430.

"Deconstruction in Philosophy: Has Rorty Made It the Denouement of Contemporary Analytical Philosophy?" *The Review of Metaphysics* 39, 2 (December, 1985), 303–320.

"Telos and Teleology in Aristotelian Ethics." *Studies in Aristotle,* ed. by Dominic O'Meara. Washington, DC: The Catholic University of America Press, 1981, 279–296.

"Variations, Good and Bad, on the Theme of Right Reason in Ethics." *The Monist* 66, 1 (January, 1983), 49–70.

"Language and Ethics: What's Hecuba to Him, or He to Hecuba?" Presidential Address delivered before the Sixty-Ninth Annual Meeting of the American Philosophical Association (Western Division), Chicago, May 7, 1971. *Proceedings Addresses of the American Philosophical Association* 44 (1971), 45–62.

A review of *Reason and Morality,* by Alan Gewirth. *Ethics, An International Journal of Social, Political and Legal Philosophy* 89, 4 (July, 1979), 401–414.

"The What and the Why of the Humanities." An Address delivered before the American Catholic Philosophical Association. *Proceedings of the American Catholic Philosophical Association* 47 (1973), 21–36.

"Natural Law: Dead or Alive?" *Literature of Liberty* 1, 4 (October–December, 1978), 7–29.

A review of *Natural Law and Natural Rights*, by John Finnis. *The American Journal of Jurisprudence* 26 (1981), 247–251.

"Natural Law and the 'Is–Ought' Question: Queries to Finnis and Grisez." *The Catholic Lawyer* 26, 4 (Autumn, 1981), 251–265.

"A Poor Benighted Philosopher Looks at the Issue of Judicial Activism." *The American Journal of Jurisprudence* 31 (1986), 1–19.

INTRODUCTION: ON TRYING TO BE AN ARISTOTELIAN OR A THOMIST IN TODAY'S WORLD

Given the present dispensation in philosophy, both here and abroad, which of us anymore would quite dare to let it be known that our philosophical affiliations were simply those of an Aristotelian or a Thomist? For would we not be likely to be written off as little more than some kind of crank or, if not a crank, then possibly someone whose philosophic convictions were determined more by religious considerations than by strictly philosophical evidence and argument? Oh, this is not to say that there are not many of us—yes, perhaps even most of us in the profession of philosophy—who find ourselves to be afflicted at times with moments of doubt and depression, and in such a way that the entire present-day scene in philosophy sometimes seems to resemble nothing quite so much as a kind of zoo, made up of the most curious and even unbelievable specimens of philosophical animals! But even into such a zoo, the poor Aristotelians or Thomists of the present day would appear to fit either oddly or not at all. For would they not stand out as little more than philosophical dinosaurs of a sort, all of the other beasts around them being so much more favored, as a result of the long, slow process of what we might call a kind of philosophic natural selection?

More seriously, though, let it be announced right at the outset that nearly all of the essays and papers that follow in this volume have a common concern—a concern with how either an Aristotle or an Aquinas might be made philosophically respectable and competitive once again—and philosophically respectable not merely as eminent figures in the history of Western philosophy, but rather as actual contemporary philosophers themselves. "How, though, is such a thing either possible, or even conceivable?" you will ask. For to judge from the philosophical developments within the last fifty years or so, particularly in the English-speaking world, but no less so on the Continent, the very last thing that one might either suspect or expect would be that either Aristotle or Aquinas were in any way about to come into their own again philosophically.

Oh, this is not to say that directly within the ranks, and even among the leaders of today's regnant Analytic and even Post-Analytic Philosophers, there are not many who have been markedly influenced by Aristotle[1]—John Austin, Gilbert Ryle, Peter Strawson, Elizabeth Anscome, Peter Geach, and more recently perhaps, and each in his own way, Donald Davidson and Alasdair MacIntyre. Still, we would all of us recognize that being influenced by Aristotle is one thing, and being an Aristotelian is quite another; and surely, among Analysts, both past and present, it would be hard to find any who would not think it to be most compromising of their reputations were they to be referred to as Aristotelians, *tout court*!

Yes, for the matter of that, we should perhaps take further note, especially in recent years, of any number of Analysts who have proved themselves to be singularly competent historians of philosophy, and whose historical research has often been centered directly on Aristotle—John Cooper, for example, or Terence Irwin, or Edwin Hartman, or J. L. Ackrill, or Montgomery Furth, or Jonathan Lear, as well as various others. Moreover, as regards St. Thomas Aquinas, while it would scarcely be accurate to say that he has ever been taken seriously by very many contemporary Analysts or Post-Analysts, nevertheless, so far as Roman Catholic philosophical circles in the present day are concerned, there can be no denying that St. Thomas does still give at least the appearance of enjoying what can only be described as an almost officially sponsored renown and pride of place. And when it comes to research in the history of philosophy, where today can one find anyone to outdo the work of the great Etienne Gilson and a whole host of others, who wrought so mightily in the matter of rehabilitating and keeping alive the philosophical reputation of St. Thomas Aquinas? And as for Aristotle, there are few who could be said to rival the achievement of the redoubtable Father Joseph Owens, particularly when it comes to making clear what the incalculable import for phi-

---

1. For these and any number of other suggestions that I have profited from in writing this Introduction, I am particularly indebted to my friends and sometime adversaries, Robert Turnbull and Jorge Gracia. They were both commentators on an earlier would-be defense that I had sought to give of Aristotelianism, and that was one of the subjects for discussion at a conference held at SUNY-Buffalo in April 1987—a conference devoted to the overall topic of "Doing Philosophy Historically." The papers of this conference have since been published under the same title and under the editorship of Peter H. Hare (Buffalo, NY: Prometheus Books, 1988). See especially pp. 92–136.

losophy has been of "the doctrine of being in the Aristotelian metaphysics."

But again, let me repeat that in the general argument of the essays that follow, it really has in no way been my concern even to pretend to contribute to a better understanding of either Aristotle or Aquinas, considered historically. For important as such historical rehabilitations may be, my concern is directed not toward questions of history, but rather toward the question of whether it might be possible to bring both an Aristotle and an Aquinas directly into contemporary debates, as if they themselves were no less than contemporary philosophers.[2] For why should it not be possible to consider either Aristotle or Aquinas as entering into an actual dialectical interchange with the likes of a Bertrand Russell, say, or a G. E. Moore, or a Ludwig Wittgenstein, or a W. V. Quine, or a Wilfrid Sellars, or a Gustav Bergmann, or a Richard Rorty, or whomever? Not that we have ourselves in what follows either the space or the wit to stage jousts between an Aristotle, or an Aquinas, and all and sundry of these contemporary worthies. But that at least has been the general idea.

Once more, however, I can imagine your objecting, "Oh, but the whole enterprise is nothing if not altogether fanciful! After all, neither Aristotle nor Aquinas are our contemporaries in fact. How, then, can it be pretended that they are so, save but by a sheer fiction? And while fiction may be all right for historical novels, in philosophy fiction can surely be no better than an irrelevance, if not even a downright impertinence."[3]

And even if you were to grant me my indulgence in such a fiction, must not that very fiction have the effect of posing for me a most uncomfortable dilemma? This is just the dilemma of having to choose between trying to be a historian of philosophy or just a philosopher. That is to say, either I must give myself over to researches aimed at determining exactly what it was that Aristotle or Aquinas, each in his own day, either may have intended to say or actually did say; or, as an

---

2. In thus speaking of the philosophical reputation of St. Thomas, I would in no way imply that St. Thomas does not have a theological reputation as well, or that the latter does not indeed outdo the former. It's just that for the purpose of this volume our concern is only with St. Thomas as a philosopher. In somewhat the same vein also, it doubtless should be remarked that, for purposes of the argument of this book, we are regarding both Aristotle and St. Thomas as being Aristotelians. Again, this is not to imply that there may not be considerable differences between St. Thomas and Aristotle, even when one considers them simply as philosophers. It's just that such differences we would not consider to be of particular moment, so far as the essays in this book are concerned.

3. For the sort of issue implied here, see the papers of the Buffalo conference referred to in note 1 above.

alternative, I might try playing at being an Aristotelian or a Thomist even today, with the result that my philosophy would appear to be but little more than history, and my Aristotle and Aquinas would be turned into but living anachronisms.

However, such a dilemma, I believe, can be got around, and got around most effectively, by employing a device or tactic in philosophy that Aristotle himself used repeatedly—or at least so I would think.[4] This is the device or tactic of so-called dialectic, which Aristotle employed at the very outset of any number of his major treatises in philosophy. True, in Aristotle's hand dialectic was hardly the kind of tool or method in philosophy that it later became for a Hegel or a Marx, say. Rather, Aristotelian dialectic was a direct heritage from Socrates, and thus also in a sense from Plato as well.

Moreover, as Aristotle conceived and practiced dialectic, it was something to be regarded, not so much as central to philosophical investigation itself, as rather only preliminary to it. Thus it consisted for Aristotle in his beginning each of his major treatises on *Physics*, on *Metaphysics*, and on *Ethics*, for example, with a summary review of his predecessors. In this sense, it could be said that taking the history of philosophy seriously is to be reckoned as essential to any use of an Aristotelian dialectic. Thus in Book I of the *Physics*, for example, Aristotle devotes his attention to the views, among others, of Parmenides and Melissus, they being, as it were, among Aristotle's recognized forebears or predecessors in what he regarded as being physics or natural philosophy. Moreover, the reasons for Aristotle's thus resorting to such a review of the opinions of various of his predecessors is that for Aristotle, physics or natural philosophy was that domain or region of being or reality in which things are subject to change and motion—*ens mobile* as the Scholastics called it. But Parmenides had argued that change or motion was simply an impossibility, because self-contradictory. Hence, it is understandable why Aristotle should have felt that he needed to turn his attention to the views of someone like Parmenides; for until and unless he could somehow get around or get over the sort of roadblock that, as it were, Parmenides had placed in the way of any investigation into the nature of change and

---

4. Once more, it is conceivable that perfectionists among present-day historians of philosophy might question whether the use in Scholastic philosophy of an elaborate scheme of objections and replies could have had any very direct affinity, either historical or conceptual, with Aristotle's use of dialectic at the beginning of several of his major treatises. To such a historical challenge, I would unfortunately feel largely incompetent to respond—certainly not in terms of any adequacy or sufficiency of historical scholarship. All I can say is that as a comparatively amateurish historian of philosophy, I find such an affinity to be not just discernible but even strikingly so.

of changing beings in the physical world, it would be impossible even to get started with anything like physics or natural philosophy in any proper sense.

And similar considerations would apply in the case of Aristotle's use of dialectic in various of his other treatises. Thus in the area of what Aristotle called metaphysics, the so-called materialists held that when it came to a question in metaphysics of the causes of being—*i.e.* of why things in the world are the particular kinds of things they are—the materialists answered that the only cause of things, or beings, being the things they are is just their matter, or the stuff they are made of. That is to say—to use a crude analogy—if one wants to know why a house or a particular structure is the kind of thing it is, one needs to point simply to the materials out of which it is made as being the only really significant causes of the house. In contrast, Plato, another of Aristotle's predecessors, had contended against the materialists that the true cause of the house had to be the *form* of a house. That is, the architect's plan or design, Plato in effect contended, was the real or true cause of what made the house to be what it was or is. Accordingly, against both of these views Aristotle argued dialectically that the cause of anything—say, a house—could be neither merely the materials out of which it was constructed, nor merely the plan or design or form of the house into which it was made. Rather still another cause needed to be reckoned with, namely the builder who was the actual agent or efficient cause of the house finally coming to be a house.

From these crude examples, then, one may perhaps be able to begin to see both why and how dialectic was used by Aristotle. First of all, any use of dialectic had to involve a certain review on Aristotle's part of various views of his predecessors. And yet Aristotle did not engage in such exercises in the history of philosophy in any spirit of either historicism or of wanting to pursue the history of philosophy merely for its own sake. Nor, of course, did Aristotle, as one might say nowadays, undertake to "do" the history of philosophy simply in order to make a display of, and thus to preen himself on, his own historical learning and erudition. No, Aristotle engaged in such a review of his predecessors because the opinions of the likes of Parmenides, or the materialists, or Plato, had become received opinions in Aristotle's own day. That is to say, they were taken seriously by philosophers and thinkers contemporary with Aristotle, with the result that Parmenides and the materialists and Plato, through their then latter-day representatives, had come to be reckoned as themselves no less than contemporaries of Aristotle.

But not only were these philosophical forebears of Aristotle's functioning as if they were his own contemporaries. In addition, in their role as his contemporaries, they had raised philosophical difficulties and complications that tended to confuse and confound things in such a way as to make it quite baffling how one might ever be able to win through to a recognition of what the true principles and causes might be, be it in either physics, or metaphysics, or ethics. And so it was that Aristotle considered that he needed to use his instrument of dialectic, in order to clear a way through, or make a passage through, the philosophical difficulties and roadblocks that had been created by his predecessors. It was just this, then, that was the function of dialectic for Aristotle: to utilize the insights, and at the same time remove the obstacles, created by his predecessors, so that one could then come to a proper view of, and so attain a genuine insight into, the true principles and causes that underlie our scientific knowledge of being and the world.

Nor in this connection could we do better than to quote a couple of passages characterizing the nature and character of this Aristotelian kind of dialectic, appearing in Fr. Joseph Owens' truly magisterial work on *The Doctrine of Being in the Aristotelian "Metaphysics"*[5]:

Aristotle had already developed the theory of this procedure in the *Topics*. He calls it "dialectic." He uses the Platonic term, but, as often, introduces a considerably different sense. For the philosophical sciences, the function of dialectic is to consider the views of other thinkers, because "being able to draw up the aporiae in the face of opposite views, we will observe in every one of them more easily the true and the false. This holds moreover in regard to the first principles in each science. For it is impossible to say anything about these on the basis of the proper principles of the science in question, since the principles in every case come first; and it is through the 'commonly received notions' (ἐνδόξων) about each that we have to proceed in dealing with them. This is the proper or most appropriate function of dialectic. For dialectic, being an ability of scrutinizing, holds the path towards the principles of all scientific treatments." [*Topics* I, 2, 101 a34–b4.] The last metaphor appears somewhat mixed. The original notion of "path" (ὁδός) has become quite obliterated. The word is simply taken in its acquired meaning of method or procedure. Dialectic is said to "possess" or to "have" this path.

Because dialectic is an ability to "pass in review" or to "scrutinize closely" (ἐξεταστική) the received opinions or notions, it possesses the way, the path to the principles of all sciences. According to the wording, dialectic does not possess the principles themselves, but only the *way* towards them. It is the ability to make a passage (διαπορῆσαι) in the face of the aporia—"lack of passage"—arising from conflicting views.

---

5. Joseph Owens, *The Doctrine of Being in the Aristotelian "Metaphysics"* (Toronto, Canada: Pontifical Institute of Mediaeval Studies, Third Edition, 1978), p. 205.

So much then by way of an account of Aristotelian dialectic, and why and how it can and should function in philosophy. Moreover, recalling again that earlier-stated dilemma with which I seemed to be confronted, in so far as I sought to treat Aristotle and Aquinas simply as contemporary philosophers, I wonder if, by availing myself of a dialectic of the kind used by Aristotle, I cannot escape between the horns of the dilemma. Thus of course the use of dialectic requires that one avail oneself of the history of philosophy, in so far as one needs always to begin one's philosophizing by reckoning with the received opinions of past philosophers, in so far as these continue to be operative in the present. At the same time, it is just the resources of dialectic that enable one to get through and beyond the inescapable aporias[6] that are left by previous philosophers in any given age or time, and thus win through to a proper insight into the necessary principles and causes that are to be reckoned with in philosophy itself and not in the mere history of philosophy as such.

Still, it perhaps needs to be considered somewhat further just how such a use of dialectic enables one to get beyond the aporias of the received opinions of our predecessors and so to progress toward the sought-for recognition and insight into what the true principles and causes of the philosophical science in question must be, whether it be a science of physics, or of metaphysics, or of ethics, or of whatever. For recall how Fr. Owens puts it: for Aristotle, "dialectic does not possess the principles themselves but only the way towards them." In fact, dialectic could not possibly provide any sort of proof or demonstration of such principles, for the reason that, the principles being literally "first," there is nothing that could precede them in such a way as to provide a proof or demonstration of them. Instead, it would seem to be a case of dialectic having to function in such a way as only to clear away the aporias which obstruct our vision of the principles; and then, as a result of the obstructions being thus removed, the principles should be able thereby to become somehow visible and intelligible simply in and by their own light.[7]

Still, we need to consider rather more concretely just how dialectic, by removing the aporias of the contemporary received opinions, thus points the way to the principles, without itself providing the actual insight into those principles. And to this end, we might examine very briefly just how it was, in the case of Aristotle's physics, that his use

---

6. The word *aporia*, taken over from the Greek, means literally "lack of passage"— i.e., a blockage or a difficulty. Considering that the term has come to be recognized as being now Anglicized, I propose to write the plural simply as "aporias."

7. For the entire discussion, cf. Owens, *op. cit.*, pp. 205–206.

of dialectic at the beginning of the *Physics* enabled him to win a passage through or around the Parmenidean aporia to the effect that change was simply an impossibility because self-contradictory; and then, having by reason of the dialectic removed the confusions, he was able thus to emerge into a clear path leading to an eventual recognition of the true principles and causes of change as being evident simply in themselves.

Thus begin by considering the question: how and on what grounds was Parmenides able to argue that change or motion was impossible because self-contradictory? Briefly, it would seem that the Parmenidean argument was something like this. "How could Being or the Real possibly change?" he asked in effect. "For if Being or the Real were to change, it would surely have to become other and different. But how could the Real ever become other than what it simply is, since that would mean that it would have to become other than real, which is to say it would have to become unreal? And how could the Real possibly be said to be unreal, without patent self-contradiction?"

In short, it is little wonder that Aristotle should have needed to reckon with such a Parmenidean denial of the possibility of motion, that denial being nothing less than a commonly "received opinion" in Aristotle's time, a received opinion among both philosophers and thinking people generally. Nor was that the only received opinion that Aristotle must have felt that he needed to reckon with. For surely, it must have been an equally received opinion—something patent and obvious to all—that it was nothing if not simply a plain fact of nature that of course things in nature do change; nor can it possibly be denied that in this sense the real does change and things do become different.

In short, what more dramatic aporia could there possibly be than this one that Aristotle found himself confronted with at the very outset of his philosophizing in physics? For it was precisely the aporia created by the open and seemingly insuperable conflict between two currently received opinions from the past, those opinions being (1) that motion and change were a downright impossibility, and (2) that motion and change were an inescapable fact of nature. How, then, could this aporia be circumvented? To all of which Aristotle's response was to scrutinize dialectically those two received opinions. And what was it that such a scrutiny revealed, if not that it was possible to view the whole situation in a new light? For why not consider that the things or entities existing in the natural world, in addition to being just what they are at this, that, or the other point in time, are also and at the same time *able* to be and become other than they are—which is to say that they thus have a potentiality for becoming other and different. In other words, recognize such an additional principle or cause in things as *matter* or potentiality, and immediately the Parmenidean difficulty over the possibility of change is nicely dissolved. Moreover, in thus dissolving the difficulty, Aristotle's dialectical scrutiny manages at the same time not just to remove the Parmenidean aporia but also to point the way to a recognition of that new and hitherto unappreciated first principle that is an absolutely necessary principle and cause in all matters of physics—namely, matter or potentiality.

In other words, what such a philosophical dialectic in Aristotle's hands has managed to do is both to clear away the aporia created by the conflicting received opinions inherited from past philosophy and also to point the way or the path to what is a necessary first principle in the science of physics, the principle of matter or potentiality.

And now to consider briefly—and in a way that I trust may be rather more immediately and directly prefatory to the essays that follow— just how the use of this particular variety of dialectic is able to subserve our overall objective. This is simply that of trying to introduce Aristotle and Aquinas directly onto the scene of contemporary philosophy and thus make of them contemporary philosophers.

First of all, note how the use of such a dialectic should enable one to slip between the horns of that earlier mentioned dilemma of a person's supposedly being constrained to do either history of philosophy or philosophy but not both. For clearly the requirement in any employment of an Aristotelian type of dialectic is that the history of philosophy, in the form of such received opinions of the time as have been inherited from past philosophy, has to be taken with the utmost seriousness. After all, the activity of philosophy of whatever age or culture never begins in a vacuum. Instead, it has to begin in a context of such prevailing philosophical views and opinions as have been inherited from the past, but which also have come to be recognized as largely true and therefore still unavoidable. Such, for example, was that received opinion in Aristotle's day of Parmenides and his denial of motion. For this view, as we have seen, could not be taken other than seriously, in as much as there were telling arguments in its support, and as a result of which Parmenides' position in regard to change and motion seemed disarmingly true, because unanswerable.

And so it is that dialectic in Aristotle's sense is unquestionably historically oriented. And yet the orientation is not toward history in any mere historicist sense, it being only such history as is relevant in and for the present, and consisting of such received opinions from the past as are nonetheless operative in the present. All the same, and for all of dialectic's being oriented to the history of philosophy, the dialectician, in thus using the history of philosophy, in effect turns that history into but so many contemporary philosophical views and opinions. Yes, and in so treating figures in the history of philosophy, the dialectician treats them as, and so turns them into, but so many contemporary philosophers. And so it is that in our own use of dialectic in what follows, we shall treat Aristotle and Aquinas as being no more and no less than our contemporaries.

Moreover, suppose that someone wants to object that the philosophical dialectician in thus utilizing figures in the history of philosophy, as Aristotle utilized Parmenides, or as we for our part shall try to utilize Aristotle and Aquinas, may often be either inaccurate or just plain wrong in his or our historical facts: Parmenides, for example, may not in fact have taken quite the sort of position that Aristotle attributed to him, or Aristotle himself in turn may have been seriously misrepresented in the sort of account that I am inclined to give of him. To which the dialectician's rejoinder need be only as follows: Maybe I have got my facts in the history of philosophy somewhat awry. But even if my account of the origins of a so-called "received opinion" be wrong, the opinion, as I have represented it, is nonetheless operative in the present, and hence needs to be reckoned with. And immediately it would be the business of the dialectician to take them up and deal with them in the present. Not only that, but the dialectician—or even I in my would-be role as a dialectician—might even go further and insist that if some historian of philosophy were to dig up historical opinions and views (say, even views of Aristotle) of which the engaged dialectician may never even have heard, much less treated, all that would be necessary would be that these views now be acknowledged in the present, and then dealt with dialectically.

Nor is that all, for granted that the Aristotelian dialectician is under obligation to deal with any historical views and opinions of philosophers, provided only they have come to be reckoned as being of philosophical import in the present, we also need to explain and underscore just why and how the dialectician needs to deal with such received opinions as he is thus obliged to deal with. The reason the dialectician needs to deal with such things is first that such received opinions are somehow philosophically inescapable in the present, having been taken up as opinions that are regarded as being somehow true, and even compellingly so, and thus as needing to be reckoned with.

Moreover, the second reason that the dialectician needs to deal with these received opinions is not just that, as we have already suggested, they come across as being somehow inescapably true, but also that, as we might say, they seem intolerably true at the same time. And how are they intolerably true? It is simply because in addition to being received as true opinions, they are also recognized as hopelessly in conflict with other equally received opinions; and thus it is that, as noted earlier, these conflicting, historically received opinions generate what Aristotle called aporias, which palpably block the way to a systematic and ordered knowledge of the particular philosophical domain or subject matter that is in question, be it physics, or metaphysics, or ethics, or whatever. And so it is that the "how" of an Aristotelian dialectic is, as we saw earlier, entirely a business of getting around or getting through these aporias, so that the way or the path ahead becomes clear, and the philosopher will then be able to proceed to an actual apprehension and recognition of the true principles and causes and elements of the philosophical science in question.

Yes, in this very connection it might be well for all of us to recall Aristotle's rather famous characterization of how it is only in the light of a grasp or apprehension of what might be called first principles that anything like a properly scientific body of knowledge becomes permissible:

> Knowledge and science are able to be brought about in all those areas of investigation in which there are principles, causes, or elements. In effect, we think we have understood a thing only when we have penetrated to its primary causes, its first principles, and even its elements.[8]

Accordingly, it is just in this connection that the final and the most important feature of the "why" and the "how" of an Aristotelian type of dialectic needs to be both pointed out and pointed up. Thus already we have been at some pains to show that dialectic as such does not grasp the first principles and causes and elements of a body of knowledge. Instead, dialectic is competent only to remove the aporias that block the way to a recognition of the true principles and causes. But once the aporias are removed, it turns out that the very removal is such as to make possible a disclosing and an apprehending of the relevant necessary principles and causes both in their own right and in their own light.

And so it is that dialectic, as a necessary propaedeutic to a science, is still not itself a part of the science, be it either physics or metaphysics or whatever. But all the same, it needs to be stressed that dialectic is indeed a propaedeutic, and even a necessary one, to any and all of the philosophical sciences. For as we were at pains to try to show earlier, in the sketch we presented of how Aristotle used his dialectic

---

8. *Physics*, Bk. I, ch. 1, 184a, 10–15.

in order to get round the Parmenidean aporia, it was solely as the means of, and in the course of, removing the aporia that the idea of matter or potentiality as a necessary principle of all change first suggested itself as being the obvious solution of the aporia, and therefore as being a necessary first principle in natural philosophy itself. In other words, that same first principle of matter, as a necessary first principle in all change, was not anything that could have been grasped as self-evident apart from the dialectic of removing the aporia; nor was it anything that was or could be evidenced simply from experience. No, it was only after and against the background of the dialectical scrutiny of the relevant aporia that the principle was first rendered something that was evident just in itself. In the light of the foregoing, I wonder if it may not be possible now to make a rather large claim on behalf of such a dialectic? It's simply the claim that without dialectic as its forerunner and its necessary propaedeutic, there can be no such thing as genuine philosophy, at least not any philosophy that is properly adequate or successful. But why not? Is it not simply because, without a preliminary dialectical scrutiny of received opinions inherited from the history of philosophy, it would seem that the very principles themselves upon which any such philosophy must necessarily rest could not be successfully disclosed or made evident. Besides, if any philosophy in any age or period of human culture cannot very well arise, save out of a matrix or context of so-called received opinions from the past, and if such received opinions inevitably confront the engaged philosopher with what can only be described as so many aporias of one sort or another, then surely dialectic would seem to be a "must" in any and all philosophy.[9]

---

9. A comment would seem in order here with reference to the contention in the text that, without a prior dialectical scrutiny of the views of one's predecessors in philosophy, one cannot very well hope to achieve an insight into the very principles of philosophy itself. For one reason that one might experience no little puzzlement, and even scepticism, on this score is that when it comes to modern natural science, there would surely seem to be no comparable reliance upon dialectic as being in any way a necessary propaedeutic to science, such as we are contending must be the case in philosophy.

Moreover, to confirm the point, just consider the striking differences that there are, at least on the surface, between the opening of Newton's *Principia Mathematica* and the opening of Aristotle's *Physics*. Already we have seen how Aristotle begins not only his *Physics*, but nearly all of his major philosophical treatises, with a dialectical review and scrutiny of the views of his predecessors. But with Newton there would seem to be nothing like this. Instead, Newton begins his *Principia* by simply laying down, as it were, what he calls his Definitions, followed by a short Scholium. And immediately thereafter, he proceeds to formulate his Axioms or Laws of Motion, of which the first Law is: "Every body continues in its state of rest or of uniform motion in a right line unless it is compelled to change that state by forces impressed upon it."

Now why, one might ask, does Newton not feel—as Aristotle certainly felt—that a

With respect, then, to this present volume and the essays and discussions that follow, may I simply say that my own program ought perhaps to be regarded as amounting to little more than exercises in dialectic, and in a dialectic directed to the overriding purpose of trying to rehabilitate Aristotle and Aquinas as contemporary philosophers right in our own day? Moreover, being a program confined thus to the use of dialectic, our tactic will be one of trying to confront Aristotle and Aquinas with all sorts of received opinions, drawn from both modern philosophers generally and present-day philosophers particularly—Descartes, Hume, Kant, Russell, Quine, G. E. Moore, Richard Rorty, *et al.* Then having made the confrontation, and having made it in various of the different areas of philosophy, but principally in the areas of what today would be called epistemology[10] and ethics, our

---

dialectical preparation is necessary before one can ever formulate the principles of one's science? Is it because Newton considered that the first principles of his system of physics were somehow immediately evident just in themselves—either self-evident, that is, or else evident directly from experience? In contrast, as we have been at such pains to show in our text, Aristotle was convinced that there could be no insight whatever into first principles, unless and until a prior dialectical scrutiny of received opinions in philosophy had cleared away the aporias that blocked the way to an insight into any proper first principles in philosophy.

Now why this apparent striking difference between science—at least modern natural science—and philosophy, so far as a knowledge of its first principles are concerned? Needless to say, any such "why"-question we do not propose to try to answer here—certainly not in any mere footnote. And yet is not the fact of such a difference, as opposed to its "why," quite patent and obvious in the light of our examples? Oh, it's true that one might well enter a demurrer at this point and claim that even the mere suggestion that there might be a difference between science and philosophy would be only a glaring anachronism, at least with respect to thinkers like Aristotle and Aquinas. For surely, in the context of both ancient and medieval philosophy, no distinction between science and philosophy, as kinds of knowledge, was ever drawn. However, any such equation of science with philosophy, or of philosophy with science, is an equation which, if it has not been given up entirely these days, so far as either modern science or modern philosophy is concerned, is certainly no longer just taken for granted.

That being the case, why might it not be illuminating in these days in which science and philosophy no longer tend to be simply equated with one another, simply to think of the difference between philosophy and science as being a difference between such knowledge, as cannot very well be attained without presupposing a dialectical preparation and prelude, and such knowledge as at least pretends to find itself generally indifferent alike to dialectic and to history? This way there need be no question of confusing science with philosophy, or philosophy with science: each would be seen to be a horse of a very different color.

10. It will immediately strike many as being a rather serious misnomer to speak of "epistemology" as being a branch of philosophy in the eyes of either Aristotle or Aquinas. Certainly, the term "epistemology" designates an area of philosophy that was not explicitly recognized by either Aristotle or Aquinas, and that can trace its rise to a concern with problems largely of modern origin, notably the sorts of problems generated by a work such as Descartes' *Discourse on Method*. But even though there may be a certain anachronism in the use of the term "epistemology" in connection with either Aristotle or Aquinas, there can surely be no denying that many of the discussions of

attempt will then be, so far as we are able, and as well as we are able, to carry out a dialectical scrutiny of the aporias in philosophy which these various latter-day philosophers have created, and which we wonder if just such an Aristotelian dialectical scrutiny may not be able to dissolve, and dissolve so as to enable the truth of properly Aristotelian and Thomistic principles in these areas of philosophy to shine forth and thus come to be evidenced in their own light.

For instance, as a mere foretaste of the sort of thing that is to come, I put forward a couple of prefatory indications and examples. Thus, for one thing, surely no one will deny that in areas like those of present-day epistemology, one does not find much exhibited in the way of an ordered and systematic science of human knowledge and cognition, both what it is and how it is. Instead, the aporias are so ubiquitous as to make the field little better than a confusion worse confounded. Thus consider: will we not all admit, in a loose and general sort of way, that if there is to be such a thing as human knowledge, human beings presumably will have to achieve that knowledge in terms of coming to understand the things of the world in terms of *what* those things are and *why*? However, that anything should be what it is, or the kind of thing that it is, be it fish or fowl or good red herring, our affirmation of such "whats" of things would have to be in terms of propositions characterized by what Kant called universality and necessity. Thus, supposing that there are beings in the world that we call human beings, and supposing further that we come to learn or discover that human beings are rational animals, the natural question is, "But just how can we come to know something like this—namely, that there are such beings as human beings, and that what they are are rational animals?"

Of course, the most natural answer to this latter sort of question might be, "Oh, we come to know this sort of thing through experience." But no sooner is that answer given than we must recognize that a large part of the history of modern philosophy has been devoted to showing that such an answer is patently indefensible. For one thing, our senses, just as such, do not acquaint us ever with such things as human beings, but only with mere sights and sounds and smells and feels, etc.; and if we want to reckon in the common sense as well as the external senses, we might then add things like shape, size, motion, etc. to the list. But notice that none of these deliverances of our senses ever yields that universality, much less the necessity, that are seemingly

---

Aristotle and Aquinas, pertinent to human knowledge, are germane to what today could be called questions of epistemology.

necessary characteristics that our judgments must have if they are to be judgments either of what things are or why they are. And besides, not only is our human experience not able to sustain judgments that are characterized by a universality and necessity, but in addition our sensory experience is as often illusory and deceptive as it is veridical.

So what to do? Well, we all know that in the history of modern Western philosophy, it appears to be impossible to find any basis in sensory or perceptual experience just as such for universal and necessary judgments as to what things are or why they are. Accordingly, the obvious alternative that has suggested itself has been: Well, if we can't rely upon experience to yield truths about the world, why not rely on something like pure reason rather than experience—on something on the order of Cartesian clear and distinct ideas, if you will? Thus it is not from experience—so this line of consideration runs— that we know that the sum of the angles of a triangle is equal to two right angles; or that, of p, and $p \supset q$, then necessarily q; or that a whole is greater than any of its parts. No, these truths seem able to be shown to be evident just in themselves, in their own right, and without any appeal having to be made to experience by way of their confirmation. Unhappily, though, no sooner is such a rationalist alternative, if we might so label it, adopted in place of the empiricist alternative, than it promptly collapses in turn—though for rather different reasons than the collapse of the empiricist alternative. For although the rationalist alternative does seem able to guarantee a knowledge that is universal and necessary, it turns out to be a knowledge that is not about the world at all. Rather, it proves to be an affair only of analytic truths, or linguistic truths, or purely formal truths, with the result that while such truths may exfoliate the sense and meaning contained within the words and terms used in formulating the propositions, the resulting truths tell us no more than how we are using our terms, and not at all whether what is signified by such words or terms is that way in reality or not.

Accordingly, empiricism and rationalism having both failed to explain how we can gain any knowledge of the world through the use of our supposed cognitive faculties of either sense or reason, there is still another major alternative that has been resorted to in modern philosophy, and particularly in recent philosophy just in our own day. This is the alternative of what might be called the Kantian "transcendental turn." Granted that a knowledge of the world or of reality, as these are in themselves, is simply out of the question for us human beings, perhaps we can make do instead with a knowledge of the world only as it *appears* to us to be, or simply as it gets structured by us in terms of our own human language forms or logical forms or thought forms or whatever. In other words, we know the world not as it is in itself, but only as it is for us and as we fashion it to be or make it to be, according to how we talk about it or think about it—which is to say according to what categories or conceptual frameworks we use by way of merely picturing things to ourselves, rather than by way of our ever actually coming to recognize the things of the world for what they really are in reality and in themselves.

So far as the area of what we are calling philosophical epistemology goes, the history alike of modern and of contemporary philosophy presents us with nothing so much as aporias, aporias, and aporias. Accordingly, in several of the succeeding essays I shall be trying to apply my own version of an Aristotelian dialectic by way of dissolving these aporias, and thereby disclosing the possibility that sense and reason, so far from being divorced from one another and operating entirely independently of each other, actually both can be made to work together, and indeed do work together, so that the very data of things in the world, which our senses present us with, at the same time come to be understood both for what they are and why they are by the discernment of our human intellect and reason. It is just such a cooperative work as this that, in the various discussions that follow, I hope to be able to show can be effected by an Aristotelian dialectic, which serves to obviate, as well as to penetrate, the various aporias, and so to disclose, even if only indirectly, what the true principles and causes and elements of our human knowledge are.

There is one more instance of an area in contemporary philosophy that is fraught with countless aporias, generated by countless of the fashionable received opinions of the present day, but which a judicious use of an Aristotelian dialectic should be able to penetrate and so to point the way through to the true principles and causes, this time not in epistemology, but in ethics. Once more, everyone—not just philosophers, but almost every one else as well—knows what the concerns are of ethics and of moral philosophy, whether he be actually given to using those particular terms or not. For our human ethical concerns surely are nothing if not concerns with what the true values in life are, and with what as human beings we ought to do and be, and how we ought to conduct ourselves, as we live out our lives as human persons. However, just as there is almost universal agreement as to what the concerns are of ethics and moral philosophy, when one turns to the received opinions among philosophers past and present as to how these concerns are to be understood and dealt with, it is once more a case of philosophers seeming to be utterly bogged down in the countless aporias that the currently received truths in ethics would seem to have generated.

Accordingly, following our own Aristotelian dialectical procedure, note that an initial source of the present difficulties and aporias in connection with current ethical theory would seem to be that, as soon as one nowadays wants to learn the facts, as it were, about the true values in life, or about what it is that human beings ought to do and be, or what the differences are between right and wrong, say, one finds oneself initially thrown off by the fact that there seemingly is just no place that one can go to, or nowhere that one can turn to, to find out what the facts are in matters of morals and ethics. No, for the universally received opinion nowadays seems to be that distinctions such as those between good and bad, or right and wrong, etc., are unfortunately just not matters of fact at all, and that therefore there is just nowhere that one can turn to learn the facts about such matters. After all, is it not the universally received opinion today that it is to the sciences, and only to the sciences, that one needs to turn, in order to learn what the real facts of nature and reality are? But science—again by the universal testimony of well-nigh all modern scientists—never discovers such things as values, or "oughts" and "ought nots," or rights and wrongs, in the world of facts.

So what to do? Well, one answer that is a perennial one, and one that has been taken up and exploited by so-called latter-day utilitarians of one sort or another is that for human individuals to know what's good for us, and therefore what the values in life are for us, we need only consult what we like and desire, and find to be to our taste, and then set about pursuing that. Values in life, in other words, ultimately come down to no more than what one likes for oneself, or what one personally values or enjoys. And so ethics, accordingly, reduces simply to what we might call a mere "desire-ethic": what one ought to do in life amounts to no more than figuring out what one wants to do or most likes to do, and then doing that, without worrying in the least about whether this is what one "ought" to do, in some fancied moral sense or other.

Unfortunately, though, a desire-ethic, despite all of its confident pretensions, just cannot quite eliminate the nagging doubt and concern that a person has that perhaps what one simply likes to do or wants to do may not always be what is morally right for one to do, or even what is best for one to do. And so, as a reaction against such a mere desire-ethic, one finds any number of present-day moral philosophers insisting that morality is not an affair of merely doing what you want or like, but rather an affair of doing what you ought. In other words, on this view, morality is essentially an affair of an "ought-ethic," or a "duty-ethic," and thus really not a desire-ethic at all.

But unfortunately, no sooner is such a theory of ethics formulated—one that is frequently called a deontological, as opposed to a so-called teleological or utilitarian, type of ethics—than it all seems to collapse for want of a proper basis or foundation. For obviously, the supposed "oughts" or "ought-nots" which are thus supposedly binding upon us seem to have no basis in fact, the scientists having told us that there just are no distinctions between right and wrong, or "ought" and "ought not," to be found anywhere in the facts of nature or in the real world. And so the question then presses, "But why should I imagine that there is anything that I ought to do, or am obligated to do, or that it is right for me to do? What possible justification is there for such a supposition, or does it amount to any more than a mere superstition?"

Oh, it's true that the deontologists among our present-day moral philosophers frequently claim, as a justification for supposing that certain duties and obligations are binding upon them, that they just have a kind of intuition—or if you will a deep-seated feeling or hunch or sentiment—that certain things are morally right for them to do, and others morally wrong. Clearly, though, if our morality and ethics rest on nothing more than intuitions and hunches, then that would almost seem tantamount to saying that our ethics rests on nothing at all. And with that, our deontologists, or partisans of a duty-ethic, would seem to be no less undone by our dialectic than are their opposite numbers among the partisans of a desire-ethic or a utilitarian type of ethics.

Accordingly, this being the stage-setting of so much of present-day ethical theory, is it surprising that it should resemble nothing quite so much as a situation involving one aporia after another? And of course, for ourselves we do not think that an Aristotelian dialectic need be in any way without resource when confronted with such aporias as have been generated from the received opinions of modern moral philosophers. Instead, in various of the essays which follow, the way in which such aporias might be able to be circumvented by an Aristotelian dialectic is by simply reviving once again the old Aristotelian notion of a natural end or goal in human life. And obviously, once it be recognized that human beings have no less than a proper end or goal—*i.e.* something which they not only do desire by nature, but which they ought to desire—then the characteristic weakness of any mere desire-ethic would seem to be effectively obviated: ethics is seen once more to be an affair of what human beings ought to do, and not merely of what they may happen to like to do, or what it pleases them to do.

On the other hand, and at the same time, once ethics is seen to be an affair of a natural end or goal that all human beings are ordered to and obligated by nature to pursue, then the characteristic aporia that afflicts the usual variety of a duty-ethic or deontological type of ethics is obviated as well: the warrant or justification for our human duties and obligations is found to reside in natural law in the traditional sense, and not in any mere fancied intuition of duty, or sentiment or feeling of duty. Oh, it's true that any such natural law ethic as an Aristotelian dialectic thus surely points to, in its scrutiny of the aporias of such rival ethical theories as utilitarianism and deontology, requires, in turn, for its own justification, that the claims of modern natural science to be the sole source of any knowledge that we human beings may claim to have of the laws of nature—that these claims be questioned and that the way be pointed to a broadened conception of nature, in which natural moral laws will be discoverable, no less than such natural laws as modern science traffics in. But this again is something to be taken up, after various reprieves, in the dialectic of several of the ensuing essays.

One final word of apology. I should repeat that the claims I would make respecting my use of an Aristotelian dialectic in the essays that follow are but modest claims. For as Fr. Owens suggested in the passage quoted earlier: dialectic as such does not provide one either with an insight into the first principles of any philosophical science, or with the further articulated development of such principles into a full-bodied system of philosophical knowledge. The most that the use of dialectic can do is to clear a way past the present-day aporias, so that the true principles of a philosophy can then be seen in the light of such principles' own evidence.

Nor is the enterprise that follows limited only in the way in which the use of the devices of an Aristotelian dialectic are limited. In addition, it must be frankly confessed that I can make no claim to having dealt with anywhere near all of the aporias that beset and block the vision of contemporary philosophers, or even with all of the eminent contemporary philosophers whose vision has been thus blocked from winning through to the relevant Aristotelian or Thomistic insights. All that I have done is to take samples—and but occasional samples at that, and not always necessarily the best samples—of those among contemporary philosophers, who, as I see it, have been unhappily chained to the wall of the cave and thus not able to emerge into the full light of the sun.

Nor is even that all. For just as I have not been able to consider a full, or even a properly representative, selection of modern philosophers in the papers that follow, so also there are any number of the major areas of philosophy that I have pretty much neglected even to touch upon in the ensuing essays—logic, metaphysics, philosophy of mind, natural theology, philosophy of religion, and others. And why these omissions? Well, it may be recalled how Dr. Johnson, when a certain lady asked him why in his *Dictionary* he had defined "pastern" as "the knee of a horse," replied, "Sheer ignorance, Madam, sheer ignorance." Well, so far as my own negligences and omissions in the ensuing discussions go, hopefully they may not all be due to sheer ignorance. But that they are due to my own limitations I will not deny, be these of time, or of space, or of philosophical competence. But enough by way of introduction and apology, and now on to the business of swimming against some of those fashionable currents in present-day philosophy.

PART I

QUIETING VARIOUS OF THE ALARMS AND EXCURSIONS IN RECENT PHILOSOPHY

1
CAN PHILOSOPHY EVER BE A THING FOR HOOSIERS?[1]

Let me begin by confessing to an impertinence and a presumption. These are that I have actually given a title to these foreseeably somewhat empty and rambling remarks of mine: I have called them, "Can Philosophy Ever be a Thing for Hoosiers?" And immediately, I can hear our chairman, Wilfried Ver Eecke, muttering to himself, "But who or what, in God's name, is a Hoosier?" For being, shall we say, the inveterate and almost irredeemable Fleming that he is, the last thing that Wilfried would ever allow himself to clutter his mind with is information to the effect that a Hoosier is someone from the State of Indiana. Yes, Wilfried, and I am afraid that the business may be a still more complicated one than that: for, after all, there are Hoosiers and Hoosiers, just as there are Belgians and Belgians; and so it is that a true Hoosier, as opposed to a mere Hoosier, is someone who is not just from Indiana, but from Southern Indiana!

With that, though, the question immediately becomes, "But why, and how come, this odd notion implied in my title that philosophy might possibly be a thing for Hoosiers?" For does not the very suggestion sound like a downright inanity, if not an actual contradiction: Surely, philosophy can only be a thing for intellectuals; and the one thing a Hoosier—at least a Southern Indiana Hoosier—neither is, nor should ever pretend to be, is an intellectual! No, for a Hoosier is, almost by definition, one who is sadly benighted, and often proud of it!

Before, though, I undertake to do the impossible by way of showing, not just that the poor Hoosiers need philosophy, but even that philosophy itself, oddly enough, needs the likes of Hoosiers—before getting caught up in demonstrations to this strange effect, let me first

---

1. This was an address delivered at The Georgetown Symposium on Ethics, which was held at Georgetown University in 1983 on the occasion of my retirement from the faculty.

stop to pay just a few of the many thank-yous that I certainly owe on a happy occasion such as this—for it is an occasion that is a peculiarly happy one for me, even if for no one else. Not only the dinner this evening, but the entire Symposium of the last two days have been billed as being "in my honor." Why? Well, some of you have doubtless got the impression that the business has begun to take on the appearance of "much ado about nothing." Perhaps so. But, then, I being the nothing on this occasion, is it any wonder that I should be most grateful!

Of course, it has occurred to me that given the circumstances, I probably could do no better by way of showing my gratitude tonight than to follow the example of General Grant at a testimonial dinner that was given in his honor some 120 years ago in St. Louis. In the words of Grant's most recent biographer, William S. McFeely:

After the toast to the general, the band burst into "Hail to the Chief." Grant rose, there were cheers, and he spoke—combining his distaste for speaking in public with a magnificent sense of how appealing unexpected brevity could be, "Gentlemen, in response, it will be impossible to do more than thank you."[2]

And he sat down!

Note, though, that I am not sitting down! Alas no! Nor is it because, I assure you, I am any less sensitive than was General Grant to how "appealing an unexpected brevity" can be. Rather it is that in my case such a brevity would be so unexpected, so utterly out of character, so totally incongruous, as to be almost too great a shock for any and all of you. And so rather than shock you thus unexpectedly, I prefer to carry right on, boring you quite expectedly.

Accordingly, let me say, first off, how particularly grateful I am to Georgetown University as a whole, and to the Philosophy Department in particular, and, most particularly of all, to my beloved friend, Rocco Porreco—and grateful not just for this Symposium of the last two days, but even more for the fact that they all—Georgetown, the Philosophy Department, and my friends in the Department—have provided me, quite literally, with a haven of refuge for all of these last 10 years. Yes, 10 years ago I was indeed the proverbial stranger, and Georgetown took me in!

At the time, as it happens, Georgetown was looking for a new chairman. True, in fairness to Georgetown, let me hasten to add, they were in no wise looking for me! Quite the contrary. Rocco Porreco, whom I then did not know too well, had called me about another matter.

---

2. William S. McFeely, *Grant: a Biography* (New York: W. Norton and Co., 1982), p. 154.

And what did I do but quite confound poor Rocco right over the long distance telephone, when I had the temerity to suggest that maybe Georgetown might consider me for the chairmanship! And what was the response? Well, I will only say that at that point the phone went dead! Or if not the phone, then it was Rocco—or at least Rocco's voice—that went dead! Happily, though, communication was soon re-established; and one thing then leading to another, I eventually did come to Georgetown—but not without the general feeling in the air, particularly among the Jesuits, that maybe the Philosophy Department, if it had not been "had," at the very least had bought a pig in a poke! In fact, I still remember the gruff, bluff Father Henle, who was then President of Georgetown, remarking at the interview that I had with him for the job: "Why, yes, I guess maybe you'll do. After all, I once used a book you wrote in one of my classes." Now even to this day I don't believe I quite know how to interpret this remark of Father Henle's: was it a reason, or a nonreason, that he was giving for hiring me?

Still, of all the Jesuits then at Georgetown, the one who really had to worry with that pig, once it had come out of the poke, was none other than poor, long-suffering Father Davis, the Dean of the College. Verily, I proved to be a heavy cross for him to have to bear—and for all I know, to have to bear vicariously for the entire Jesuit Community! Nor was Father Davis' cross-bearing in any way alleviated, until one fine day he chanced to meet my good wife at some campus function or other. As usual, Father Davis wore his look of long-suffering on my account—at which Janie said to him cheerily: "Oh, Father Davis, you mustn't let such things worry you. For just consider that I am the only roommate whom Henry has ever had, who has not suffered a nervous breakdown in consequence!" Well, that seems to have done it! From then on Father Davis found his lot to be not such an unhappy one after all. True, he could not be said to have been made any less miserable as a result of my wife's remark; and yet he did find that misery, when it has company, is somehow easier to bear!

But to return to the subject of my own gratitude. For on this particular occasion my gratitude is not just my long-standing one toward Georgetown, it is also the immediate one of my being grateful to all of those, my friends and former students and sometimes associates, who have been good enough to give so generously of their time and effort as lecturers and participants in the symposium of the last two days. True, for them it may have been more of an occasion to roast me than to toast me. But then that's just fine! In fact, nothing could be better, if that be what it takes to get the likes of Father Owens and

Alan Donagan and Alan Gewirth and all of the rest of you to come to Georgetown merely for such a much-ado-about-nothing. Thanks, and thanks again!

And now having paid my tributes and my thanks to both Georgetown and to the symposium participants, what is it that I can possibly say on the score of that egregious topic of mine having to do with Hoosiers and philosophy? Already I have remarked—and I am sure that none of you will hesitate to acknowledge it to be a fact—that philosophy, as it tends to be practiced nowadays, is scarcely meet for Hoosiers—neither "meet" nor "meat." And with that, I can hear you rejoining, "But why should philosophy be either "meet" or "meat" for Hoosiers? Why not recognize that by its very nature philosophy is a subject solely for intellectuals, and indeed, even for the elite among the intellectuals?"

But no, I am afraid I just could not accept the notion of philosophy as being only for intellectuals. And that, not just because I am a Hoosier, but also because I have never been able to make the grade of being an intellectual! Indeed, will it surprise you if right here and now I make a frank confession of the fact that throughout my whole professional career as a teacher of philosophy, I have had no end of trouble with philosophy and philosophers, particularly with the really sophisticated ones among them, especially the great philosophers—with Descartes, with Spinoza, with Leibniz; yes, especially with the likes of Hegel or Nietzsche, and even in our own day with Wittgenstein and Heidegger and all the rest. And what has my trouble with them been? Well, simply that I couldn't understand them!

Yes, even in my student days in the 1930s, when I was taking courses in philosophy, both undergraduate and graduate, it so happened that I was fortunate enough to be able to study under some of the most eminent among the then philosophers—Alfred North Whitehead at Harvard, Karl Jaspers in Germany, the remarkable pioneering logician, Henry M. Sheffer, C. I. Lewis, R. B. Perry, A. O. Lovejoy, *et al.* The only trouble was that, though lucky enough to be able thus to sit at the feet of some of the great—and there is no doubt about their all having been truly sophisticated philosophers and intellectuals—I, alas, found myself singularly unable ever to figure out quite what they were talking about! And even if on rare occasions I did manage to make some vague sense out of what Whitehead, for example, might be driving at with his talk of "actual occasions prehending the entire past actual world," or Jaspers with his notion of *Existenz*, or Sheffer with his "logic of forms and structures," I am afraid that the only sense I could make out of these esoteric doctrines was but a very feeble, remote, and even abstract sense, and not any firm, concrete sense that could in any way be related to my own fund and background of downright Hoosier experience.

Nor was it until after I had gotten my doctor's degree, and before I could find a regular job, that I came under the influence of my longtime, and I am afraid my sometime, friend at Harvard, the late John Wild. He it was who started me reading Aristotle, really for the first time. And with that, believe it or not, it was as if the scales began to fall from my eyes! At last, it seemed that a bit of philosophical light—not much, to be sure, but just a bit—began to penetrate my thick, dull, dense Hoosier skull. "Why," I said to myself, "Aristotle is a philosopher who really talks like a Hoosier."

Or maybe it is not quite accurate to say that Aristotle talked like a Hoosier, since he probably only spoke Greek; and even what he wrote was, of course, a very forbidding "Greek to me." Not only that, but the standard translations of Aristotle in those days had been done into the English of the eminent Aristotelian scholar and Oxford don, W. D. Ross. Alas, though, it must be said that the English of Oxford has never been quite the English of southern Indiana, no, not by a long shot! Still for all of that, whatever the language of Aristotle may have been, what he wrote certainly made good Hoosier sense—at least to me.

Likewise, somewhat later, I found myself able to say somewhat the same thing of St. Thomas Aquinas. For recall how St. Thomas in the Prologue to his mammoth theological *Summa* cites, as being his guiding principle in the work, the declaration made by St. Paul in *First Corinthians*: "For my part, my brothers, I could not speak to you as I should speak to people who have the Spirit. [No,] I had to deal with you on the merely natural plane, as infants in Christ. That is why I give you milk to drink, instead of meat (or solid food). For you are not yet ready for that." Very well, I ask you—or rather I put it to the formidable array of Thomistic scholars who are scattered through the audience this evening: when St. Thomas thought of himself as addressing people "on the merely natural plane," was he thinking of addressing people on any other plane than that of his master, Aristotle, and indeed in much the same vein as Aristotle? And what was this plane if not that of the natural man or, if you will, of the ordinary man, and not the plane of any mere sophisticated few among philosophers and intellectuals? Accordingly, why could one not say that very milk, as opposed to meat and solid food, which St. Thomas proposed to offer in his *Summa,* was, and is, nothing if not just such philosophical nourishment as even Hoosiers might be ready for?

Perhaps, also, the record as I am here reporting it would not be quite just or complete if I were not to tell you of the somewhat caustic comment that still another of my Harvard professors once made many years ago about Aristotle. "Why," he said, "Aristotle is really the only great philosopher who was able to enunciate the perfectly obvious, and still get away with it." True, the remark was not made so much in either irritation or disparagement, as rather in sheer amazement that a philosopher of Aristotle's presumed stature could ever have supposed that philosophy needed to be structured out of little more than commonplace truths, capable of being understood and appreciated by the common sense and common intelligence of all men everywhere—yes, doubtless even of Hoosiers. And need I add that the professor who made this remark was, after all, a Harvard professor, and as such was one who certainly fancied himself to be very much the philosophical sophisticate, if not actually a member of those select groups of professors and intellectuals, that seem to recur in almost every age, and that invariably think of themselves as constituting a philosophical elite. Hence for him the philosopher of all people was hardly one to traffic in the mere commonplace, but rather one to deal in the new, the original, the recondite, the abstruse—as, shall we say, only a Harvard professor can! Yes, for all I know, this particular professor may very well have gone along with the ever-fashionable view of the philosopher, as being nothing if not the creative thinker, the original genius, the one who spurns anything like common sense, and who is determined to shake the world with his brilliant insights and startling new ideas. To all of which I believe the pertinent retort is one made by the late great French Catholic thinker, Etienne Gilson, many years ago, when he said, "Just consider, is not one commonplace truth worth more than a hundred original errors?"

But enough by way of an account of my own Hoosier's difficulties with the elite among the great philosophers, as well as with the high-powered intellectuals among my own professors. And now let me come right out and say what it is that my thesis about Hoosiers and philosophy really amounts to. It amounts simply to the contention that philosophy is not really, and therefore ought not to be allowed to become, the mere resort or preserve of gifted intellectuals. Rather philosophy is for all men everywhere, and its teachings should speak directly to the common sense or common intelligence of all mankind. Oh, immediately, I can hear all of you muttering to yourselves that I am saying this only because, given my own self-confessed lack of even normal intelligence, much less of anything like a minimal competence for a subject like philosophy, I want to peddle a view of philosophy that will be largely by way of a self-justification, or maybe just a kind of protective coloration for my own philosophical limitations.

And yet I do not think that that is entirely it. For is it not simply a fact, whatever my own self-interest in the matter may be, that philosophy just is the one subject in the curriculum that is and ought to be for anyone and everyone? Thus so far as any college or university curriculum is concerned, philosophy is surely not the sort of thing that is for specialists only, or solely for those of superior talents and intellectual abilities, or even for those who have a kind of taste or liking for the sort of discipline that nowadays goes by the name of philosophy. Rather philosophy is a subject that is decisively and peculiarly for human beings, and indeed for all human beings, simply in virtue of their being human.

After all, if man is a rational animal, then just what may that be taken to mean, if not that a human being, unlike any and all other beings in nature—trees, rocks, orangutans, or squirrels—is just such a being as is not only able to know what he is about, but actually is under obligation—yes, a moral obligation—to find out what he truly is about and ought to be about, just as a human being. For surely, no human individual can qualify as a fully and properly rational animal, if life for him consists in no more than merely being aware that he has various desires, impulses and tendencies, and then being able to muster the necessary wit and ingenuity to figure out how he can best gratify these inclinations and tendencies. No, to be a truly rational animal, one needs to see to it that one's very desires and inclinations are the right ones for a human person to have, and therefore that one's very ends and purposes in life are rationally determined. In other words, for any human being—Hoosiers included—the business of living needs to be an affair of coming to desire and seek after those things which one ought to desire and aim for, and not merely a matter of figuring out how to get what you want, and then getting it.

Just where, though, is a human being—yes, any and every human being, insofar as he needs to be a rational and responsible agent—where is he ever to come by such knowledge of how to be and become human, if not from philosophy? For is not any and all human moral knowledge—*i.e.* any knowledge of what is required of a man, of what his very business in life is as a human person simply by virtue of his being human—must not any really basically human knowledge be thus a moral knowledge? And does not a moral knowledge in this sense call for a still further and all-embracing knowledge, or what one might call a knowledge of the whole—a knowledge of nature, man, and God, no less? For surely, how could a person ever hope to know, in the sense of rationally to understand, what he really ought to do and be as a human person—what it is that it is truly incumbent upon him to be, as over against merely responding to what his interests and inclinations impel him to be, or what his family or his community or his society try to condition him to be, or what he himself somehow fancies that his own conscience or supposed moral intuitions prompt him to imagine that he should be? How could one ever hope to arrive at any such genuine and right knowledge of the moral and the ethical, if this moral knowledge be not set in the context of a knowledge of the entire order of being, and thereby of man's place in that order? And where else is such knowledge to be had, and what else is the nature of such knowledge, if not simply the knowledge that has traditionally been called philosophy?

Besides, is there not another point that needs to be made as regards this reputed philosophical knowledge which turns out to be, as we have been suggesting, both a moral knowledge and a knowledge such as we have loosely termed a knowledge of the whole, in the sense of being a knowledge of the very order of being itself—of nature, man, and God? For in addition to its being a knowledge such as all men need to have, is it not also a knowledge, which all men, even if they don't have it, nevertheless can have, at least in the sense that they can all appreciate the truth of such things, once the truths be pointed out to them. To be sure, this proposition that there need be nothing especially abstruse or esoteric about philosophical knowledge—it being a knowledge that is both indispensable to everyone, as well as available and intelligible to everyone—this may strike many of you as being somewhat far-fetched, if not downright wrong-headed, at least at first hearing and at first glance. And yet I wonder if such be not the conception of philosophy that is fundamental to Aristotle and Aquinas alike. For would they not both say that philosophy is somehow a properly and distinctly human knowledge, in that the very test of truth of philosophical knowledge is that such knowledge must somehow be ascertainable and certifiable by the common sense and common understanding and common testimony of all mankind? It is in just this sense that philosophy should be the concern of all men, and not the mere preserve of any intellectual elite. Or at least, they would say, philosophy could be and should be the concern of all men, unless by chance their economic or cultural circumstances might somehow prevent it.

Thus suppose, for example, we consider very cursorily some of the salient truths that are set forth in any Aristotelian type of physics, metaphysics or ethics. For would not both Aristotle and Aquinas hold that of course we human beings find ourselves simply to be and to exist in a world of people and things, that such things or substances, as Aristotle called them, have all sorts of characteristics or accidents attaching to them: they are of various sizes and shapes, are located in various places, are subject to change and motion, sometimes being acted upon by other substances, and sometimes being themselves the agents of changes in other substances. Of course, too, when substances thus undergo change, it is possible to determine roughly the sorts of causes that operate to produce these changes. For one thing, nothing could possibly undergo any change, be it of place or of quantity, or of quality, or even of substance, without its being able to be other and different, or without its having a capacity or potentiality to be in a different place, or to become larger or smaller, or to take on a different quality, say. Likewise, there could be no such changes in a thing without some force or agent or active power to effect the change.

Similarly, what we have designated as being the potentialities of things to be or become other and different from what they presently are—these potentialities can also be recognized as being what a substance might be or could be—what, in other words, it has a capacity to become. Thus a young plant has a potentiality to attain to its full growth, and thus to enjoy a naturally flourishing condition. Or again, a human infant or young child has a potentiality to become a truly rational and responsible adult. Accordingly, we may say that the potentialities of any substance represent what that substance might be or could be, and thus what it ought to be or should be—though not necessarily an "ought" here in any moral sense. On the other hand, if we are talking about a human being's capacity or potentiality eventually to become and to act as a truly rational and responsible human person—this does represent what that individual ought to be, this time in an unmistakably moral sense, and what he therefore is under an inescapable natural and moral obligation to try to be and become simply as a human individual. In other words, the moral responsibilities of human beings are built right into their natural condition, or better these moral responsibilities are determined in the light of no less than the entire natural order of things as this pertains to men. Likewise, this same natural and moral order of the universe can surely be seen to be an order that would be scarcely intelligible, or even able to exist, without God, or the operation of a divine causality.

Oh, I realize that no doubt at this point I ought to go down on my hands and knees to all of you, and beg your forgiveness and indulgence for my thus rehearsing to you all of these several commonplace truisms drawn from Aristotelian philosophy. And yet does not the very point that I wished to make lie just here? Are not all of these truths of Aristotelian philosophy—almost all of them—little more than truisms, when you come right down to it? Moreover, if one should ask, "But how do we really know that as human beings we do exist in a real world of persons and things, that these things are, many of them, in process of change, and that when such changes pertain to human beings we have a responsibility for what we are to be and become—for what we make of ourselves?" Once this sort of question is put to us, do we not find ourselves constrained to answer such a challenge as to how we know such things, by responding, "Why these are things that are simply evident to us from our experience as human beings. Indeed, that is why they strike us as being little more than truisms and commonplaces, for what are they if not things that are palpable and evident just to the common sense and common intelligence of all men everywhere?"

But surely by this point, if not long before, there are many of you who will want to draw me up short and to say: "Is not, though, this whole business of philosophy as supposedly being a properly human knowledge in the sense of being a knowledge that is of and for all men—does this not run into one very obvious difficulty? For what about science and scientific knowledge, as these are purveyed by the modern natural sciences? For supposing that this reputed philosophic knowledge that we have been talking about is a knowledge that pretends to locate the moral and the ethical right within the very order of being itself—within the order of nature, man, and God, as we have termed it—how in the modern age can one possibly claim to a knowledge of man and of nature without one's relying heavily, if not exclusively, on the natural sciences?"

Surely not, though! And indeed, must not the answer to such a query be: "No, scientific knowledge, as we understand it today, is in no position to be in any way a substitute for philosophical knowledge. For scientific knowledge, instead of being what we have called a knowledge of the whole—a knowledge of the very order of being itself—is, of all things, a highly specialized knowledge. Rather than a knowledge that could ever purport to be in any way an all-encompassing knowledge of nature, man, and God, science necessarily restricts itself, and should restrict itself, to its own sphere. Accordingly, even to the extent to which science may rightly and properly be said to occupy itself with what might be called the order of nature, it does not and cannot envisage that order in such a way as to include the moral and the ethical. Instead, scientific knowledge in the modern sense is a knowledge that is radically value-blind and virtue-blind. And so the last thing that one could ever hope to learn from modern science is what it is that we human beings, simply by virtue of our human nature, ought to do and be, or of what our natural, human moral responsibilities in life are. No, for to take but a trivial example, it is of course possible to learn from physics that water seeks its own level. But the one thing that one cannot possibly learn from any modern scientific study of physics is whether it is either right or wrong, or good or bad, that water should seek its own level—or for that matter that anything else in the scientific universe should either be the way it is or do the things that it does.

Moreover, as a consequence of all of this, is it not now clear how scientific knowledge is to be contrasted with philosophic knowledge as being a specialized knowledge, rather than a knowledge for all? After all, in modern physics or chemistry or biology, the test of truth could never be based on the fact that scientific findings and principles are simply confirmable by the common sense and common experience of all mankind. Imagine submitting such things as the principle of complementarity in atomic physics, or Einstein's formula $e = mc^2$, or the business of recombinant principles of DNA in molecular biology—imagine submitting these to the test of their being directly evident to human experience everywhere—yes, even to the experience of Hoosiers! Why, the very idea of such a thing is ridiculous in the context of science. But in philosophy—at least in Aristotelian or Thomistic philosophy—it is surely quite different. There the test of truth just is its evidence to the common experience and common intelligence of all men everywhere.

No sooner, though, have we thus distinguished scientific truth and scientific knowledge, than immediately another objection suggests itself from another and very different quarter—this time an objection coming not from the scientists, but from the theologians, and maybe, for all I know, particularly from the Jesuit theologians! For why may we not imagine the theologians as contesting directly our fundamental contention in these remarks that it is philosophy, and philosophy alone, that is able to provide men with such knowledge as they need regarding the entire order of nature and being—a knowledge of nature, man, and God in short—a knowledge which men simply have to have if they are ever properly to know themselves, as Socrates would say, and thus be able to know what they ought to do and be simply as human beings? But no, we can imagine such theologians saying: any instruction for human beings that pretends to be an instruction in what we have called a universal and all-embracing knowledge, and that includes a moral or ethical knowledge as well—any such instruction can only be an instruction that must be based solely on faith, and be communicated only in the Faith.

Nor is it to be denied that such a theologian's objection is a difficult one to handle, particularly for me. For just as I confessed to you earlier my ignorance and lack of sophistication in the usual subtleties of intellectuals and of philosophers, so also must I now confess that I do just happen to be a Christian. Or perhaps if these words would seem to imply that one ever could be a Christian by mere happenstance, then let me just say that I happen to be a Christian, thank God, by the grace of God! Moreover, as a Christian I would certainly have to admit that there is just no way a human being can very well live as a human being ought to live, unless it be in the Faith. That, I think, is true. On the other hand, I would hardly take this to mean that the Faith which all men need to guide them is a faith that should ever be construed to the absolute exclusion of philosophy, to say nothing of being necessarily in opposition to the teachings of any and all philosophy. Quite the contrary, I would certainly want to affirm that the Faith needs philosophy—maybe not as much or as acutely as philosophy needs the Faith; but still in its own way, I should be inclined to say that I find it hard to see how the Faith could ever really dispense with philosophy at all!

And at this I don't doubt that the theologians will immediately come back at me, raining down upon my head all of those Pauline imprecations and condemnations in *First Corinthians*, where, quoting Isaiah, St. Paul says, "I will destroy the wisdom of the wise, and bring to naught the cleverness of the clever." For whom else and what else did St. Paul have in mind here, one will say, if not precisely philosophy and the wisdom of the philosophers?

Nevertheless, in my Scriptural ignorance and temerity both, I would venture to suggest that St. Paul is not here condemning philosophy as such, but rather a mere pseudo-philosophy, or philosophy as practiced by those whom we might call "the intellectuals," those who tend to be wise only in their own conceits, and whose philosophy turns out to be little more than a cleverness of the clever. For if we but undertake to supplement what St. Paul says in *First Corinthians* with what he affirms in the *Epistle to the Romans*, we there find that, although St. Paul complains and complains bitterly, that "in their wickedness men are stifling the truth," he promptly goes on to affirm in the very same passage, and in no uncertain terms, that "all that may be known of God lies plain before [men's] eyes. . . . [Indeed] His invisible attributes, that is to say His everlasting power and deity, have been visible, ever since the world began, to the eye of reason, in the things that He has made."

And so St. Paul concludes—if we may here render St. Paul's words in the rumble of the old King James version: "Thus men are without excuse!"

But now I ask you—and without my claiming to make even any minimal claims for myself in matters of Biblical exegesis—Is it not patent and obvious that St. Paul is here affirming that there is indeed such a thing as a true philosophic wisdom and knowledge of just the sort we have been advocating and even pleading for up to now? It is a knowledge and wisdom of the sort that we have termed a universal and all-embracing knowledge, in that it is a knowledge of the entire order of nature and being, as these have been "visible to the eye of reason ever since the world began." Besides, such a knowledge and wisdom of things as things visible to the eye of human reason—why is this not just that sort of philosophic knowledge which we have been claiming is both indispensable and accessible to all men everywhere, and accessible to them simply because, in their capacity as rational animals, all men—even Hoosiers—possess that eye of reason; and accessible to them, precisely as truths that are confirmable and verifiable in the common experience and common understanding of all mankind?

Not only that, but following St. Paul's lead still further, suppose we ask why it is that such philosophic truth as is thus available to all mankind would seem no longer to be recognized and appreciated by all men everywhere? Is not St. Paul's answer that this natural truth, this universal truth, available to all mankind, has nonetheless been "stifled by men in their wickedness"? And who and what is it that is thus primarily responsible for this stifling of the truth? Why, is it not just that "wisdom of the wise" and "cleverness of the clever" of which St. Paul speaks? In other words, is it not just those whom we have all along been calling the intellectuals among the philosophers—those who would scorn the idea that philosophy is after all something for human beings, yes, all human beings, and who would insist instead that philosophy is very much a thing only of intellectuals, by intellectuals, and for intellectuals?

Yes, in this very connection why might we not venture to spot what I would suggest is, doubtless, the telltale mark of the so-called "intellectual"—not just the intellectual in philosophy, but the intellectual generally, as being a somewhat distinct phenomenon of modern culture? For why not say that the intellectual is just such a one as ever seeks to replace our ordinary, everyday human and common sense criterion of truth with a criterion that is peculiarly the intellectual's own, or at least that of his own circle? Thus the common sense criterion of truth might be thought to be simply one which holds that those things are most basically and fundamentally true in human life that are evident to the common experience and common intelligence of mankind. In contrast, the intellectual would replace this everyday human standard of truth and meaning with some more or less private or esoteric standard that has been tailor-made, shall we say, in some one or other of those sophisticated circles in which intellectuals tend to move—for example, the cafes of the Left Bank in Paris, or maybe some literal "Vienna Circle," or perhaps the gatherings of the Bloomsburies in London, or maybe that one-time group of American neo-Marxists clustering around the *Partisan Review*? Or, still more prosaically perhaps, the intellectual's circle might be any one of those ever emergent cliques of professors and graduate students that are forever springing up in any of the various great multiversities of the modern world, Oxford, Berlin, Harvard, Berkeley, Chicago, Princeton, or wherever.

Why, though, rest only with these mere generalities? Why not consider at least one or two concrete cases of how in the course of modern philosophy, intellectuals have ever been prone to set up their own sets of truth-conditions or meaning-criteria by way of replacing the more traditional standards of truth as being evident to the common sense and common experience of mankind? And first off, why not consider the case of the great French philosopher, Descartes, the very founder of modern philosophy. For Descartes was nothing if not thoroughly convinced and imbued—if not even obsessed—with the idea that all of the knowledge and learning of his day, as well as all of the knowledge and learning inherited from the past, as the sort of common knowledge of Western culture—that all of this supposed knowledge was something so inadequate, so messy and confused, so haphazard and ill-ordered, that it really could not claim to be a proper knowledge at all. And so what did Descartes do? Well, he simply undertook to tear down the whole fabric of the then common fund of human knowledge, and to reconstruct it all from the ground up, simply according to his own, Descartes', method and specifications. For, as he said, the idea "that occurred to me was that frequently there is less perfection in a work produced by several persons than in one produced by a single hand. And so we notice that buildings conceived and completed by a single architect are usually more beautiful and better planned than those remodeled by several persons using ancient walls that had originally been built for other purposes" (*Discourse on Method*, Pt. II).

Really now, is not the import of such a Cartesian declaration almost breathtaking in its sheer assurance—yes, one might almost say in its very *hubris*! No longer was philosophic knowledge and wisdom to be the common heritage of mankind; instead, it was now to be a new creation set up by a single intellectual—*viz.*, that exceedingly smart Frenchman, René Descartes! Nor is that all, for one might almost say that what Descartes thus did was to provide the very charter and title deeds for what I might well call no less than "philosophy in a new key"—*i.e.*, philosophy for and by intellectuals.

For in effect, what did Descartes do, if not simply erect as his own standard of truth—which was to say really nothing but the standard of clear and distinct ideas, as this might be said to operate in mathematics? Accordingly, for Descartes nothing was to be taken as true regarding the natural world, unless it could measure up to Descartes' own mathematical standard of truth. In contrast, Aristotle specified those things as being truths that are simply evident to the common sense of mankind, *viz.* such truths as that, as human beings, we live in a world of substances and their accidents, that these substances undergo change, that such changes always have their proper causes—there is always a something that undergoes the change, an agent of the change, and a proper terminus or end of the change, *etc., etc.* But not so Descartes! He would have none of this. Instead, he insisted that none of these commonsense truths of Aristotle could possibly meet his (Descartes') mathematician's standard of clear and distinct ideas. And so Descartes simply read onto the face of nature a purely mathematized conception of matter as being no more than geometrical extension, the matter being simply disposed in countless different geometrical configurations, which are forever succeeding one another from instant to instant. And as for the causes of these successions of geometrical configurations one after the other, there of course could be no natural causes here of any sort at all. Instead it had to be no less than God Himself who needed to be invoked by way of quite literally recreating the entire physical world from instant to instant, each time with a slightly different material configuration from the one immediately preceding it.

Now, of course, such a Cartesian world is no longer a world in which any ordinary man can ever experience himself as actually living in, or being in, at all. Instead, it all turns out to be no less than a "brave new world" designed by Descartes, and aimed at providing the new physics with a framework within which the newly emerging modern natural science might be able to operate, and has indeed continued to operate pretty much right down to the present day.

Alas, though—or maybe happily—there is no time for me to adduce other examples than that of Descartes, by way of showing how our modern philosopher-intellectuals have ever been given to setting up their own, often most ingeniously devised standards of truth, in order thereby to undermine completely the testimony of our common everyday human experience and human intelligence. For no less than Descartes, I could have used countless other examples—Bertrand Russell, Jean-Paul Sartre, F. H. Bradley, W. V. Quine, Karl Marx, Wilfrid Sellars, John Dewey, you name them—each and every one of them, each with his own standard or criterion of truth; and yet all of them to the same effect, *viz.* that of transforming the everyday world, in which we all of us as human beings live, into a world that is largely unrecognizable by the common sense and common experience of mankind.

And if now you should want to ask, but what's wrong with all of this? Why shouldn't different philosophers each set up their own private and personal and esoteric truth conditions? To this the answer surely is that if it be but a case of *suum cuique*—"to each his own"—in the matter of the philosophers' criteria of truth, then the upshot of this is to turn philosophy into no more than a matter of fashion, rather than truth. Nor is such mere fashion and arbitrariness necessarily the worst fate to befall philosophy when it thus forsakes the truth of common experience for truth as determined by the latest fashions of the intellectuals.

No, even more sinister would appear to be the new wrinkle that present-day philosophy has come increasingly to take on ever since Kant, and largely as a result of that transcendental turn which contemporary philosophers, nearly all of them, now tend to make largely as a result of Kant's influence. For one might indeed say that the decisive issue that our latter-day Kantian intellectuals have injected into philosophy is just the issue of whether there can really be any criteria of truth about the real world at all, be these criteria those simply of common human experience, or be they those of this, that, or the other passel of intellectuals. No, for perhaps no criteria of the truth of human experience will ever do, simply because, as Kant saw it, human experience, however conceived and however hedged about with criteria of truth and error, is somehow radically and in principle incapable of ever telling us anything about the way things really are, or the way the world is in fact and in itself.

Instead, what the Kantians insist upon is that the very framework or structure of the real world—the very order of being and of nature, if you will—is not anything that is even in principle ever discoverable in and through human experience. Why not? Why, it is simply because what we fancy that we experience as being out there, and in the facts, and in reality, is but a function of that order, or structure, or categorical framework, that the human mind itself brings to experience rather than finds in experience. Or if it be not the human mind that should thus be said to fashion the entire world, together with our experience of the world, then perhaps we might say that it is our human logical thought-forms or language forms by which we think about the world or talk about the world that are responsible for the world appearing to be the way that it is. Indeed, as Kant himself suggested, rather than for human scientists and philosophers and human knowers generally having to worry about bringing their theories and ideas into conformity with objects, it is far better, to say nothing of being far easier and more fruitful, for scientists and philosophers simply to make objects conform to our own scientists' or philosophers' ideas of the way they would have objects in the world to be and to appear.

Clearly, with this Kantian development in modern philosophy, the triumph, then, of the so-called intellectual in philosophy—and indeed in science and in human knowledge generally—would appear to have become total and complete. No more need the intellectual worry about having to defer to the judgments of men's common human experience. Instead, it is now the intellectual who calls the tune, setting up his own standards and criteria of truth; and even determining what the very character of the world and the very order of nature shall be, according to the particular set of categories or hypotheses or theories with which he, the philosopher-intellectual, now approaches reality, and so makes it conform to his own conceptual patterns and frameworks.

With this, though, is it not now unmistakable what the consequences must be for philosophy of this determination and domination of all truth simply by the intellectuals? No longer will the truth men live by be in any way God's truth. Rather it will be only man's truth. Nor will it even be man's truth or a human truth, so much as it must now be but a truth cut to the cloth and to the measurements of the intellectuals' own standards and criteria. That is to say, it becomes largely a private truth, tailor-made and fashioned at the hands of whoever or whatever may be the regnant group of scientist-intellectuals or philosopher-intellectuals, whose particular world view happens to be the fashionable one at a particular time or place. For remember, if our human ideas are no longer to be brought into conformity with objects, but rather objects into conformity with our ideas, then there is just no way in which there can any longer be any objective standards of truth at all. Instead, truth will no longer be truth about the world or reality, or the truth of things as they are in themselves, but rather only such truth as but reflects the way things chance to appear to be when seen from the perspective of, and as filtered through, the particular hypotheses and theories and conceptual frameworks from which the currently fashionable philosophers and intellectuals may have chosen to view the world.

And so in conclusion I would but wonder, and at the same time, rather shudder to think, at what must be the eventual outcome of this whole notion of philosophic truth as something that is only cut to the particular specifications of philosophy's intellectuals. For as different intellectuals come to put forward their own very different and diverse standards of truth and evidence, and advocate their own radically different ordering schemes and conceptual frameworks for the picturing and structuring of reality and the world, just which standard, or which world-view, will it be that comes to prevail? For after all, if our present-day philosophical intellectuals are right, there is no longer anything like what we might call the fund of our ordinary human experience, or the common sense and intelligence of mankind as a whole, that now may be appealed to by way of deciding which world-view is the true one, or which set of intellectuals we should cast in our lot with.

Instead, all truth must become utterly arbitrary on this basis; nor will our own decision as to which truth we will go along with ourselves be anything more than a thing merely up for grabs. Yes, if there be no objective standards of any kind by which we can judge as between the innumerable rival truth-schemes and world-views of the intellectuals, then the only consideration that presumably can carry the day in favor of the one intellectual's scheme as over against another's will have to be none other than a consideration of mere persuasive force and power. And so what else does philosophy come down to in this present dispensation of our philosopher-intellectuals, such as we find ourselves to be in in today's world, if not simply the pursuit of what Nietzsche called "the will to power."

Is it any wonder, then, that in philosophical circles nowadays, real dialogue as between different philosophical schools and positions has tended to go pretty much by the board? And why should this sort of thing not have gone by the board? For so far from it being supposed that philosophic discussion should ever lead to greater knowledge and understanding, its only function is, as Richard Rorty would say, "to keep the conversation going" as between rival philosophical groups. And yet I ask you: why bother to keep the conversation going as between rival philosophies, if your own fashion in philosophy happens to be in the ascendancy—and in the ascendancy just in the sense that you and your own group control all the jobs, the promotions, the publication outlets, and just about anything and everything else in the profession—or indeed in the culture as a whole?

No, rather than keep the conversation going with your rivals, why would not the sensible thing be simply to concentrate on keeping your own in-group and its partisans in power, and your rivals out? After all, if the entire philosophic enterprise, as practiced by our present-day intellectuals, amounts to no more than a pursuit of the will to power, then why not do just that, and forget about anything so old-fashioned as the pursuit of truth? Yes, remembering Matthew Arnold's well-known concern with what he called "culture and anarchy," why not say that nowadays our philosophical culture in the West bids fair to giving way to anarchy, indeed, and the anarchy to tyranny!

For myself, though, I am afraid that rather than merely acquiescing in this state of affairs, and even though I now be much too superannuated to do much of anything about it—I am still determined to go right on insisting that, notwithstanding all current philosophical fashions being to the contrary, I do believe philosophy to be a thing for Hoosiers after all. Nor is it merely a case of Hoosiers, and of ordinary men generally, needing philosophy; it is no less a case of philosophy needing Hoosiers, and indeed of its needing once more to respect the judgment of the common sense and the common experience of mankind, instead of being forever mesmerized by all the different sorts of ingeniously invented and imposed standards that today's philosopher-intellectuals would try to gull us into accepting.

Of course, I realize that in insisting that the criterion of truth in philosophy should be the common judgments of all men everywhere, I can hardly maintain that always and in each individual case the judgments of human beings will invariably reflect the ability of ordinary men to see the truth clearly and to see it whole. Far from it. And yet just recall how it was Abraham Lincoln who said that while you can fool all of the people some of the time, and some of the people all of the time, what you cannot do is fool all of the people all of the time! And surely Lincoln was right! Indeed, in enunciating as his standard of truth that no one can fool all of the people all of the time, was not Lincoln really only articulating a conviction that was common alike to Aristotle and to St. Thomas?

No, I would not go so far as to claim that Honest Abe ever read Aristotle; and I am almost as sure as I am standing here that he doubtless never even heard of St. Thomas Aquinas. And yet, need I remind you once again of what I have already remarked on before, and that is that Aristotle was most unmistakably a Hoosier in spirit, if not in geography? And where was it, I ask you, that Lincoln grew up as a boy? Why, of course, you have already guessed it! He grew up in Southern Indiana, not far from the little town of Gentryville. Why, then, should it be so surprising that Aristotle and Lincoln should both have thought so much alike as regards the nature of philosophic truth, and whether such truth be not a thing for Hoosiers and for all men alike, and so is not just a thing merely for sophisticates and intellectuals? After all, anyone who has been to Gentryville, Indiana, can readily understand how that mere wide place in the road could have been a proper enough training ground for Honest Abe. But what it never was, and presumably never could be, would be any sort of rendezvous for intellectuals. No, not Gentryville, Indiana!

2

FOLLY AND SENSE IN PRESENT-DAY PHILOSOPHY[1]

How would it be, if, at least for tonight's occasion, we as philosophers undertook to concentrate on the task of trying "to see ourselves as others see us"? Unhappily, I am afraid the experience may not be too reassuring! For the way others see us is anything but flattering to ourselves. Thus consider what the title theme is for this entire annual meeting of the American Catholic Philosophical Association: "Philosophical Knowledge: *an sit et quid sit?*" Suppose now that such a question about philosophical knowledge were put to nonphilosophers? What would the likely answer be? Would it not be that there really is no such thing as philosophical knowledge? For just imagine a nonphilosopher putting to us the blunt question: "What is it, after all, that present-day philosophers can claim to know? What kind of knowledge does a philosopher have? A physicist claims to know about physics, and an accountant about accounting, and a computer expert about computers. But what exactly is a philosopher supposed to know about or be expert in?" To which we philosophers might imagine ourselves trying to give the somewhat cheery reply, "Oh, the philosopher is supposed to know about philosophy! What else?" Of course, and yet just what sort of a body of knowledge is it that one is knowledgeable about, when one is knowledgeable about philosophy? After all, everybody recognizes the kind of information, or the kind of facts, one comes to be informed of through the study of physics or biology, or even through accounting or computer science, or through history or psychology or medicine or whatever. But what are the facts that philosophy informs us about?

Of course, such questions nowadays are likely to be of little embarrassment to anyone except to the philosophers. For who takes philos-

---

1. Presidential address delivered before the American Catholic Philosophical Association, 1979.

43

ophy seriously anymore, unless it be the poor benighted philosophers, and perhaps not all of them either? And even the philosophers—at least the academic philosophers—being in general a rather smug and self-important lot, may not be too disturbed by the fact that as philosophers they really know nothing and have nothing to say. For having nothing to say is the last thing that would ever deter a contemporary philosopher from going right ahead and saying it—so much so in fact that it is tempting to suggest that just about the only saving grace left to today's philosophers is that nobody listens to them!

Still, it has not always been so. In the ancient world, for instance, it was assumed that it was to philosophy that one needed to turn in order to know anything. Yes, the very business of philosophy was no less than a knowledge of reality, of the world, and of the nature of things. And the point of philosophy was that from such a knowledge and understanding of the nature of things, the philosopher should be able to gain an insight into ethics, *i.e.*, into how we human beings ought to live, and what the things are that matter most in our human lives and human existence. For how can anyone, be it in the ancient world, or today, or whenever, ever hope to know how to order his life, or what the real values in life are, without first knowing, as it were, what the score is, or what the truth is about both the nature of things and the nature of our human situation? Thus it was that the Latin poet, Lucretius, being an Epicurean philosopher, could entitle his great poem, *De Rerum Natura,* "On the Nature of Things"; and in that poem could then think of himself as actually demonstrating how a hedonistic type of ethics—basically an "eat-drink-and-be-merry" sort of thing—must needs follow inevitably from an Epicurean state of nature, in which infinite atoms were incessantly, and indeed meaninglessly, raining down in an infinite space.

But as we all know, so all-embracing a conception of the business and role of philosophy as that which prevailed in the ancient world pretty much came to an end with the advent of the modern world, and particularly with the onset of modern science. Just ask anyone today whom we might best apply to, if what we want to know is what reality is like, or what the nature of things is. Of course, we shall be told we must apply to science and to the scientists. It is physics, chemistry, biology, geology, even the social sciences, that tell us what the facts are about our world, and in this sense what the nature of things is. Yet there is a major reservation to be appended to such advice: whereas in ancient times a philosophical knowledge of reality and the nature of things was thought to provide a ground and basis for ethics and for a knowledge of how to live, in modern times it has come to be generally recognized that a scientific knowledge of the nature of things really gives no guidance at all as to what ultimately we human beings ought to do and be. Modern physics, for instance, can assure us that, say, water seeks its own level, or that the atom can be split; but it gives us no inkling as to whether atomic fission is right or wrong, or whether water's seeking its own level is good or bad. Not only that, but even a social science like economics, while it may well be able to demonstrate that slave labor can be most productive under certain circumstances, and comparatively unproductive under others, does nothing, if not simply evade the issue, when it comes to demonstrating that slave labor is either morally right or morally wrong.

Still, does not this very state of things suggest a possible deal and division of labor, as between science and philosophy, that could possibly serve to rehabilitate the poor, dispossessed philosophers, and really give them something to do again, so far as their making a genuine contribution to knowledge is concerned? Granted that the modern scientists have pretty well taken over from the ancient philosophers when it comes to providing us with a knowledge of the nature of things, then why not let the modern philosophers, for their part, take over when it comes to a knowledge of ethics? Yes, we can even imagine the rich and well-placed scientists making a magnanimous gesture toward the comparatively bankrupt and unemployed philosophers: "Let us deal with the facts, and you deal with questions of morals and ethics!"

Scientists being generous, however, are rather like Greeks bearing gifts! For the original business of the philosopher was knowledge, and even today it still tends to be recognized that if the philosopher can't deal in knowledge, he can't deal at all: he might as well just go out of business as a philosopher. Is it any wonder, then, that today's scientists should appear so willing to deed to the philosophers the whole domain of ethics? Is it not because, in the scientists' eyes, ethics is really not a proper matter of knowledge at all? Distinctions between good and bad, and right and wrong, just aren't to be found in the facts; nor is there any way in which so-called scientific evidence could be brought to bear on such questions. And so it is that a philosopher like Bertrand Russell, in the course of his exceedingly long and, shall we say, quite colorful intellectual career, could make countless speeches, and turn out any number of books and pamphlets dealing with ethical and political questions, and yet at the same time be quite frank to admit that in none of all this could he (Russell) really claim to know what he was talking about. Why, then, did he talk about it? Well, his own answer was that he just wanted people to know how he felt about such matters—as if even the mere feelings and prejudices of so great a man were somehow worthy of expression and advertisement!

Besides, be it said to the credit of the third Earl, that when he did thus address himself to issues of ethics and politics, he was nearly always scrupulous in not claiming to be doing so as a philosopher. For to Russell the business of the philosopher was nothing if not knowledge; and if there can be no proper knowledge in regard to matters of ethics and politics, then ethics and politics are no proper business of the philosopher as such. But then what is the business of the philosopher, and what is his particular area of knowledge, if anything?

This is not to say, of course, that any number of the most eminent philosophers of recent years, at least in the English-speaking world, have not occupied themselves with, and even made their reputations on the basis of, their work in ethics—G. E. Moore, Stephen Toulmin, R. M. Hare in England, and in the United States R. B. Perry, Charles Stevenson, Richard Brandt; and more recently, perhaps, John Rawls and Robert Nozick; and more certainly, and still more recently, Alan Gewirth and Alan Donagan. Yet curiously enough, while all of these philosophers would insist that ethics is a legitimate area of knowledge, and in this sense a proper area of occupation for themselves as philosophers, their insistence on this score has been not a little compromised by their having to admit that ethical knowledge is not really in any strict sense a factual knowledge, and cannot be said to rest on empirical evidence in the manner of scientific knowledge. But why then call it knowledge? To such a question, it is true, there have been no want of answers on the part of various of our recent and currently fashionable ethicists. The only trouble is that these answers have tended to be, if not downright sophistic, at least disturbingly unconvincing!

And so the question still presses: is it the case that present-day philosophers really don't know anything? And to obviate their embarrassment with respect to this question, not a few such philosophers, rather than beat any hasty retreat into ethics, have chosen the course of casting about for a more or less new and even somewhat recondite area of knowledge, which the scientists may perhaps have either overlooked or disregarded. For while it may be conceded that the scientists have indeed done a good job, and still give every promise of continuing to do an even better job, in telling us all about the facts of our world, have the scientists been at equal pains to consider the very means and implements that they themselves and everyone else cannot very well avoid using in the acquisition and articulation of knowledge, be it scientific or otherwise? These are the implements of logic and language. Why, then, might not the philosopher busy himself with investigating these things?

Remember, it isn't just the scientist who uses language and logic; we all do. Not only that, but the language of everyday life is different from the language of science; the language of music and art is different from the language of morals; and all of these are different from the language of religion and religious devotion. Moreover, what is significant in all this is that it is not just our knowledge about the world and about ourselves, but in addition our every expression of any kind—of our feelings, and of our reactions to anything and everything—that are inevitably shaped and colored and determined by the incredibly diverse and largely unnoticed language games that we tend to play in these many and varied contexts. Here, then, is business for the philosopher, surely! And who can say that contemporary philosophy is bankrupt, when the philosopher has such a host of logical and linguistic issues to busy himself about?

Unfortunately, however complacent the present-day philosopher may feel about having now got something really to do at long last, is it likely that such to-do over language and logic is ever going to impress the ordinary person or the ordinary citizen that the philosopher really has any serious business to perform? For does it not all sound like so much ado, if not about nothing, then certainly about very little? To go in for a knowledge, not of the world and of the nature of things, but only of the linguistic and logical devices associated with our experience of the world and of the nature of things—is this anything but a distraction from the real *stuff* of knowledge to its mere *form*, a fascination with only the shadow and not the substance? What, then, is the present-day philosopher to say to this? Well, whatever he may say—and certainly it is apparent on the face of it that he cannot say much—the fact remains that any number of the most distinguished names in contemporary philosophy are names of people who first won their spurs in philosophy largely on the basis of their work in logic and language—Russell, Wittgenstein, Quine, Kripke, and in a somewhat different way, perhaps Austin, Ryle and Davidson, among the philosophers in the English-speaking world; and of course on the Continent there has long been a preoccupation with questions of language among the phenomenologists, the existentialists, and now among the emergent varieties of French structuralists.

Is it any wonder, then, given the prestige, to say nothing of the overweening sense of greatness, of so many of these persons and parties in recent philosophy, that philosophers such as these would hardly be content to let themselves be written off by their contemporaries as but largely concerned with mere logico-linguistic trivia and inconsequentials? Quite the contrary, in recent years it would seem that philosophers of this general persuasion were trying to make some sort of a comeback, even if it meant pulling themselves up by their own bootstraps! "Language games and logical systems are mere trivia," do you say? "Far from it," the answer is, "for how else do you think we can talk about things, or even in any way organize and order our experience, save in terms of the very sorts of language or logic that we happen to be using? And what does this imply, if not that the very form and shape of things, indeed the very character of the world as different people see it and interpret it, is simply a function of the logical and linguistic devices in terms of which various language users react to it and thereby structure it?"

Accordingly, it is considerations of this sort that have led any number of recent philosophers—Heidegger, Wittgenstein, Sartre, Popper, Quine, Strawson, Sellars, and various lesser lights as well—to say, each of them in their respectively different ways, that the proper way to regard the philosopher nowadays is no less than as a man of vision. For if things are pretty much the way we take them to be, or the way we see them as being, depending upon our linguistic and logical modes of vision and interpretation, then why is not the philosopher just the one to supply us with such made-to-order visions in the sense of ways of seeing? And while the scientist, of course, will still be the source of our knowledge of the facts, the philosopher—at least so the argument runs—must now be the one who, so far from being able to discover ever new facts, is rather the one to get us to see the same old facts in ever new ways. Besides, who would want seriously to dispute this new role for the philosopher? For we all must acknowledge that the facts the scientists ply us with are so numerous and so heterogeneous that no one can take them all in, not even the scientist. And so it is that the philosopher is seemingly just made to order to come to the rescue here: he will supply us with ways of organizing the facts, ways of getting a purchase on them, thereby giving us a kind of synthesis, an overview, a *Weltanschauung*, if you like. Conclusion: the philosopher must be our twentieth century visionary! And remember that we have it on the very best authority that "without vision the people perish!"

What, then, have we here! From having been down and out, our new-day philosophers would suddenly seem to be up and on top. From having had to play second fiddle to the scientist, it now appears it is the scientist who must play second fiddle to the philosopher. For what can the scientist do but grub and grind about among the facts, whereas it is the philosopher who comes forward as the great seer and man of vision, the man (or woman) who teaches us how to see the facts, how to get a perspective on them, how to interpret them! Of course, there is but one fly in this soothing ointment for philosophers. True, we will none of us deny that in today's world we do need visions all right. The only trouble is that when we reflect upon the matter a bit, it turns out that the people seem to perish *with* visions, no less than *without* them. For was not Hitler a visionary, no less than Winston Churchill, say? And what about Mao Tse Tung or Karl Marx; or perhaps Napoleon or Oliver Cromwell or Mahommet and certainly the Ayatollah Khomeini! Yes, one might even venture to say that the anti-Christ must have been a visionary no less than the Christ! Hence no sooner does one ascribe a visionary role to the philosophers than one must hasten to reckon with the fact that visions as such are not necessarily unmixed blessings. And who is to judge between the true visions and the false ones?

Nor can our newly self-appointed philosopher-visionaries suddenly take thought and try to claim to be the judges of their visions, no less than their creators. For any such judgment would presumably have to be on the basis of knowledge. And have we not seen how the new-day philosophers chose quite cavalierly to toss over to the plodding scientists the humdrum business of a mere knowledge of facts, whereas they, the philosophers, elected to soar over and beyond the facts and into the wide-blue yonder of their own visions? With this, then, the poor philosophers would appear to be brought right back once again to square one! For have we not seen how the predicament of the philosopher, ever since the advent of the modern period, has been nothing if not this: how can philosophers claim to know anything; and if there be nothing that philosophers can rightly and properly claim to know, then what good are they?

But no, the wily present-day philosopher is still not done for! For when taxed with the dubious character of his role as a visionary, he is likely—and this is indeed something that has happened just in the last few years—to reverse his field and say: "So far from discrediting myself by claiming to be a visionary as contrasted with the slow but sure scientist, it is really the scientist who is just as much the visionary as the philosopher. Hence if the philosopher is to be suspect on account of his visions, the scientist cannot avoid coming out tarred with the same brush." Moreover, the way the contemporary philosopher is thus able to reverse his field, and suddenly associate himself with the scientist for protection, as contrasted with his earlier tactic of distancing himself from the scientist, in order to pretend to a superiority over him, is simply to follow the lead of a number of philosophers of science, and scientist-philosophers, of recent fame and fortune—men like Sir Karl Popper and the late N. R. Hanson, and still more recently Thomas Kuhn and Paul Feyerabend.

It was a singularly ingenious line of argument that these men developed. For is it not obvious, they said, that apart from low-level scientific laws like "Water boils at 100°C," or "Silver melts at 960.5°C," the great overarching theories and hypotheses of science are not established by induction, or on the basis of observation at all. Kepler, for instance, did not go out and observe a number of the planets to be moving in elliptical rather than circular orbits, and then generalize that all the planets must surely be moving in that same way! Nor did Newton first observe several physical bodies, that happened not to be acted upon by any external forces, just continuing on indefinitely in motion, and then from such data proceed to infer his (Newton's) first law of motion. Rather it was a case of Kepler's having devised, right out of his mathematician's imagination, his hypothesis as to the elliptical orbits of the planets. And likewise, Sir Isaac Newton—at least so the new historians and philosophers of science are wont to tell us—did not arrive at his laws of motion from experience. Instead, he simply invented his laws out of his own head, he dreamed them up, as it were, much as one might think up the movement of a symphony or the plot of a novel. In other words, the really great scientists—the Keplers, the Newtons, the Einsteins, the Heisenbergs—were nothing if not true visionaries. Not only that, but their visions—that is to say, their great revolutionary scientific hypotheses and theories—could scarcely be said ever to be definitively verified by subsequent observation. Quite the contrary, considered logically, the very process of verification of hypotheses in experience commits a simple and unmitigated fallacy. And no less than verification, falsification would seem to be out too, so far as basic scientific theories are concerned, and that for the simple reason that such a scientific theory is really like a vision: it represents an entire way of seeing things, a framework in terms of which we view them, so that the facts or the data can only appear to us to be the way they are in terms of the theory or conceptual scheme or framework through which we view them. In other words, no data but what they are already theory-laden, and no data but what they can always be made to seem to confirm, and never really to falsify, the theory in terms of which they took on the character of being data in the first place.

And with that, presto! It looks as if maybe the philosophers had done it again. Having run the danger of being discredited in their claim to knowledge, simply because as philosophers they had put themselves forward as little better than wheelers and dealers in visions, rather than in hard knowledge like the scientists, the philosophers would appear now to have deftly turned the tables: "You say that in contrast to the scientists we are mere visionaries and dreamers? But are not the great geniuses of science no less dreamers and visionaries than the philosophers, and in exactly the same sense? Yes, for the matter of that, there would seem to be no basic difference at all any longer between the kind of knowledge that philosophers claim to have and that which the scientists claim. For has not Professor Quine of Harvard—certainly one of the most eminent of contemporary American philosophers today—declared flat out that science and philosophy, so far from being different cognitive enterprises, are really all of a piece? In fact, so far as the visionary hypotheses and conceptual schemes and world views in terms of which we order the data of our experience are concerned, it makes really no difference whether such theories and hypotheses be called the work of philosophers or the work of scientists. It's very much six in one, half-a-dozen in another!"

Surely, though, this is nothing if not astonishing! Indeed, why may we not even ask at this point, "But isn't this just where we all came in!" For the original difficulty that we seemed to be up against, so far as philosophy was concerned, was just the difficulty as to whether philosophy could any longer claim to be a legitimate body of knowledge. In other words, what is it that the philosopher, *qua* philosopher, can properly be said to know about? And the source of this difficulty was traceable to the fact that whereas in the ancient world the philosopher claimed a knowledge of reality and the nature of things, such a claim, it would appear, could now no longer be sustained in the modern period, simply because we have all come to recognize that it is the scientist and not the philosopher who has taken over the business of providing us with a knowledge of nature and reality. How, then, can it possibly be a defense of philosophy, and philosophic knowledge, for contemporary philosophers suddenly to start telling us, "Oh, but you see, we philosophers really are no different from scientists after all: we do much the same things; we investigate many of the same problems; we make the same knowledge claims!" But what is this if not mere word juggling? If philosophy, as men once knew it, is now generally taken to be bankrupt, then it is not likely that the bankrupt philosopher can very well hope to restore himself to respectability and solvency by baldly putting the story about that he is nothing if not a full-fledged business partner of his very scientist creditors after all.

Why, though, need we say more about what so-called informed

opinion among nonphilosophers is nowadays, as regards philosophy and philosophers? Isn't it obvious that when as philosophers we thus make an effort to see ourselves as others see us, the spectacle is hardly likely to be a flattering one? Remember that that very line from the poet Robert Burns about seeing ourselves as others see us is taken from a poem entitled "To a Louse." And the occasion that prompted the poem was Burns' having been in church and observing on the hat of a fine lady, seated in the pew in front of him, a louse suddenly crawling out from under the masses of flowers and tulle on the hat! Perhaps, therefore, we philosophers ought to let that be an object lesson for ourselves, when we pause long enough to see ourselves as others see us.

What, then, ought we to conclude from the fact that the present spectacle that we make of ourselves is comparable to that of a fine lady with a louse on her hat? Must we simply acknowledge, after following all of these incredible twists and turns that modern philosophers have resorted to, in order to save themselves and save philosophy, that they have not managed to save philosophy after all, and that philosophy itself in the present day is nothing if not a largely bankrupt venture in the matter of knowledge? Hardly. Instead, why not just say that rather than its being philosophy that has gone bankrupt, it is the somewhat bemused and confused present-day philosophers who have done so? For haven't they let themselves be persuaded into selling their very birthright as philosophers—*i.e.* their birthright to what may properly be called simply a knowledge of nature and reality? Haven't they pretty much relinquished knowledge of this sort to the scientists? Or why not just carry through with our earlier metaphor and say that the philosophers are like no one so much as Esau in the Bible: they have sold their birthright for a mess of potage—potage handed them by the scientists!

For just what exactly is the knowledge of nature and reality that the philosophers have given over to the scientists? Is it really a knowledge of nature and reality? True, it has only come to light in very recent years, and that light is none other than that associated with what has sometimes been called "the new image of science." But still, what this new image of science would appear to light up is just the fact that the term "knowledge" probably should no longer be considered a univocal term at all—*i.e.* univocal as between scientific knowledge on the one hand and philosophical knowledge on the other. Yet how many philosophers in the present day have taken the trouble to think through the implications of this new image of science? True, the image itself is largely the work of philosophers rather than scientists—of philosophers of science, that is to say. Yet have the philosophers themselves really considered the full import of this their "new image of science"? For the most striking feature about this "image" is that it tends definitely to establish the fact that "science," at least in the sense of the most up-to-date, contemporary natural science, is fundamentally a visionary—not to say even a largely speculative—enterprise and activity. Rather than being basically empirical and inductive in its procedures, science now seems given over largely to following the hypothetico-deductive method. For how often have we not been reminded that the overarching theories and fundamental hypotheses of science, so far from having been arrived at, or in any way logically inferred from, any evidence, are rather said to be simply dreamed up, invented, made up out of whole cloth, as it were? And while, once a scientific hypothesis has been propounded, it is insisted that empirical observation and evidence are of course relevant to the establishment of the hypothesis, the exact nature of this relevance is difficult to determine, at least logically. For it can hardly be said that empirical evidence is ever able to verify the hypothesis, since that would involve a logical fallacy. And while using empirical evidence to falsify hypotheses commits no logical fallacy, it unfortunately would seem to be a procedure that in principle is quite incapable of ever yielding an unequivocal and definitive instance of such falsification in regard to hypotheses.

And so what to do? Well, there would seem to be no alternative but to fall back on what can only be called a transcendental method of justification, so far as scientific theories and hypotheses are concerned. That is to say, a theory or hypothesis in science is accepted, ultimately, for scarcely any other reason than that it enables us to introduce at least some sort of order and intelligibility into what would otherwise be a sheer welter of experience. Or as a Kant might put it, our basic categories and categorical schemes are accepted finally for no other reason than that they make experience possible, or at least experience of anything that in any proper sense of the word could be called a "world."

Given, though, such a transcendental mode of justification—or as Quine might prefer to call it, such a purely pragmatic justification—of the truth of science and scientific theories, then the consequence would appear to be at once clear and inescapable: science and scientific knowledge are logically precluded from ever being a knowledge of nature and reality as they really are, or as they are in themselves; instead, scientific knowledge amounts to no more—and in fairness one needs to add, to no less—than a knowledge of but the appearances of things. That is, of things as they appear to us to be, when seen through the medium of our particular scientific hypotheses and categories and conceptual schemes, but not of things as they really are.

So be it, then, for science and scientific knowledge. But what of philosophy and philosophical knowledge? Why assume that it needs to be at all in a like case with scientific knowledge? True, this is an assumption which most present-day philosophers would seem to make—shall I say "Critically" with a capital "C," or "uncritically" with a lowercase "c"? But why? Why should present-day philosophers, or at least so many of them, allow themselves thus to be led down this Kantian primrose path to everlasting bonfire? Or why should philosophers be inclined to assume that their knowledge claims in philosophy are largely on all fours with the knowledge claims of scientists in science? Indeed, might not this be just that mess of potage that present-day philosophers have let the scientists hand them, and in exchange for which the philosophers gave up their ancient birthright to a knowledge of nature and reality as these really are in themselves?

Oh, it's true, no doubt, that one reason the philosophers have let themselves be thus beguiled into accepting such a mere potage of transcendental knowledge, rather than a knowledge of being, is that philosophers, ever since the impact of Kant and of the Romantic movement generally, have liked to fancy themselves as playing the role of great visionaries in matters of knowledge, as original geniuses who teach us to see things in ever new lights, or perhaps as mighty and supreme manifestations of some Hegelian Spirit of the Age. But no! Surely, philosophers ought to have none of that. Such indulgence in heady transcendental modes of thinking may be all right for the "new-image" scientists, but for philosophers it is hard to think of it as anything other than indulgence in sheer vanity and folly. Such need not be—and indeed in the main tradition of Greek and Christian thought it never was—the accepted mode and manner of philosophizing, or of philosophical knowledge.

Thus just by way of example, consider Aristotle's classic description and account of change in terms of the three principles of matter, form, and privation. Did Aristotle arrive at this by an ingenious use of the hypothetico-deductive method, and then proceed to justify his hypothesis in regard to change and motion by invoking some sort of transcendental argument? Of course not. Instead, he simply came to see, as I am sure each and everyone of us cannot help seeing, that the very fact of change itself requires that there be something that changes, and that it change from something to something else. So, far from being any hypothesis devised to explain the fact of change, this is rather something written on the very face of change itself—that's just it, in other words!

Or consider an example from metaphysics—say, the principle that for anything to be, it must be something, *i.e.* it must be the kind of thing that it is, or be what it is, or be essentially of the nature that it is and not something else. Surely, such a principle of the connection or identification of a being with its essence is no hypothesis that is put forward but hypothetically, and then demands to be subjected to a subsequent verification or falsification in experience. Nor is this principle of the character of a synthetic judgment *a priori*, that ultimately can be justified only on the ground that without it our human experience, rather than being in any way intelligible to us, would be no more than a mere "booming, buzzing confusion." True, our experience would make no sense, if nothing were what it is. And yet the very justification of such a principle of being and essence does not turn on considerations to the effect that, however things may be in themselves, nevertheless for us and for our human experience of the world, things must always appear to us as somehow being what they are—and that simply in virtue of the transcendental exigencies of our logic or of our human language games.

Nor need we limit ourselves only to examples drawn from physics and metaphysics, if we want to exhibit what is distinctive about what I might call a realistic philosophical knowledge, as opposed to a scientific knowledge of the transcendental type, such as is associated with the new image of science. For take ethics: Is it not evident to us, simply as human beings and not just as philosophers, that various of the things or substances in the world round about us, for better or worse, just are not all that they might be or could be? A tree may be sickly or stunted in its growth, an animal lame or maimed in its gait, or a fish half-starved for lack of food—just a poor fish, in other words! And what goes for trees and fish and brute animals, of course, goes for human beings as well, except that in our case our deficiencies and inadequacies may well be of a sort that we ourselves are more often than not responsible for. For instance, is it not true that throughout this entire harangue of mine this evening, any number of you in the audience have been muttering to yourselves, "Poor Veatch, he ought not to go on raving and ranting like that! He ought to have better sense." And at the very same time that you are making these judgments of censure with respect to me, just think how in the very moment of your severest condemnation of me, you have right before your eyes and ready for your most enthusiastic commendation all the many and varied and shining examples of virtue and good sense right up here at the speakers' table—Fr. Sweeney, Sr. Clark, Fr. Norris Clarke, Fr. Owens, Fr. McLean and all the rest! For are they not, each and every one of them, veritable paragons of moral virtue, not to mention philosophic wisdom and insight? Yes, what are they if not unquestioned manifestations of the very Aristotelian ideal of the great-souled man, or woman!

But now I ask you, as the rest of you sit out there in front of us up here at the table, making your judgments as to the contrasting types set before you of human excellence and human deficiency, can you honestly say that these moral judgments that you thus make so surely and so justly are judgments that ultimately have no warrant save in terms of some involuted transcendental argument or other? In conclusion, then, why should not all of us, simply as philosophers, seek once more to reclaim our philosophers' birthright, and thereby to let sense prevail over folly in the matter of philosophic knowledge? Why not recognize, let us say, that philosophic knowledge just is not cut to the same cloth as scientific knowledge? So far from being a transcendental knowledge of but the way nature and reality appear to us to be, a philosopher's knowledge is a knowledge of nature and reality as they really are.

True, this philosopher's knowledge of being and of the natural world may not extend very far, or be able to acquaint us with too many, or even scarcely with any, of the details of nature. For this region we surely need to admit quite candidly that much of nature and the natural world remains opaque to philosophic penetration, just as, at the other end of the philosophic spectrum, it has long been acknowledged that a knowledge of God and of the divine nature is largely inaccessible to philosophy, at least apart from revelation. And so it is that our philosophic knowledge of the natural world does indeed need to be, as it were, massively supplemented by a scientific knowledge, which, while it may be able to acquaint us with no more than appearances, nevertheless does provide us with the most incredible technologies for our human control and manipulation of nature. Still, for all of that, the philosopher is able to achieve a knowledge of the nature of things, at least in its principles and fundamental causes. Why, then, as philosophers do we not stand on our own two feet and profess that knowledge of fundamental principles regarding nature, man, and God—a knowledge such as is accessible to philosophic understanding, and such as is not amenable to treatment by any of the natural sciences so-called; and yet such as does truly mount up to a knowledge of "the things that matter most," alike to us as men and in our lives as human beings?

3

IS QUINE A METAPHYSICIAN?

The title question of this essay to many may sound impertinent; and besides, is it not a gratuitous question as well? For has not Professor Quine himself repeatedly characterized his philosophical concerns as being concerns with ontology? Nor would there seem to be any doubt that Quine takes "ontology" to be largely synonymous with "metaphysics." True, he may not come right out, beating his chest and shouting, "I am a metaphysician, and damned be he who first says 'No' to that!" Rather his way is one that at least by Quinean standards can only be described as *suaviter in modo*. Thus he frequently insists that, as he sees it, the enterprise of ontology is really indistinguishable from that of science, and that in consequence a part of his philosophical activity may be seen as having the effect of "blurring the supposed boundary between speculative metaphysics and natural science."[1]

Nevertheless, for all such reassurances to the effect that Quine indeed is a metaphysician, there could well be not a few old mossbacks who would refuse to be thus reassured. Time was—though this was surely years ago—when so far from Quine's being hailed as a member of the ancient and honorable order of metaphysicians, he was instead roundly cursed for being almost the very heresiarch of the anti-metaphysicians! And while nearly all such oldsters as may once have uttered such curses are now either dead or at least among those who could be said to have given up the ghost philosophically, still the question persists, "Is Quine's philosophical activity that of a metaphysician?"; "Does he ask the same sorts of questions, and is he trying to get at the same sorts of things as, say, Plato or Aristotle, as Descartes or Spinoza, or even as Whitehead or Bergmann?"

Put the question this way, and I would wonder if an initially seeming inappropriate question might not prove to be a new and comparatively fruitful way of illuminating just what it is that Quine's philosophy is

---

1. W. V. Quine, "Two Dogmas of Empiricism," in *From a Logical Point of View* (Cambridge, MA: Harvard University Press, 1953), p. 20.

all about. For to the uninitiated it may not be immediately apparent quite what Quine is up to philosophically. Raise the question, though, as to whether and how Quine might most properly be reckoned a metaphysician, and maybe a new light will begin to dawn. For must it not immediately occur to one that in some ways "metaphysics" is perhaps not a univocal term, and that while, in one sense, Quine could well be a metaphysician, in another sense, he just wouldn't make the grade at all and wouldn't even want to!

Thus, for instance, we surely do not need to be reminded that for many the concern of metaphysics is simply with being or reality—perhaps in Aristotle's sense of being *qua* being, or perhaps in the sense of Being or ultimate Reality, or perhaps in the sense of the logical atomists, where a concern with being might be characterized as a concern with the ultimate entities, or the ultimate simples, or "the ultimate furniture of the world." In sharp contrast, though, with such conceptions of the subject matter of metaphysics, is that very different notion of metaphysics, associated with what might simply be called the tradition of Kantian transcendental philosophy. Thus, on the latter view of metaphysics—this being more or less consequent upon the so-called transcendental or epistemological turn in philosophy that was effected largely as a result of Kant's efforts—it tends to become an exercise in futility for metaphysics any longer to occupy itself with trying to discover what being is in itself, or what the nature of things is, or with the ultimate entities as these are in themselves. For how can such things ever come to be known, at least in any proper sense of "know"? Accordingly, on the Kantian and post-Kantian conception of metaphysics, the prior business of metaphysics has got to be with whether and how a metaphysical knowledge in the more traditional sense is even possible—*i.e.*, with what the conditions must be of human knowledge in general and of a metaphysical knowledge in particular. In other words, the first business of metaphysics is not with trying to achieve a knowledge of being *qua* being, but rather with trying to determine the conditions under which such a knowledge becomes possible. And so it is that metaphysics on this Kantian model comes to be identified with the enterprise of so-called transcendental philosophy.

Supposing, then, that "metaphysics" is a term fraught with the sort of ambiguity that has been somewhat crudely roughed out in the preceding paragraph, what are we to say of Quine? Is he a metaphysician in the more traditional Aristotelian sense, or is he rather to be classified as a metaphysician in the more up-to-date and fashionable sense of the transcendental philosopher? Immediately, the reaction will be that since just about the last thing Quine could ever be accused of being would be an Aristotelian, the only alternative left would be but to write him off as a transcendental philosopher of the inevitable Kantian stripe—if not an overt and acknowledged Kantian, then perhaps a covert or crypto-Kantian! To which suggestion we may imagine that any and all Quineans, including Quine himself, would react at first with utter astonishment; and then perhaps, quickly recovering themselves, they might be heard to cry out in anger about how dastardly it is in philosophy to try to victimize a thinker through the fallacy of complex question. Or more in character, they might complain about the impropriety of anyone's ever invoking anything even suggesting "natural kinds" in philosophy or metaphysics. Yes, it is conceivable that Quineans might even become technical at this point and quote the master to the effect that

> ... the notion of kind, or similarity, is crucially relevant to the notion of disposition, to the subjunctive conditional, and to singular causal statements. From a scientific point of view [these latter] are a pretty disreputable lot. The notion of kind, or similarity, is equally disreputable. Yet some such notion, some similarity sense, was seen to be crucial to all learning, and central in particular to the processes of inductive generalization and prediction which are the very life of science. It appears [thus] that science is rotten to the core.[2]

And from here the Quineans might go on to admit that if such "rot" as is associated with kinds, with similarity, with dispositional properties, etc., be as indispensable in science as it is unclean in itself, one might even tolerate for a time the still greater rot in philosophy of classifications like "Aristotelian," or "transcendental philosopher," in an effort to understand philosophies and philosophers. Still, there is a way, Quine tells us, in which the rot can be, if not exactly eliminated, then at least rendered harmless in science, and perhaps in philosophy too. For he explains how in chemistry a notion like solubility in water can "get its clean bill of health." "One can redefine water-solubility by simply describing the structural conditions of that mechanism." And "once we can legitimize a disposition term by defining the relevant similarity standard, we are apt to know the mechanism of the disposition, and so bypass the similarity."[3]

Why not, then, follow a like procedure in matters of metaphysics and philosophy? Just learn what the structural conditions are that determine the mechanism for producing an Aristotelian or a Kantian or whomever, and then, no doubt, one can simply bypass such classifications altogether. Unfortunately, the mechanism of a disposition

---

2. W. V. Quine, "Natural Kinds," in *Ontological Relativity and Other Essays* (New York and London: Columbia University Press, 1969), p. 133.
3. *Ibid.*, p. 136.

toward water-solubility might prove to be rather easier to determine than is the mechanism of any disposition toward Kantianism, or even toward transcendental philosophy generally, with the result that dispensing with such a similarity as that, say, between philosophers of a transcendental bent might be far less easy in philosophy than would be, say, the bypassing of classifications and similarities in chemistry. But be all that as it may, our latter-day Quineans do seem to have taken the instructions of their master almost too much to heart. For they never bother to tell us what kind of a philosopher or metaphysician Quine is. Doubtless they would prefer that one not try to type Quine at all, as being a philosopher of this, or that, or even of any kind, but rather treat him as simply *eine Nummer für sich*! And maybe even Quine himself would wish to be known as just the philosopher *non pareil*! But whatever the motive, the fact remains that if you take a Quinean interpreter, or neo-Quinean philosopher, such as Professor Gilbert Harman in the two articles he published in the *Review of Metaphysics* several years ago,[4] it is perhaps not without significance that while Harman goes to great pains to expound Quine's critique of analyticity, his elimination of meanings and intentional objects, his notion of ontological commitment, etc., he says not a single word about what all of these specific Quinean doctrines add up to philosophically. What sort of a philosopher do such teachings on specific points make of Quine, and just how does Quine come out smelling philosophically, given his notions about analyticity or about intentional objects or about ontological commitment or whatever—does he smell like a Platonist or a Cartesian or a Humean or a Nietzschean, or what? To such questions one finds no answer in Harman or, for that matter, in any of the other contemporary commentators on Quine that we know of. And while such a self-denying ordinance with respect to making comparisons between Quine and other figures in the history of Western philosophy may well serve to seal off contemporary philosophy from the obvious "rot" of kinds, of similarities, and other enormities of that ilk, the unhappy result is that contemporary philosophy, at least in its Quinean form, will remain largely unintelligible to any save only a happy few among the cognoscenti.

Very well, we propose to rush in where angels, no less than Quineans, would apparently fear to tread and try to classify Quine for the kind of metaphysician that we think he really is. And as we have already implied, we think he is a metaphysician simply in the mode

---

4. "Quine on Meaning and Existence," *Review of Metaphysics* 21 (September 1967): 125–151; 21 (December 1967), 343–367.

or manner of a transcendental philosopher.[5] Moreover, to sustain such a thesis, we would propose, at the start at least, to follow the very lead that Quine himself has suggested in his repeated assertions that for him science and speculative metaphysics are to be regarded as being, if not one and the same, then certainly as continuous with one another. Accordingly, in any enterprise aimed at determining what sort of a metaphysics Quinean metaphysics is, would it not make sense for us first to determine just what sort of an enterprise modern natural science is?

Fortunately, with respect to the latter question we need do little more than follow the lead of several of the more up-to-the-minute philosophers of science among our contemporaries. For what seems to be common to many if not most contemporary philosophers of science is their tendency to characterize science, not in terms of subject matter or a set of doctrines, but rather in terms of method. Thus physics, for example, is not to be thought of as being concerned with *ens mobile,* say, in the manner of the Aristotelian Scholastics, or with being, in so far as it is quantifiable, or possessed of so-called primary qualities, as was characteristic of the seventeenth century. Instead, the current fashion is to think of science, and particularly physical science, in terms of the methods which the scientists rely upon in order to arrive at their so-called scientific knowledge. Of course, these methods are all held to be "empirical," in at least some sense of that poor, jaded term. Still, the interesting thing about the more contemporary philosophical discussions of scientific method is the way in which these philosopher-scientists, or scientist-philosophers, would appear to want to qualify, to reinterpret, and even in a measure to "do down" the presumed empiricism of modern science. Sir Karl Popper, of course, is the name that immediately comes to mind as being the one who pretty much set the stage for that whole spate of recent discussions by philosophers of science of the nature and character of modern scientific method. As we all know, the hallmark of *The Logic of Scientific Discovery* was its discrediting of induction as the decisive resource of

---

5. Lest the thesis of this present article be thought to be entirely without precedent, it should be noted that a few years ago there appeared in the *Philosophical Review* 81 (October 1972), 484–97, an article entitled "Kant, Quine, and Human Experience" by Kenton F. Machina. However, Professor Machina's objective and method of procedure are both rather different from our own. For Professor Machina's concern is much more with the letter of the *Critique of Pure Reason* and with whether Quine might possibly be reckoned a Kantian in this literal sense. In contrast, we have concerned ourselves with the spirit rather than the letter of that so-called transcendental turn in philosophy for which Kant might be held ultimately responsible; and it is only in this larger sense that we are asking whether Quine might perhaps be reckoned as a metaphysician of a markedly Kantian persuasion.

empirical science. Not only is induction said to be of a dubious reliability logically, but in addition and simply as a matter of historical fact in the history of science, it would appear that the major hypotheses and theories of science—as contrasted perhaps with mere low-level scientific laws—were not arrived at by any process of induction on the part of the scientist who devised the theory or the hypothesis. That water boils at 100°C or that silver melts at 960.5°C may, in a sense, be said to have been established by induction from experience. In contrast, a basic hypothesis like Kepler's, that the planets move in elliptical orbits, or like Newton's first law of motion, that a body not acted upon by an external force will continue indefinitely in motion or at rest—these certainly are not established by induction. After all, Kepler did not observe first one planet and then another moving in ellipses, and then generalize from these cases to his hypothesis. Nor did Newton observe, nor could he have observed, the behavior of a number of physical bodies not acted upon by external forces, in order then to infer his law by an induction from experience. No, Popper insists that scientific hypotheses and theories of this nature are neither derivable from experience nor verifiable in experience. Nor would Quine presumably demur in any way at such Popperian qualifications regarding the empirical bases of science. Quite the contrary, Quine constantly insists that not only are scientific hypotheses, but even everyday judgments about the nature and identity of ordinary objects—yes, even the judgment that what we are perceiving are, shall we say, ordinary objects like tables and chairs and people, etc.—all such judgments, Quine would insist, are *underdetermined* by experience.

To return, though, to Popper and his account of what he chooses to call the logic of scientific discovery. Supposing that the theories and hypotheses of modern science are neither derived from experience nor verified by experience, how then is it that the scientists come by their theories and hypotheses in the first place, and what is their warrant for accepting them, once they have been propounded? In answer to the former question, Popper insists that scientific hypotheses are not arrived at by any logical procedure of any kind, be it either inductive or deductive. Instead, he compares their initial invention or discovery to the devising of a plot for a novel, or the dreaming up of a theme for a symphony. In other words, the basic principles and overall frameworks of modern science are not really to be thought of as being either inferred or discovered in any way, so much as they are simply invented or dreamed up or made up, as it were, out of whole cloth.

Of course, once a scientific hypothesis has been thus devised and propounded, the second of our two questions just mentioned above immediately becomes pertinent: granted that there is no logical or empirical basis for the invention of a scientific theory or hypothesis, must there not be at least some reason or basis or ground for our accepting it, once it has been so devised or thought up? And to this question, Popper gives an emphatically affirmative answer. True, our hypotheses cannot be said to be warranted on the ground of their being subsequently verified in experience. For any procedure of trying to verify a hypothesis commits the obvious logical fallacy of affirming the consequent. On the other hand, scientific hypotheses, while they cannot strictly be verified in experience, can be, and often are, falsified in experience. And this procedure of falsifying a hypothesis is as logically impeccable as the former procedure of trying to verify an hypothesis was indefensible.

Thus it is that Popper comes out with his celebrated hypothetico-deductive method as being the decisive method of science and scientific discovery. Science, in other words, in its ongoing procedures must not be thought of as involving a process of trying to discover in experience or through observation just what the order of nature is. Rather, the true way to think of scientific procedure is to think of the great overarching theories and hypotheses of science as having been thought up and devised by the occasional scientific genius; and then, following the projection of such theories by the scientists of genius, their more mine-run fellow scientists turn to and seek to put these theories to the test. And putting them to the test means trying to upset them or falsify them. Suppose, then, that a given theory sustains the initial tests to which it is subjected; the theory may then be said to have been corroborated by the evidence thus far and, hence, may be allowed to continue on as the operative scientific theory within a particular domain or epoch of scientific investigation. Moreover, it will continue on as the presiding theory within that domain until such time as the ever-renewed testing processes come to turn up such contrary or negative evidence as will serve to falsify or upset the then regnant theory or hypothesis. In other words, as Popper sees it, the ongoing process and advance of science is essentially an affair of new theories and hypotheses being first dreamed up, all of this being then followed by an intense and continuing concern on the part of practicing scientists to see if they can not falsify or knock out such theories.

And what would Quine say to this second feature of Popper's account of scientific practice and procedure? Well, it is true that while Quine never seems to let himself in for the usual fervid paeans to the creative genius of the great scientists, who according to Popper are supposed to have invented and devised the great overarching hypotheses of science, he would nonetheless agree with Popper that it is not by any logical procedure or as a result of any sort of compelling evidence that the scientist thinks up or dreams up his theories and hypotheses in the first place. No, for Quine, no less than Popper, would insist that the business of trying to understand how hypotheses or theories occur to scientists is a matter of psychology and not of logic. It is just that Quine, unlike Popper, is not inclined to go in for the usual romantic rhetoric about the "creative" aspects of this process.

Nevertheless, even as Quine would agree with Popper as to the absolutely decisive role in science of so-called hypotheses or theories—and of hypotheses and theories for which there could be said to be at the time of their inception no sort of decisive evidential warrant, be it either logical or empirical—Quine at the same time would probably part company with Popper as to the possibility and even the necessity for scientists to attempt ever to find decisive falsifications of their hypotheses in the ongoing process of theory-testing or hypothesis-testing that is characteristic of science. For Popper's insistence upon the crucial role of falsification in science has become increasingly suspect among any number of more recent philosophers of science, coming after Popper. And indeed, years before Popper's name had even so much as been heard of, the eminent French physicist and historian of science, Pierre Duhem, had argued that a decisive falsification of a scientific theory or hypothesis was exceedingly dubious, if not a downright impossibility. Now Duhem's reason for this was that no scientific theory or hypothesis is ever a simple statement or proposition, but rather a whole intricate web of interrelated principles and propositions. Hence, if on the basis of a given theory or hypothesis it could be deduced that a certain event would have to occur at a certain time, and yet the predicted event did not occur, then one could indeed infer from this that something was wrong with the hypothesis. But just what it was that was wrong, one could not say, for the simple reason that of all of the interrelated propositions making up the hypothesis at least one would have to be given up as a result of the adverse evidence; and yet one could not possibly tell which one, or ones, would need to be revised, merely on the ground of a particular predicted event's not occurring after having been deduced from the theory or hypothesis considered as a whole.[6]

---

6. Quine has frequently associated himself with this view of Duhem's. *Cf. From a Logical Point of View*, pp. 41 ff.

However, Duhem's line of argument is not the only one that has led recent thinkers to question the feasibility of the falsification of hypotheses as being the decisive resource in scientific knowledge and procedure. Instead, it has become increasingly fashionable of late to stress the fact that while the falsification of a hypothesis is a perfectly valid logical procedure, it is nevertheless always possible in practice persistently to refuse ever to invoke the procedure. Thus as Quine himself has observed somewhat tersely, "Any statement can be held true come what may, if we make drastic enough adjustments elsewhere in the system. Even a statement very close to the periphery can be held true in the face of recalcitrant experience by pleading hallucinations or by amending certain statements of the kind called logical laws."[7] And what Quine means by this might be illustrated in part by a more or less trivial example. Recurring to our earlier instance of Kepler's theory of the elliptical orbits of the planets, as we all know, this theory was designed to replace the old Ptolemaic theory that the only possible motion for the planets would have to be circular motion, inasmuch as on the Aristotelian view no other motion than a circular motion would presumably be appropriate to a heavenly body. But suppose that a Ptolemaic astronomer should simply choose—as indeed in the 17th century many did choose, including Tycho Brahe, who, in terms of the then available observational data, was reputed to be the best informed astronomer of his time—not to accept the new Keplerian theory and to stick with the old Ptolemaic theory instead. Would there be any way in which such a holdout for the ancient theory could ever be refuted by adverse or contrary data? Presumably not, for given that a certain planet failed to appear at the particular point on its orbit where it might be expected to appear if it were travelling in its presumed circular orbit, all that the Ptolemaic astronomer would need to do would be to account for the deviation by positing an epicycle. Nor is there any reason in principle, presumably, why even today someone of Ptolemaic persuasion might not work out an elaborate scheme of planetary motion involving cycles and epicycles and, for all we know, epi-epicycles almost without end, in order, thereby, to save the appearances. True, such a Ptolemaic scheme would be so cumbersome as to be hardly workable, thereby lacking those features of simplicity and elegance to which scientists have so long been partial. But so what? For any scientist must needs admit that whatever his personal preferences might be in the matters of simplicity or elegance, so far as nature and reality are concerned, there would seem to be no

---

7. *Ibid.*, p. 43.

compelling reasons a priori to suppose that the order of nature must necessarily be the simplest or most tidy order conceivable.

Clearly, then, the upshot of such a line of thought would appear to be in further confirmation of the view that scientific theories and hypotheses are no more subject to a decisive falsification than they are to a decisive verification. Indeed, it is in just this connection that Quine's earlier quoted statement comes to have peculiar pertinence, "Any statement can be held true come what may, if we make drastic enough adjustments elsewhere in the system."[8]

So be it, and yet consider just where considerations of this sort leave us, when it comes to questions of the logic, not just of scientific discovery, but of the scientific enterprise as a whole. For if all scientific theories and hypotheses, in the very nature of the case, are underdetermined by experience, and if they are susceptible to no verification or falsification in experience that is logically compelling, then just what sort of warrant do scientific theories have? Surely, no one would propose, least of all Quine, that we return to what Kant would call the "dogmatism" of his (Kant's) predecessors, according to which one relies simply on "pure reason" alone to authenticate the principles and hypotheses of science. But if neither experience nor pure reason suffices when it comes to providing a justification for so-called scientific knowledge, what other sources of justification are there? Indeed, is there any alternative but to go right down the primrose path with Immanuel Kant and opt for some kind of a transcendental mode of justification? For put in Kantian terms, what are the so-called conceptual schemes or categorical frameworks of the modern scientific enterprise, if not just so many tissues of synthetic judgments a priori? And how are synthetic judgments a priori possible? The Kantian answer is that they are possible only in virtue of a transcendental justification. And what such a mode of justification presumably amounts to is a frank recognition that since all of our theories as to reality and the nature of things lack any direct evidence in their support, they can at best claim but a kind of indirect evidence, according to which it is acknowledged that if through our various theories and hypotheses we did not manage to make sense of our world somehow, then our world would quite literally make no sense at all. Indeed, there could not even be said to be a world either to make sense or to make sense of, or of which we could be said even to have any experience, at least not in any proper sense of "experience."

Moreover, the significant implication of any such reliance upon a

---

8. See n. 7 above.

transcendental mode of justification, be it in science or in philosophy or in human knowledge generally, is that a transcendentally justified knowledge can only be a knowledge of *appearances* and not of *reality* or of the thing in itself. And the reason is that, in the very nature of the case, what thus comes to be justified in a transcendental justification are but our own human schemes or conceptual frameworks, or the ways in which, through our various theories or hypotheses, we human beings have come to order things and to put them together and thus, in a quite literal sense, to have placed a certain construction upon them. Consequently, the knowledge of things that we attain by such means can only be a knowledge of things as they appear to us to be, in the light of the theories and hypotheses through which we view them and come to regard them, and hence not necessarily a knowledge of things as they really are in themselves at all.

And what, you will ask, does all of this have to do with Quine? Well, clearly if our line of exposition thus far be correct, then the conclusion would seem to be inescapable: Quine is nothing if not a transcendental philosopher. For does he not insist that for him there is no difference in principle between philosophical (or metaphysical) knowledge and scientific knowledge? And would he not appear to be equally committed, at least by implication, to the particular contemporary view of science that we have just been outlining? Surely, he would acknowledge that any scientific account of the world can never be other than underdetermined by experience and, as such, must be ultimately susceptible of neither verification nor falsification in experience. And what does this entail—if not in so many words, then surely in fact— but a thorough reliance on Quine's part upon the transcendental method in both science and/or philosophy?

"Oh," but you may retort, "one can scour the whole of Quine's writings from beginning to end and find not so much as a single mention of such typical Kantian notions as 'synthetic judgments a priori,' 'transcendental deduction of the categories,' 'phenomena and noumena,' 'empirical reality' vs. 'transcendental ideality,' etc., etc." So be it, but might not the answer be that Quine is a Kantian not of the letter but of the spirit? And if it might appear overly harsh, not to say wrongheaded, to accuse so thoroughgoing a behaviorist as Quine of being in the spirit of anything or anybody, then we might consider a still further counterconsideration. For the protest might be made by true blue Kantians, no less than by Quineans, that for Kant the scheme of the categories is an absolutely invariant one, deduced in a "metaphysical deduction" from the Table of Judgments, and hence like the law of the Medes and Persians in that "it altereth not." In contrast, for Quine such categorical schemes and conceptual frameworks as we happen to employ in science or philosophy are open alike to partial change and even to complete discard, subject only to what Quine would call pragmatic considerations, and nothing more.

Thus, consider the celebrated, not to say perhaps even puckish, passage from "Two Dogmas of Empiricism":

> As an empiricist, I continue to think of the conceptual scheme of science as a tool, ultimately, for predicting future experience in the light of past experience. Physical objects are conceptually imported into the situation as convenient intermediaries—not by definition in terms of experience, but simply as irreducible posits comparable, epistemologically, to the gods of Homer. For my part I do, qua lay physicist, believe in physical objects and not in Homer's gods; and I consider it a scientific error to believe otherwise. But in point of epistemological footing the physical objects and the gods differ only in degree and not in kind. Both sorts of entities enter our conception only as cultural posits. The myth of physical objects is superior to most in that it has proved more efficacious than other myths as a device for working a manageable structure into the flux of experience.[9]

Surely, it does not take too much imagination to see in this passage, if not a literal Kantianism, then certainly a full-blown transcendentalism. True, Kant would no doubt say that what Quine calls "the myth of physical objects" is a myth that we cannot possibly dispense with, that such physical objects being but functions of the Table of Categories, and the Table of Categories being deducible from the Table of Judgments, the Categories represent nothing if not the ineradicable furniture of the human mind. In contrast, Quine would simply dismiss out of hand any such Kantian view of the permanence and fixity of the categories, replacing it with a complete tolerance for countless alternative myths or Tables of Categories, the choice between them being dictated by purely pragmatic considerations as to which might seem the better "device for working a manageable structure into the flux of experience." But whether categories so conceived be regarded as fixed or changeable, in either case, the method of knowledge in-

---

9. Quine, *Logical Point of View*, p. 44. It perhaps needs remarking that in his article, entitled "Quine's Philosophy of Science," in the Davidson and Hintikka volume, *Words and Objections* (Dordrecht, Netherlands: D. Reidel Pub., 1969), J. J. C. Smart makes much of the fact that Quine in *Word and Object* would appear to have happily eradicated even such "lingering traces of a phenomenalism and instrumentalism" (p. 8) as are still evident in his earlier writings, notably in the above-quoted passage from "Two Dogmas of Empiricism." Instead, Smart would represent Quine as having now returned to a position of sober, respectable "realism," after his bouts with both phenomenalism and instrumentalism. What Smart fails to note, however, is that the realism to which Quine has presumably thus returned is hardly distinguishable from that very "empirical realism" which Kant once insisted was to be closely correlated with a "transcendental idealism."

volved is a transcendental method. For as Kant would insist—at least as Wolff paraphrases him in his commentary—"knowledge is the 'determinate relation of given representations to an object.' But an object is merely a 'that which'; it is 'that in the concept of which the manifold of a given intuition is united.'"[10] In other words, the object in such a case is, as Quine would put it, a posit which is "conceptually imported into the situation," in order that, as Kant would say, some unity in the manifold may be effected. The unity, in other words, is something that we bring to the experience and not anything that we find in experience. Thus Quine elsewhere, arguing against the sense datum philosophers, remarked, "our [sense datum] philosopher may try, in a spirit of rational reconstruction, to abstract out a pure stream of sense experience and then depict physical doctrine as a means of systematizing the regularities discernible in the stream."[11] However, no flux of experience ever constitutes such a pure stream; nor are there any regularities discernible in it: "For the trouble is that immediate experience simply will not, of itself, cohere as an autonomous domain. References to physical objects hold it together."[12] In other words, it is we human beings who, in seeking to know the world, import objects into the situation, and so effect a unity and a regularity in the flux or manifold of experience that simply are not there in the experience just as such.

Surely, therefore, Quine's distancing of himself from Kant on the matter of the alterability, as opposed to the fixity, of the scheme of the categories, so far from discrediting him as a transcendental philosopher, only serves to confirm the radically transcendental thrust of his entire metaphysical enterprise.

And if you want to insist that nowhere in Quine is there ever any talk of any transcendental deduction of his categories, that, far from it, Quine talks of nothing more than purely pragmatic considerations as being the only grounds on which one set of categories, say, is to be preferred to another—this again would seem not so much to go counter to the transcendental character of Quine's metaphysics as rather to sustain and support it. After all, what is a reliance upon pragmatism or pragmatic considerations if not an appeal to a kind of transcendental deduction, albeit by another name? Thus if one says that the key feature of any transcendental procedure in science or philosophy

10. Robert Paul Wolff, *Kant's Theory of Mental Activity* (Cambridge, MA: Harvard University Press, 1963), p. 187.
11. W. V. Quine, *Word and Object* (Cambridge, MA: Technology Press of MIT, 1960), p. 2.
12. *Ibid.*

is that in any such procedure our very understanding and account of the nature of things is justified not by the fact that its truth is made decisively evident either by reason or by experience, but solely by the fact that, without some such conceptual scheme or ontological frame of reference, we just could not make sense of things at all, or even talk about or discourse meaningfully about our world in any way—yes, there would not even be a world that we could discourse meaningfully about—if such be the thrust of a transcendental method of justification, then let us but remind ourselves of the following passage from Quine:

> The fundamental-seeming question, How much of our science is merely contributed by language and how much is a genuine reflection of reality? is perhaps a spurious question which itself arises wholly from a certain particular type of language. Certainly we are in a predicament if we try to answer the question; for to answer the question we must talk about the world as well as about language, and to talk about the world we must already impose upon the world some conceptual scheme peculiar to our own language.[13]

Surely, the "must" of this last clause is a "must" whose cogency is derived from an implicit transcendental argument. Be it so-called or not so-called, a rose by any other name would smell as sweet! Nor is that all, for continuing right on with the same passage from the same essay, Quine in the very next sentence utters a demurrer that in our immediate present juncture in philosophy one might be tempted to interpret as both reflecting back in time upon Kant and prophetically reflecting forward in time to someone like Strawson: "Yet we must not leap to the fatalistic conclusion that we are stuck with the conceptual scheme that we grew up in." And then he continues:

> We can change it bit by bit, plank by plank, though meanwhile there is nothing to carry us along but the evolving conceptual scheme itself. The philosopher's task was well compared by Neurath to that of a mariner who must rebuild his ship on the open sea.
>
> We can improve our conceptual scheme, our philosophy, bit by bit while continuing to depend on it for support; but we cannot detach ourselves from it and compare it objectively with an unconceptualized reality. Hence it is meaningless, I suggest, to inquire into the absolute correctness of a conceptual scheme as a mirror of reality. Our standard for appraising basic changes of conceptual scheme must be, not a realistic standard of correspondence to reality, but a pragmatic standard. Concepts are language, and the purpose of concepts and of language is efficacy in communication and in predictions. Such is the ultimate duty of language, science, and philosophy, and it is in relation to that duty that a conceptual scheme has finally to be appraised.[14]

13. Quine, *Logical Point of View*, pp. 78–79.
14. *Ibid.*

Need more be said by way of making it clear that Quine's pragmatic standard does indeed function in the manner of a transcendental standard? The transcendental standard must be understood in sharp contrast to any realistic standard and would require the users of such a standard to settle for a knowledge of reality, not as that reality is in itself, but only as it appears to us to be in the light of the categories and conceptual schemes in terms of which we attempt to deal with it or to make sense of it or, as it were, to live with it. On Quine's pragmatic standard, the legitimacy of any linguistic or conceptual scheme is not going to lie in any fancied correspondence that it may have to reality, but solely in its efficacy in facilitating what Quine likes to call "communication and prediction."

And now for still another possible objection to our proposal that Quine's version of metaphysics be regarded as no more than a type of transcendental philosophy. For the passage that was quoted above, in which Quine raises the question as to how much of our knowledge of reality reflects but the linguistic or conceptual scheme in terms of which we view reality and how much of it is a genuine reflection of reality—this might prompt some to say that Quine's entire treatment of language and of the linguistic component in our knowledge is one that differentiates him sharply from the tradition of transcendental philosophy. For has it not been the hallmark of this latter sort of philosophy, particularly in comparatively recent years, that it has ever been concerned with securing for philosophy a distinctive type of knowledge that could be considered a truly a priori knowledge, as contrasted with a scientific knowledge which is basically and principally a posteriori? Thus a thinker like C. I. Lewis, for example, in discarding Kant's claims to a synthetic a priori knowledge, proceeded to direct attention to the analytic a priori element in knowledge, which so many would associate with what they would call the logical and linguistic component in knowledge. And indeed, in the case of any number of the older logical empiricists, as well as with the so-called linguistic philosophers of more recent years, there has been great stress laid upon the decisive difference between so-called conceptual studies or investigations, on the one hand, and so-called empirical studies on the other, the former being the area of so-called a priori knowledge and the latter, that of a posteriori knowledge.

Quite patently, however, Quine, with his slashing attack upon analyticity in all of its forms and his by no means unsuccessful attempt to banish the entire analytic-synthetic distinction from the domain of philosophy altogether, would appear to have deprived philosophy of its last haven of refuge within the sacred precincts of the analytic a priori—as if here, at last, philosophy could do its own thing by confining its attention solely to linguistic and logical questions and leaving it to science, and to science alone, to speak with authority on questions of substance.

But Quine, of course, will have none of this. Instead, he has tried to force the philosophers to come out from behind their protective covering of the a priori, and to face again the bright light of day along with the scientists. Indeed, this is the very point of Quine's insistence that there should no longer be any line of demarcation between science and philosophy, that they are both alike concerned with questions of substance, and this even in matters of logic and language no less than in physics or biology or sociology or whatever. And what must all of this be interpreted to mean, if not that Quinean philosophy and metaphysics, so far from being a variety of transcendental philosophy, is really a philosophy that has effectively exorcized the a priori, alike from philosophy and from everywhere else?

To this, though, the retort is easy and obvious. It is true that Quine has sought to banish the analytic a priori from out of the realm of knowledge altogether. At the same time, we surely need none of us to be reminded that Kant, as the great progenitor of transcendental philosophy, hardly thought of analytic truths as playing any very major role within the compass of such a philosophy. On the contrary, the a priori knowledge that he was concerned to salvage was the knowledge he called synthetic a priori. And so, turning again to Quine, can one say that, in his unremitting opposition to anything like the analytic a priori, he is no less opposed to any and all alternative forms of a priori knowledge as well? Surely not! Thus, consider Quine's well-known pronouncement:

> The Aristotelian notion of essence was the forerunner, no doubt, of the modern notion of intension or meaning. For Aristotle it was essential in men to be rational, accidental to be two-legged. But there is an important difference between this attitude and the doctrine of meaning. From the latter point of view it may indeed be considered (if only for the sake of argument) that rationality is involved in the meaning of the word "man" while two-leggedness is not; but two-leggedness may at the same time be viewed as involved in the meaning of "biped" while rationality is not. Thus from the point of view of the doctrine of meaning it makes no sense to say of the actual individual, who is at once a man and a biped, that his rationality is essential and his two-leggedness accidental or vice versa. Things had essences, for Aristotle, but only linguistic forms have meanings. Meaning is what essence becomes when it is divorced from the object of reference and wedded to the word.[15]

---

15. *Ibid.*, p. 22.

Abstracting, for the moment, from any implied criticism of the Aristotelian notion of essence proper that there may be in this passage, and confining attention simply to what Quine says about essences when these are "divorced from their objects of reference and wedded only to the word," then Quine is surely right: there just is no way in which such mere meaning and intentions can be made the resource for a knowledge that is a priori in Kant's sense of being universal and necessary. After all, even an Aristotelian would probably be as emphatic as Quine in insisting that essences, divorced from all reference to what Aristotle would call being, could never be considered as guarantors of universality and necessity. Yet clearly, the universality and necessity that are thus excluded are but the universality and necessity of so-called analytic truths. And whereas an Aristotelian would seek to recover a proper universality and necessity by returning to a consideration of real essences, be they either actual or potential, Quine has already placed a "Road Closed" sign in front of that possible route, by his earlier declaration that he simply will not accept any "realistic standard of correspondence to reality."[16] Instead, his course is to rely only on "a pragmatic standard," as he calls it. And have we not already seen how Quine's pragmatic standard really functions in the manner of a transcendental justification? And what must such a transcendental justification be a justification of in Quine's case? It presumably could be none other than a justification of those very universal and necessary truths that make up our scientific and/or philosophical hypotheses and theories. To be sure, such pragmatically and/or transcendentally justified truths are not necessary truths in the sense that they could never be false, or that their opposites are to be pronounced self-contradictory. But then neither are synthetic a priori truths necessary in this sense. Not only that, but it would seem that Quine's pragmatically and/or transcendentally justified truths are a priori, not just in the sense of being universal and necessary in the manner of synthetic a priori truths, but also in the sense of their being, as one might say, "prior" to experience. For would not Quine be the first to insist that such scientific and philosophic truths as make up the planks in his and Neurath's famous ship of knowledge, and that must be replaced one by one on the open sea—are not these truths, all of them, prior to experience, in that they are all of them underdetermined by experience and none of them either conclusively confirmable or disconfirmable in experience?

No, let it never be said that Quine is one to depreciate the a priori

16. *Cf.* n. 14 above.

element in knowledge—and that, precisely in the Kantian or transcendental philosophical sense of the synthetic a priori!

And now for a final difficulty. For it is not hard to imagine that many of those who might fancy themselves to be transcendental philosophers should be outraged that so thoroughgoing and hard-bitten a behaviorist as Quine should ever be permitted, not to say encouraged, to sail under the illustrious flag of transcendental philosophy. Is not the tradition of transcendental philosophy precisely a tradition in which the rights of subjectivity, of consciousness, of mind, etc. have always been most jealously guarded and protected? Yes, one might even say that, so far as Kant himself is concerned, the key notion running through both the Transcendental Aesthetic and the Transcendental Analytic is the ever-recurring notion of synthesis. Further, this synthesis can only be thought of as a somehow spontaneous act of unifying; and what gets unified is nothing other than the so-called manifold of perception or sensation or whatever; and the agent of such synthetic unity has presumably got to be, in some sense, a subject or a consciousness—be it the imagination, the understanding, or whatever. Moreover, without allowing ourselves to get bogged down in the morass of Kantian considerations bearing on the synthetic unity of the manifold and just how it is brought about, may it not still be safely affirmed that in their persistent and overarching concern with trying to find the "a priori conditions of the possibility of experience,"[17] the Kantians tend ever to trace these conditions of the possibility of experience right back to the conditions of that synthesis and that unification that is effected in the manifold by the agency of consciousness? Nor is that all, for having thus traced the conditions of the possibility of experience back to the conditions for the synthesizing of the manifold of experience, it is as if the Kantians, or at least some of them, tended to forget, or at least to blink at, their own cherished principle to the effect that no human knowledge can ever be a knowledge of things in themselves, but must always be a knowledge of things only as they appear to us to be under the conditioning forms of human intuition and human understanding. Indeed, in blurring this principle of theirs, it is as if the Kantians often seem to suggest that, while knowledge of the world and even of our own selves must always be a conditioned knowledge, still the knowledge which the transcendental philosopher has of these very conditions of knowledge and of the synthesizing activity of consciousness that effects these conditions of knowledge—these last are somehow not a conditioned knowledge at

17. *Cf.* Wolff, *Kant's Theory of Mental Activity.* p. 94.

all. Instead, let us say that knowledge of this latter type, such as it is achieved by the transcendental philosopher, is sometimes held to represent a true insight into the conditions of human knowledge as these conditions really are, and not merely as they appear to be.

Not so Quine, however. As a behaviorist, he would not only brush aside all talk of the possibility of knowing how the synthesizing activity of consciousness works, but in addition he would doubtless deny that his, Quine's, philosopher's knowledge of the conditions of our human experience and of our human knowledge, as conditioned by the particular categorial schemes or conceptual frameworks that we happen to be using, is in any way a privileged knowledge. That is to say, for Quine to know that we know nothing of the world or of reality save in terms of the hypotheses and theories through which we come to see or view reality—this knowledge itself is no more than a hypothetical knowledge all over again, in the sense that this very conception of human knowledge as being but a conditioned knowledge is still one more hypothesis that itself needs justification in terms of a reapplication of the familiar pragmatic standard.

Indeed, is not this just the import of Quine's characteristic invocation of Neurath's figure:

> Neurath has likened science to a boat which, if we are to rebuild it, we must rebuild plank by plank while staying afloat in it. The philosopher and the scientist are in the same boat.[18]

Surely, the implication of this last statement is that the philosopher, with his vision of our human situation as if we were in a boat on the open sea, is just not to be considered as being in any sort of privileged position in regard to knowledge as contrasted with the scientist—as if the philosopher, say, had a nonhypothetical knowledge of our overall human situation of being in the boat on the open sea, whereas the scientist had but a hypothetical knowledge of which planks in the boat would seem to need replacing and when. No, for the question of whether the supposedly all-encompassing metaphor of the boat is an appropriate one for understanding our human predicament in regard to knowledge—this very question in turn can only be answered by applying the pragmatic test to the philosopher's hypothesis of the boat metaphor, just as the scientist's hypotheses regarding the several individual planks and their need for replacement are likewise subject to exactly the same sort of pragmatic test.

But, then, does this refusal on Quine's part never to claim more

---

18. Quine, *Word and Object*, p. 3.

than a purely pragmatic and hypothetical knowledge, even of our overall human situation, preclude him from being a true blue transcendental philosopher? Of course not! If anything, it only serves to show that Quine is much more consistent in his transcendentalism even than many professed transcendentalists. For if it be a principle of transcendental philosophy always to insist that no human knowledge can ever be more than a knowledge of ourselves and of reality, only as these appear to us to be in the light of some transcendentally justified categorial scheme, and not as they really are in themselves, then how can a transcendental philosopher ever claim to have a knowledge of the human mind, or of our human situation vis-à-vis reality, or even of the conditions of the very possibility of human knowledge, that is more than a conditioned knowledge? Such a claim could not be other than a violation of his own transcendental principles. That is why a thinker like Quine, who regards even his own overall account of human cognitive situations in terms of his metaphor of the boat as being itself a mere hypothesis that is justified only in the light of pragmatic considerations—it is just this that should stamp Quine as nothing less than a transcendental philosopher par excellence.

Still, is it not possible to imagine someone like Harman raising a final objection at this point:

> Quine observes that in the end all of one's views are posits. ... But this does not mean that what one posits is not real. To say one *posits* the existence of molecules is to make an epistemological remark. To say that molecules exist, are real, is to make an ontological remark. To say a view is a posit is not to say it is a fiction. To make a posit is to think something true.[19]

But again, rather than being an objection to Quine's transcendentalism, this is but a further confirmation of it. For one has only to recall Kant's distinction between empirical reality and transcendental ideality, construing this as meaning that to speak of the ideality of things and objects as schematized under the categories is really to make an epistemological remark, whereas to speak of physical substances in space and time acting and reacting upon one another is to make an ontological remark—or, as Kant would have it, to ascribe to such things an empirical reality, as contrasted with their transcendental ideality. Yes, in this very connection we might even quote a remark of Cartwright's which bears directly on Harman's insistence that Quine's posits have ontological import and are thus not to be thought of as mere epistemological devices. Cartwright observes: for Quine, "to enquire into the ontological commitments of a theory is not to ask

---

19. Harman, "Quine on Meaning and Existence," p. 350.

what there is, but only to ask what that theory *says* there is."[20] Surely, this is decisive as to any ontology of Quine's being but an ontology set within an overall transcendental framework.

With this, though, it is perhaps high time that we returned our discussion to the considerations from which we first set out. For supposing that our thesis is correct and that Quine is indeed to be reckoned as no more and no less than a transcendental philosopher and, for this reason, but a chip off the old Kantian block, so what and then what? At the beginning of our discussion we suggested that for us to be able to classify Quine in some such way as this might be to render his philosophy somewhat more intelligible, not to say more accessible to the uninitiated. At least it could be illuminating to consider both the family resemblances, as well as the family differences, between Quine and other members of the family of transcendental philosophers. And already we have made various passing suggestions as to such family resemblances and differences in the course of our discussion. But we need not stop with the suggestions thus far. For what about Strawson? True, in the current literature, we are, all of us, accustomed to think only of the points in respect to which Quine has argued against Strawson, or Strawson against Quine, each thereby differentiating himself strongly from the other. And yet, has it not occurred to anyone that in terms of the characterization of transcendental philosophy that we have been following in this paper, Strawson is no less a transcendental philosopher than is Quine? And so, also, perhaps are various of the so-called linguistic analysts, who take their philosophical cues from the Wittgenstein of the *Investigations.* Nor is it necessary to stay only on the one side of the Channel. For surely, Sartre and Heidegger, as well as various of the latter-day French Structuralists, could definitely qualify as philosophers whose philosophizing is unmistakably in the transcendental mode. "But these are strange bedfellows for Quine," you will say. True enough, and yet must we not all acknowledge that when one gets into the business of family resemblances, the resemblances can embrace some very strange types indeed, and that it is no less than the very family resemblances themselves that serve to point up the strangeness of the differing types?

"Oh," but you will say, "if one's notion of transcendental philosophy is so broad as to enable one to bring Quine and Strawson and Heidegger and Sartre all within the same family, then has not the classification become so trivial as to cease to be illuminating?" Besides, such

20. Richard Cartwright, "Ontology and the Theory of Meaning," *Philosophy of Science* 21 (October 1954), 316–25.

a criticism might be reinforced from the side of the Quineans themselves, by their invoking the master's teachings in regard to radical translation. For is it not a kind of enterprise in translation that we have been engaged in throughout most of this paper, trying to see, in effect, if we could not get Quine to speak more or less in the language of the Kantians, and so qualify as a member of the Kantian family? Thus where the Kantians would use "transcendental deduction," we have sought to render this in Quinese as "pragmatic justification"; or where the ones would say "synthetic a priori propositions," we would have the others say "conceptual frameworks underdetermined by experience"; or where the ones would talk of "a priori conditions of knowledge," we would translate this into something like "myths and posits"; or the insistence of the one upon "empirical reality" goes over into "ontological commitment" on the part of the other, etc.

With this, though, we could easily imagine the Quineans beginning to chide us for not properly reckoning with the problems of radical translation. For do we not realize that when the linguist-anthropologist says,[21] "There's a rabbit," "There we have a rabbit," "Lo! a rabbit," "Lo, rabbithood again," and the native speaker says "Gavagai," what the one speaker is referring to may be quite different from what the other is referring to? Thus the one might be referring to a physical object like a rabbit, whereas the other might be referring only to "the various temporal segments of rabbits," or perhaps to "the integral or undetached rabbit parts." In other words, how can the linguist-anthropologist be sure that what he is referring to with his expressions is the same as what the native refers to with his? Not only that, but isn't there always the danger that in carrying the "necessary job of lexicography forwards and backwards, [the linguist-anthropologist] has read [his] ontological point of view into the native language"?[22]

And so, we can imagine the Quinean rounding on us and saying, "You see in your more or less elaborate exertions to translate Quinese into Kantese, and Kantese into Quinese, you really have no way of knowing that what the transcendental philosopher refers to with his expressions is at all the same as what the Quinean philosopher refers to with his. And so, does not the whole enterprise of trying to make Quine out to be a transcendental philosopher come down to but an enterprise in futility?"

But no! The Quineans could hardly press such an argument in their own defense, at least not in a defense against the allegation that they

---

21. *Cf.* Quine, "Speaking of Objects" in *Ontological Relativity and Other Essays,* pp. 1–6; also *Word and Object,* pp. 26 ff.
22. *Ibid.,* p. 22.

might be transcendental philosophers, after all. For when it comes to Quine himself, it will be remembered that while, on the one hand, he has deftly argued that one never can be sure that what the speaker of the one language refers to by his expressions is the same as what the speaker of another language is referring to by the use of his own supposedly corresponding expressions, on the other hand, he has also been equally emphatic in suggesting that the whole issue of a discrepancy of reference could well turn out to be a bogus issue simply because of "the inscrutability of reference":

> I have urged in defense of the behavioral philosophy of language, Dewey's, that the inscrutability of reference is not the inscrutability of a fact; there is no fact of the matter. But if there is really no fact of the matter, then the inscrutability of reference can be brought even closer to home than the neighbor's case; we can apply it to ourselves. If it is to make sense to say even of oneself that one is referring to rabbits and formulas and not to rabbit stages and Gödel numbers, then it should make sense to say it of someone else. After all, as Dewey stressed, there is no private language.[23]

Very well, to paraphrase Quine himself, if it makes sense for me to say of myself that when I speak Kantese I refer not to things in themselves but only to phenomena or appearances, then it should make sense to say it of someone else, say, Quine: when Quine speaks Quinese, it surely makes sense to say that his references are to the sorts of things that transcendental philosophers refer to and not to what more traditional metaphysicians of a realistic bias would refer to at all. Not only that, but when it comes to the business of criticizing Quine, particularly with respect to the more specific topics in his philosophy, or when it comes to assessing his overall philosophical and/or metaphysical achievement and accomplishment, it would seem wise always to keep in mind that he is a transcendental philosopher, and that therefore one has to try to handle him only in the way one would go about trying to handle a Kantian. Yes, should one think that one can properly address oneself to Quinean metaphysics in the way one would address oneself to, say, Aristotelian metaphysics, or even to Bergmannian metaphysics, or perhaps Whiteheadian metaphysics, or whatever, then one's address can only be misdirected and strangely at cross-purpose. Save by understanding him as a transcendental philosopher, there is just no understanding of Quine as a metaphysician at all.

23. *Ibid.*, p. 47.

4

RICHARD RORTY'S WOULD-BE DECONSTRUCTION OF ANALYTIC PHILOSOPHY

What is deconstruction? So far as the mere term goes, most of us would doubtless associate it with various current assaults upon the humanities that would appear to be taking place in several quarters these days. It is particularly from English Departments, as it would seem—notably perhaps those of Johns Hopkins and of Yale—that one hears the noise of "wars and rumors of wars" that are presumably being fought between those, on the one hand, whom one might call the traditionalists with respect to the Humanities, and those, on the other hand, who are loud in their boasts that they are marching to the newly fashionable tunes of Deconstruction. Again, though, just what is Deconstruction, and just who are the Deconstructionists?

Unhappily, such questions are not easy to answer. And little wonder, considering that even the so-called traditionalists would appear scarcely to know what the presumed tradition is in regard to the Humanities that they are wont to uphold, or why they want to uphold it. And no less so for the Deconstructionists. For who are such people, and what is it that qualifies them to be numbered among the disturbers of the peace in the Humanities? True, one has but to ask the question and the name of the incredible, not to say in the mouths of some the unspeakable, Jacques Derrida immediately comes to mind. But then, pray tell, who is it who can say what it is, either in God's name or in the Devil's name, that the eminent Derrida himself purports to say?

Alas, those of us who are no more than benighted souls, and who can in no way claim to be among the elect of God, so far as the latest Parisian intellectual fashions go, of course, cannot aspire ever to penetrate those seemingly deliberate enigmas that Derrida himself is given to propounding. But what about the books of Derrida disciples, or near-disciples, that even now are beginning to flood the market in this country? There are titles such as: *Saving the Text: Literature, Derrida and Philosophy*; or *Hermes: Literature, Science and Philosophy*; or *Displacement: Derrida and After*. Once more, though, what are even such works reminiscent of, if not a latter-day cabalistic literature, which we who are among the uninitiated and unwashed can surely never hope to penetrate?

All the same, it may be that we need not be altogether daunted by our own failed efforts to figure out what it is that Deconstruction is all about. Instead, taking to ourselves a somewhat deliberately perverted motto to the effect that discretion is perhaps the lesser, rather than the greater, part of valor, why don't we boldly shift the scene, and see if we may not find striking, and rather more intelligible, evidence of both the fact and the nature of Deconstruction—this time right within the confines of some of the immediately contemporary movements in American philosophy? Thus surely we are all familiar with Richard Rorty's brilliant and truly seminal book, *Philosophy and the Mirror of Nature*. And in a like spirit there is Richard Bernstein's *Beyond Objectivism and Relativism*. In Bernstein's case, to be sure, his title could well signal more a slogan than an achievement. But still, could not one say that it is supposedly no less than a technique of Deconstruction that Bernstein would regard as being his very means of getting beyond what he calls objectivism and relativism? For the matter of that, does not Bernstein, right in the book, give his applause to his friend, Rorty, calling him "one of the most astute deconstructive critics of our time"?[1]

Nor are Rorty's and Bernstein's names the only ones that we might mention as being among those who seem to have certain affinities for a program of Deconstruction in philosophy. For what about Alasdair MacIntyre? Or coming from a somewhat different quarter, there is Arthur Danto, with his intriguing book on Nietzsche, which, right on the cover, is openly billed as "an original study." Indeed, in token of that same originality, directly in the preface to the Morningside Edition of his book, Danto makes the following rather startling pronouncements:

> The pages of *Mind* would have been one of the forums in which what we think of today as analytical philosophy took shape, with its central teaching that the problems of philosophy are *au fond* problems of language, however heavily disguised. But just this, I came to believe, was Nietzsche's own view, that the structures of language determine what are the structures of reality for those whose language it is, and that the deep order of the world, so sought

---

1. Richard J. Bernstein, *Beyond Objectivism and Relativism* (Philadelphia: University of Pennsylvania Press, 1983), p. 197.

by philosophers of the past, is but the cast shadow of the deep order of their grammar.[2]

True, the word "Deconstruction" is nowhere used in this passage. And yet is it going too far to imagine that, be it consciously or unconsciously, Danto, in likening Analytical Philosophy to Nietzsche, means to be placing in the hands of the up-to-the-minute Analyst any number of Nietzschean instruments of Deconstruction? Indeed, following hard upon the passage just quoted from his preface, Danto propounds the thesis on behalf of Nietzsche, to be sure, but presumably no less on behalf of today's Analysts and Philosophers of Language,[3] that "a change in human reality cannot be expected until there is a change in language."[4] And so it is that Danto then goes on to remark on how Nietzsche insisted that "we shall not get rid of God . . . until we get rid of grammar."[5] Moreover, he continues, it was in terms of just such a "change in language" that Nietzsche "polemicized . . . by submitting the realities of his tradition to the most devastating criticism it had ever sustained: the demolition of idols, the moral arson, the brash defacement of sacred writ by brilliant graffiti"[6]—all of these were part and parcel of Nietzsche's program of Deconstruction, at least as Danto pictures it. Moreover, what was the instrument of such a Deconstruction? Danto's answer seems to be that it was nothing less than Nietzsche's philosophy of language. And why shouldn't this be a particularly potent instrument of Deconstruction, considering that a "change in language" is able to effect no less than "a change in human reality"?

Accordingly, taking up these summary indications of Danto's, in view of the all-important role ascribed to language by the Philosophers of Language in our own day, no less than by Nietzsche, it would seem to follow that the phenomenon of Deconstruction could well turn out to be a feature no less of contemporary Anglo-American philosophy than of what, to so many of us, would seem to be the utterly baffling and recondite speculations of Continentals like Derrida, whose affinities with Nietzsche are presumably rather more obvious. Yes, for that matter, is it not significant that Rorty repeatedly likes to trace his own

---

2. Arthur C. Danto, *Nietzsche as Philosopher* (New York: Columbia University Press, Morningside Edition, 1980), p. 8.
3. Throughout this paper we shall be using the terms "Analytical Philosophy" and "Philosophy of Language" only in a very loose sense. That we should even compound such looseness by treating both of these types of philosophy as largely equivalent, for this our justification, is what Danto would appear to be saying in the passage just quoted.
4. Danto, pp. 8–9.
5. *Ibid.*, p. 9.
6. *Ibid.*

philosophical lineage back to Heidegger, no less than to Wittgenstein, and even more directly to John Dewey as well. "All, all honorable men," as Mark Antony might say, so that if a philosopher is to be judged by the company he keeps, then the Deconstructionist program of Richard Rorty can boast of some of today's most eminently fashionable antecedents, at once English, Continental, and American.

For that matter, when Danto, in the name of Nietzsche, talks about how "the deep order of the world, so sought by philosophers of the past, is but the cast shadow of the deep order of their grammar," are there not many of us who might fancy that they hear echoes of the great Willard Van Orman Quine in such words? For do we not all recall Quine's account of what he says are the daunting problems of translation, particularly in the case of translation from a language of, say, some "newly discovered tribe whose language is without known affinities"[7] into our own? Thus in trying to translate into our own language what a native speaker is supposedly saying, how can we possibly avoid using the "object-positing pattern"[8] of our own language, a pattern that has built right into it all of our own logico-linguistic devices of identity, quantification, *et al.*? And yet what possible reason have we to suppose that in the native's language there are anything like the same object-positing devices, or that they are used in his language in the same way as they are in ours? In short, it would seem that it is no less arbitrary, than it is inevitable, that we find ourselves reading "our [own] ontological point of view"[9] into the language of the native speaker whom we are seeking to translate, thereby missing altogether what may be the distinctive ontological point of view of that same native speaker himself. Accordingly, what does such an acknowledgment on Quine's part amount to, if not that the ontology of "physical objects,"[10] which objects, Quine would insist, we tend, in our language, to regard as constituting nothing if not "the deep order of the world"—that this same ontology of physical objects is, after all, no more than "the cast shadow of our grammar"?

Accordingly, by exploiting hints of this sort drawn from the likes of Danto and of Quine, to say nothing of Rorty's own entire general line of argument, we may feel safe in saying that Deconstruction need no longer be regarded as a phenomenon that is confined to the Continent and to sophisticated literary critics and philosophers such as Derrida,

---

7. W. V. Quine, *Ontological Relativity and Other Essays* (New York and London: Columbia University Press, 1969), p. 1.
8. *Ibid.*, p. 2.
9. *Ibid.*, p. 3.
10. See quote from Quine given below, n. 14.

whose contacts with Analytical Philosophy, or the Philosophy of Language, at least as we know it in this country, are presumably minimal.

Very well, are we not safe in saying that so-called Deconstruction has come to be thoroughly domesticated, if not in name, then certainly in fact, right within the current fashions of an analytical or linguistic type of philosophy? Besides, has not Rorty, in turn, carried such a Deconstruction one step farther? For has he not shown it to be not merely at home in, but even the veritable denouement of, much of present-day Analytical Philosophy?

First, though, perhaps we should pause just a bit longer in order to spell out in somewhat more detail just how it is that what we are calling a philosophical Deconstruction is even now at work within the very bowels and in'ards of contemporary Analytical Philosophy and Philosophy of Language. Consider the title of Rorty's major work, *Philosophy and the Mirror of Nature*. Now as we all know, the thesis of that book boils down to the contention that it is singularly wrong-headed for philosophy to try to be, much less to go on any longer claiming to be, anything like a mirror of nature. And what is this if not an effort at deconstruction on Rorty's part, and of deconstruction with respect to one of the most ancient and honorable theses of Western philosophy—the thesis of what might be called a traditional Aristotelian realism and empiricism?[11] Indeed, Rorty seems to be saying: it is not so much ill-founded and ill-argued as it is just downright silly and gratuitous for us any longer to bother our heads about whether there is a reality "out there," existing in itself, and having the nature and character that it does, independently of whatever we human beings may think or say about it.[12] And no less foolish and gratuitous is it for us to suppose that our human cognitive faculties of sense and intellect are capable of disclosing to us—of mirroring for us, if you will—the nature and character of things as they really are in themselves. No, all of this is clearly *passé*, Rorty is saying, and *passé* simply in terms of the very developments within the tradition of Analytical Philosophy itself.

Moreover, if we ask what the instruments are that Rorty avails himself of to effect such a deconstruction of traditional realism in both physics (and/or metaphysics) and epistemology, may we not say that

---

11. In saying that Rorty, by castigating the notion of philosophy as being the mirror of nature, is really repudiating a metaphysical and epistemological realism like that of Aristotle, we would not wish to imply that in such an Aristotelian realism philosophy is indeed taken to but "mirror" nature, either literally or metaphorically.

12. In saying this, we should certainly not wish to prejudge the issue of whether Rorty is more a Kantian or an out-and-out idealist.

they are just those instruments that our present-day philosophers of language have so painstakingly hammered out, and that Rorty has now had the wit—yes, even the genius—to use and exploit with what can only be described as an incredible panache? After all, as Danto says, speaking alike for Nietzsche and for our latter-day philosophers of language: "the structures of language determine what are the structures of reality for those whose language it is, [with the result] that the deep order of the world, so sought by philosophers of the past, is but the cast shadow of the deep order of their grammar." Or if one wants to evoke an even more formidable authority, and one to whom Rorty is careful often to defer, at least in name, why not just say that reality, or the world as it is for us, speaking the language that we do, and speaking it in the age and time in which we live, is but the reflection, not to say even the creation, of our particular "form of life." Surely, pronouncements to this effect point to nothing less than an attempt at a thoroughgoing deconstruction of anything like a genuine realism in philosophy. Ours should indeed be a "world well lost," as Rorty would say.

And now let us consider a second step, or a second moment, in what we are choosing to call Rorty's program of Deconstruction in philosophy—a program which in so many ways would seem to herald but the late blooming (or some might say, the last, final, faded, fatal blooming) of contemporary Analytical Philosophy. This second step consists simply in the recognition that just as the world, or nature, or reality, as these are for us, are nothing but the reflections, or better, the creatures of our language, so also it must follow that if we want to change our world, all we need do is change our language.

Here again, we have only to turn to Danto, and to what Danto says about Nietzsche, if we want to grasp the full import of this second step or moment in Rorty's program of what presently will begin to sound like a radical Reconstruction, as well as a Deconstruction, in both science and philosophy. Thus Danto remarks on how "Nietzsche liked to speak of himself as philosophizing with a hammer." And so Danto continues, "His purpose was in part to crack the habitual grip on thought in which language holds us, to make us aware of how much our minds are dominated by concepts from which we can hardly escape, given the rules our language follows. Then, realizing the conventional nature of our language, we might try to create fresh concepts, and so whole new philosophies."[13] Directly we can see in the final turn of this quotation how any Deconstruction in philosophy will

13. Danto, p. 12.

naturally be correlated with a Reconstruction or, perhaps better, a Re-creation as well. But of this more in a moment.

For the time being, it might be remarked in passing that "philosophizing with a hammer" is hardly Rorty's own style. No, for that would be bad form for any contemporary Analyst or Philosopher of Language. But form apart, it does not have to be to someone like Nietzsche necessarily that Rorty either does or needs to appeal, when it comes to his wanting to exploit "the conventional nature of language," and then move on to the business of undertaking to "create fresh concepts and whole new philosophies." No, for right within present-day Analytical Philosophy, particularly in the area of the philosophy of science, have we not become accustomed to thinking in terms of what Thomas Kuhn has termed "paradigm changes"?

And what are these paradigm changes but such as what Kuhn himself calls "scientific revolutions"? And why "revolutions"? Is it not because such paradigm changes in science cannot properly be said to be based on considerations either of logic or of evidence in any proper sense? On the contrary, the great over-arching hypotheses in science—the hypotheses or theories that determine the scientific paradigms of a given age or time, say Aristotelian and Ptolemaic science, or Newtonian science, or Darwinian evolution, or whatever—as Sir Karl Popper would insist, cannot properly be said to be derived either directly from observation or from inductions from observations. Instead, they are like free creations of the human mind; they are dreamed up or invented or, as it were, created out of nothing by the great scientific genius. Moreover, once invented and then projected upon the face of nature, there is no way that they can be verified, Popper insists, because to suppose that one could ever verify a hypothesis would be to commit the patent logical fallacy of affirming the consequent. Nor can they really be falsified either, as Kuhn in turn would insist. Because, while a procedure of denying the consequent, and so of falsifying a hypothesis, is quite impeccable logically, still in practice any such falsification can never be carried out, at least not decisively and definitively.

Accordingly, relying as he does upon a method of falsification in regard to scientific hypotheses, Popper is in effect forced to acknowledge that the most the scientist can do is to tell you what nature is not like, not what it is like. And on the other hand, with Kuhn's questioning of the possibility even of a falsifying of scientific theories and hypotheses, it would seem to follow that science is largely unable to give information either as to what nature is like, or what it is not like. Rather all that science can do is to project for us certain fanciful pictures of nature or the world, mere schemes of nature, which so far from revealing the truth about nature are justified only pragmatically—*i.e.*, they pay off in terms of enabling us to make predictions, and thus to attain a greater measure of control over nature. Again, recall Quine's rather jaunty, and yet sobering, words:

> As an empiricist I continue to think of the conceptual scheme of science as a tool, ultimately, for predicting future experience in the light of past experience. Physical objects are conceptually imparted into the situation as convenient intermediaries—not by definition in terms of experience, but simply as irreducible posits comparable, epistemologically, to the gods of Homer. For my part I do, qua lay physicist, believe in physical objects and not in Homer's gods; and I consider it a scientific error to believe otherwise. But in point of epistemological footing the physical objects and the gods differ only in degree and not in kind. Both sorts of entities enter our conception only as cultural posits. The myth of physical objects is epistemologically superior to most in that it has proved more efficacious than other myths as a device of working a manageable structure into the flux of experience.[14]

In the light of such considerations, then, does it not begin to emerge how, right within the bosom of present-day Analytical Philosophy, the techniques alike of a scientific and of a philosophical Deconstruction and Reconstruction are not only ready at hand, but in actual operation and full sway? Again, recall Danto's contention that "the structures of language determine what are the structures of reality for those whose language it is." Accordingly, granting, as the Analysts doubtless would grant, that there is no basic difference between the method of science and that of philosophy; that in both domains reliance has to be placed ultimately and exclusively upon something like the hypothetico-deductive method; and granting further that our conceptual schemes, our categories, our theories and hypotheses, be they in science or in philosophy, are but part and parcel of the language that we use to talk about reality and about the world; and recognizing finally that not only do the structures of our language determine the structures of our world, but also that such language structures are no more than "conventional"—then there is nothing to prevent us from going about a work of deconstruction with respect to any particular world-view that happens to prevail at a given time, and that we may happen not to like as it is, and so want to change, either in part or in its entirety. Moreover, just as the way is thus opened for us, be it either as scientists or philosophers, to go about deconstructing any world-view that our prevailing language uses may have set for us, so also the way is opened

---

14. W. V. Quine, *From a Logical Point of View* (Cambridge, MA: Harvard University Press, 1953), p. 44.

for us to go about following up such a work of deconstruction with a concomitant or subsequent work of reconstruction, such reconstructions, or perhaps better such new constructions or even new creations, being aimed at providing ever new world-views to take the place of those just deconstructed.

Again, it is Danto's authority that is to be invoked at this point. For in paraphrasing Nietzsche, Danto lays it right on the line that once such ongoing prospects and possibilities, alike of Deconstruction and of New Construction, are thus disclosed to us, it is then that "men [need] to be made to understand that everything is possible, if they [are] to be moved to try anything at all."[15]

Immediately, this very phrase "everything is possible" has overtones of almost a Sartrian freedom. And indeed, Danto himself has emphasized that in such a context as we have been depicting, where there is a sort of ongoing business of philosophic deconstruction and reconstruction, the situation for the deconstructors and reconstructors is nothing if not one of a "total conceptual permissiveness."[16] Accordingly, may we not say that we can now begin to glimpse something of the full import of Rorty's treatment and assessment of Analytical Philosophy? For the very denouement of such a philosophy is that it turns out to be a philosophy of just such a total intellectual permissiveness.

Moreover, what is even more interesting, to say nothing of ingenious, at least so far as Rorty's own particular achievement is concerned, is that he has managed to exploit the possibilities of this kind of total intellectual permissiveness, not only with respect to the sciences, but even more with respect to philosophy and the humanities generally. Yes, one might even say that Rorty has managed to convert into a kind of working capital for the humanities much the same intellectual permissiveness that, in recent years, it has become fashionable to credit the sciences with. For but consider: does it not have to be acknowledged that it is not just within the confines of science, but also within what we might loosely call the parameters of our modern culture as a whole—or of any culture for that matter—that the denizens of that culture cannot but find themselves caught up in a whole web of ideals, basic beliefs, prevailing world-views, and so on, all of which together tend to channel and govern the lives and activities of those within the culture, much as scientific paradigms can be said to channel and govern the investigations of scientists within any given period of scientific activity?

15. Danto, p. 12.
16. *Ibid.*

And surely, too, just as within the confines of science, it has come to be recognized as pertaining to the very life and health of science that there should be a continuing possibility of ever new deconstructions and reconstructions of scientific paradigms, so also why should there not be a comparable openness to radical deconstructions and new constructions with respect to our overall cultural paradigms as well? Indeed, why might it not be said that what is so novel and exciting about what Rorty is advocating is that when it comes to paradigm changes, not in science alone, but in our culture as a whole, it is to the humanities that we should turn, and not so much to the scientists? For why should it not be our poets, our novelists, our sculptors, our historians, our philosophers, our composers, *et al.*, to whom appeal is made, as being those who have it within their power and capacity to be the proper agents either of the maintenance of our cultural traditions, or of their deconstruction and then of their concomitant or subsequent reconstruction, or new construction, or even new creations, as the case may be?

Moreover, if one asks just how this "ministry of all the talents"— *i.e.*, of musicians, poets, philosophers, architects, yes, and scientists too—[17] is supposed to work in any given culture as the means for effecting either a conserving of cultural traditions or a creating of new ones, Rorty answers that ideally it should be an affair simply of "keeping the conversation going."[18] That is to say, from continuing cultural interchanges among the so-called humanists within any given culture, it should be possible either to keep the basic "cultural posits" of a society alive, or else replace them with new and presumably better ones.

And if this prompts the question as to just how the several representatives of the humanities, as they keep their conversations going, are ever to know which cultural ideals or posits are the truly better

17. In insisting that it is the philosophers and humanists who should participate in the determination of what our cultural paradigms shall be, Rorty would surely not mean that scientists should be systematically excluded from such deliberations or "conversations." No, for in the determination of cultural paradigms there is no reason why the scientists should not have an input into such conversations, along with humanists and philosophers. Whereas, when it comes to the determination of properly scientific paradigms, it would seem that only the scientists might be presumed to have an input there. For rather similar sentiments stemming from some of the Continental Deconstructionists, see Michael Serres, Hermes: *Literature, Science and Philosophy*, Harari and Bell, eds. (Baltimore and London: Johns Hopkins University Press, 1982).

18. This metaphor of "conversation" Rorty repeatedly employs throughout his book. However, it is in the final chapter of the book that Rorty appears to be singularly eloquent and persuasive regarding the need to "keep the conversation going." *Cf. Philosophy and the Mirror of Nature* (Princeton: Princeton University Press, 1979), Ch. 8, esp. pp. 377–78.

ones for their own particular culture, Rorty could only answer that, of course, there can't be any such thing as *knowledge* in regard to matters such as these. True, on a more traditional view of the humanities than that to which Rorty would subscribe, it has long been held that the whole point and purpose of the pursuit and practice of the so-called humanities is that through such pursuits and practices men can come to no less than a genuine knowledge of the human— *i.e.*, of what man is and what he ought to be. Clearly, though, it is not any knowledge of this sort that Rorty would ever imagine could be derived from humanistic pursuits. From Rorty's perspective it would have to be acknowledged that just as it is a total intellectual permissiveness that needs to be thought of as prevailing in a scientific context—when scientists have to decide between a paradigm preservation, say, or a paradigm change—so also a like permissiveness needs to be extended to the humanists when in their "conversations" they seek to determine what our cultural paradigms should be, and should not be.

Wait a minute, though! For is it literally a total conceptual or intellectual permissiveness that may be said to prevail in the matter either of scientific posits or of cultural posits in the broad sense? What, then, about that business of so-called pragmatic considerations we talked about earlier? Certainly, in a scientific context such pragmatic considerations do provide definite restrictions on any supposed total permissiveness, such as scientists might be thought to enjoy, when it comes to the business of their either sticking with their old theories and hypotheses or propounding new ones. Instead, we are told that it is only on the basis of whether the new theory "works" or not—*i.e.*, whether it pays off in terms of more reliable predictions and a more effective control over nature—that scientists are led to accept a new theory or paradigm, or reject it. Accordingly, will it not be comparable pragmatic considerations that will be determinative of the humanists' deliberations when, in "keeping their conversations going," they go about the business, which Rorty assigns to them, of seeing to it that our ideals and basic cultural posits are in order?

To this latter question, the answer must surely be, "Yes." At the same time, is it not necessary to recognize a not insignificant difference between what might be called the pragmatism that would appear to be operative in the case of general cultural paradigm changes (or preservations), and the pragmatism that is operative in the more narrowly scientific paradigm changes? Thus the paradigm changes that take place in science, as we have seen, are such as need to be determined almost exclusively in terms of whether the changes are likely to pay off in terms of a greater control over nature. Surely, though, when it comes to human cultures and human societies generally, and the paradigm changes that might occur there and occur at the behest not so much of the scientists in the community as of the philosophers and the humanists generally, at least according to Rorty's account of things, surely the pragmatically controlling factors that are operative with respect to these overall cultural paradigms would not be as precisely specifiable as they are in science. For rather than a greater technological control over the forces of nature as is the case in science, surely in the case of general cultural paradigm changes, considerations of technology and of social control in the ordinary sense of these notions would scarcely be operative at all. Instead, it would appear to be little more than the vaguest and loosest kinds of considerations of possible benefits or advantages that would here come into play—*e.g.*, whether one world-view might give promise of being somehow more "congenial" than another, or whether one set of basic beliefs might strike people as rather more "attractive" or as "a better one to live by" than some other.

Accordingly, then, what could Rorty say about the sorts of control that presumably would be restrictive or directive of paradigm changes in the sphere of human culture generally? Would he not have to recognize that the sorts of pragmatic advantages that might be said to justify our favoring one world-view over against another would seem to be so vague and so imprecise as to be practically indistinguishable from that total conceptual or intellectual permissiveness that Nietzsche talked about so confidently and so brashly? In other words, the "conversations" that philosophers and humanists are supposed to keep going could not be conversations involving any sort of rational or objective grounds for their eventual decisions and choices that hopefully might emerge from them.

What, then, is one to make of such a conclusion? In a way, is it not a conclusion that is frightening in its implications, not to say even downright intolerable? Thus it has been our continuing contention throughout this paper that the underlying thrust and thesis of Rorty's *Philosophy and the Mirror of Nature* is that present-day Analytical Philosophy cannot end in anything other than a philosophy of radical Deconstruction. And what is the import of such Deconstruction if not that, although Aristotle may well have taught that "philosophy begins in wonder," it must now turn out that present-day philosophy can only end in a total conceptual or intellectual permissiveness? That is why for ourselves we cannot but wonder whether, if Deconstruction indeed be the denouement of contemporary Analytical Philosophy, it must not also spell philosophy's effective destruction and demise as well.

For but consider: if philosophy cannot claim to be a proper knowledge, then how can it claim to be anything at all? Surely, philosophy can never, or ought never, settle for being relegated to the role of mere picture-projection, or world-view projection, simply as the product of continually engaging in some amiable and gentlemanly business of "keeping the conversation going." All the same, it does begin to look as if both contemporary philosophy and contemporary science have allowed themselves to be led down the garden path, as a result of their having made what has sometimes been termed the Kantian "transcendental turn." For the import of making such a turn is that neither science nor philosophy can any longer claim to be in any way a knowledge of things in themselves—*i.e.*, of things as they really are. Not only that, but the entire human cognitive enterprise must be radically reconceived, if it be Kant who is calling the tune. No longer must it be thought that "all our knowledge must conform to objects." Instead, "we must [now] make trial whether we may not have more success ... if we suppose that objects must conform to our knowledge."[19]

So much for Kant himself. But in recent times, as we all so well know, it has become increasingly fashionable to push Kant somewhat further and to construe science, and often by implication philosophy as well, as having to rely upon the hypothetico-deductive method, as if this were somehow the most reliable and authentic way of following Kant's lead in making the transcendental turn.[20] Unfortunately, though, as we have seen, once the hypothetico-deductive method comes to be put into practice, it proves to be sadly incapable of yielding a knowledge either of what nature and reality are or of what they are not. Instead, the only reason for ever accepting any hypothesis or theory or world-view, be it either in science or in philosophy, would appear to be the merely pragmatic reason that it works. But this, so far from ever yielding what Aristotle would have called a "theoretical knowledge" of being or of fact or of reality, can at most provide a "practical knowledge" of—to put it crudely—how to get what we want!

Moreover, even with respect to such a purely practical knowledge, it would seem that, for the reasons we have already adduced, philosophy will prove to be decidedly worse off than science in such a context. After all, the criteria for "working" in science are comparatively specific: a scientific theory works if it leads to a greater predictability

---

19. Immanuel Kant, *Critique of Pure Reason*, Norman Kemp Smith trans. (London: Macmillan, 1929), Preface to Second Edition, B XVI.

20. *Cf.* Sir Karl Popper, more or less to this effect, in *Conjectures and Refutations* (New York and London: Basic Books, 1962), pp. 188–89.

with respect to the observable phenomena, as well as to a greater technological control over nature. Yet in philosophy even this limited specificity of the criteria for a theory's "working" or paying off in terms of results—even this—is lacking.[21] Instead, the implications of Rorty's recommendations apparently are that in the sphere of human culture, when it comes to a question of what our basic beliefs and ideals are to be, we enjoy nothing less than a total intellectual permissiveness: those ideals and beliefs may be whatever we want them to be; or more specifically, they are whatever the philosophers and the humanist guardians of our culture in their recommended ongoing intellectual exchanges and conversations may decide or determine them to be. Nor can the determination of such fundamental cultural posits be based on any intellectual or cognitive considerations of any kind; we just go about the business of creating, or preserving, or deconstructing, or reconstructing cultural posits entirely at will and arbitrarily: they are what they are because the humanists in their conversations have decided that that is what they want them to be. Clearly, though, once the idea of a philosophical knowledge of being and the world gets transmuted into any such activity of sheer creation and deconstruction with respect to our world and its values, then philosophy must surely renounce all claims to being a knowledge, and arrogate to itself something almost like the role of God in creation.

Nor is it only Kant's transcendental turn that could be said thus to have started Rorty down this primrose path, so far as his interpretation of present-day Analytic Philosophy is concerned. For in addition, one might say that as much as Rorty may have been uncritical (though certainly not un-Critical) in simply subscribing, like so many others today, to something more or less like Kant's Transcendental Deduction of his categories, so also it would seem that Rorty has been rather differently, and yet no less equally, uncritical in his emphatic repudiation of anything like Kant's so-called Metaphysical Deduction of his categories.[22] Thus as we all know, in his Metaphysical Deduction Kant thought that he had succeeded in establishing the absolute fi-

---

21. For an illuminating general discussion of whether and how a pragmatic criterion of truth might be extended, or would need to be extended, to theories other than those in the physical sciences, see Mary Hesse, *Revolutions and Reconstructions in the Philosophy of Science* (Bloomington and London: Indiana University Press, 1980), especially Ch. 8.

22. It should perhaps be noted that, although throughout his book Rorty constantly inveighs against Kant and Kant's influence, I believe that a careful scrutiny of such passages in Rorty will reveal that it is not Kant's use of a Transcendental Deduction to justify categories and conceptual schemes, but rather the use of his Metaphysical Deduction as a means of demonstrating that there can never be any change in the categories one uses, that Rorty objects to.

nality and immutability of his own list of the categories. But of course, this Metaphysical Deduction of Kant's has long ceased to be taken seriously by either present-day philosophers or scientists. In fact, the very reliance upon anything like the hypothetico-deductive method in either science or philosophy must involve one in the notion, so taken for granted on almost every hand nowadays, that, regarding any such thing as a categorial scheme, or conceptual scheme, as the popular term now is, so far from being anything fixed and immutable, it is rather the sort of thing that we can perfectly well conjure up, employ, and then repudiate simply at will. Yes, that very mark of repeated deconstruction and of new creation that Rorty so heralds as being characteristic of present-day Analytical Philosophy and Philosophy of Language—this very openness on the part of both science and philosophy to such ever renewed deconstruction and construction—is nothing if not a function of the general repudiation of anything like Kant's Metaphysical Deduction.

Yet note, what Rorty seems not to have realized is the embarrassing, not to say compromising, aspect of all of this. For if our categories and conceptual schemes can be created, and then again deconstructed largely at will, what possible grounds or reasons do we human beings have for what would seem to be the ever ongoing business of our now embracing and then dispossessing ourselves first of one conceptual scheme and then another? Of course, as we have already seen, we can always adduce pragmatic reasons for such categorial preferences. And yet we also noted that when it is an affair of category preference in philosophy, as distinct from science,[23] the pragmatic considerations that determine our choices turn out to be so indeterminate as but to confirm the utter arbitrariness and permissiveness of those category choices: we choose them and then repudiate them, because now they appeal to us, and now they do not.

But given such a total intellectual permissiveness, when it comes to anything like a choice between categorial schemes or cultural posits, how else may we explain the fact that now one cultural paradigm

---

23. I note, in passing, that insofar as Rorty imagines that it is not just in science, but in philosophy generally, that the only justification of our supposed knowledge of nature and reality must be in terms of some version or other of a Kantian transcendental deduction of categories, to this same extent, Rorty's own entire philosophical position could well be questioned on the basis of a familiar type of self-referential argument. After all, Kantian philosophy has often been questioned on just such grounds. And surely if Kant is not immune, then why should Rorty be? However, this particular line of refutation of Rorty's position we propose not to press in this paper. Indeed, a point to much this same effect has already been pressed against Rorty by Alvin Plantinga in his presidential address, *Proceedings and Addresses of The American Philosophical Association*, Sept. 1982.

comes to be the prevailing one in a given society or community, and now another? If it not be as a result of any sort of rational choice that one set of cultural posits comes to prevail over another, then what else can account for this other than something like the exercise and operation of a sort of sheer Nietzschean Will-to-Power? And what must this do to a program like that of Rorty's in which the responsibility for keeping our cultural paradigms in order—for preserving them, no less than for changing them—should be entrusted to the humanists and the philosophers? Alas, it would seem that so far from being able to claim any intellectual competence for such a task, the poor humanist-philosophers would need to take a crash course in how to execute sheer power plays. For these presumably are really the only ultimate determinants of what our cultural paradigms will be.

To be sure, we rather doubt that Rorty has ever faced up to this possible denouement of his own philosophical position and program. Or if he has faced up to it, it is just conceivable that he might come back with a possible ready answer. "Why," he might ask, "does one necessarily have to assume that, just because ultimately it is only something like the Will-to-Power that is decisive in determining what it is that men are to live by, it must therefore follow that the exercise of such a Will-to-Power must always be a ruthless, and never a benign one. Indeed, is this not just the point of insisting that when considering what our ideals and cultural posits are to be, we need simply to keep the conversation going, and not necessarily give ourselves over to the practice of mere power plays? Will this not guarantee a benign exercise of the Will-to-Power rather than a ruthless one?"

Fine! The only trouble is that the methods used in *Nineteen-Eighty-Four* for changing our language and thus altering our basic beliefs and our notions of the very structures of reality would seem no less available, and also no less justifiable (given that there are no objective bases for justification anyway), than the method of "keeping the conversation going." Both alike would need to be reckoned, in the present context at least, as being no more than alternative ways of exercising a Will-to-Power. Nevertheless, I would suggest that, human nature being what it is, something like Newspeak would be bound to win out over Rortian conversations every time! Not only that, I would even presume to make this judgment on the basis of what I would say is a genuine knowledge of human nature, and not any mere cultural posit *à la* Rorty!

PART II
WHAT PRICE ETHICS IN THE EYES OF MODERN MORAL PHILOSOPHERS?

5

TELOS AND TELEOLOGY IN ARISTOTELIAN ETHICS

What possible point could there be to the title of this paper? For while *telos* and *teleology* are not exactly synonyms, it is quite inconceivable that there could ever be any sort of teleology without reference to some sort of telos, and given that, in the context of ethics, one were convinced that something like a telos or end or purpose or goal in human life needs to be reckoned with, then immediately one's ethics could hardly be considered to be anything other than a teleological ethics.[1] True enough, and yet for all of that, I believe it no less true that, when it comes to the varieties of so-called teleological ethics that are prevalent today, anything like a telos in Aristotle's sense is strangely absent. Still, it is not so much the specific content or make-up of the Aristotelian telos that I want to consider in this paper as it is rather the way in which that telos serves to determine what it would seem to me is the distinctive character of a teleological ethic of the Aristotelian type. For though I lack either the classical scholarship or the philosophical acumen necessary to substantiate my contention in terms of the Aristotelian texts, I would still, sunk as I am in my deplorable ignorance, like to make frank confession of a hunch that I have that Aristotle's teleology is of a radically different character from most, if not all, of the going varieties of teleology that are fashionable in present-day ethical theories, be these contractarian or utilitarian in character. Not only that, but I also suspect that most modern commentators

---

1. It is interesting that in his book *Reason and Human Good in Aristotle* (Cambridge, MA: Harvard University Press, 1975), p. 87, John Cooper explicitly states that "Aristotle does not stand with the teleologists as is usually assumed, but is in fact in certain respects closer to Kant and the deontologists." However, it would seem that Cooper's judgment is based entirely on the particular sense he attributes to the terms "teleologists" and "deontologists." And goodness knows, the Protean character of these terms has become so pronounced as to render them almost useless for continued philosophical classification—a fact which the argument of this present paper should make particularly manifest.

99

on Aristotle, or even contemporary philosophers who glibly discuss Aristotle, have somehow misconceived and misconstrued the very nature and character of what I would simply call Aristotelian teleology. Thus I believe that these strictures of mine would extend to scholars like Cooper and Hardie in the present day, as well as to a Ross and a Prichard of a yesterday, and even to contemporary sympathizers or critics of Aristotelian teleology, thinkers as different, say, as Rawls and B. A. O. Williams. But again in this paper I have time only for a voicing of my suspicions in this regard and not for any proper documentation. Instead, I must confine myself to but a very abstract and speculative "structural history," as the Bergmannians might call it, in which I will attempt to work out the very different way in which, as it would seem to me, the human telos is conceived and understood, by someone like Aristotle on the one hand and by so many modern teleologists on the other. Moreover, as a result of their conceiving the telos so differently, modern teleologists, it seems to me, tend to work out a type of teleological ethics that is not only very different from Aristotle's but one that is palpably odd on its face, and perhaps exceedingly dubious as well.

And so to come immediately to my central point, let me pose the direct question: What is the nature of the difference between an end or telos, as Aristotle conceives it, and the various sorts of candidates for the role of ends or purposes or goals in ethics that modern teleologists tend to put forward? Unhappily, I find the difference rather hard to state, not because the difference is not a striking one but rather because the very notion or concept that must play the decisive role in any teleological ethics, whatever the kind, is a notion that would appear to be fraught with a rather frustrating ambiguity. The concept is simply that of "interest" or "desire." And must it not be agreed that any telos or purpose or goal or end for anyone who actually has that purpose or goal or end cannot be other than the object of that person's interest or desire? Yet so to characterize things tends to slur over a possible radical difference, alike in the kinds of ends and the kinds of desires involved. Invoking what I sometimes like to call "the *Euthyphro* test," we need only remind ourselves of how in that dialogue Socrates raised the question: Are things good because they are beloved of the Gods, or are they beloved of the Gods because they are good? Applying such a test, then, in the instant case, are such ends or goals as we human beings happen to have to be pronounced good because we go for them or desire them, or is it rather the case that they are ends that we should desire or seek simply because in themselves, and independently of what our own interests and desires may happen to be, they really are good and hence are just such things as ought to be desired?

Picking up, then, on the terminology of the last clause—terminology that may come across as a bit odd to many of us nowadays, namely, that certain ends might be such as we should desire or ought to desire, whether we actually desire them or not—suppose I introduce a new term into the picture, that of "obligatory ends." Admittedly, this is an odd-sounding term, and yet it is not a term that is wholly novel. In fact, it is a term that Robert Paul Wolff of all people has used, albeit somewhat grudgingly, in his commentary on Kant's *Groundwork*.[2] True, Wolff speaks of obligatory ends only in order to deny that there are any such. And yet whether the expression has referents or not, it does have a sense. Or at least it has one for Wolff, and if it can make the grade with the likes of Robert Paul Wolff, it surely then ought make sense to the rest of us. Moreover, the sense that it makes is, I believe, pretty much the sort of thing that Aristotle has in mind whenever, in the context of his ethics, he has occasion to think or speak of the telos of human life or human existence. An Aristotelian telos, in other words, is nothing if not an obligatory end.

And if this still strikes many of us as odd and as scarcely sounding like Aristotle, consider the following comment by R. A. Gauthier, with reference to Aristotle's ethics:

The great question which determines the whole of our moral life is just this: 'Which is the highest good that human action can propose for itself by way of an end?' And it is here that [the notion of] happiness appears. But it is absolutely essential to note the manner—for us somewhat disconcerting—in which it appears in the *Nicomachean Ethics*: it appears, in effect, only as a *word*. Happiness is the *name* which most men . . . are agreed should be given to the supreme good, the ultimate end of human life. Certainly, Aristotle will take the trouble to show that they are right to give this *name* to the supreme good; but in fact when he undertakes to define the *essence* of the supreme good, the fact that it has the *name* happiness will play no role at all. One can see from this how wide of the mark are the objections that one sometimes makes respecting Aristotelian eudaemonism: it is entirely accidental to the supreme good in Aristotle's sense that it should be called "happiness"; the determination of its nature owes nothing to this *word*, but rests entirely on a metaphysics of finality.

And that is why one can speak, in Aristotle's ethics, of a *duty to be happy*. The expression, to be sure, is not Aristotle's; but it translates his thought very well. For in his eyes, man is "happy" when he realizes that for which he is

---

2. Robert Paul Wolff, *The Autonomy of Reason: A Commentary on Kant's Groundwork of the Metaphysics of Morals* (New York: Harper Torchbooks, 1973).

made; and to realize that for which he is made is the duty of man, for it is that which reason prescribes for him.[3]

Supposing, now, that Gauthier is right in placing such a construction upon Aristotle's notion of man's end or telos, is it surprising that a telos of this sort just doesn't enter into the councils of latter-day teleological ethicists at all. "'A duty to be happy,'" we can imagine a modern utilitarian or contractarian exclaiming, "why, the very idea of such a thing is preposterous!" And no less preposterous would appear to be the idea of "an obligatory end." Instead, happiness is something that no one needs to be persuaded that he ought to seek after. On the contrary, it is something that everyone just does seek after. And as for duties, if they so much as enter the picture at all, they do so not as obligating us to pursue our own happiness but rather as obligating us somehow not to pursue our own happiness, or at least not to pursue it unrestrictedly and without due regard for what Nozick might call certain "side-constraints" that obligate us by way of restricting our own pursuit of happiness in deference to the rights of others to pursue their happiness. Or putting it the other way around, so far from there ever being any duty incumbent upon us to pursue our own happiness, it would seem rather to be exclusively the case of duties always being incumbent upon others to allow us to get on with our own pursuits of happiness, without undue let or hindrance from them.

Yes, if we were to take either R. M. Hare as a contemporary exemplar of a utilitarian type of ethics or John Rawls as a champion of an updated contractarianism, might we not imagine either of them manifesting just such an incomprehension and disbelief regarding either the notion of "a duty to be happy" or the notion of "an obligatory end" as we have just indicated? "Aristotelian teleology," they would say, "at least as that is construed by Father Gauthier, has simply got the relations of happiness and duties, or of ends and duties, entirely inverted, if not perverted: it is not our own ends and our own happiness that we have a duty to pursue, but rather the ends and the happiness of others that we have a duty to let these others pursue." And no less would they say that any teleological ethics, rightly conceived, is precisely an affair of trying to show, not that any Tom, Dick, or Harry has a *duty* to pursue his own end or telos but rather, that every Tom, Dick, and Harry has each of them the *right* to pursue his own end or telos. Indeed, just to the extent to which an ethical teleology of the Aristotelian type would have us suppose that a person's

---

3. R. A. Gauthier, *La Morale d'Aristote* (Paris: Presses Universitaires de France, 1959), pp. 47–48.

own telos is something that he is obligated to pursue, to that same extent Aristotelian teleology is really a kind of inverted or even perverted teleology, and old Aristotle might just as well put that in his pipe and smoke it!

So much, then, for the imagined initial and pained reactions that contemporary teleologists might well experience with reference to Aristotle's notion of man's end or telos, at least as that is expounded by Gauthier. Ironically enough, though, if we were to listen to the late Leo Strauss—and apparently all too few professional philosophers did listen to him—it is not Aristotle who should be accused of having inverted the teleology of the moderns, but rather the moderns whose teleology is to be understood as a curious perversion or inversion of Aristotle's—and, for that matter, of Plato's as well, no doubt. And historically, of course, Strauss is entirely right. After all, it could hardly be the ancients who may rightly be accused of having inverted or perverted what the moderns managed to say many years after them, so much as it must be the moderns who can be said to have perverted or inverted the supposed wisdom which the ancients had uttered many years before them. But be this as it may, as Strauss analyzes the situation, there was one particular ploy which the moderns, particularly in the person of Thomas Hobbes, would appear to have resorted to and which had the precise effect of upsetting the traditional ancient and medieval view of man's telos or end. And the way the moderns brought off their ploy was first of all to challenge directly what earlier we found Gauthier referring to as "the metaphysics of finality" and which was so integral a part of both the Platonic and Aristotelian view of things. For with the rise of modern science and modern philosophy, as we all know so well, final causes were simply eliminated from the natural order altogether. And once final causes were removed, both root and branch, then any and all natural obligations or duties or "oughts" disappeared as well. As Strauss put it, "Classical political philosophy had taken its bearings by how man ought to live [i.e., by man's natural finality, and hence his obligatory end or ends]; the correct way of answering the question of the right order of society consists in taking one's bearings by how men actually live."[4]

And how do men actually live? Surely, the answer to such a question would perhaps strike us in the present day as even more obvious than it was to Thomas Hobbes in the seventeenth century. For what is the life of man, according to the usual contemporary way of looking at

---

4. Leo Strauss, *Natural Right and History* (Chicago: University of Chicago Press, 1953).

things, if not simply the pursuit of his own interests and desires, so far as this is possible? And what else does any man do just naturally, and if left to his own devices, if not simply to go about doing what he wants or trying to get what he wants, so far as he can and as much as he can? Clearly, there is nothing of duty or obligation in all of this; instead, it is but a simple fact of nature that human beings just do what they are impelled to do or what their very interests and desires incline or lead them to do. Again, to quote Strauss, and this time with reference to Hobbes specifically, what Hobbes did "was to maintain the idea of natural law but to divorce it from the idea of man's perfection; only if natural law can be deduced from how men actually live, from the most powerful force that actually determines all men, or most men most of the time, can it be effective or of practical value. The complete basis of natural law must be sought not in the end of man, but in his beginnings."[5]

With this, then, we can begin to see just what the modern perversion or inversion of the Aristotelian notion of man's telos or end amounted to. Ends, purposes, and goals of human beings there still are, of course. But such ends are no longer in any sense things that men ought to pursue; rather, they are but the things that men actually do pursue simply in virtue of the natural forces and impulses acting upon them. In other words, there is nothing either right or wrong, or good or bad, about such human goal-seeking or pursuit of ends; rather, human goal-directed behavior is but an inescapable fact of nature.

Very well, then, but if anything like obligatory ends, or the so-called natural perfection of human beings, is eliminated altogether and can no longer serve as the moral standard for our human conduct and behavior—to say nothing of the natural basis for our human duties and obligations—then how are morals and ethics to be got into the picture at all? If duties and obligations have been dissociated from natural ends and extruded from nature altogether, is there any way to get them back into the picture? Or maybe our contemporary teleologists feel there is no need to get them back into the world, or even into the picture, considering how onerous and disagreeable things like duties and obligations are! Could it be, then, that the import of modern teleology is and ought to be simply the elimination of ethics altogether? "Not so; not so at all!" say the modern teleologists, be they contractarians or utilitarians. "For granted that each of us, just as a matter of fact, is bent on, if not hell-bent on, pursuing his own ends and gratifying his own desires, then inevitably and quite

---

5. *Ibid.*, p. 180.

inescapably the basic concern with all of us must necessarily be with whether we can actually bring off what we are thus each of us naturally purposed to do. And will not the great threat to each of us thus getting what he naturally wants out of life stem from nothing if not the clearly foreseeable conflict that inevitably arises from your pursuing your ends and interests and my pursuing mine? True, the conflict need not assume necessarily the proportions of a Hobbesian 'war of all against all,' but a conflict it will certainly be nonetheless. Hence, why not suppose that morals and ethics—and with them the whole array of moral duties and obligations—are to be thought of as emerging first in connection with some sort of political or social arrangement that would guarantee to each of us the right to pursue each his own ends or goals, so far as this might be possible? That is to say, it would be acknowledged that I would have no less than a veritable right to pursue my ends and purposes, and to gratify my desires and interests, so long as I was scrupulous about not interfering with a comparable right on your part to do the same thing. Yes, it would even need to be said that you had no less than an actual duty or obligation to respect my right to gratify my interests and my desires, so long as I recognized a corresponding duty or obligation to respect your right to gratify your interests and your desires."

Nor need it make any particular difference, so far as the basic understanding of the general scheme of reciprocal rights and duties in a teleological ethics of the modern type is concerned, whether it be a utilitarian or a contractarian who might here be calling the shots. For the contractarian will say that my right to pursue my ends and my interests, as well as my duty to recognize the rights of others to pursue their ends and interests, is but a function of a proper social contract. In contrast—though still perhaps not in a radically dissimilar vein—the utilitarian, while not invoking anything like a social contract, will nonetheless try to devise some sort of argument to show that it does not have to be as a result of any actual contract, but rather that it follows from the very logic of the human social situation, that the members of any society are each of them obligated to restrain themselves, at least in part, in the gratification of their own inclinations and desires; and this, just so that all and all alike may enjoy just that maximum gratification of as many of their respective interests as may be possible under the circumstances. And so it is that, be it on the ground either of a contractarian or of a utilitarian type of ethical teleology, what we might call the gravamen of the moral and the ethical would appear to have shifted from the one-time supposed moral responsibility of the individual to try to make something of himself and so to become the human person that he ought to be by nature, or is cut out to be in the light of the supreme good that is the ultimate end of human life. For rather than any individual's being said to have an obligation to pursue his proper end or telos as a human being, on the newer teleology, the human individual will have only his own private or personal ends or objectives or τέλη, and, with respect to such ends or personal objectives, he has no duties or obligations of any kind, but only rights. In fact, as Strauss remarks, the new teleology has the effect of introducing and injecting into consciousness the picture of "a social order that is defined in terms of the rights of man. For the rights in question express, and are meant to express, something that everyone actually desires anyway; they hallow everyone's self-interest as everyone sees it or can easily be brought to see it."[6]

With this, then, need we say more by way of bringing out the radical contrast between the older and more Aristotelian type of teleology and the newer and more modern type of either utilitarian or contractarian teleology? In the one case, it is insisted that there is a natural finality in human life and human existence—that is to say, a natural human end or natural human perfection, which, if a person does not achieve, he can hardly be said to be fully human and, in this sense, could hardly be said to have become what he might be or could be and, hence, ought to be just as a human being. In the other case, so far from there being any natural end or telos in human life which any and every human being is somehow obligated or has a duty to try to achieve, it is rather a case of each individual's having his own end or *telos*—or even more likely of his having any number of possible ends or τέλη from which he can choose according to his taste or inclination, or between which he does not even have to choose but with respect to which he can first follow one impulse and then another, or go first for one end or goal and then for another, according to the whim of the moment and perhaps even in the manner of Plato's "democratic man." Here, of course, there can be no talk of duty or obligation or even of ethics or morality at all. Instead our pursuit of ends and goals and purposes will simply be as nature dictates, relatively to each one of us—and all of this in the modern sense of "nature" too and not at all in the ancient sense of "nature" as involving natural finalities.

Yes, one can further say that in teleologies of the modern type there has been a radical displacement or shift of incidence of duties and obligations and, hence, of morals and ethics as a whole. The moral life is no longer thought of as consisting principally in the individual's

---

6. *Ibid.*, pp. 182–83.

pursuing his rightful end or goal or telos just as a human being and trying not to be deflected therefrom by the myriads of chance impulses and drives and inclinations and likings and preferences that never cease to manifest themselves in the life of any one of us. No, morality will instead be largely an affair, if we might so put it, of the individual's having to try to bring himself to be other-regarding rather than self-regarding. His duties, that is to say, are not towards himself at all, but only towards others, in that morally he must needs be careful to try not to impede or wrongfully interfere with others in their pursuit of their ends and interests, just as they in turn are in duty bound not to interfere with him in his pursuit of his ends and interests. Accordingly, so far as the individual himself is concerned, he will of course never cease to be occupied with his own interests and purposes and ends, but now, in the context of the new teleology, he will regard such a concern with his own ends not as a matter of duty but of right. For just as morally his duties will now consist solely in his respecting the rights of others to pursue their own ends and interests, so correspondingly his pursuit of his own ends he will come to regard as being exclusively a matter of right and not of duty at all. Again, to quote Strauss: "If we may call liberalism that political doctrine which regards as the fundamental political fact the rights, as distinguished from the duties, of man and which identifies the function of the state with the protection or safeguarding of those rights, we must say that the founder of liberalism was Hobbes."[7]

Enough, though, by way of putting the contrast between the Aristotelian conception of the human telos and of teleological ethics on the one hand and the very different modern views of teleology and teleological ethics on the other. But is the contrast a mere contrast in fact, or is it a contrast in worth as well? That is to say, is the contrast possibly one between teleologies of which the one is definitely the superior of the other? Let me say that for myself I cannot help opting for an Aristotelian type of teleology, as over against teleologies of either the contractarian or utilitarian type. Nor do I consider it a mere affair of opting for one view as over against another. No, for I believe that it can be shown that, with reference to the very foundations of ethics, modern teleological theories are radically deficient and that it is only by a return to something like an Aristotelian telos that a teleological ethics—or for that matter, any type of ethics—can find a proper grounding and justification.

Have no fear, though! I have no intention, in what remains of this

---

7. *Ibid.*, pp. 181–82.

already labored paper, of completely outrunning my allotted time, and your long exhausted patience, by attempting to offer a full-dress justification of an Aristotelian type of telos as being the one and only defensible basis for any sort of teleological ethics. For one thing, as our earlier quotation from Gauthier has implied, any justification of a telos or obligatory end in Aristotle's sense must needs presuppose a prior justification of an entire "metaphysics of finality," as Gauthier calls it. And for another thing, any justification of an ethical teleology in Aristotle's sense would require not simply a defense of a general metaphysics of finality, but also a defense of Aristotle's specific view of man's natural end or telos as consisting in "the activity of the soul in accordance with virtue" and, more specifically still, in accordance with both intellectual and moral virtue. However, such undertakings in justification of an Aristotelian telos are not for this paper. Instead, in what remains I shall simply confine myself to trying to show what, as it would seem to me, the prohibitively high cost to ethics and to ethical theory must be if one chooses, in the manner of modern teleologists, to repudiate anything like a natural telos or a naturally obligatory end, whether that end be conceived precisely in the manner of Aristotle or not.

In the first place, I would wonder whether, when in the manner of Hobbes—or even for that matter of any of the modern teleologists—anything like a naturally obligatory end for human beings has been eliminated from the ethical picture altogether, there then any longer is, or even can be, any ethics in the picture at all. Thus recall how, on Strauss's analysis, it is characteristic of modern ethical and political theory that the order of priority of rights and duties comes to be curiously inverted. With Aristotle one might say that there is a natural priority of duties over rights. For supposing that there be a natural end or telos of human life—a naturally obligatory end as we have already called it—then what might be called the logic of our human moral situation will thereby be at once clearly and cogently determined: necessarily there will be certain things which it will be right for us human beings to do, namely, such things and such actions as will lead to the attainment of our naturally determined end or telos. Not only that, but such courses of action and modes of behavior as it will thus be "naturally right" for us to follow and to engage in could scarcely be considered as "rights" in the modern sense at all. Instead, they will be more on the order of natural duties and obligations—*i.e.*, things that as human beings we must do and ought to do if we are ever to attain our natural fulfillment or perfection as human beings.

At the same time, given that we have such natural duties and obligations, then consequent upon them will presumably be various rights—*i.e.*, various guarantees and protections that we might be said to be naturally entitled to, if we are ever to live our lives as we are supposed to do and as it is incumbent upon us to do, just insofar as we are human beings. For instance, to use a more or less Aristotelian example, if as a human being I am naturally obligated to live courageously and temperately and justly and if, in addition, I am so obligated not merely in the sense that I have a duty to perform courageous and temperate and just actions but also in the sense that I must love courage and temperance and justice, and love them for their own sakes, then surely I can be said to have the right not to be forced to perform unjust actions, or not to be prevented from ever coming to understand what courage and temperance and justice are, or not to be subjected to such conditioning as might make me uncritically choose to do merely what others want me to do and without my really exercising my own better judgment at all.

Granted that such Aristotelian examples are somewhat vague and abstract, still it may be hoped that they suffice to show how, within the framework of an Aristotelian teleological ethics, it is our duties and obligations as human beings that are logically prior, and, hence, that it is from such duties and obligations—*i.e.*, from such things as it is "naturally right" for us to do—that all of our "rights" in the more modern sense of that term might be said to be derived. In contrast, in modern teleologies, as Strauss suggests, it is just the other way around: it is our human rights that are prior, and what might be called our human duties and obligations are consequent upon these.

And here let us pause to ask whether such a priority of rights over duties, and the consequent derivation of duties from rights, as is characteristic of most modern teleologies, be really a defensible ethical position at all. Or "defensible" may perhaps be hardly the right word. For the issue here is almost whether what we might call the very "logic" of modern teleological ethics be a possible logic at all. So far as an Aristotelian teleology is concerned, given the natural telos or the natural finality of human life, it is possible, as it were, "logically" to derive our human duties and responsibilities from such a telos or end and our human natural rights and privileges, in turn, from our duties and responsibilities. In contrast, suppose that, in the manner of our modern teleologies, we eliminate anything like an Aristotelian telos or obligatory end, as Wolff would call it; the next step, as we have seen, is to say that just as human beings we now have a natural right to pursue our own interests and ends and goals and purposes, whatever these may be. And given that such a pursuit of our own interests be our natural right, then consequent upon such a right will be a corresponding duty that is incumbent upon our neighbor—or, perhaps better, a whole set of corresponding duties incumbent upon all mankind—to respect these our prior rights as individuals. What, though, is the logical ground or basis for this affirmation of such prior and inalienable rights of ourselves just as human individuals?

Suppose, for example, that, being the true and loyal American patriot that I would hope I am, I find myself in the very forefront of those who would maintain and even fight for their supposedly natural and perhaps God-given rights to life, liberty, and the pursuit of happiness. Still, on what grounds may I assume that I have any such natural rights to life, liberty, and the pursuit of happiness, much less any God-given rights to the same? Placing myself in the context of any of the modern teleological types of ethics, I must acknowledge that such things as life, liberty, and the pursuit of happiness do not constitute any natural telos in the Aristotelian sense. That is to say, they are not in any way what could be called a naturally obligatory end for me, or, as Gauthier might put it, I certainly do not have any such thing as a "duty to be happy." All the same, however much my pursuit of life, liberty, and happiness may not be a duty for me, they certainly are things that I want and cherish. Not only that, but availing myself of the modern sense of "natural," as contrasted with anything like the Aristotelian notion of a "natural finality," I can very properly claim that I have a natural inclination toward life and liberty and the pursuit of happiness, and not just a natural inclination, perhaps, but even an all-consuming passion for such things, such that nothing means more to me in life—there is nothing that I cherish more—than precisely my life and my liberty and my happiness.

So be it. And yet remember the relevance of the *Euthyphro* test in this connection. Applied to my pursuit of life, liberty, and happiness—at least as these are to be thought of within the framework of a modern teleology—the *Euthyphro* test forces me to recognize that such ends and goals are not to be regarded as things that I pursue or cherish because they are naturally or intrinsically good; rather, they are things that I only call "good" because I happen to like them and to cherish them. In other words, ends or goals that I may thus be said naturally to go for or to be inclined towards—yes, even though they be things that I find myself actually driven to pursue just by some irresistible force of nature—are for that very reason ends or goals that are of no moral import whatever. Not only that, but whatever success I may have in my pursuit of a life, liberty, and happiness so conceived, I cannot possibly consider myself to be one whit better off morally, or even one whit better as a human being, for all of my success or proficiency in thus attaining my desired ends or in getting what I want. But then, if my ends and goals and purposes have no moral weight, on what possible basis can I claim that I have a moral right to pursue them? To be sure, if I have such a right, then, by the very logic of the moral situation, others will have a corresponding duty or obligation to respect my right. And with this, I shall indeed find myself caught up in an entire context of moral rights and duties, both mine and others. But still, what is the source of those initial individual rights, upon which the entire structure of modern teleological ethics is erected?

I suggest that there is no basis whatever for these rights claims that are the very basis and starting point of modern teleological ethics. Apparently, the only argument that modern teleologists would seem prepared to give in support of such rights would seem to take the following form: (1) Let it be granted that there is no natural telos or end for which man is made and which he, therefore, has a natural duty or obligation to try to attain. (2) The consequence of this would surely be that the human individual must be considered free to do whatever he wants and to pursue whatever ends or goals he chooses. (3) Nevertheless, even though, when seen in this light, it must be regarded as being all right for a person just to follow his own inclinations and simply do as he pleases, there is little or no likelihood that any individual can ever actually gratify many of his interests or desires, unless that which it is now recognized as being all right for him to do be further understood as being something that he has an actual right to do. (4) Accordingly, once it is acknowledged that it is not merely all right for a person, say, to devote himself to the pursuit of life, liberty, and happiness, but that doing so is a matter of his individual right as well, then an answering or corresponding duty on the part of others to respect this right of the individual will follow immediately, and the result will be that an entire moral context of rights and duties becomes thereby established.

And yet what sort of an argument is this? That there should be no obligatory ends which it is my duty to pursue and that I am thereby free just to pursue my own life, liberty, and happiness if I so desire—that is one thing. But to say that I therefore have a moral right to pursue such ends is surely another thing. Again, to quote from Strauss, it would seem that, in the modern period, "a social order [tends to be] defined in terms of the rights of man. For the rights in question express, and are meant to express something that everyone desires anyway . . . they hallow everyone's self-interest as everyone sees it or can easily be brought to see it."[8] But clearly, there is a fallacy

---

8. *Ibid.*, pp. 182–83.

contained in any such argument. The mere fact that as human beings we all of us have various interests and desires—and this simply naturally and as a fact of nature—that certainly does not mean that the pursuit of our interests and desires is a matter of right. What could be a more flagrant instance of an attempted conversion of a fact into a right or, if you will, of an "is" into an "ought" or of fact into a value?

Perhaps, though, the latter-day teleologist might claim that such an attack on his rights-claims for human individuals is grossly unfair. Thus, he might readily concede that no one can possibly establish his own rights-claims—say to that of pursuing life, liberty, and happiness—merely on the ground that life and liberty mean everything to him and are things that he loves and cherishes above all else. No, merely wanting something and wanting it passionately is no ground for claiming that one has a right to it. And yet our teleologist might insist that such is not really the basis of his claim. Instead, he will say that his own claim to life and liberty is validated only to the extent and on the ground that he concedes to others the same right to life and liberty that he claims for himself.

Surely, though, this will not do the trick either. For why should a mere concession to others that they have similar rights be a way to validate my own claim to have rights in the first place? Is this anything more than merely trying to find safety in numbers? Besides, are not one's problems merely increased a hundredfold, if, being at a loss to show how one has any rights in the first place, one then blithely takes on the task of showing that everyone else has such rights as well? After all, of what significance is it that I merely concede to others the same rights to life and liberty that I want to claim for myself? The mere fact of my conceding such rights to others scarcely proves that they really do have such rights, anymore than my original affirmation of my own rights proves that I do in fact have such rights myself.

What, then, must we conclude from all this if not that the very logic of the modern teleologist's case is a faulty one? True, if you grant him to begin with that human beings, just as individuals, do indeed have rights in the very nature of the case, then an entire ethical framework of reciprocal rights and duties can be erected on this basis alone. And yet on what grounds may it be granted that there are such rights of individuals in the first place? The answer is that, given the logical structure of modern teleological theories of ethics, there is just no way in which such an initial concession of rights to individuals can ever be legitimated or justified.

Nor is it merely a case of modern teleologies thus not being able to make out a case for themselves in logic. In addition, and particularly as one considers them in comparison with an Aristotelian type of teleology, it would seem that they might be hard put to it even to make out much a case for themselves on what I might call psychological and motivational grounds as well. For is it not ironical that, in those modern versions of teleology that we have been considering, the very projects that as human beings we occupy ourselves with most intensively and are most concerned with in our daily lives—our businesses, our professions, our families, our country, our religion, yes, even our general well-being—these are, none of them, things that we may regard as being of any moral import for us at all? And vice versa, whatever things be of moral import for us, and that we may consider it morally incumbent upon us to try to do—these, in turn, are all precluded from being things that in the first instance we may be said to love or cherish or even to reckon as desired ends or goals in any really proper sense.

And if at this point you make rejoinder, insisting that I am here forcing all utilitarian and contractarian teleologists into an impossible mould of the most exaggerated Kantian deontologism, I would respond by simply recalling again that "structural history," as the Bergmannians might call it, of modern teleological ethics. For the lesson of such a structural history is that modern teleologies are to be understood as taking their rise directly from the repudiation of anything like Aristotle's notion of a natural or obligatory end or telos of human life. So far from there being any end or ends that we are naturally obligated to pursue, in the ancient sense of the word "nature," there are nothing but countless ends and purposes which in the modern sense of "nature" we are naturally inclined to pursue. And ends and purposes of the latter type are simply devoid of moral import altogether: they are not immoral but just plain amoral or nonmoral. In other words, there is something about a naturally desired end in the modern sense that precludes and excludes it from ever being properly moral or ethical at all.

And on the other hand, when we look at the other face of the coin and ask ourselves just what sorts of actions those are that, from the point of view of modern teleological ethics, may be regarded as partaking of this moral quality, the answer must be that they have to be such actions as in the first instance are not directed to the attainment of our own ends and purposes really in any sense at all. The reason is that morality is thought to enter the picture only at the moment when the pursuit of our own ends and interests tends to interfere with others in their pursuit of their ends and interests. And so it is that in the first instance moral action must be reckoned as action that is not at all what we are naturally inclined to do or tend to do or that involves us in the pursuit of our own ends and purposes. Rather, it needs to be conceived of precisely as action in which we do not follow our own inclinations and interests but rather give place to others in their pursuit of their interests.

Moreover, if you try to counter this by saying that there is nothing to prevent our discovering that we ourselves like helping others, or that we may find ourselves to be actually disposed toward checking our own inclinations in order that others may gratify theirs, the answer is that of course such a thing is possible. And yet the point is that even supposing such a possibility to have become a reality and that in a given instance an individual finds that he actually has developed a liking for doing for others and hence for restraining himself from only doing for himself, still such a new-found liking as this—such as may have come about, as it were in the second instance—must itself in turn be reckoned as no more than a natural inclination and thus a fact of nature. But as a mere fact of nature, my now having come to like to do what I have all along been obligated to do in no wise increases the moral worth of my action. Nor does my loving to do my duty either validate the fact that it is my duty in the first place or enhance the moral worth of my doing my duty in the second place. Nor would there seem to be any way that the modern teleologist might overcome the opposition between nature and morality that he himself has set up in the first instance: what we naturally tend to do, or what for us is a natural end or goal, has no bearing whatever on what it is morally right for us to do, and what it is morally right for us to do is neither validated nor enhanced by the fact that we may happen to be naturally disposed to doing what is thus morally right, or to like or enjoy doing what it is held that we ought to do.

"But," you may ask, "what about those of our ends and inclinations, our purposes and objectives, our loves and our hates, as do not appear to bring us into conflict with others and that are thus not subject to moral restrictions of the kind admitted by modern types of teleological ethics? With respect to such supposedly harmless and thus socially acceptable aims and inclinations, may we not say that we are under a kind of moral responsibility at least to pursue these? After all, it is the hallmark of modern teleological theories to maintain that we have a right—yes, a moral right—to do as we please and to follow our inclinations, so long as we don't injure others. Very well, then, must not those things which we have a moral right to do be things which it is morally right for us to do?"

Immediately, the non sequitur contained in this last question becomes apparent. For we have already had occasion to see how a right to do as we please, and to follow our own inclinations, which modern teleological ethics are so concerned to establish—even if *per impossibile* such rights could be established—still would not mean that what we might thus be said to have a right to do was also something that it was right for us to do in the sense of being our duty to do. No, for the incidence of morality, in such teleological theories, is strictly speaking not with respect to the person who is said to have the right to perform a certain action but, rather, with respect to such others as may be said to have a duty not to interfere with the other's rights. Morality, in other words, is an affair simply of those who are under obligation and not, as such, of those who are the objects or beneficiaries of that obligation.

But does not all of this merely confirm our earlier suggestion as to the psychological, no less than the logical, untenability of contemporary teleological ethics? Imagine how implausible and even counterintuitive it must be for all of us when we are told that our goals, our purposes, our objectives in life—all that we love and cherish and hold most dear—these are things of no moral import whatever. In other words, our responsibilities extend no further than the business of respecting the rights of others. But we ourselves, and what we may be and become, as well as what we may make of ourselves and do with our own lives—these are all things for which we have no responsibility whatever and in regard to which we can simply do as we like, so long as we do not injure or interfere with anyone else. Is it any wonder that, in the present day and under the influence of such currently fashionable utilitarian and contractarian teleologies, young and old alike are so often baffled and frustrated and confused, not knowing what to do with themselves or how to go about living their lives? And why shouldn't they be baffled when they are told it makes no difference what they do, that it makes not the slightest difference morally or ethically what a person does with himself or how he leads his life. For so far as human goals and purposes and ends are concerned, pushpin is, after all, just as good as poetry, and each person has only to take his pick. So do what you want to do; only remember it will not be of any intrinsic worth, nor will it do you any real good; and, indeed, it is of no moral significance whatever.

Now what counsels but these would seem better calculated to make all of our strivings and concerns seem utterly futile and to turn all of our most cherished accomplishments into but a list of so many moral irrelevancies? Isn't it high time, then, that we returned once again to something like an Aristotelian telos or a naturally obligatory end? For what else can give meaning to our lives as we actually live them and in terms of the actual purposes and projects to be pursued and striven for?

6

VARIATIONS, GOOD AND BAD, ON THE THEME OF RIGHT REASON IN ETHICS

In his comparatively recent and altogether remarkable book, *The Theory of Morality*,[1] Alan Donagan would appear to have managed quite to astound, not to say confound, the better part of his colleagues and *confrères* in the present-day moral philosophical establishment. For what is the thesis of his book, if not that the fundamental precepts of traditional Hebrew-Christian morality—The Ten Commandments, the Golden Rule, the Summary of the Law, *et al.*—are all of them nothing if not precepts simply prescribed by right reason! "Incredible!", you will say. "Worse than that, it is downright presumptuous!" one can imagine the typical, present-day moral philosopher exclaiming. "For such precepts as those that Donagan cites and talks about are unmistakably religious precepts; and in the very nature of the case, a religious precept presumably derives such authority as it has only from its being thought to be by Divine command.[2] How, then, can Donagan maintain that the typical religious precepts of Hebrew-Christian morality don't have to be regarded as being religious precepts in the usual sense at all? No, for he takes them to be grounded on nothing less than the authority of right reason!"

Now to this kind of characteristic secularist, not to say prejudicial, professional philosophical reaction, Donagan's answer consists simply

---

1. Alan Donagan, *The Theory of Morality* (Chicago and London: University of Chicago Press, 1977).
2. William Frankena in his well-known little book, *Ethics* (Englewood Cliffs, NJ: Prentice-Hall, 2nd ed., 1973), pp. 28–29, notes that one major variety of ethical theory, alongside of various kinds of deontological theories, teleological theories, etc., might simply be called "Divine-Command Theory." Speaking but impressionistically, I wonder if nowadays it be not commonly assumed by religious moralists, no less than by secular ones, that any system of morality that is taken to be integral to a religious tradition could not possibly be other than a Divine-command theory. Long gone is the day, in other words, when a religious or theological tradition could think of itself as incorporating philosophy within itself, and yet doing so on philosophy's own terms—*i.e.*, the terms simply of right reason.

in the subtle and sustained argument of his entire book. Nor is there any denying the impressiveness of his performance. Still, for all of its impressiveness, I wonder if perhaps even one who is in every way sympathetic with Donagan's conclusions might not question whether the right reason which Donagan appeals to in his argument is altogether a reason that is right for his purposes. Thus many of his typical examples are examples of actions that everyone would acknowledge to be, in their various ways, harmful to others—stealing, murder, adultery, bearing false witness, etc. Unmistakably, these are examples of actions drawn right from the Decalogue. Not only that, but they are presumably also actions of a kind that everyone of us would unhesitatingly pronounce to be wrong. But what is distinctive about Donagan's treatment of such actions is that in his eyes the basis on which we can recognize them to be wrong is simply that they can be seen to be "contrary to reason."[3]

And yet is this entirely correct? Is it true that all such actions and others like them may be recognized as patently contrary to reason? After all, the relevant reason here would admittedly have to be the kind of reason that for Aristotle, no less than for Kant, would need to be reckoned as being a practical reason, rather than a theoretical reason. And clearly, so far as theoretical reason is concerned, no one presumably would have too much difficulty with the idea that it would clearly be contrary to right reason for one to suppose that the way to double the size of a square would be simply to double the length of the sides. But in contrast, suppose that one has stolen the towels from a motel in which one had just spent the night, could it be said that such an action could be seen to be no less contrary to right reason? That is to say, one can actually see (with "the mind's eye," or by "the natural light of reason," or whatever) that an act of theft is wrong, in just the same way in which one is able to see that one simply cannot double the size of a square by doubling the length of its sides? In other words, is contrariety to right reason no less patent than, and patent in exactly the same way as, contrariety to theoretical reason?

Confronted with such a question, it would appear that Donagan makes a first move, by way of answer, that is not unlike a move that is made by Aquinas no less than by Kant. Both of these thinkers, that is to say, would seem to feel that, in order to meet the challenge of the above sorts of questions, one needs first to show how the very considerable number of our diverse moral precepts—in the present case, for instance, the precepts of Hebrew-Christian morality—can be

---

3. *Cf.* Donagan's unequivocal statements to this effect, work cited in n. 1, above.

reduced to a comparatively few first principles. Thus Donagan shows how Aquinas, for instance, would consider that the Ten Commandments, and more specifically the commandment, "Thou shalt not steal," can all be reduced to a more basic moral principle expressed in the second part of the Summary of the Law: "Thou shalt love thy neighbor as thyself."[4] Nevertheless, although Donagan summarizes Aquinas' general line of procedure in this connection, for various reasons Donagan says that he would prefer to follow the lead of Kant, rather than of Aquinas, when it comes to showing how the manifold moral precepts can be reduced to a comparatively few first principles. Indeed, the moral first principles that Donagan comes out with are, by his own admission, not unlike Kant's two formulations of the Categorical Imperative. For example, the Golden Rule Donagan construes as being a purely formal principle, not unlike Kant's first formulation of the categorical imperative. "Do unto others as you would have others do unto you," Donagan thinks, amounts in effect to, "So act that you will be able to will that the maxim of your action should become a universal law." In other words, the Golden Rule may be held to be warranted by right reason in much the way in which the principle of universalizability—which has become such a favorite among contemporary ethical writers—is held to be a purely rational principle of morality, *i.e.*, a principle justified simply by right reason. The only trouble is that this Golden Rule Principle, or Principle of Universalizability, is a purely formal principle, and as such is quite incapable of providing warrant or justification for any truly substantive moral principles. That is to say, to put it rather baldly: *if* there are such things as distinctions between right and wrong, good and bad, etc., to which human beings are subject, or *if* there can truly be said to be duties and obligations that are incumbent upon human beings, or *if* it be supposed that there really are such things as rights, which human beings may be said to enjoy, then by the principle of universalizability, any right that I may claim to have must be adjudged to be no less a right that my neighbor has as well; or if there be certain duties and obligations that I consider to be incumbent upon my neighbor, then I cannot but acknowledge that these same duties are no less incumbent upon me as well, given similar circumstances.

Unfortunately, though, it should already be apparent, as we have remarked, that such a principle of morality, considered as a first prin-

---

4. Needless to say, in what follows we are presenting but a very summary statement of what in the book is a most subtle and sophisticated treatment of St. Thomas' position, as well as of Donagan's own reasons why he feels Kant's account of ethical first principles to be superior to Aquinas'. *Cf. The Theory of Morality*, esp. Chapter 2, 2.3–2.5.

ciple, is a purely formal one: if there are rights, duties and obligations pertaining to any human beings, then they pertain to all human beings alike, given similar circumstances; and yet such a formal principle alone gives no indications of what such rights and duties might be, substantively and concretely. Worse yet, the principle does not even indicate whether there are any such moral obligations or rights—this latter quite apart from the question of what they might be, supposing there to be any. After all, this particular principle of morality, be it formulated as the Golden Rule, or as the Categorical Imperative, or as the Principle of Universalizability, is basically hypothetical in character: if human beings can properly be considered to inhabit what might be called a moral universe,[5] then there is no denying that they are obligated to do unto others as they would be done by; or that they do need to act from maxims that they can will to be universal laws; or that whatever it be that one is obligated to or entitled to, all other human beings, *mutatis mutandis*, are no less obligated or entitled to as well. Is it surprising, then, given this purely hypothetical character of morality, insofar as it gets expressed in such a principle as the Golden Rule Principle, or the Principle of Universalizability, that contemporary discussions of morals and ethics are forever being plagued by the nagging question, "But why should I be moral?"

Very well, then, given this obvious insufficiency of the Golden Rule Principle to serve as the sole first principle of morality, Donagan—and in his own way, Kant as well—sought to formulate another and rather more adequate first principle for morals and ethics. Thus as Kant put the principle: "So act as to treat human nature, either in your own person or in that of others, always as an end, and never merely as a means." Moreover, as the equivalent of this, Donagan puts forward the second part of the Summary of the Law, as this has long been recognized in Hebrew-Christian morality: "Thou shalt love thy neighbor as thyself."[6] Stated in more secular language, what Donagan says that this first principle amounts to is no more and no less than a principle of respect for human nature, or human life, or human ex-

---

5. Perhaps it would be a more fashionable mode of speech to say, "If they should subscribe to the moral point of view."

6. It goes almost without saying that in his selection and discussion of examples of moral precepts drawn from Hebrew-Christian morality, Donagan is ever careful to confine his attention solely to those precepts of which it may be said that they are "independent of any theological presupposition" (p. 60). Accordingly, in the so-called Summary of the Law, Donagan regards only the second part, "Thou shalt love thy neighbor as thyself," and disregards the first part, "Thou shalt love the Lord thy God with all thy heart, and with all thy soul, and with all thy strength and with all thy mind" (Luke 10:25-28). *Cf.* Donagan, cited in n. 1, above.

istence: "Act always so that you respect every human being, yourself or another, as being a rational creature"; or "It is impermissible not to respect every human being, oneself or any other, as a rational creature."[7]

Clearly, once Donagan, thus following Kant, proceeds to formulate what he, Donagan, considers to be the supreme principle of morality, he is forthwith able to claim (1) that such a principle is no mere formal principle of morality, but rather one that provides morality with both substance and content, and (2) that all of the various more specific and concrete moral precepts that Donagan had earlier, and by way of example, cited from the Decalogue may now be seen to be readily derivable from the supreme first principle.[8] For clearly, is it not readily understandable how such actions as murder, theft, bearing false witness, *et al.*, are at once actions directed against others, and at the same time actions that quite patently do not involve a respect for those others, considered as rational creatures? Certainly, if it be contrary to right reason for one to fail to respect either oneself or one's fellows as rational creatures, then it will be no less contrary to reason for one to perpetrate acts of murder, or of adultery, or even of stealing towels from a motel! And with this, may not Donagan be reckoned to be in a fair way toward having succeeded in his basic enterprise of demonstrating that such a system of ethics as may be held to be exemplified by traditional Hebrew-Christian morality, is, through and through, an ethic whose precepts are based simply on right reason?

But no, Donagan is still not entirely out of the woods, so far as his being able to show that the ethics of Hebrew-Christian morality is indeed an ethics of right reason. True, if that supreme principle of morality which Donagan would set up—call it the principle of unfailing respect for human, rational nature—be a principle that is certified by right reason, then it would seem that Donagan could unquestionably show that all of the more specific precepts of the Decalogue, that obviously are derivable from the first principles, are themselves, in turn, clearly founded on right reason. But still, this does not show us that Donagan's very first principle—or, as Donagan represents it as being, Kant's principle as well—is, or can be, certified merely by right reason. Recall our earlier example drawn from the sphere of theoretical reason: to imagine that one might be able to double the size of a square by doubling the length of the sides is something that can clearly be seen to be contrary to reason. But when one moves from

---

7. *Cf. ibid.*, pp. 65–66.
8. Donagan, of course, is careful to discuss the comparable sort of derivation that one finds in Aquinas. See Donagan, work cited in n. 1 above.

such an example to the example of what Donagan and Kant would both of them hold to be a first and basic principle of practical reason, is it equally and in like manner evident that for one not to show respect for the rational nature of human beings is nothing if not contrary to reason? Thus suppose that I just say that I don't see any reason why I need always, or even ever, show any particular respect for rational human nature, be it my own or that of other human beings as well? For instance, recall the Earl of Rochester's caustic lines:

> Were I, who to my cost, already am
> One of those strange, prodigious creatures, Man,
> A spirit free, to choose for my own share
> What sort of flesh and blood I pleas'd to wear,
> I'd be a dog, a monkey or a bear,
> Or anything but that vain animal,
> Who is so proud of being rational.

Granted that we may not share Rochester's depreciatory sentiments regarding the rational nature of ourselves and of our fellows, must we also say that even to entertain such convictions as those of the cynical Earl is as self-contradictory and contrary to right reason, as to entertain the belief that you can double the size of a square by doubling the lengths of its sides? Surely, when looked at in this light, it would seem that the contentions of both Kant and Donagan are just plain overdrawn. No, there just doesn't seem to be anything contradictory, or contrary to reason, for one just to refuse to accept as an imperative that one ought to love one's neighbor as oneself.

But wait a minute! For even supposing that we may have cast doubt on what might be called the Kantian or Donagan first principle of morality, have we really succeeded in making our challenge to the self-evidence of that principle thoroughly cogent? For does not this, like any other dispute over the self-evidence[9] of supposed first principles, seem alike futile and unconvincing? Thus on the one side, it is insisted that the principle in question just is evident to reason, and to deny it is nothing if not contrary to reason; and on the other side, the opposition counters by simply pontificating that there is nothing self-evident about such a principle at all, and that its opposite is nothing if not entirely conceivable by reason. Very well, rather than let ourselves in for any such futile back and forth of denials and counter-

---

9. Unhappily, this is no longer a term that is fashionable in present day logic. Suffice it to say that I am using it in much the way St. Thomas used the notion of a proposition or principle *per se notum*. However, in such a paper as this on ethics, I hope that I may be spared having to discourse on whether such self-evident principles as I shall be referring to are analytic or synthetic, or whether their necessity is *de dicto* or *de re*, etc.

assertions about the evidence to reason of a principle such as that of respecting human nature, or loving one's neighbor as oneself, let us see if we cannot analyze the situation rather more carefully, so as to lay bare just how and why both Donagan and Kant, in their respective ways, would seem presumably to have been misled into supposing that what they take to be the first principle of morality is a principle guaranteed and certified by right reason. For might there not be a certain ambiguity and confusion generated by the fact that a first principle in ethics presumably has to be one that is guaranteed by practical reason, whereas such self-evident principles as those of logic and mathematics, for example, and perhaps even metaphysics, are such as must needs be evident to theoretical reason? Moreover, no sooner does one ask just what sort of a right reason that of practical reason is, than it seems impossible to avoid thinking of practical reason as being anything but a reason that is somehow ordered and oriented entirely to action. And action, in turn—considering that it is a properly human action—would surely have to be an action that in some sense or other is purposive, or directed to some end. Must not the consequence, then, be that in the exercise of so-called practical reason what such a reason comes to disclose or to determine must always be such things as one might say need to be done or not done, or ought to be done or not done, if a given purpose is to be attained?

In contrast, what one ordinarily understands by theoretical reason would seem to be a reason that is not necessarily ordered toward action at all. Instead, abstracting entirely from all concerns as to what needs to be done or left undone, theoretical reason is concerned only with things as they are, or better with the natures of things and what it is that pertains to the natures of things, given that the things in question are the kinds of things that they are.

Given this background, then, what if I were now to hazard a suggestion as to just where and how it is that both Kant and Donagan—and, for that matter, most so-called deontological thinkers as well—would appear to have been led astray in their understanding of practical reason. Well do I know, of course, that trying to interpret Kant is notably difficult, if not downright hopeless. And even Donagan, alas, seems to become studiously opaque, when it comes to saying just what sort of a self-evidence it is that pertains to practical principles. Nevertheless, let me in all tentativeness, no less than in all temerity, try to sketch out what it seems to me is the general sort of pattern or connection of ideas that tends to be operative in the minds of most deontological thinkers when they try to understand the way human reason works in the practical sphere. The key problem here, it would seem, is simply one as to whether and how what might loosely be called our human desires or purposes—the ends that we seek to attain—have relevance to what practical reason might tell us needs to be done or ought to be done in given concrete cases.

In this connection let me but quote a few passages from Robert Paul Wolff's commentary on Kant's *Groundwork*.[10] For as Wolff represents Kant—and I believe that a similar kind of difficulty or ambivalence afflicts nearly all deontological thinkers—Kant clearly saw (1) that any instruction that practical reason might be able to give us with respect to what we ought to do or ought not to do can only be made understandable in terms of the ends and objectives that we seek to attain by our actions. Yet at the same time, Kant was no less plagued by the notion that (2) human desires and purposes are hopelessly "subjective" and relative, and hence not at all of a sort that can provide a basis for duties and obligations that are objectively binding upon all human beings, and binding regardless of, and even in spite of, what our human inclinations and purposes might happen to be.

For instance, Wolff says:

> Since according to Kant there is an objective good which all rational agents *qua* rational take as their end (the so-called obligatory ends), it follows that the principle of practical reason corresponding to such an imperative is a valid principle for all rational agents whatever.[11]

But having said this much, Wolff goes on to aver that Kant seems to take back with his left hand what he has just given with his right:

> The principal source of the confusion [in Kant] is his habit of describing imperatives as commanding actions without reference to ends. In paragraph 16 [Kant] writes: "A categorical imperative would be one which represented an action as objectively necessary in itself apart from its relation to a further end." ... Finally, in paragraph 22, Kant repeats, "there is an imperative which, without being based on, and conditioned by, any further purpose to be attained by a certain line of conduct, enjoins this conduct immediately."[12]

On this, Wolff's comment is at once sharp and decisive:

> Now this way of talking just doesn't make any sense. Rational action is purposive action. It is behavior which is caused by the agent's conception of the state of affairs to be brought about by that behavior. ... So a categorical imperative cannot "directly command a certain conduct without making its condition some purpose to be reached by it," for that is the same as saying

---

10. Robert Paul Wolff, *The Autonomy of Reason: A Commentary on Kant's Groundwork of the Metaphysics of Morals* (New York: Harper Torchbooks, 1973).
11. *Ibid.*, p. 130.
12. *Ibid.*, pp. 130–131.

that it commands an agent to engage in purposive action which has no purpose. Instead, the logic of Kant's theory of imperatives ought to lead him to define a categorical imperative as an imperative which commands us to pursue a purpose which we *must* (insofar as we are rational) adopt.[13]

Certainly, as Wolff here depicts him, Kant is caught in a well-nigh hopeless dilemma: Rational action—*i.e.*, action that is dictated by practical reason—cannot be other than purposive action; yet any action that is directed toward human ends and purposes, at least as we are familiar with them in the ordinary course of nature, cannot possibly be a rational action, simply because, as Kant sees it, there is no way in which such an action could ever be seen to be "objectively necessary." That is to say, again paraphrasing Kant, the imperative of any action directed toward any sort of natural purpose or goal that an individual might have could be no more than "a hypothetical imperative," never "a categorical imperative." Moreover, the action proceeding from such a merely hypothetical imperative could only be "heteronomous" and never "autonomous."

Now how Kant himself may or may not have extricated himself from his own dilemma, or how Wolff or any other Kantian commentator would wish to extricate his master from the predicament he has got himself into, need not concern us. Instead, let me but cut short the whole discussion by simply observing that so far as most present-day ethical deontologists are concerned, the way they would appear to have chosen to meet this Kantian dilemma is simply to accept the second horn of the dilemma, and then to close their eyes and grit their teeth as they let themselves be gored unmercifully by the other horn! In other words, what the latter-day ethical deontologists have tried to do, by and large, is simply to say that the duties and obligations which practical reason prescribes for us are duties to perform certain actions without any reference to ends at all. In other words, what we are morally obligated to do we are obligated to do just because we are, and not because of any purpose or objective that we may attain through the performance of any such actions.

With this, then, we can begin to see why it is that when we considered those earlier examples of moral first principles, such as were proposed by both Kant and Donagan, it seemed that, when put to the test, principles such as "Always respect human nature," or "Love your neighbor as yourself " turned out not to be certified or authorized by right reason at all. True, they were supposed to be moral principles whose only warrant was supposed to lie in the fact that to disregard

---

13. *Ibid.*, p. 131.

them would be contrary to reason. And such contrariety to reason as was generally admitted to be the only kind that could here be relevant—such a contrariety to reason would have to be a contrariety to practical reason. However, practical reason, as we have seen, by its very nature can only prescribe what needs to be done or ought to be done, in the light of some purpose or end to be achieved. But now if I am right in my suggestion, most contemporary deontologists, almost unconsciously, and apparently often without really facing up to the implications of what they are doing, tend simply to deny, or at least to suppress, the fact that the prescriptions of practical reason can only be made with reference to some purpose or end.[14] And then the consequence is inevitable: so-called categorical imperatives, and moral prescriptions, generally, can never be imperatives or prescriptions of practical reason at all!

But what, then, of theoretical reason? If practical reason cannot suffice—or rather is just plain incompetent—to issue categorical moral prescriptions, then maybe one should fall back on theoretical reason after all. True, as we remarked earlier, it would hardly seem to be in the nature of theoretical reason to lay down prescriptions for action. But waiving this point, why could not one say—perhaps following Donagan more or less—[15]that, given what it means to be a human being, it is self-contradictory, or contrary to reason, for a human being to act out of disrespect towards his neighbor? Clearly, though, this just won't do: there is nothing contradictory about the supposition of a human being having little or no respect for himself or his fellow man. On the contrary, it happens every day! Moreover, we can now see why such an appeal to right reason in support of a moral principle such as "Love thy neighbor as thyself" (or for that matter, in support of any derivative moral precept either) just will not work. The only way such a principle, or such precepts, could ever be shown to be contrary to right reason would have to be in terms of an appeal to practical reason. However, deontologists by their very Kantian-induced exclusion of all consideration of ends and purposes, so far as the determination of moral obligations and requirements are concerned, have precluded themselves from appealing to right reason in the sense of practical reason altogether. And if they then in desper-

---

14. It is true that as a deontologist, Donagan may not entirely conform to this customary pattern. However, we shall return to the rather exceptional case of Donagan later.

15. It may be that this is not an entirely accurate representation of Donagan's position. And yet there is no denying that he seems to come dangerously close to saying just the sort of thing we are here suggesting. But of this, more later.

ation try to fall back on theoretical reason, it is obvious in principle that right reason in this sense is incompetent and irrelevant, and, in terms of examples, just won't work! What, then, is the conclusion to be drawn from all of this? Must it not be that in the so-called deontological tradition of ethics, any and all appeals to right reason in the final analysis simply fail altogether!

Very well, supposing that our moral precepts, together with the entire array of human rights, duties and obligations, simply cannot find any proper footing in right reason—at least not within the context of a deontological type of ethics—what happens when we turn to a more teleological type of ethics? True, the contrast between deontology and teleology is an all-too-shopworn item in contemporary ethics. But perhaps for that very reason it is an almost indispensable one, particularly since, on a superficial level at least, nearly everyone has a fairly common understanding of what the contrast involves. For may not one say that this common understanding of the contrast turns pretty much on the very question of the relevance to a determination of our moral obligations and duties of what, in the paragraphs immediately preceding, we referred to loosely as being our human ends, desires, purposes, and so on? Thus ethical deontology, as we saw, might be interpreted as insisting upon the thoroughgoing irrelevance of anything like ends, interests, or purposes in the ordinary sense, so far as the determination of our moral obligations are concerned. In contrast, in a teleological type of ethics it would seem that the only way our duties and obligations could ever be determined would be by reference to what our human ends and purposes might be. Moreover, given the difficulties associated with a deontological ethic, the transition to a teleological view seems eminently plausible. For given just any situation in which something presumably needs to be done, or, in a broad sense, ought to be done, how can one possibly figure out what the situation calls for, save by reference to some good or benefit or advantage that one supposes might be brought about from such a situation? And so with respect to those more basic concerns as to what we ought to do, or how we ought to conduct ourselves in the very living of our lives, must not our responses to such concerns be in terms of what we want from life, or of what our aims and ends and objectives in life are?

Turning, then, to the question of practical reason, and of its relevance to ethics, the teleologist presumably need have no difficulty with this at all. For recognizing that we have ends and purposes to accomplish, there can surely be no question of our being able to determine, and to determine rationally, what sort of things we need to do or ought to do. In fact if one wants to establish that our determinations of what we ethically should do or ought to do are, at least in principle, entirely rational, one has only to point up the clear analogy that exists between practical reason, as it functions in the moral sphere, and practical reason, as it functions in the context of art or technology.[16] Given, say, that it is a bridge to be built, or a case to be tried, or a patient to be healed, or even a fisherman's lure to be cast into just the right spot on the shoreline—in all such cases there are obviously various right ways of doing such things, as well as various wrong ways. Moreover, it is just the relevant art or skill or technology that determines what these ways are. In other words, what else does an art of medicine, or of bridge-building, or of bait-casting, consist in, if not simply the relevant set of how-to-do-it rules, which have come to be determined in the light of experience and by right reason? Nor is the so-called right reason that functions in such cases anything other than a practical reason.

Moreover, just as we do not question the capacity of practical reason to determine how things ought to be done, or what actions need to be performed, in all of the various arts and technologies like medicine, engineering, military science, business, *et al.*, why should it not be equally the case, *mutatis mutandis*, that in the domain of ethics, or of "moral science," practical reason is no less able to determine what ought to be done, and what actions need to be performed, or how generally as human beings we should conduct ourselves? In fact, what does the qualification of *mutatis mutandis* here involve, when one moves from the domain of the various arts and skills to that of morals and ethics, if not that in the former context practical reason attempts to instruct us in the arts of how to be good butchers, or bakers, or candlestick makers, whereas in the context of morals and ethics practical reason instructs us simply in the art of living, or of how to be good men?

In the light of considerations such as these, then, might we not be said to be in a fair way toward having re-integrated right reason into the context of morals and ethics again? Apparently, what was required was no more than a shift from a deontological to a teleological perspective, so far as ethical theory is concerned. For in a deontological type of ethics with its tendency to exclude from the sphere of morals

---

16. As is well known, in the Aristotelian tradition of philosophy, it is customary to distinguish between "a practical reason" in matters of ethics and politics, and a "productive reason" in matters of art and technique. However, I don't believe that it will cause any serious misunderstanding if we use the same term "practical reason" to describe both kinds of non-theoretical reason.

and ethics all consideration of what our human ends and purposes might be, we found ourselves deprived of any possibility of guidance by right reason in the matter of our moral obligations, or of what we human beings ought to do or might need to do in the matter of actually living our lives. But now by shifting to a teleology in ethics, we would seem happily to have recovered all of the ground that was lost in ethical deontology. Moreover, the key to the recovery was just the reintroduction of ends and goals—of a human *telos*, if you will—into the ethical picture. For no sooner is there a recognition of an end or purpose to be achieved, than right reason immediately resumes its rightful function of providing us with a proper instruction as to what we ought to do, or how we ought to act, if that end or *telos* is ever to be achieved.

Alas, though, having come this far down the pike toward full-blown ethical teleology, would we not suddenly seem to have come a cropper! True, practical reason can be shown to have a proper and decisive role to play in any ethical teleology. Yet no sooner is this role established, than it begins to appear that that same role might well turn out to be a thoroughly nonmoral or extra-ethical one. Yes, teleological ethics itself could well be threatened with being unable to claim to be even an ethics at all! Remember that integral to our entire argument for the role of practical reason in a teleological ethics was our continuing insistence upon the seemingly unmistakable analogy between ethics, considered as a sort of art of living, and all of the various other arts and skills and techniques. Indeed, it was just this analogy that provided us with the basis for our contention that if our various human technologies could be said to consist in a genuine know-how and technical knowledge, and could therefore provide grounds for properly rational judgments as to what we ought to do or ought not to do, were we ever to be successful in such things as bait-casting, stock-brokering, or bridge-building, then so also it would seem that there would have to be a comparable know-how in what we called the art of living—*i.e.*, in the living of our lives successfully and well, as contrasted with merely playing tennis well, or marshalling an army well, or whatever.

Suddenly, though, having reached this point, we are faced with a veritable *dénouement*, not to say *peripateia*, of our whole argument. For clearly, in the various special arts and techniques, although the judgments of practical reason tell us what we ought to do, or ought not to do, by way of accomplishing the purposes of the relevant art or technique, these same judgments, by no stretch of the imagination, can be considered as moral judgments. Instead, they are no more than judgments of skill, involving, as Aristotle would say, only intellectual virtue and not moral virtue. But then supposing there to be a strict analogy between the judgments of practical reason that we make in pursuing what we have been calling the art of living, and such practical judgments as we make in the other arts, then it must surely follow that properly moral or ethical judgments could no more enter the picture in the former case than they do in the latter.

Thus, for example, suppose that someone does not play tennis too well, or is not a very good doctor, or just isn't too successful when it comes to trading shares on the stock exchange, we surely do not condemn such a person morally for such failures or shortcomings, do we? But then, must it not be in a like case, so far as someone's living well is concerned, or, so far as his being successful in life, or perhaps achieving a true happiness, are concerned? Given the analogy with the other arts, how could such an overall success or achievement simply in life itself be reckoned as being in any wise a moral achievement? Instead, the rational judgments that we make respecting such actions as need to be taken, to say nothing of the overall success of our policies and programs—these all involve no more than purely "prudential" considerations, as they tend to be called, and not moral considerations at all.

Clearly, then, the shift that we made from a deontological type of ethics to a teleological one would appear to have gained us nothing, so far as our being able to find a footing for ethics in right reason is concerned. True, in a deontological ethic, there seemed to be no way in which practical reason could be brought into the picture, whereas in a teleological ethic, practical reason was certainly found to have a role to play, and a most decisive one at that. The only trouble was that it was not at all a moral role; and indeed, the very concept itself of a teleological ethics has seemingly turned out to be not really a concept of an ethics at all so much as one of a mere skill or art. Nor can there be much question as to just what the diagnosis has to be of this failure on the part of a teleological type of ethics. For although, by returning ethics to a rightful concern with ends and purposes, it would seem that teleological moralists had indeed found a place for right reason in the sense of practical reason, still this same practical reason, by the very nature of its situation as a teleological ethics, would appear to be restricted to operating solely with reference to prior and already given ends or purposes. But this must mean that reason is thereby precluded from ever passing judgment on those ends themselves. For whether my end be the destruction or the welfare of mankind, whether it be the attainment of a Socratic self-knowledge on my part, or merely the pursuit of wine, women, and song, in either or in all of these cases practical reason is entirely competent to give instruction as to how such ends may best be achieved, but is entirely incompetent to make any judgment as to the rightness or wrongness of the ends themselves.

Is it, therefore, at all surprising that a contemporary moral philosopher of the stature of Professor Frankena should be led to make the rather tendentious, not to say quite prejudicial, judgments that he does regarding any and all forms of a teleological ethics:

> A teleological theory says that the basis or ultimate criterion or standard of what is *morally* right, wrong, or obligatory, etc. is the *non-moral* value that is brought into being.

Or again:

> For a teleologist, the *moral* quality or value of actions, persons or traits of character is dependent on the comparatively *non-moral* character of what they bring about.[17]

Surely, such pronouncements by Frankena would appear to amount to little more than just his way of writing off the entire project of a teleological ethic as being hopeless one, if not one that is actually self-contradictory. For how could nonmoral ends ever be such as to provide a proper ground and justification for what it is hoped will be morally right means to those ends?

Happily, though, we just do not have to accept Frankena's summary dismissal of such teleological theories, as if his word were the last word on the subject. For it requires but little reflection on the history of Western ethics to realize that Frankena's generalizations in regard to teleology are both overdrawn and historically inaccurate. Not any and every teleological theory fits into the impossible pattern that Frankena lays down, according to which our moral values and obligations can be justified only in terms of non-moral ends. On the contrary, it may be supposed that there have been at least two quite divergent types of teleological theories in the Western tradition. On the one hand, there have been what for want of a better term I will simply call teleologies of a "hedonistic" or "interest-theory" type, and on the other hand, those of a "natural-law" type.[18] Moreover, as a sort of touchstone for distinguishing these two types I propose to apply what I have sometimes been wont to call "the *Euthyphro* test."[19] Thus in the *Euthy-*

---

17. *Cf.* Frankena, work cited in n. 2 above.
18. Admittedly, these terms are far from felicitous, but it may be hoped that both their sense and their aptness may become clear from the ensuing contexts.
19. I have discussed this at some length in my paper, "Telos and Teleology in Ar-

phro, it will be recalled, Socrates voiced the question as to whether things were to be called good, because they were beloved of the gods; or is it rather that they are beloved of the gods because in themselves they really are good? Returning, then, to Frankena's characterization of teleological theories, what he says would appear to be accurate enough, but only with respect to what I would call the hedonistic or interest theories. For in this type of theory, things are held to be good or of value only because we like them, or they give us pleasure. So far from there being anything objectively good about them, things are only labelled "good," or called good, according as they chance to suit our interests or desires. In contrast, teleological ethical theories of the sort that Plato would doubtless have subscribed to, and probably Aristotle as well,[20] and certainly St. Thomas Aquinas—these would all be theories in which it is maintained that there are objective goods, or things which are of value or worth just in themselves, and whether we happen to like them or not, and which for that very reason are the sorts of things that we ought to like, or should learn to appreciate, supposing that we do not actually do so.

Moreover, having said this much by way of fleshing out what we have called our natural-law alternative to the more common hedonistic type of teleological theory, is it not just possible that this might ring a bell with respect to those earlier questions which we cited from Wolff respecting Kant's ethical theory? For Wolff argued that Kant, on the one hand, seemed to be inclined to recognize that there somehow had to be "an objective good which all rational agents, *qua* rational take as their end (the so-called obligatory ends)." On the other hand, it would appear that in the final analysis Kant himself drew back from any such happy inclinations of his, not quite having the courage of his convictions! But suppose that Kant had had the courage of his convictions, and had recognized unequivocally that there was such a thing as an objective good, then it would have immediately become intelligible how human beings could be said to be objectively obligated and thus morally bound to perform such actions as would bring about such a good. That is to say, an objective good could perfectly well function as an obligatory end. For consider a rational moral agent who recognized that certain things would need to be reckoned as good, not because they just happened to be liked, or that people tended to go

---

istotelian Ethics." This has appeared in *Studies in Aristotle*, ed. by Dominic J. O'Meara (Washington, D.C.: The Catholic University of America Press, 1981). This is reprinted in the present volume.

20. *Cf.* Joseph Owens, "The Grounds of Ethical Universality in Aristotle," *Man and World*, vol. 2 (1969).

for them, but rather because they were no less than such things as people ought to like or to appreciate, whether they actually do or not—would this not be tantamount to recognizing such ends as being obligatory? And what in turn does this do to Frankena's contention that in a teleological ethics, all ends have to be admitted to be nonmoral ends, simply because practical reason must first presuppose ends, before it can make recommendations as to what needs to be done; and the ends thus having to be presupposed, there is no way in which practical reason could ever assume a jurisdiction of ends, as compared with mere means to ends? Well, this contention of Frankena's may now be considered to have been simply by-passed in a so-called natural-law type of teleology: as Kant suggests in the above quotation, it is no less than rational agents, *qua* rational, who are able to recognize things as being objectively good and hence as being obligatory ends in a moral sense. Not only that, but given such a rationally determined obligatory end, practical reason can determine what the actions are that we are now morally obligated to take, if such an obligatory end is ever to be attained.

With this, then, have we not at long last found the very thing that we have been searching for throughout the course of our entire paper thus far—a proper answer to the question of just how and where right reason may be taken to be integral to ethics and to provide a ground for true moral judgments as to what we ought to do or ought not to do? Granted that this was not to be found in the ordinary varieties of deontological ethics. For there was apparently just no way in which Kantian categorical imperatives, or Donagan's first principle of morality, could be seen as being grounded in right reason. Granted, too, that this was not to be found in a teleological ethic of the hedonistic or interest-theory type either. For although in the context of such an ethics, it is indeed possible and legitimate to make appeal to practical reason by way of justifying all of the various recommendations, precepts and how-to-do-it rules, which, were we to follow them, would enable us successfully to attain our ends, still such purely prudential judgments of reason cannot claim to be moral judgments in any sense, or to specify any sort of properly moral duties and obligations. Accordingly, that leaves only a teleological ethic of what we have termed the natural-law type, as being the one place where right reason can properly be said to enter into ethics and to prescribe genuine moral rules for our human conduct and behavior. In fact, such an ethics may even be said to combine the virtues, while discarding the weaknesses, of both ethical teleology and ethical deontology. That it is a teleology is clear in that all our human duties and obligations need to be understood with reference to that proper end or telos toward the achievement of which all of our human actions and behavior must be ordered. At the same time, that it may be considered a deontology as well may be seen from the fact that this presumed end or telos of human life and human existence is what Wolff could call an objective end; and as objective, it is thus an obligatory end, just in the sense that it is an end which human beings are under obligation to pursue, and hence is not the kind of end which men just happen to be inclined to, or disposed towards, from psychological, or sociological, or physiological, or economic, or other mere natural causes.[21]

Once again, though, our would-be conclusions have quite outrun our evidence. True, if there are such things as objective and obligatory ends in human life, to use Wolff's terminology, then it might indeed be possible to envisage a teleological ethics that could clearly be seen to be based on right reason. And yet are there such obligatory ends? Remember that by Wolff's account, Kant seemed to acknowledge that there needed to be such ends, if his supposedly deontological type of ethics could even get off the ground. And yet for all of the acknowledged need of such an end or telos for his entire system of ethics, Wolff implies that Kant waffled badly, when it came to actually pointing to and actually specifying any such thing as a truly objective and obligatory end. Instead, it was as if he seemed to weasel and to back away, suggesting that somehow categorical imperatives had to be thought of "as commanding actions without reference to ends," or that "a categorical imperative" just is such a one as "represents an action as objectively necessary in itself apart from its relation to a further end."[22] But if Kant was thus forced to wink and to blink, and perhaps even to equivocate as regards actually recognizing any obligatory ends—and this, despite the fact that the very logic of his position, according to Wolff, would seem to demand such things—might this not all have been for the simple and obvious reason that there just "ain't no such animal" as an obligatory end! And indeed, Wolff himself comes flat out with the declaration, "There is nothing good in itself; there is therefore no valid theory of the objective good to be found, and hence there are not and could not be any obligatory ends."[23] Besides, we have already noted how most, if not all, deontological thinkers of a more or less Kantian persuasion tend simply to

21. For a further discussion of this confluence of both deontology and teleology in natural law ethics, see my article cited above, "Telos and Teleology in Aristotelian Ethics."
22. Wolff, cited in n. 10, above, pp. 130–131.
23. *Ibid.*, p. 132.

repudiate anything like an objective, and hence obligatory, end or good in human life, even though this tends to force them into what would seem to be the altogether indefensible ethical position of arguing, again to paraphrase Wolff, that moral precepts command moral agents to engage in purposive action which has no purpose![24]

Despite, however, all of this seeming mountain of difficulty over recognizing such a thing as an obligatory end for human beings, St. Thomas Aquinas would appear to have experienced no difficulties on the score of such a notion at all. True, he uses no terms or expressions that are quite comparable to what Wolff calls "an obligatory end"; but the thing itself, by whatever name it be called, he not only recognized, but even provided a kind of demonstration of. Unhappily, though, so far as I know, not only are there no discussions of these Thomistic doctrines in the contemporary literature; but there does not even seem to be an awareness that they so much as exist.[25] Accordingly, let me try to provide but a very summary account, and one couched very much in my own words, of St. Thomas' teaching respecting these issues. And be it noted, first of all, that in Aquinas' view the investigation and determination of that which is objectively good, and hence qualified to function as an obligatory end, is something that needs to be carried out in metaphysics, rather than in ethics proper. Likewise, such an investigation is one that calls for the exercise of theoretical reason in the Aristotelian sense, rather than practical reason. Nor is this anything but proper, considering that Aquinas is attempting to understand how good or *bonum*, and indeed how ends generally, can have a proper status directly in being or in reality. Moreover, inasmuch as being *qua* being, or being just as such, is the proper subject matter of metaphysics, it is important that goodness or value be seen as an inescapable feature or aspect of being.[26] To demonstrate this, Aquinas notes that in any and all beings that may be said to be basic or primary[27]—*i.e.*, in what Aristotle would call substances—the very

---

24. *Ibid.*, p. 131.
25. St. Thomas's most important texts bearing on these issues may be found in the *De Veritate*, Qu. I, art. 1, and Qus. XXI and XXII, *passim*. *Cf.* also *Summa Theologiae* I, Qu. V. Perhaps I should also confess that I have already tried to summarize and discuss these Thomistic Doctrines myself. *Cf.* my *For an Ontology of Morals* (Evanston, IL: Northwestern University Press, 1971), esp. ch. 6. See also *Human Rights: Fact or Fancy* (Louisiana State University Press, 1985).
26. Anyone familiar with Thomistic doctrine will recognize that what I am here calling features or aspects of being (*ens*) are nothing other than what the Scholastics would call "the transcendentals," such things as *bonum* and *verum*. Now, that these are hardly "features" or "aspects" of being goes almost without saying. But what other terms ought one, or can one, use?
27. We are relying here simply on the Aristotelian doctrine of so-called "*pros hen*

being of substance involves the distinction, or perhaps one should say, the polarity, of potency and act. For is it not a simple fact of all such beings that they are somehow subject to change and development:[28] they are able to become other and different from what they are; they are not all that they might be or could be; and as thus lacking perfections which they are capable of having or possessing, but which they do not yet have, may not such beings be said to be lacking in something, to be imperfect in their being, and thus not to be all that they are capable of being, or, in a fully analogous sense, ought to be? Accordingly, given this duality of potency and act that pervades and characterizes all beings, why may not one simply "define" good, or excellence, or worth, or value as being nothing if not just the actual as over against the potential, or, if you will, as the complete as over against the incomplete, or the perfect as over against the imperfect? In other words, the good of any thing or substance is simply that which that being or substance by its very nature may be said to be potentially. In other words, it is just that being's full actuality, which such a thing may therefore be said by its very nature to be ordered toward being, or aimed at being, and which it thus ought to be, but is not yet.

And now for a further note that attaches to this Thomistic account of goodness or value or perfection, as these are considered to pertain to any and all beings. For in so far as the goodness or perfection of any thing is simply its full actuality, and thus the very actuality toward which that thing or being is naturally ordered in virtue of its characteristic potentialities, why may not the complete fulfillment or actualization of a thing's potentialities be just that which that thing may be said to "desire," or for which it may be said to have an *appetitus*,[29] in the fully analogous sense of those terms? And so what the good, or the natural perfection, or the completion or fulfillment of a thing may be said to be is nothing other than what it truly and properly desires. In other words, it is its end, or that which it tends towards by nature.

Of course, in saying that the good of any thing or being is just what that thing desires, we must not be unmindful of the *Euthyphro* test.

---

equivocation." On this, see Joseph Owens, *The Doctrine of Being in the Aristotelian Metaphysics* (Toronto, Canada: The Pontifical Institute of Mediaeval Studies, 3rd ed., 1978), esp. ch. 3.

28. Of course, neither Aristotle nor Aquinas would have acknowledged that all beings or substances are subject to change or development. But for our present purposes, we need hardly stop to take account of the analogous manifestation of act-potency in such unchanging beings.

29. This is Aquinas's term. *Cf. Summa Theologiae*, I, 5, 1, ad 1. *Cf.* also my discussion of this notion in *For an Ontology of Morals*, cited in n. 25, above, ch. 5, esp. pp. 110–17.

For clearly, goodness or value in this metaphysical sense is not to be construed as being good merely because it is desired. Rather it is desired because it is objectively good. Potentialities, after all, have their proper actualities: fire is disposed to burn, copper to conduct electricity, and human beings to act rationally. These are what in an old-fashioned sense might be said to be the "natural" dispositions of such things or substances. Hence the activities toward which beings are thus naturally disposed are nothing if not the natural and obligatory ends toward which these substances are oriented by their very natures, and which they may be said to desire in the sense just indicated.

Such, then, might be said to be the fundamental metaphysical framework or justification for a teleological ethic of what we have termed a natural-law type of teleology. All of the basic notions of "good," of "desire" (*appetitus*), of "end," or telos, particularly in the sense of obligatory ends, are provided with both a grounding and an ordering of the one with respect to the other, directly in being and in reality just as such. But what now of ethics specifically, as contrasted with metaphysics, or what of a specifically ethical teleology, as contrasted with what might be called that universal teleology, or general teleology, that is treated of in metaphysics? Quite obviously, what one needs to do at this point is to get from the notion of good in general to that of the human good, and from that of natural and obligatory ends in general to that of man's proper end or good, or the human telos. Moreover, in the light of our earlier discussions of both ethical deontology and ethical teleology, it should be obvious that with respect to the latter, one needs first to recognize what man's natural good or end or telos is, and then one should be in a position to invoke so-called practical reason in order to determine what one ought to do or ought not to do, if one is ever to attain one's natural and obligatory end as a human being.

Needless to say, this is scarcely the occasion, nor mine the competence, to give any full-scale account of this human good, which, of course, has to be the keystone of any ethical teleology of the natural-law type.[30] Instead, suffice it only to recall the outlines of the Aristotelian discussion of this. For in effect Aristotle says that the good of man—which is to say man's proper end or perfection or actuality—must be something quite different from that of a fish, or a dog, or a daisy, or even of earth, air, fire or water! Indeed, why not simply recognize that the good or end that is proper to a human being, as a rational animal, is none other than that of being rational, or of living

---

30. *Cf.* also *Human Rights, op. cit., passim.*

intelligently or rationally? And for Aristotle, it will be recalled, this is to be unpacked in terms of the notions of both intellectual and moral virtue, so that Aristotle's summary description of human happiness or perfection is the celebrated one of "the activity of the soul in accordance with virtue."[31] Nor is that all, in that, for Aristotle, a human being as a rational animal is not just an individual animal, but a political animal as well, with the result that built right into the individual man's goal or end, just as an individual, is not only that individual's own perfection or well-being, but the perfection or well-being of his fellow citizens as well. Indeed, it might be argued that one could perhaps flesh this out still further with some of the formulas Aristotle uses in connection with his celebrated discussion of human friendship—for instance, when he says, in effect, that "one wants for one's friend the very thing one wants for oneself."[32] And what does this amount to, but the idea that, incorporated right into one's own end or goal, is the well-being of one's fellow human beings, no less than one's own individual well-being?

With this, then, do we not find ourselves brought back once more to that second part of the Summary of the Law, which Donagan took as being the first principle of morality: "Thou shalt love thy neighbor as thyself"? Recall that in the earlier part of our discussion, we expressed no little dissatisfaction with the way in which Donagan presumably wished to show such principle to be founded on right reason. More specifically, what we suggested was amiss about Donagan's efforts was that he apparently thought that such a justification in terms of right reason could be exhibited from within a framework of a so-called deontological or Kantian type of ethical theory. But this, we argued, was in all ways impossible, and simply would not work. Now, however, and after all of our intervening pages, the ball would seem to have been put back into our own court! For as an alternative to a deontological type of ethical theory, we have now sketched both the general nature and some of the implications of teleological theory of a so-called natural-law type. And so the question for us now becomes one of whether, from within the context of such a teleological theory, one may be able to show that the moral obligation or imperative to love one's neighbor as oneself is just such an imperative as may be certified by right reason.

Responding to this challenge, let me first note that, in the light of our earlier discussions, it would seem that the only way in which any

---

31. *Nicomachean Ethics*, Bk. I, ch. vii, 1098 a, 17–18.
32. *Cf. ibid.*, Bk. VIII, ch. 4.

judgment as to what needs to be done or ought to be done can ever be rationally justified would have to be in terms of some prior end or good. Accordingly, that it is a moral obligation for us to love our neighbors as ourselves can only be shown if it first be demonstrated that the well-being of ourselves and of our neighbors is already something that we have a desire for, or a natural *appetitus* with respect to. Or to put this just a little differently, if our own well-being, together with that of our neighbors, is indeed a part of our natural end and goal in life, practical reason may then be invoked to show what needs to be or ought to be done in order that such an end be achieved. In fact, if we understand him aright, Aquinas' way of ordering any demonstration of a moral obligation such as that of loving one's neighbor as oneself would be something like this. First, one relies on theoretical reason to exhibit what the good for man is, or what man's natural end is—namely, the well-being alike of oneself and one's neighbor. Then, as the first principle of what he calls practical reason, St. Thomas lays down his well-known guideline to the effect: "Good is to be done and pursued, and evil avoided."[33] Accordingly, on our own account we have already sketched out how the good alike of oneself and of one's neighbors just is a part of one's own goal, as being the natural end of any human being: it just is what any one naturally desires. Very well, if in the light of theoretical reason this is seen to be the true good for man, and if by the first principle of practical reason the good is that which is to be pursued just as evil is to be avoided, then practical reason may therewith move in to demonstrate that one does indeed have a moral obligation to love one's neighbor as oneself, as well as all of the further and derivative obligations not to murder, not to steal, not to commit adultery, not to bear false witness, and so on. In other words, our obligation to love our neighbors as ourselves may be seen to be clearly founded upon right reason.

Moreover, against the background of such a teleological type of ethics, it should now be even more clear how not only deontologists generally, but even a rather more sophisticated and subtle deontologist such as Donagan, have gone astray regarding this very business of right reason in ethics. For what the deontologist invariably tries to do is to maintain that our moral obligations may be seen ultimately to be rationally justifiable just in themselves, and without any appeal to any prior notion of the good or of an end. But this may now be seen to be in all ways impossible. There just can't be any categorical imperatives in the literal sense: instead, all imperatives need to be justified

---

33. *Summa Theologiae*, I–II, 94, 2.

by practical reason, but practical reason must necessarily appeal to the notion of an end or good, which can only be established by theoretical reason.[34] In other words, imperatives, in order to be rationally justified, have to be seen to be hypothetical. It is just what right reason in ethics requires, no less!

34. Germain Grisez in a very remarkable paper, "The First Principle of Practical Reason" (reprinted in *Aquinas*, ed. by Kenny, Anchor Books, 1969, pp. 340–82) has questioned whether theoretical reason should be thought of as supplementing practical reason, when it comes to establishing the foundations of ethics. This whole question I have discussed somewhat tangentially in my paper, "Natural Law and the 'Is–Ought' Question," *infra*.

7

LANGUAGE AND ETHICS: "WHAT'S HECUBA TO HIM, OR HE TO HECUBA?"[1]

Many years ago in the hills of southern Indiana, in the days when linguistic analysis had scarcely even been heard of, much less encountered, by the then unsuspecting Hoosiers, a rather odd event occurred: Prof. John Wisdom arrived from Cambridge to address a small gathering of philosophers assembled at Indiana University. That Wisdom probably had no idea of where he was, and that his audience had indeed not the slightest idea of what had descended into their midst, go both of them almost without saying. Nor was the mutual incomprehension in the least lessened when Wisdom rose to speak and, instead of producing a typescript, casually declared that rather than read a paper he would merely answer any questions.

Now whereas it can hardly be denied that such a prescription for a public address would constitute a most admirable precedent for presidents of the American Philosophical Association to follow, when each year they must face their rather bored and semi-captive audiences, it was hardly a prescription calculated to win friends and influence people for Prof. Wisdom on the occasion of his advent into Hoosierland. Indeed, Wisdom's words had the effect of rendering his audience completely speechless, and left him standing up there in front of everyone, with nothing to say. Finally, someone in the audience, quite obviously oppressed by the deepening embarrassment, and anxious to relieve the tension at all costs, stammered out a question of sorts: "Would Prof. Wisdom perhaps mind characterizing and even explaining to his comparatively ill-informed and behind-the-times audience some of the more obvious changes and developments that had taken place in philosophy in Great Britain from the days of idealists like

---

1. Perhaps it should be noted, with some apologies, that this paper was the presidential address delivered at the 69th annual meeting of the then Western Division of the American Philosophical Association, as far back as the year 1971.

Bradley and Bosanquet, down through realists like Moore and Russell, and so on to the present day?".

No sooner, though, was the question put, than the answer came back, "Sorry, I am not a historian of philosophy. I cannot answer the question." Again, silence descended upon the stunned and by now incredulous audience. Presently, though, another questioner took heart, or better felt a compulsive obligation to say something—anything to break the tension—and accordingly asked about the sort of reception which contemporary English philosophers were inclined to give to the writings of the political scientist, Sir Ernest Barker. This time the answer was simply "I've never read the man." With that, though, a few further questions did begin not so much to flow from the audience as rather to come painfully one by one, much as if it were a pulling of eye teeth. One person asked something about metaphysics, someone else asked about the philosophical import of some recent remarks by the physicist, Werner Heisenberg. And so on it went for a while, each question seeming to elicit—if that were possible—an even more negative response from the speaker than the one before, until finally Prof. Wisdom did open up just a little. As if chiding his listeners for being so ignorant of anything so obvious, he remarked: "In philosophy one does not study physics, but the language of physicists; not political science, but the language of political scientists; not history, but the language of historians; not religion or theology, but religious or theological language." And that was it! With those few terse words, linguistic philosophy had penetrated even to the fastnesses of Indiana, and a new day was ready to dawn.

But let us now leave those dear, dead days beyond recall, when men, or at least Hoosiers, had not yet realized that philosophy was the study of language, and when it devolved, somewhat accidentally and perhaps rather ill-advisedly, upon no less a messenger than John Wisdom to bring this gospel to the heartland of Indiana. For surely we all know the good news by now; and we have all learned—even the most retarded among us—to mouth the familiar words about language games and linguistic uses, or to exercise ourselves to the familiar locutions, "We do not say ... unless we mean ...," or "When we ask ... we imply ...," etc. Such turns of phrase have now become, if not the accomplishment, at least the pretension of practically everyone nowadays. Particularly, though, it would seem that it is with respect to ethics that the linguistic approach has by now pretty well carried the day, so that the up-to-date moral philosopher occupies himself not so much with morals as with the language of morals; and the study of ethics has tended to become at once admittedly and supposedly quite fruitfully a study of ethical language.

Why, though, and in just what sense should such investigations of the language of morals and of ethics be supposed to hold the key to an understanding of morals and ethics themselves? It's true, of course, that even to raise such questions may seem to be little more than a courting of irrelevancies and a return to issues long ago disposed of and laid to rest. But for all that, I cannot seem to deflect my own concerns—or perhaps they are my obsessions—from the thought that the whole enterprise of a language or logic of morals as somehow determinative of morals, or the view that the linguistic or logical rules of ethical uses are somehow determinative of what we ought or ought not to do—all of this, it seems to me, rests on a basic presupposition which is as dubious as it has been largely unrecognized and unacknowledged by moral philosophers of the linguistic tradition. What this presupposition is, I would venture to suggest, is no less than a kind of transcendental turn or perhaps a transcendental argument in virtue of which—if I may at once cite and then misapply an oft quoted sentence from Kant's *Prolegomena*—"the understanding is enabled not so much to draw its laws from nature, as rather to prescribe them to nature."[2]

But having thus misapplied Kant to serve my own purposes, I must quickly take precautions lest I appear to have misinterpreted the entire history of modern ethics for no other purpose than merely to convict it of having made the transcendental turn. Actually, however, I wonder whether, when one passes in quick review some of the major figures and developments in ethics over the last 50 or 60 years, one may not be struck by two rather salient features of that history. On the one hand, there would seem to be a progressive determination to eliminate from ethics and ethical judgments anything like an objective or factual status—yes, one might even say an ontological status—for values and obligations. And on the other hand, there would seem to be an equal determination to fend off all charges to the effect that this would but reduce ethics to being a purely relative matter, as if there could be no rational basis for ethics anymore—no, not even any reasoned judgments in ethics at all. Quite the contrary, it has come to be insisted upon with an ever-increasing sureness, not to say vehemence, by a whole series of writers from Toulmin through Hare, and right on down to John Searle, that all properly moral or ethical judgments must in the very nature of the case have a rational basis.

Still, let us consider briefly just a few examples by way of illustration of what I am claiming are concurrent, and yet seemingly rather com-

---

2. Immanuel Kant, *Prolegomena to Any Future Metaphysics*, trans. by Lucas (Manchester: Manchester University Press, 1953), p. 82.

petitive, tendencies in modern ethics, or rather metaethics—tendencies we might simply label the nonobjectivist tendency on the one hand and the rationalistic tendency on the other. And first of all, how about G. E. Moore? One need only mention the so-called naturalistic fallacy to recognize how Moore made what was perhaps the first, if not also the most decisive, contribution to the nonobjectivist tendency of modern ethics. It's true, he did not deny that goodness was an objective property of things, but he certainly did deny that it was a natural property. And from this, it was but a step to denying that it was a property at all. Nor did those who came after Moore hesitate to take this step. For how could anyone, they seemed to say, ever swallow so dubious a notion as that of a nonnatural property? Would it not be much more sensible simply to recognize that to call a thing "good" is not as such to ascribe an objective property to the thing at all, but rather simply to express one's approval of it, or perhaps to commend or recommend it?

Moreover, just as Moore laid the groundwork—albeit perhaps somewhat unwittingly—for the eventual scuttling of anything like an objective status for goodness, he also might be accused of having seriously endangered the possibility of finding anything like a genuinely rational basis for our ethical judgments. For if the value or goodness of a thing is never to be defined or understood in terms of any of the natural or even supernatural properties that that thing might have, then how could those same features, properties, or characteristics of that thing ever be considered to be proper grounds or reasons for our calling the thing "good"? In other words, our judgments of value, all of them, would suddenly seem threatened with having to be simply written off as at once irrational and without any possible ground or basis of any kind.

But no, as we all know, the various species of analytic and linguistic philosophers who came after Moore seemed to be united in their determination to save what were wont to be called "good reasons" in ethics. Indeed, hardly had the first wave of emotivism in ethics crested, when a whole series of moral philosophers of varying kinds of linguistic persuasion started to bob up—Toulmin, Hare, Mrs. Foot, Searle, *et al.*—all of them equally insistent, albeit in their respectively different ways, on the role of good reasons in ethics. Nevertheless, what is interesting for our present purposes about this almost unanimous determination on the part of more recent metaethicists to try to preserve a rational basis for our moral and ethical judgments is that it seems never to have occurred to them that if there were to be a rational basis for ethics there would presumably need to be an objective basis as well. For after all, was it not Moore's undermining of the natural, and hence ultimately of the objective, bases of ethics that originally seemed to threaten the rational bases as well? Yet considerations of this sort seem not to have impressed the linguistic philosophers at all, they having been at some pains to show that there can be perfectly good reasons for calling something good or right, even though neither goodness nor rightness is ever an objective feature of the world.

Nor has the situation been an altogether dissimilar one when it has come to questions as to the possibility of truth and falsity in the case of ethical judgments. For if such judgments be not factual judgments, and if in attributing ethical predicates to things we are not, strictly speaking, saying anything about those things, so much as we are merely commending them or commanding them or recommending them, or what not, then how can such judgments be either true or false? Or if, in calling something good, we are not describing the thing at all, but only expressing our approval of it, then how can such a judgment be contradicted? After all, if with respect to a given thing one person manifests his approval and another his disapproval, that can hardly be taken to mean that the one person has contradicted the other. Accordingly, if ethical judgments are not to be considered as making any claims as to what is or is not objectively the case, then would not the ordinary logical relations between judgments simply break down in the case of ethical judgments?

Once again, though, the linguistic analysts have tended to meet this sort of challenge to what might be called the very rationality or logical character of ethical discourse by showing at great lengths how judgments which make no factual or objective claims are nonetheless quite capable of entering into entirely unexceptionable and proper logical relationships with other judgments.

Finally, too, there is the issue of the universalizability or generalizability of ethical judgments. For once more, it might seem to be the case, at least superficially, that if a judgment of value, say, made no objective or factual claims for the value or values that were being predicated, then the judgment would not be universalizable. That is to say, what in the judgment was being adjudged to be of value would presumably be adjudged to be of value only to the person making the judgment, and to him only at the time of his judgment, and hence could not be regarded as being in any way compelling or binding either in respect to anyone else or in respect to the man himself on a different occasion. But here again, the reaction of linguistic philosophers to the charge that a denial of objective status in reality to things such as value and obligation must entail a corresponding denial of what Kant might call universality and necessity to ethical judgments—such a charge the linguistic moralists would most emphatically rebut on the ground that it fails to respect the peculiar logical grammar or linguistic use of ethical terms and expressions. Thus to say that X is an action that ought to be done is very different from saying that X is something that I would like to see done: the former is clearly universalizable, the latter not.

And so it is that what might be called the linguistic turn in so much of recent metaethics, while it admittedly and even boastfully has had the effect of depriving ethical judgments of at least one kind of objectivity, at the same time has been held not to deprive such judgments of their character of being reasoned judgments, or even of their potential universality and necessity. For all of this, though, one cannot but wonder whether this effort at a reconciling of what I have called the nonobjectivist tendency in modern ethics with its rationalistic tendency may not have taken some doing, and perhaps even some dubious doing. In any case, would it not be fair to say that linguistic philosophers, when called upon to explain just how such nonobjective judgments of value, say, could at the same time be reasoned judgments, as well as universalizable, have been more content with insisting *that* such a thing is possible than they have been zealous to explain *how* such a thing is possible? The ploy nearly always seems to have been simply to say, "Well, that's just the way the ethical language game is played," or "That's the way words like 'ought,' 'good,' 'right,' etc. are used, as contrasted with words like 'pleasant,' 'desired,' 'agreeable,' 'liked,' etc."

For example—to choose just one illustration—consider the grounds on which a moral philosopher like Philippa Foot seeks to upbraid someone like R. M. Hare for his rather uncritical acceptance of the fact-value distinction, and for his tendency to turn the relation between evaluative judgments and the factual considerations upon which they are based into a mere "external relation," as Philippa Foot calls it. No, she insists, the relation must be an internal one and not merely external: you simply may not (or perhaps cannot), she suggests,[3] base your "beliefs about matters of value entirely on premises which no one else would recognize as giving any evidence at all"; or again, "given the kind of statement which other people regard as evidence for an evaluative conclusion," you may not (or cannot) simply "refuse

---

3. Philippa Foot, "Moral Beliefs," reprinted in *Theories of Ethics*, ed. by Philippa Foot (Oxford: Oxford University Press, 1967), p. 84.

to draw the conclusion because *this* does not count as evidence for [you]."

Yet just what is the nature of these "may-nots" or "cannots" which Philippa Foot here invokes, and what is the source or basis of their implied universality and necessity? So far as I know, she nowhere chooses to answer such a question directly. And yet by implication her answer would appear to be that it is but a case of our linguistic rules being such as to require an internal and not a mere external relation in such instances. And what does this amount to, if not to an admission that the reasoned character and the universalizability of our ethical judgments, while they may turn on internal rather than external relations between the terms and notions involved, must nonetheless find their warrant for being considered as internal relations simply in the nature of the language game as it is played, rather than in the nature of the realities which our ethical judgments are judgments about? Or to put it a little differently, it would appear to be an exclusively logical or linguistic, as opposed to an ontological, warrant, a warrant derived from the way we have to speak about things, rather than from the way the things themselves are. Thus as Philippa Foot has herself put it rather unambiguously:

> Anyone who uses moral terms at all, whether to assert or deny a moral proposition, must abide by the rules for their use, including the rules about what shall count as evidence for or against the moral judgment concerned. For anything that has yet been shown to the contrary these rules could be entailment rules, forbidding the assertion of factual propositions in conjunction with the denial of moral propositions. The only recourse of the man who refused to accept the things which counted in favor of a moral proposition as giving him a reason to do certain things or to take up a particular attitude, would be to leave the moral discussion and abjure the use of moral terms.[4]

Surely, from statements and declarations of this sort, the like of which one so frequently encounters in the writings of linguistic moralists these days, it begins to become clear just what the resource of these philosophers is when they are called upon to account for what they claim is the reasoned and reasonable character of moral and ethical judgments. Their resource is to fall back on the device of what has sometimes been called the linguistic turn. Again, to paraphrase Philippa Foot, why is it that certain facts of the case provide me with a reason for doing certain things or taking up a particular attitude? It is not because the facts themselves are indicative of any such reasons, but rather because the rules of the moral or ethical language

---

4. Philippa Foot, "Moral Arguments," reprinted in *Ethics*, ed. by Thomson and Dworkin (New York: Harper and Row, 1968), p. 17.

game require that the assertion of certain moral propositions be conjoined with the assertion of certain factual ones.

But no sooner is the linguistic turn seen in this light than one begins to wonder whether it is quite the innocent device that it might appear to be. So far from being only a linguistic turn, could it be that what is operative here is no less than a veritable transcendental turn; and as for linguistic philosophy itself—at least in its ethical reaches—is it any less than a full-fledged transcendental philosophy? For does it not seem that present-day linguistic philosophers, in their effort to secure what I have chosen to call the rationality of moral and ethical judgments, have allowed themselves to be maneuvered into a situation not unlike that in which Kant fancied he found himself at the outset of the First Critique? Thus Kant asked, "How are synthetic judgments a priori possible?" and the peculiar bite of this question for him lay in the fact that he was thoroughly convinced that neither through pure reason nor through experience could one ever discern in things any basis or ground for the universality or necessity that would seem to be proper to judgments in mathematics and in physics. And similarly—albeit *mutatis mutandis*—would it not seem that contemporary linguistic philosophers must face up to the question of how reasoned and universalizable judgments in ethics are possible? Moreover, the bite of such a question in their case is surely traceable to that very conviction—seemingly so widespread among the linguistic moralists—that ethical judgments are not primarily objective judgments about the world at all, with the result that what superficially would appear to be the only seemingly possible ground for their universality and necessity is thereby removed.

Nor would it appear that one could stop with a mere similarity in the questions. For must not something like Kant's answer to his question impose itself upon the linguistic analysts when they attempt to answer their comparable question in the domain of ethics or meta-ethics? Now Kant's answer, as everyone knows, was what might be called a transcendental one. And as he himself explained, a transcendental principle is "just that sort of principle through which is presented the universal condition [Bedingung] a priori under which alone things can become objects of our knowledge."[5] In other words, the way we know the universality and necessity of the causal principle, for example, is that without such a principle we simply would have no experience of a world at all, it being a necessary condition of such

---

5. Immanuel Kant, *Kritik der Urteilskraft*, ed. by Vorländer (Leipzig, G.D.R.: Felix Meiner, 1924), *Einleitung*, V.

experience that it be ordered and structured in accordance with just such a principle as that of cause and effect.

Similarly, then, when linguistic analysts are challenged to explain how ethical judgments can ever be reasoned judgments and universalizable at the same time that they are not objective (or descriptive) judgments about the world, and when these same philosophers respond by saying, in effect, "But that is just how the language game of ethics is played," are they not thereby making a transcendental turn, no less than Kant? And does not their argument in such a context really amount to no less than a transcendental argument, according to which one seeks to show that reasoned and universalizable judgments are possible in ethics, precisely in that without them we would have no moral or ethical experience at all? That is to say, they are no less than the conditions a priori under which alone people and things can ever appear to us in a moral or ethical light in the first place. Yes, if we may take the liberties of paraphrase with respect at once to both Kant and Wittgenstein, we might say that the linguistic rules that govern the moral or ethical language game are no less than "the conditions *a priori* of the possibility of [moral] experience,"[6] and that these same rules being thus the conditions a priori of the possibility of moral experience are at the same time the sources from which all the reasoned and universalizable laws of ethics may be derived.

And so it is that we would hazard the conclusion that modern linguistic philosophers are really, whether they know it or not, but so many crypto-Kantians. Moreover, the contention of these philosophers that the philosopher's study of morals and ethics ought properly to be a study of moral and ethical language is really to be interpreted as the contention that moral philosophy itself is but a species of transcendental philosophy, and that contemporary metaethics so-called is but another name for what might more properly be called a transcendental ethics.

"But why not?" you will say. "What's wrong with linguistic philosophers being but so many crypto-Kantians? After all, Kant was surely a great philosopher, was he not, and presumably so was Wittgenstein; and supposing great minds to run in the same channel, then what of it if Wittgenstein somehow got sucked into the Kantian current and eventually floated up not so far away from old Kant himself, albeit without his (Wittgenstein's) ever quite knowing where he was or how he had got there?" To all of which the answer is that of course it really doesn't make the slightest bit of difference, provided, of course, that

---

6. *Cf.* Kant's *Prolegomena, op. cit.,* pp. 55–56.

a resort to the transcendental turn in ethics and a recourse to something like a transcendental argument will indeed suffice to salvage and secure that rationality of morals and ethics which it was supposed to be the very business of such a transcendental turn to provide a guarantee of. True, I am not myself convinced that Kant himself in his ethics, as contrasted with his Critical philosophy generally, ever did fall back on anything like a transcendental mode of argument. But surely this is the sort of thing that the latter-day linguistic philosophers have indeed tried to do and do directly in ethics. Consequently, the instant question for us now becomes: Will such a transcendental turn work with respect to ethics? And to this question, I am afraid that the answer must be, "No, it will not work." That is to say, whatever may be the defensibility or indefensibility of a transcendental mode of justification in science or in philosophy generally, I just don't think that it will do, when it comes to matters of ethics. But why not?

Well, I think there are two main reasons why it will not work, depending pretty much on how one understands the business of a transcendental turn in the first place—that is to say, whether one takes it in a more or less orthodox Kantian sense, or in a somewhat more relaxed and heterodox sense. As for the orthodox sense, we all know that, having derived his categories and his pure forms of the understanding from the Table of Judgments, Kant felt that, like the law of the Medes and Persians, they were a law "which," as the King James version has it, "altereth not." Not only that, but the very universality and necessity of synthetic judgments a priori were, in Kant's eyes, directly a function of the invariance and the universal scope of the categories. For if our experience were not structured according to the categories, it would not be structured at all. Thus to take the causal principle as a familiar example, this principle simply could not be other than universal and necessary, for the very reason that an experience of uncaused events or occurrences just would not be an experience of anything real or objective at all. That is to say, it would not even be an experience.

Suppose, though, that one now tries to consider moral or ethical categories as functioning in a manner analogous to the regular Kantian categories, and suppose likewise that one imagines that the universality and necessity attaching to ethical categories can be justified by a transcendental argument analogous to that employed with respect to the other categories—alas, the thing just won't work out. Moreover, where the analogy or the similarity breaks down is just at that point where Kant construes his categories as being the very "conditions a priori of the possibility of experience." So far as moral or ethical categories are concerned, however, these could never be construed as being the conditions a priori of the possibility of experience, but only of moral experience.

And this limitation and restriction would surely seem to be at once decisive and disastrous, so far as any and all efforts to justify morals and ethics through a transcendental argument are concerned. For a transcendental argument has cogency presumably only with respect to principles through which, as Kant says, "is presented the universal condition [Bedingung] a priori under which alone things can become objects of knowledge." But moral principles surely can never be principles that function as universal conditions through which alone a thing can ever be even so much as an object of knowledge. Quite the contrary, one might say that so much of the thrust of recent metaethics is precisely one of delimiting and demarcating the sphere of values and of the moral and ethical, if not by a crude and old-fashioned separating off of values from facts, then at least by such new-fashioned and more subtle distinctions as that which would distinguish prescriptive judgments from descriptive.

Very well, then the inevitable consequence of this is that the a priori rationality—or if you will, the universality and necessity—of moral principles and of norms and standards of value can no longer be justified by any sort of Kantian transcendental argument of the orthodox type. Instead, the linguistic rules that might be presumed to guarantee the a priori possibility of reasoned and universalizable judgments in ethics are rules that are determinative only of moral experience and not of experience generally. And yet the whole question is why we should ever let ourselves in for anything like moral experience at all. Indeed, as Philippa Foot would seem to imply, if anyone should refuse to abide by the rules of moral discourse, then such a person would have no alternative but "to leave the moral discussion and abjure the use of moral terms" altogether. Granted. But again, why shouldn't one leave it or abjure it altogether? The thing is that if we have any option in the matter at all, then a Kantian justification of the strict type can no longer be either relevant or operative, so far as a justification of ethics is concerned.

Nor is this question of the justification of the rationality and universalizability of ethical judgments reducible to the somewhat more superficial and trivial question of "Why should I be moral?" For as Frankena and others have observed with respect to this latter question, it is a question that is ambiguous as to whether it is asking for a motivation or for a justification. And if it is the former that is being asked for, Frankena suggests, then the question is irrelevant; and if the latter, then it is question-begging.[7]

Unfortunately, however, such an answer is hardly telling as a reply to someone who does not understand why he is in any sense obliged to enter into the language game of morals and ethics in the first place. For by his very challenge to such a moral language game as being in any way binding upon him, such a person is implicitly questioning no less than the basic tenet of the linguistic ethicists—namely, that the binding character of morals and ethics is relative only to certain language games which conceivably one may either choose to play or not. Hence for a linguistic analyst to reply to such a challenge by insisting that when a challenger asks why he ought to engage in the moral language game in the first place, he has already entered the game—and that simply in virtue of having used the word "ought"—it is surely the linguistic analyst who has this time begged the question. For having admitted that the language game or conceptual scheme of morals or ethics is limited in its scope, the linguistic philosopher cannot then rule out all second-order questions about the morality of this very game itself, as if such second-order questions were already included in the first-order domain. This would seem to be no less than a case of bad logic.

So much, then, for the first reason as to why it would seem that a transcendental mode of justification of the orthodox Kantian type could be of little avail to linguistic philosophers—at least not when it is applied in the domain of ethics. Still, to all this it is easy to retort, "But why worry about a transcendental justification of an orthodox type?" For who any longer is hobbled by a notion of categories—or if you will of linguistic rules—as being fixed and unchanging after the manner of the law of the Medes and Persians? Indeed, one need only think of Hegel's paean to the French Revolution, which Alasdair MacIntyre has recently quoted in his book on Marcuse: "Never since the sun had stood in the firmament and the planets revolved around it had it been perceived that man's existence centers in his head, i.e. in thought, inspired by which he builds up the world of reality. . . . This was accordingly a glorious mental dawn. All thinking beings shared in the jubilation of that epoch."[8] Moreover, MacIntyre goes on to explain that the occasion for this jubilation was in part due, as Hegel

---

7. William K. Frankena, *Ethics* (Englewood Cliffs, NJ: Prentice-Hall, 1963), pp. 87–88, 96–98.
8. Alasdair MacIntyre, *Herbert Marcuse* (New York: Viking Press, 1970), pp. 21–22.

saw it, to a certain sense of liberation from the fixity and invariance of Kant's categories:

> Kant had argued that we are able to understand the world and to know truth about it only because the mind brings to its task of understanding a set of categories by means of which it organizes what is given in experience. Experience never comes to us raw, but mediated by the categories. We experience things as having determinate qualities and relations, because the conceptual structure which thought imposes on the world gives determinate form to what would otherwise be formless. Moreover the categories are fixed once and for all; the mind itself has a determinate unchanging constitution.[9]

Now it was just this fixity of the categories, this supposed unchanging constitution of the mind that needed to become unfixed and to become subjected to change, if that jubilation and "glorious mental dawn" of the epoch of the French Revolution were to be made understandable. And so MacIntyre continues:

> Hegel attacked the notion that the categories are timeless and unalterable. The history of thought is a history of changing conceptual structures. Elucidating the categories of a given age must not be confused with elucidating the structure of thought as such. To elucidate the structure of thought, a history has to be written, a history exhibiting growth both in consciousness and self-consciousness. For it is by becoming conscious of their present mode of thought that men are able to criticize it and rationally to transcend it. The end and culmination of such a history would be the rational comprehension of the whole process.[10]

And so it is, one might say, that Hegel has bequeathed to us the resource of a new and much more flexible means of transcendental justification than that which Kant had envisaged. True, the contemporary thinkers are few indeed who have any particular concern with working out the history, as Hegel calls it—to say nothing of the dynamics of that history—of human thought as it progressively discards what happen to be its present prevalent categories or, if you will, forms of life, for ever new and different ones. But indifferent as they may be to this kind of history and the laws of such a history, nearly all contemporary philosophers, whatever their different persuasions, seem to be agreed that our categories, our conceptual schemes, our "bliks," our basic linguistic rules, or what have you—that is to say, all of those collections or repositories of the a priori which provide us with the basic forms we impose upon the world so as to "give determinate form to what would otherwise be formless"—all of these are in no wise fixed and unchanging. It makes no difference whether one

9. *Ibid.*
10. *Ibid.*, p. 23.

is concerned with scientific revolutions in the sense of Thomas Kuhn, or of world horizons or world constitution in the sense of the existential phenomenologists, or of forms of life in the sense of the Wittgensteinians—in all such cases the operative consideration is the same: our human a priori's are subject to change, and while a given a priori scheme or project or language game may well be the guarantor of universal and necessary truths within the confines of that scheme, it is nonetheless a strictly limited and relative universality and necessity.

And now back to ethics and more particularly to the ethical theories of the linguistic philosophers. Is it possible that this somewhat more relaxed and permissive mode of transcendental justification might give them just the resource they need, when it comes to justifying the reasoned and universalizable character of moral and ethical judgments? To answer this question, I suggest that it might be interesting and instructive to consider the case of Prof. Searle. For we are all familiar with how in his brilliant and provocative writings of the last few years, he has sought to show how in the language game of promising, the very rules of this game serve to guarantee the legitimacy of no less than a derivation of "ought" from "is." Indeed, availing himself of the distinction between "brute facts" and "institutional facts," Searle makes it clear that, so far as brute facts are concerned, there is nothing discoverable in them that could in any way legitimate the derivation of moral obligations from the brute facts of the case—for example in the case of promising. No, it is only because the constitutive rules of our language and of our social institutions generally have resulted in the institution or constitution of certain institutional facts, such as the fact of the so-called promising game, that a so-called fact like that of promising seems to entail an obligation to keep such a promise.

Accordingly, if Searle were to be asked whether the fact of promising does, indeed, provide a ground or reason for a moral obligation—that is to say, as to whether a judgment to the effect that one ought to keep one's promises is a judgment that is at once a reasoned judgment and universalizable—Searle would have to reply that it is a reasoned and universalizable judgment, and yet it is so only relative to the institution of the promising game. But what of this institution of promising itself? Is that in turn anything to which we are in any way bound, either morally or otherwise?

To such a question, Searle's answer is as honest as it is compromising:

> It is perfectly consistent with my account for someone to argue "One ought never to keep promises." Suppose for example a nihilistic anarchist argues that one ought never to keep promises because, e.g., an unseemly concern

with obligation impedes self-fulfillment. Such an argument may be silly, but it is not, as far as my account is concerned, logically absurd. To understand this point, we need to make a distinction between what is external and what is internal to the institution of promising. It is internal to the concept of promising that in promising one undertakes an obligation to do something. But whether the entire institution of promising is good or evil, and whether the obligations undertaken in promising are overridden by other outside considerations are questions which are external to the institution itself. The nihilist argument considered above is simply an external attack on the institution of promising. In effect, it says that the obligation to keep a promise is always overridden because of the alleged evil character of the institution. But it does not deny the point that promises obligate, it only insists that the obligations ought not to be fulfilled because of the external consideration of "self-fulfillment."

Nothing in my account commits one to the conservative view that institutions are logically unassailable or to the view that one ought to approve or disapprove this or that institution. The point is merely that when one enters an institutional activity by invoking the rules of the institution one necessarily commits oneself in such and such ways, regardless of whether one approves or disapproves of the institution.[11]

A fine, brave statement, surely, is this one on Searle's part, and one which quite effectively removes from him any suspected trace of that taint-of-all-taints nowadays, the taint of being a conservative, and particularly of being a conservative in respect to institutions, especially moral institutions! Alas, though, in clearing himself of this taint, has not Searle at the same time convicted himself of what amounts to little less than a radical and thoroughgoing ethical relativism? For while the upshot of his position would now seem to be that while you or I or the next man may have certain moral obligations simply as a matter of fact, we have them only relatively to our acceptance of certain institutions. But that anyone must accept the particular moral institutions that he has in fact accepted, rather than accepting quite other and radically different ones—or even that he must accept any moral institutions at all—this apparently is something which we are under no obligation or necessity of doing at all. And with that, what has become of the requisite universality and necessity, to say nothing of the rationality, of our moral and ethical principles?

Nor would it seem that this predicament that Searle has got himself into is really anything other than that general predicament which all linguistic moralists must find themselves in, if they will but take thought of this present difficult and even untenable situation as regards their ethical theory. For if our analysis and brief account of the

11. John R. Searle, *Speech Acts* (London: Cambridge University Press, 1969), pp. 188–189.

structural history of linguistic ethics be correct, these thinkers originally set out to solve a certain seeming dilemma in regard to ethics: how could moral principles, to say nothing of ethical norms and standards generally, be at once nonobjective and at the same time universal and necessary? And this dilemma they sought to meet by simply rebutting it; and the device of their rebuttal was that of the so-called linguistic turn in ethics. It was this device, they felt sure, that would enable them to make it intelligible how ethical judgments could be at once nondescriptive or nonfactual and at the same time properly universal and reasoned judgments. However, such a linguistic turn, we would suggest, has now proved to be for the linguistic philosophers no less than a concealed and perhaps even unwanted transcendental turn. And unfortunately, a transcendental turn in ethics, however one chooses to interpret it, either strictly or more loosely, would seem to commit one, either to a certain arbitrariness in one's ethics, or else to a pretty hopeless relativism. But if so, then the device of the linguistic turn in ethics, entailing as it apparently does some sort of transcendental turn, would presumably have to be written off as a failure: the nonobjective character of ethics just is not reconcilable with its rationality after all.

"But so what, and then what?" you may well ask. Surely, though, the answer is a simple one: if the supposedly prescriptive and nonfactual character of ethical judgments turns out to be irreconcilable with the rationality of such judgments, then had we not better start taking seriously once again the descriptive and objective character of such judgments? That is to say, the crying need in ethics today would seem to be, not for any language of morals, or logic of morals, or even phenomenology of morals, transcendental or otherwise, but rather for an ontology of morals.

"Oh," but you will say, "such an answer is not so much a simple one, as a silly one—and even worse, one that is terribly old-hat." True enough, but given the desperate straits of contemporary metaethics, perhaps we should bring ourselves to listen once more even to the retelling of old stories. And as for the silliness, it might just be remarked that there is at least some authority, questionable though it be, for the notion that maybe the wisdom of the wise is something that is to be confounded by the very foolishness of one whose name should perhaps in this body go entirely unmentioned.

But be that as it may, and returning again to Prof. Wisdom and his one-time advent into southern Indiana, may we perhaps say—now in the light of hindsight—that that particular advent was no true Advent, and that the gospel which he brought with him, while it may have been in some ways a good news, has since turned out to be a somewhat misleading news? Yes, reviving a now rather outmoded colloquialism, why not just say that perhaps what Prof. Wisdom did on that long-ago visit to Indiana was but to give the poor Hoosiers "a bum steer"?

8

IN APPRECIATION AND REFUTATION OF ALAN GEWIRTH'S PRINCIPLE OF GENERIC CONSISTENCY

What can one say of Professor Gewirth's book,[1] if not that it is an incomparable philosophical performance! Massive, powerful, and thorough, it seems to move onto the contemporary philosophical scene like some great tank—not necessarily with guns blazing, but certainly with multiple defenses all intact, and seemingly ready to take on all comers. The better to understand the fundamental stance of the book, it might be well to begin with a somewhat superficial sketch of the way the land lies in contemporary ethics, at least as this must presumably appear to Gewirth as he looks out from behind his heavily armored turret. What first strikes one, of course, in such a view is that ethics, in its contemporary phase, has decisively abandoned the splendid isolation of the metaethics of a time not so long past, and having come down from its one-time heights, has started to maneuver directly within the world of present-day politics and society. Nor is it hard to discern at least the major rival sets of ethical theoretical principles that seemingly inspire the different moral philosophers who carry out these maneuvers. For suppose one asks whether it might perhaps be something like the old traditional natural law principles that guide our latter-day ethical generals and field marshals in their marches and countermarches. The answer can only be a decisive "No!" For it has come to be taken as an absolute if jaded truism that there just is no way in which an "ought" can be derived from an "is." Hence not even the most exhaustive knowledge of nature, be it scientific or otherwise—no, not even a thorough grasp of the known facts about human nature—can shed light on questions as to what human beings ought to be, or how they ought to act. Instead, when it comes to current rivalries among those who inhabit today's academic establishments,

1. *Reason and Morality*, by Alan Gewirth (Chicago: University of Chicago Press, 1978).

these seem to be confined almost entirely to such issues as whether moral rules and moral values are to be conceived in terms of teleological or of deontological principles. For instance, assuming that no knowledge of the realities of our human situation can ever disclose any naturally grounded rights and duties incumbent upon us in virtue of our nature as human beings, an obvious alternative for moral philosophers is then to have recourse once again to mere utilitarianism: "Why worry whether we have any naturally grounded responsibilities or obligations merely as human beings? Rather, our concern need be with no more than getting what we want, and getting as much of it as we can, and for as many of us as possible, and regardless of whether the various goods and goals that we thus happen to fancy have any authorization in nature."

One trouble, though, is that the attractions of such a utilitarian alternative have tended to pale rather perceptibly in the last few years. "For is it not a scandal," so the objection runs, "that the maximizing of happiness for the greatest number could well be purchased at the price of the misery and suffering of the lesser number—at least when these are additively considered?" And so considerations such as these have recently boosted the stock of various deontological alternatives to utilitarian teleological theories. And indeed, so far as Gewirth is concerned, there would seem to be no mistaking that it is his intention to maneuver his mighty armament in such a way as to bring it ultimately around to the side of the deontologists.

Yet Gewirth would be the first to insist, and rightly so, that his is a deontologism with a difference! For the trouble with the mine-run of deontologisms, stemming as they do from Kant, and then flowing down into the mud flats of Oxford, and eventually broadening out into the messy, muddy delta of the many curious current varieties of deontologism—of Frankena, of Rawls, of Nozick, or of whomever—is that apparently none of them seems to deal adequately with the problem of justification. And after all, the problem is one that is forced upon the deontologist by nothing less than the very logic of his own moral language game. For supposing it to be a question of categorical, and not mere hypothetical, imperatives—and the former are of the very essence of any proper deontology—immediately, the one who is subject to such obligations as are expressed in the imperatives may well ask, "But why and on what grounds am I thus bound by such imperatives? What is there about them that makes them binding upon me, or for that matter upon anyone?"

To be sure, hypothetical imperatives pose no such problem. It is entirely intelligible why someone might be said to be obliged to do X, given the condition that he wants or is desirous of Y, and X is the best or only means of attaining it. But by definition a categorical imperative to do X can never be justified on the hypothesis of the moral agent's wanting something else, Y. In other words, there just is no way in which the binding force of a categorical imperative may be made evident through any appeal to ends or purposes outside of and extrinsic to the imperative itself. But if the binding force of a categorical imperative cannot be made evident by any appeal to extrinsic purposes or considerations, there would seem to be no alternative but to hold such imperatives to be somehow self-evident—that is, "You ought, just because you ought." But how can this be? How can the binding or obligatory character of any imperative be held to be literally self-evident?

Of course, Kant's answer was that a categorical obligation, like that of never making a lying promise, is a self-evident obligation, just in the sense that for one to deny it or to try to exempt oneself from its force, can only involve one in self-contradiction. And yet this Kantian way of construing the self-evidence of categorical obligations has scarcely carried much conviction. Hegel is not the only one who has felt that, while it might be true that a categorical imperative was one whose self-evidence could only be manifested by the fact that to deny or repudiate it would involve one in self-contradiction, nevertheless Kant was singularly unable to come forward with any concrete or specific examples of such categorical duties or obligations. Hence Kant's ethics has seemed to many to be an empty formalism, with no concrete moral content of any kind.

Moreover, to move from Kant to the Oxford Kantians, it appears that they simply gave up trying to exhibit the self-evidence of categorical duties by showing that to repudiate them would be self-contradictory. Instead, they contended that categorical duties and obligations had to be simply intuited, there being no other way that their self-evidence could be made manifest. But the seeming arbitrariness of such appeals has meant that the deontologists who have taken this line have been scarcely able to hold their own, much less to sweep the field, in the contemporary struggles between rival ethical theories. And so it is at such a juncture, and against the background of these many failed attempts to justify our categorical duties and obligations, that Gewirth would have us think of himself as entering the lists on behalf of the faltering deontologists. For he is convinced that what all earlier ethical thinkers of a deontological persuasion, from Kant on, have never succeeded in doing he, Gewirth, can now bring off, and bring off successfully. Indeed, for well over the first half of *Reason and*

Morality he is concerned with explicating and defending a single supreme principle of morality, which he terms the Principle of Generic Consistency (PGC), and which he contends is subject to just such rational justification as Kant strove for but never attained. That is to say, it is a principle that can indeed be evidenced by the fact that one can deny it only on pain of self-contradiction.

Moreover, in passing, it perhaps should be added that it is not merely the ethical deontologists whom Gewirth feels able to set right by invoking this supreme principle of the PGC. No, contemporary teleologists, no less than deontologists, have all flunked Gewirth's key test of whether or not they are able to provide a rational justification for moral principles. Thus as Gewirth understands morality, it is "a set of categorically obligatory requirements for action that are addressed at least in part to every actual or prospective agent, and that are concerned with furthering the interests, especially the most important interests, of persons or recipients *other than or in addition to the agent or the speaker*" (p. 1, emphasis added). Or again, "morality, however, is primarily concerned with interpersonal actions, that is, with actions that affect persons other than their agents" (p. 129). Clearly, though, if morality be so conceived as being primarily, if not wholly, other-directed, then teleologists must face the problem of the rational justification of their moral principles, no less than deontologists. That is to say, it can never suffice for a teleologist to offer, by way of a justification of his moral actions, the fact that such actions are those that he wants to perform, or that lead to the attainment of his acknowledged ends or goals. No, for strictly "moral" action, as Gewirth understands the term, can only be justified on the ground that it benefits others, and not on the ground that it benefits us or is somehow what we ourselves want to do. But why and on what grounds, then, may a teleologist suppose that we have duties and obligations to promote the good of others? With reference to such a question, Gewirth has an easy time disposing of the likes of Mill's questionable "argument from each individual's desiring his own happiness to the conclusion that the general happiness is desirable" (p. 203). And if Mill be not the one to set the standard that teleologists are to follow in the matter of moral justification, what other standard is to be put forward? Can one any longer simply posit with Hume the presence in all human beings of moral sentiments, or sentiments of benevolence, as supposedly providing the warrant for our other-directed actions and behavior, and in this sense for our moral behavior? Worse yet would be to invoke a so-called moral point of view à la Baier, and then say that moral behavior is justified just to the extent that we give ourselves over to the let's-pretend game of being moral. Or is the moral language game somehow one that we cannot avoid playing, with the result that morality gets its justification by virtue of a kind of transcendental argument? Or we might follow R. M. Hare, and by a kind of hocus-pocus of universalizability try to transform such actions as we happen to be personally inclined toward into actions of a truly universal, and hence moral, import.

Clearly none of these alternatives would seem to do. It is not surprising, then, that as he surveys the field of moral strategies, as these have been developed by either teleologists or deontologists, Gewirth is able confidently to affirm that in no instance, either in history or in the current discussions, has anyone been able to come forward with anything that even approaches an adequate rational justification of moral behavior. Moreover, it is precisely in this light that he would have us see his own Principle of Generic Consistency: It is a principle that is not to be thought of as revolutionizing ethics so much as one that for the first time in history provides ethics with a truly rational basis and thus turns it into a respectable discipline at long last.

Needless to say, these are no mean claims, and to substantiate them Gewirth offers a most thorough and searching scrutiny of his PGC. Reduced to its simplest terms, what this scrutiny discloses is that human action, all of it and any of it, is distinctive just in the fact that it cannot be other than voluntary and purposive. Indeed, the argument here, at least in its general features, is not unlike Aristotle's argument to the effect that change or motion must involve at least three principles. That is to say, how could one possibly conceive of change—supposing there to be such a thing—that was not somehow a change of something, from something, and to something else? So likewise, Gewirth argues that an action would not be an action, or an agent an agent, if such action were not free in the sense of being uncompelled and uncoerced, and if it were not directed toward some end or purpose, of whatever sort that might be. And not only, Gewirth goes on to argue, must an action be free and purposive, but also as agents we cannot but value such freedom and purposiveness as necessarily attaches to our actions. True, it is conceivable that an agent might seek to renounce his freedom or surrender it or otherwise deny it; but in doing so, he would literally and in the very act be doing so freely; and in thus freely renouncing his freedom he cannot but value that very freedom just in the sense that without it he could not possibly carry out even his own act of freely renouncing it. And so, Gewirth concludes, there just is no way that a human agent can repudiate or disvalue his freedom as an agent without thereby affirming the very thing he is denying, or without valuing that which he is pretending to disvalue.

Moreover, like considerations would apply to that other distinctive feature of action, its purposiveness. For an action to be purposive simply means for it to be aimed at something that the agent thinks to be in some way or other beneficial or as making for the agent's own well-being, however diverse may be the conceptions which different agents may have of what their well-being might consist in. In other words, however varied and divergent the purposes of different agents, no agent could act or be an agent without purposing and valuing his very being, and hence his well-being as an agent.

And now for the next step: just as actions could not be actions, or agents agents, without such actions being free and without their purposing the agent's own well-being, so also that very freedom and well-being, which agents cannot but value in and by their very actions, must also be things which agents cannot think of themselves as having anything other than a *right* to. After all, if as an agent I cannot but value my freedom and my well-being as being the absolute prerequisites of my being an agent, must these not be things that I therefore cannot but consider myself as being entitled to? Or, to put it still differently, since I could not even claim to be what I am without being free and without my enjoying a certain well-being just *qua* agent, then surely my freedom and well-being cannot even be conceived by me in any other light than as things to which I am basically and absolutely entitled. But no sooner is it thus established that I have rights just as an individual than therewith there are established all of the correlative duties and obligations of all other agents, past, present, and to come, to respect these rights of mine. Not only that, but just as I have rights, *qua* agent, so also will all other individuals have the same rights, *qua* agents, as well. But this means that just as all other agents have duties to respect my rights, so also must I acknowledge that I have duties toward each and every other agent to respect just those rights that he has *qua* agent. And with this there emerges that basic condition of all human agents, which Gewirth likes to call "egalitarian universalism" (p. 127): it is a universalism, because it extends to all rational agents just insofar as they are agents; and it is egalitarian in that the reciprocal rights and duties extend to agents, not in virtue of any special status or condition or qualification that any other agent may happen to have, but rather in virtue simply of his being an agent, and *in* this sense of his being on an equal footing with any and all other agents. Yes, Gewirth conceives of the exercise of human agency in the world as involving what he calls "transactions": the agent as actor acts, but in the normal human situation there are other agents, who within the context of that particular action may be said to be its "recipients." In other words, whether it be buying or selling, doctoring or lawyering, soldiering or conscientious objecting, philandering or practicing chastity, philosophizing or playing the ponies—in all such instances of human acting there are bound to be both actors and recipients.

And so with this, the way is at last prepared for the *grande entrance* of the Principle of Generic Consistency: "Act in accord with the generic rights of your recipients as well as yourself " (p. 135). "But," you will say, "does this not sound mightily like the now-hackneyed first formulation of the categorical imperative: Act so that you can will that the maxim of your action shall be a universal law?" Well, of course it does. For the matter of that, Gewirth's formulation of the PGC sounds not only like the categorical imperative of Kant; it also sounds like the second part of the so-called Summary of the Law which Gewirth's own colleague at the University of Chicago, Alan Donagan, in a book published scarcely a year before Gewirth's, has most ingeniously undertaken to exploit as a possible supreme principle of morality: "Love thy neighbor as thyself." And yet the point would seem to be not that Gewirth considers his formulation of the supreme principle of morality to be so radically different from such other comparable principles as may have been put forward by other deontologists. Rather, what Gewirth would claim is that he has managed so to construe and explicate his principle that it comes off as being in a quite literal and precise way self-evident and self-justifying. Thus Donagan, for example, would say that his supreme principle rests on intuition, and hence is not such that its very denial turns out to be self-contradictory. And as for Kant, we have already remarked how questionable it is whether he was able to make good his claim that for anyone to go counter to the categorical imperative would involve one in self-contradiction. In contrast, Gewirth, with his very careful and sustained analysis, is able to show that if one denies to another his generic rights either to freedom or to well-being, then it needs only to be pointed out how the very person who denies these rights to another cannot avoid claiming such rights for himself, just in virtue of his being an agent. But if one must think of oneself as having such rights, and on no other ground than that one is oneself an agent, then one must also acknowledge that any other agent has exactly the same rights as oneself. Hence to deny such rights to others is to fall into a patent inconsistency, so far as one's own rights claims are concerned. Q.E.D.!

Nor is that all, for Gewirth would also no doubt wish to insist that even if Kant were able to maintain that the Kantian categorical imperative cannot be challenged without involving oneself in self-contradiction, there nonetheless is the further difficulty that attaches to Kant's way of conceiving his moral first principle, in that apparently for Kant the principle remains purely formal and resists all application to concrete cases. Not so, though, with Gewirth's principle. For given Gewirth's analysis of human action, it follows that any and every agent is committed to the specific recognition of the concrete values of freedom and well-being. Accordingly, in the second half of his book (chaps. 4 and 5), Gewirth spells out in elaborate and painstaking detail various of the specific ways in which human agents have sought either to deny, or to question, or to look the other way when it comes to facing up to the generic rights of others in specific concrete cases. And in each such case Gewirth is able to show, with remarkable ingenuity, how one has but to invoke the PGC, and at once the various evasions of the generic rights of others turn out to be self-contradictory.

Unfortunately, in the comparatively narrow limits of even this long review one cannot begin either to outline or to give adequate illustration of the richness and intricacy with which Gewirth works out his account of the manifold and varied applications of the supreme principle of morality. But just by way of giving a foretaste of what may be found in this second part of the book, consider how Gewirth attempts to sort out some of the specific obligations that human beings have with respect to others' rights to well-being. Such well-being, he suggests, must involve a variety of so-called goods. For instance, there are basic goods—things like "life, physical integrity, health and its various contributing factors, general freedom, mental equilibrium and the like." These are "attributes of an individual without which he cannot act, either at all or beyond some minimum relative to his pursuing and achieving purposes" (p. 211). Besides such basic goods, there are also what Gewirth calls "nonsubtractive goods." Thus "a person has a nonsubtractive good when his status quo as to his possession of good is maintained so that his level of purpose-fulfillment is not lowered through his being made to lose something he views as good" (p. 230). And finally there are additive goods. These "consist in the means or conditions that enable any person to increase his capabilities of purpose-fulfilling action and hence to achieve more of his goods" (p. 240). Now with respect to each and every one of these varying sorts of goods, there arise rights and obligations on the part of any one agent as regards the possession of these goods, both by himself and by others. Thus specifically, in Gewirth's eyes, the PGC requires not merely that agents not interfere with the freedom and well-being of their recipients; in addition, they have a duty to contribute positively to the well-being of others, considered as recipients of their actions or possible actions. Thus the drowning man has a right to be aided and succored, assuming that others are in a position to save him without undue risk to their own basic goods of life and health, etc. Or when it comes to additive goods, as opposed to basic goods, agents have an obligation actually to forgo some of their own additive goods, in order that others' lack of these goods may be made up for: "In certain circumstances, when prospective agents are unable to provide for their additive well-being through their own efforts, the agent's obligation extends to assisting them to have such well-being . . ." (p. 241). Yes, when it comes to questions about private property and property rights, Gewirth unequivocally declares that "the right to property is limited by the PGC's requirement that agents also act in accord with their recipients' rights to well-being" (ibid.). Need it be added that Gewirth finds himself having to tread very warily here, considering that some of his own most loyal students are libertarians, and, while wholeheartedly accepting the PGC, they tend to be no less insistent that it scarcely commits one to thus helping others, as opposed to merely not interfering with them or injuring them?[2]

Particularly interesting, too, is Gewirth's concluding chapter, which he entitles "Indirect Applications of the Principle" (*i.e.*, of the PGC). What he means by indirect applications as contrasted with direct applications is that while in many instances an individual's actions and behavior are directed toward others, considered simply as individuals and as possessed of their appropriate rights and duties directly under the PGC, at other times our actions are directed toward others in terms of the roles that we and they may have, as these are determined by various social rules. For example, given the fact that in a context of such social rules a judge may sentence a criminal to prison, or an umpire declare a batter out (p. 273), would this not seem to involve a measure of actual coercion or of harm being meted out to recipients; and how is this ever to be justified in terms of the PGC? In meeting such a challenge Gewirth wishes to avoid both the extreme of a libertarian individualism and anarchism, on the one hand, and that of a mere utilitarian calculation of aggregate benefits as over against aggregate harms on the other. In general, his tactic is to argue that "all persons have a prima facie right to participate in activities or associations whose rules they have freely accepted" (p. 286). For is this any more than a specification of any agent's right to freedom

---

2. See the interesting series of articles by Roger Pilon that is scheduled to appear in the *Georgia Law Review*, vol. 13 (Summer 1979), and is entitled, "Corporations and Rights: On Treating Corporate People Justly."

under the PGC? However, if an agent has voluntarily accepted the rules of a given association, then, Gewirth argues, if he refuses to accept "the adverse impact of procedurally justified rules on himself and others, or if he violates any of the rules, then he contradicts himself " (p. 287).

But then, it soon turns out that the principle that is here involved needs to be considerably nuanced and qualified, depending upon whether the social rules that are thus voluntarily accepted be the rules of some mere voluntary association like a club or professional society, or those of the so-called minimal state, or those of the supportive state, etc. Nevertheless, Gewirth never once draws back from a careful and thorough examination of all of these situations and circumstances, showing in each case how the relevant sorts of social rules may be justified or not, in terms of an ultimate appeal to the PGC. For instance, the differences between the spheres of "retributive" and "distributive" justice, between the methods of consent in the case of, say, a basic social contract as over against specific items of legislation within a state—all of these questions are taken up and dealt with in an incredibly thoroughgoing and systematic fashion. In short, the very last accusation that could be made against a deontological ethics such as that developed by Gewirth is that it reduces to a mere formalism without concrete applications in our individual and social existence.

Nevertheless, this will have to suffice by way of indicating the extent and the subtlety of Gewirth's concern with how his PGC may be applied in concrete cases. For inadequate though our summary of this part of his book may be, it should enable one to see that however much one may be inclined to agree or disagree with Gewirth's specific applications of his principle, there can be no question of his having so construed his supreme principle of morality as to make it eminently susceptible of such application. Gewirth's ethics, in short, is no formalism. Far from it! But even though it can thus escape the charge of formalism, is it, as an ethics, really a basically successful achievement after all? For there is no mistaking the claim which *Reason and Morality* makes. It is true that Gewirth's inherent modesty forbids him to articulate the claim in all of its stark reality. And yet there is no mistaking that his book claims to do what no other major figure in modern ethics has succeeded in doing—not Kant, not Prichard, not Ross, not any of today's worthies or unworthies, whatever their stature or nonstature, be it Rawls or Hare or Frankena or Brandt or Donagan or whoever. For Gewirth would surely say that he for the first time has managed to establish a supreme principle of morality on such a footing as to make it absolutely unshakable: it cannot be denied without self-contradiction; and upon this one absolute first principle the entire edifice of ethics can be erected. Still, is Gewirth's claim in this regard really justified?

With no little hesitation and reluctance, I feel that I must answer this question in the negative. It is true that, considering the very carefully worked out dialectic that Gewirth has developed to exhibit the self-evident and self-justifying character of his supreme principle of morality, one cannot but feel that in criticizing it one may have overlooked or missed a point somewhere. But for whatever the following consideration may be worth, is it the case that he really has succeeded in showing the indefeasible right of each and every human agent to freedom and well-being? For granted that every human being does in fact cherish both freedom and well-being—yes, granted even that every human agent must value such things not just in fact, but necessarily and unavoidably, as being a part of the very notion of what it means to be an agent—still how does it follow from this that every human agent has a right to such freedom and well-being? Is there not somehow an illicit process here from fact to right, or from "is" to "ought"? Merely because I or anyone else happens to have or cherish something very dearly, surely that does not mean that I therefore somehow have a right to what I thus love and cherish, or even that it is right for me thus to love and cherish it. Recall how Hume sought to argue that all men do, as a matter of fact, tend to approve such actions as are useful or agreeable either to the agent himself, or to others. And yet surely the fact of such approbation, assuming it to be universal, still does not make it right that human beings should bestow their approbation upon such useful or benevolent actions. After all, suppose that, just as a matter of fact, human beings were inclined to approve, not so much benevolent or useful actions, as rather malevolent or sadistic ones, that of course would not serve to justify such actions or to make them right.

Of course, one knows what Gewirth's reply to all of this would be. He would say that as long as human beings just happen to approve of freedom and well-being, it certainly does not follow either that it is right for them so to do, or that they have rights to such things. But the case must be different when we recognize that as human beings we cannot avoid esteeming our human freedom and well-being, when our so esteeming them is no less than the very condition of our being agents in the first place. In other words, Gewirth would insist that it is precisely the necessity and absolute inescapability of our thus valuing our freedom and well-being that make such things a matter of right for us, and not merely a matter of liking or choice or inclination.

But again, why should something's being necessarily the case make it any more a matter of right or obligation than its merely being actually the case? Is an inference from "must be" to "ought" any more valid than one from "is" to "ought"? Indeed, suppose that an old-time psychological hedonist were actually to bring off a demonstration to the effect that human beings not merely do not, but cannot, seek anything but pleasure. That still would not mean that pleasure was for that reason a good, in the sense of being something that human beings have a right to.

Supposing, then, that there is indeed something questionable, if not downright faulty, in Gewirth's key argument in justification of his supreme principle of morality, might we perhaps go a step further and presume to offer a possible diagnosis of just where and how and why he may have gone astray in conjuring a rabbit out of the hat—or a matter of right out of a matter of fact (or necessity)? Might it be that what Gewirth failed to do was to apply what some have been wont to call "the Euthyphro test": Is a thing good because it is desired, or is it desired because it is seen somehow to be good, and quite independently of its being desired?[3] Now imagine Gewirth to have applied this test to the objects and items of value, which, as he seems to feel, are necessarily associated with all human action, namely, freedom and well-being. And imagine further that having applied the test, it should turn out that freedom and well-being, so far from being things of worth and value merely because we cannot help desiring or cherishing them, but rather because, like them or not, they are things that we ought to value and to cherish, just because in themselves they really are valuable or worthwhile. In other words, what if Gewirth's freedom and well-being were esteemed to be values, not because there was something about our situation as human agents that makes such things appear to be of value to us, but rather because they really are of value, whether they seem so or not?

With this, would not the entire situation change radically for Gewirth, so far as the grounding for his ethics is concerned? No longer would he be forced into any dubious moves from the fact of men's valuing certain things to their having a moral right to what they so

---

3. Richard McKeon once remarked that this was a principle particularly dear to moral philosophers in the eighteenth century. For example, see Kant's formulation of the same principle in the *Critique of Practical Reason*, trans. L. W. Beck (New York: Liberal Arts Press, 1956), p. 61, n. 2: "The expression *sub ratione boni* is also ambiguous. For it can mean: we represent something to ourselves as good, if and because we desire (will) it. Or it can mean: we desire something, because we represent it to ourselves as good. Thus either the desire is the determining ground of the concept as a good or the concept of the good is the determining ground of desire (will)."

value. Instead, prior to any fact, be it necessary or otherwise, that men do desire certain things, is the more basic fact that certain things just are desirable as being naturally and intrinsically good for us. And from this it would follow that such things as are naturally desirable are for that reason things which we ought to desire, and which it is therefore morally right for us to desire. In other words, whatever is thus a natural good, and thus a natural end for human beings, whether they be aware of it or not, will necessarily be something which human beings will have a natural obligation and responsibility—and therefore also a moral obligation and responsibility—to pursue and try to attain. Moreover, whatever it be thus naturally right that any human being should try to do and be—for example, to be free and to enjoy such a natural flourishing or well-being as is appropriate to his nature as a person—this may also be something which a human being may be said to have a natural right to. Does this not, then, provide us—and had he availed himself of it, would it not have provided Gewirth as well—with an entirely proper and defensible transition from nature to ethics, and from the natural to the moral? Indeed, such a transition could hardly be faulted in the way in which from our earlier analysis it would seem that Gewirth's own attempted transition is only too open to fault.

But no, for Gewirth such a line of argument would never do! True, by following such a line, he might be able to get himself off the spike on which he would seem to have got himself impaled, namely, that of trying to derive a matter of right from a matter of fact. But to get off in this way could well seem to Gewirth to be an even worse fate than that of being impaled! For in his eyes it is absolutely essential to the success of his own variety of dialectical demonstration of the supreme principle of morality that the freedom and the well-being, which he considers to be necessary conditions of our human agency, be things which as individuals we are impelled toward out of purely prudential considerations (see esp. pp. 71–73). But this amounts to saying that freedom and well-being are, in Gewirth's eyes, things of value only because we desire them; they are not things that we need to value, and hence are obligated to value, because in the first place they are valuable in themselves. In other words, our original esteem for freedom and well-being does not proceed from any sense of obligation or duty at all. Instead, the obligation and the duty come later, when from a necessary inclination toward our own freedom and well-being we are supposedly compelled to recognize that we have certain duties and obligations to promote the freedom and well-being of others.

But there is an even deeper reason why Gewirth might wish to look the other way, when it comes to applying the Euthyphro principle, and particularly to invoking that one feature of the principle according to which certain of our human ends and purposes—like freedom and well-being—so far from being valued merely because we desire them, are rather things that we should or ought to desire because of their inherent worth. For no sooner might Gewirth resort to such considerations, than he would suddenly find himself in an entirely different ethical ball game from the one we are all accustomed to today between teleologists and deontologists. Or rather than a different ball game, it might be better to stick with our earlier metaphor and speak of an altogether different battleground, namely, that of traditional natural law ethics, as one might call it, the type of ethics associated with Plato and Aristotle in the ancient world, or with Aquinas in the Middle Ages, and possibly with Hooker in the modern period.

Unfortunately, on such a battlefield Gewirth's otherwise magnificent armor would seem ill-suited and out of place. For how would he deal with a type of ethics which refuses to take for granted what to him appears so evident as to be beyond question? Thus in the context of a natural law ethic, morality is not to be thought of as being primarily, not to say exclusively, other-directed; rather, it is fundamentally, and in the first instance, self-directed. The properly human good, or the good for man, is man's own natural or proper telos; and unlike the *telē* of modern teleological ethics, such an end consists not of such objects of desire as are good only because they are desired; rather it is desired because it is seen to be good. Not only that, but a man's telos, conceived as his fulfillment and perfection as a human person, is something that the human individual has a moral obligation to try to bring about. And after all, is it so strange that, as less than perfect individuals, we should have a responsibility, as it were, to make something of ourselves, and to become that which as human persons we are naturally ordered to becoming? So it is that our development of ourselves in our jobs and in our professions, in our community and in our religious life, and indeed in our entire lives as persons, so far from being the sorts of things that can be written off as having to do only with so-called nonmoral goods, is rather that which is the very substance of the moral life itself.

And as for others—that is, our neighbors and fellow human beings—is it so far-fetched to suppose that we need to recognize that we are by nature political animals? For the matter of that, who knows but that by nature we may be children of God as well? (After all, the thing is at least conceivable!) Very well, then, our very duties and responsibilities to ourselves as persons must incorporate countless duties and responsibilities to our neighbors, to our families, to our professional associates, to our fellow citizens, and perhaps even to God. How different, and even in a way how alien, all of this is from what one finds in the context of a deontological ethics like Gewirth's. For there, having recognized that our own freedom and well-being are of course things of value to us, we must at the same time recognize that they are of value as nonmoral goods. And then, from the fact that we value these as nonmoral goods for ourselves, we are supposedly bound to recognize the equal value—but this time a moral value—of the freedom and well-being of all other human beings. But even supposing the logic of this connection to hold, is there not something questionable about such a dissociation of the objects of our duties from all objects of our love and interest? For logic aside, how binding are duties going to seem to be to us, if the objects of those duties are quite dissociated from all concern with ourselves as persons and with what we ourselves want to be and ought to be as individuals? Must not a mere duty for duty's sake eventually appear to be not really a duty at all?

Clearly, though, all of this is another story from anything that Gewirth seriously addresses himself to in *Reason and Morality*. But then, no less is it all another story from anything that contemporary moral philosophers, either teleologists or deontologists, are inclined to address themselves to either. Why, then, should Gewirth be expected to have bothered with an entire approach to ethics which is no longer à la mode, and the issues of which are scarcely heeded at all anymore? Besides, it must surely seem not just captious, but even churlish, that we should wish to fault Gewirth's achievement in *Reason and Morality*, when we would be the first to admit that what he has attempted to bring off in this book, and in such painstaking detail, is something that no other contemporary moral philosopher, be he teleologist or deontologist, has ever been able to bring off at all. Granted! Yet for all that, while we cannot deny that Gewirth's achievement would be something absolutely nonpareil, if he has really succeeded, has he entirely succeeded? And if he has not succeeded, might he not then be well advised to look to another, even if seemingly outmoded, type of moral philosophy, which though conceived very differently from his, might nevertheless provide him with a possible issue out of his difficulties? Indeed, the very "stone which the builders rejected" could well be the "one to become the head of the corner."

9

ETHICAL EGOISM, NEW STYLE: SHOULD ITS TRADEMARK BE LIBERTARIAN OR ARISTOTELIAN?

Who does not sense that a distinctive new style has begun to manifest itself in recent moral philosophy, perhaps not in Britain so much, but certainly in America. And what is this new style if not that of a veritable Ethical Egoism,[1] or perhaps Rational Individualism, as some of its proponents would prefer to call it? Moreover, what might be taken principally to characterize this new style is its determined divergence from the prevailing fashions of Ethical Altruism, which are characteristic no less of the various strains of Utilitarianism (or Ethical Teleology, as it is wont to be called in modern ethics), than of such Deontological types of ethical theory as stem originally from Kant.

Thus we are all familiar with how in the several varieties of Utilitarianism their proponents invariably begin with talk about how nothing can be reckoned to be of worth or value for an individual, save only his own good or happiness or pleasure; and then, no less invariably, these same Utilitarians end by insisting that what morally or

---

1. Throughout this paper I intend to follow the uncommon, and hence perhaps questionable, practice of always capitalizing such nouns as are used to designate anything even approximating a philosophical school or movement—yes, even a would-be such approximation. This is only for purposes of identification, and not of either advertising or approbation.

No less does my use in this paper of the terms, Egoism and Altruism, call for explanation, and perhaps even apology, right at the start. Originally of a provenance largely within the Utilitarian tradition, I am proposing to use these terms in such a way as to bend and perhaps twist their meaning to an extent that will allow any ethical position that considers the flourishing or perfection of the human individual himself to be the end or goal in ethics as being an Egoism. On the other hand, any ethical position that holds that morality is an affair of human beings being obliged to be primarily other-regarding rather than self-regarding in their conduct and behavior—such a position I will simply designate as being an Altruism. The result will be that I will even go so far as to characterize an Aristotelian type of ethics as being Egoistic, and a Kantian type of ethics as being Altruistic. True, this may be forcing things both linguistically and historically, but so be it.

ethically an individual ought to work toward is not his own good or happiness at all, but rather the greatest happiness of the greatest number. Moreover, so far as Kant and the Kantians are concerned, the pursuit of one's own interests or one's own happiness is held to be of no moral worth whatever. On the contrary, human beings being rational beings, they ought to act in accordance with what reason dictates; and clearly there can be no way that reason can be said to prescribe, as being what we ought to do, that which we are merely impelled to do by nature—*i.e.*, as a result of our natural, and, if you will, purely animal, inclinations and desires and interests. Hence the rational prescriptions of morality will be those which one can recognize as being universalizable, in the sense of their abstracting from all particular interests and desires that individual human beings may have simply by virtue of their nonrational or animal nature. Instead, a proper moral imperative such as is prescribed by one's rational nature will be one that requires one so to act that one can will that the very maxim of one's action should be nothing less than a universal law, or that one so act as always to treat human nature, whether in one's own person or in that of another, always as an end and never merely as a means. In other words, the very nature of morality requires that our actions never be merely self-regarding (*i.e.*, Egoistic), but always other-regarding, and therefore Altruistic, in the sense in which we are choosing to use that term.

Very well, then, to return to the matter of the new breed of Ethical Individualists or Egoists, it should now be easy to guess just how they tend to react to all of these prevailing fashions of Altruism. "Why," they say, "it is no less foolish than it is perverse thus to insist that a human being—*i.e.*, a being who can be said to be both rational and free—ought not (*i.e.*, it is morally wrong for him) to concern himself with simply making something of himself, with being or becoming something simply as the individual human person that he is. For what other life does a human being have to live, or what other does he need to live, but simply his own? And what else could possibly make sense to a person of sense, and having a sense of responsibility as to what he may and should do with his own life, but that he seek to make the most of it? After all, it being one's own life that is at stake, it would seem that sense and reason both would require that one take one's responsibilities in just this regard most seriously. And if this commits one to embracing an Egoism or an Individualism, so far as the living of one's own life is concerned, so what?"

Moreover, if you ask just who or what this new breed of moral philosophers might be, who would thus repudiate so decisively the prevailing fashions of Altruism in contemporary ethics, one might respond by remarking that in recent years many of them have not been averse to taking unto themselves the name of Libertarians.[2] After all, like so many whose formative years were in the '60s and '70s, not a few of the newly emergent moral philosophers found themselves captivated, often as undergraduates, by the novels and other writings of Ayn Rand.[3] Futher, it might not be too misleading to say that what one might call the spirit of the so-called "Yuppies" is a spirit that many of the new Rational Egoists or Rational Individualists in moral philosophy have found not uncongenial to themselves.

Be all of that as it may, however, the immediate point to bear in mind about our latter-day Libertarian Egoists is that, whatever their origins and antecedents may be, what they all seem to be united in now is in the repudiation of Altruism and in the championing Egoism. Unfortunately, however, no sooner does one say this than one is forced to admit that, presumably like all "true Love," the course of Ethical Egoism seems never to "run smooth"—at least not given the present dispensation in matters of moral philosophy. For it would seem that almost without exception almost all of the worthies of the present-day ethical-philosophical establishment tend for the most part simply to

---

2. Immediately, the use of this designation, "Libertarian," calls for both explanation and apology. For one thing, the term is far from having any univocal sense or application, covering as it does an almost bewildering variety of saints and sinners alike. For another thing, it might well be said that the primary incidence of the term has to do for the most part with thinkers and political activists, whose principal concerns are with questions of economics (they are so-called "Classical Liberals") and of government (they are opposed to so-called "big government"). Moreover, even among those whose primary concern is with philosophical questions of morals and ethics, one finds a wide diversity of views and opinions, ranging all of the way from Hobbesians, Lockeans, and even partisans of more classical theories of natural law, as represented by Aristotle and Aquinas. Besides, let it be noted that in speaking of "Libertarians," we are not to be taken as referring to the members of any particular political party.

Although it may not be anything if not gratuitous to mention any items that might belong in a proper bibliography, the following might be singled out as having been rather particularly helpful to me: David Norton, *Personal Destinies* (Princeton University Press, 1976); Robert Nozick, *Anarchy, State, and Utopia* (New York: Basic Books, 1974); Murray N. Rothbard, *The Ethics of Liberty* (Atlantic Highlands, NJ: Humanities Press, 1982); Tibor Machan, *Human Rights and Human Liberties* (Chicago: Nelson-Hall Co., 1975); Tibor Machan, ed., *The Libertarian Reader* (Totowa, NJ: Rowman and Littlefield, 1982); John Gray, *Liberalism* (University of Minnesota Press, 1986); Loren E. Lomasky, *Persons, Rights, and the Moral Community* (Oxford University Press, 1987). Perhaps also to be mentioned are three books in manuscript that I have had the good fortune to read, one on Rational Individualism by J. Charles King, another by John Kekes, and still a third book by Douglas Den Uyl and Douglas Rasmussen, on what they would call "a neo-Aristotelian approach to natural law."

3. For a most illuminating treatment of the implications for philosophy of the thought of Ayn Rand, see the excellent book edited by Douglas J. Den Uyl and Douglas B. Rasmussen, *The Philosophic Thought of Ayn Rand* (University of Illinois Press, 1984).

dismiss Ethical Egoism out of hand, and not just the Egoism of Libertarians, but any Egoism. "For how can it ever be a proper ethics," these establishment ethicists ask in effect, "if it takes as its point of departure the slogan 'Think first only of yourself.' But no," their answer is, "in anything that can qualify as a proper ethics, the slogan should be, 'Think always of others before yourself.'" Thus, for example, consider some of the cursory remarks that the eminent Bernard Williams makes in the opening chapter of his most recent book, *Ethics and the Limits of Philosophy*.[4] For Williams begins with a subtle and somewhat dialectical treatment of what he designates as being Socrates' question, the question simply as to how one should live. And of course, Williams observes, one cannot very well address oneself to such a question without taking account of the various kinds of considerations that have a bearing on such actions as we cannot very well avoid engaging in in the very living of our lives. Moreover, in order the better to determine just which of such considerations are of a clearly ethical import, one would do well—or at least so Professor Williams thinks—to consider first some of the considerations that are clearly not of ethical import. And of these latter, Williams asserts that "there is one very obvious candidate"—*i.e.*, a candidate for the role of "considerations that bear on action, but are *not* ethical considerations." Among these, Williams continues, are simply "the considerations of egoism, those that relate merely to the comfort, excitement, self-esteem, power or other advantages of the agent."[5]

And with that mere stroke of his pen, the eminent Professor Williams would appear to have ostracized for good and all any kind of Egoism from the assembly of reputable types of moral philosophy. All the same, having thus seemed summarily to dismiss Egoism as being a proper kind of ethics, Williams almost immediately would appear to qualify his dismissal by remarking: "We are concerned with Socrates' question, 'how one should live,' and egoism, in the unvarnished and baldly self-interested sense, is at any rate an intelligible answer to that, even though most of us would reject it."[6] And why do "most of us" thus hasten to reject egoism as an answer to the ethical question of how one should live? To which Williams' response is seemingly almost as bland as it is condescending: "However vague it may initially be, we have a conception of the ethical that understandably relates to us and our actions the demands, needs, claims, desires, and, generally,

---

4. Cambridge, MA: Harvard University Press, 1985.
5. *Ibid.*, p. 11.
6. *Ibid.*, pp. 11–12.

the lives of other people, and it is helpful to preserve the conception in what we are prepared to call an ethical consideration."[7]

Now in the face of such a pronouncement, as it were, *de haut en bas*, and from out of the obvious pride of place that Williams arrogates to himself, one can well imagine all of our latter-day young Egoists in ethics protesting at once loudly and vigorously. "Why," they will say, "it surely requires more than Williams' mere *ipse dixit* as to what 'our conception of the ethical' involves, or does not involve, for it to be determined, as it were for good and all, that Egoism, despite its admitted intelligibility as an answer to Socrates' question as to how one should live, must nonetheless be rejected as an answer. After all, why should a concern on our part with our own 'demands, needs, claims, desires'—yes, a concern with no less than our own very 'lives'—nonetheless be a concern and a consideration that is simply not relevant to ethics at all? And on the other hand, is it not equally odd that so many professional moral philosophers would appear so uncritically to accept almost the inverse of the above proposition, namely, that until people's demands, needs, claims, desires, *et al.* are clearly recognized as being those of persons other than ourselves, such demands, needs, claims, etc. cannot be recognized as properly moral or ethical concerns at all. Surely, that is nothing if not just plain farfetched!"

"Nor is that all," we can imagine the Rational Egoist or Individualist continuing, "for is it not clear that Williams would appear, at once gratuitously and uncritically, to equate any and every sort of Egoism simply with what he calls 'egoism in the unvarnished and baldly self-interested sense'? And yet surely, any Egoism that would put itself forward as offering a proper answer to Socrates' question as to how one should live would hardly be likely to be an Egoism of the unvarnished and baldly self-interested kind. Instead, one can readily imagine that the philosophically sophisticated Egoist or Individualist would be the first to recognize that almost any Egoist, in reckoning seriously with his own demands, needs, claims, and desires, such as these arise in his own life, would certainly both want and need to take cognizance of such demands, needs, claims, desires, etc. as pertain to the lives of others. After all, their needs and desires and claims can hardly be completely separated and divorced from his own, it being the case that 'no man is an island,' and that the concerns and needs of others being integral to our own are somehow inseparable from our own. So it is, therefore, that any truly sophisticated Egoist would be the first to acknowledge that to be fully self-regarding one must certainly be other-regarding at the same time."

7. *Ibid.*, p. 12.

But Is Not the Principle of Universalizability the Real Stumbling Block for Any Philosophical Egoism?

Let this then suffice—what we have just developed in the paragraphs immediately preceding—by way of an initial line of answer on the part of the present-day Egoist to the sort of casual, not to say unargued, dismissal of Egoism that one encounters nowadays in establishment thinkers such as Williams. Still, for all of that, it seems that the Egoist has a long way to go, if he is ever fully to make his case for Egoism, given the bias toward altruism that is so characteristic of fashionable moral philosophy in the present day. And particularly, what the Egoist needs to come to grips with is the classical argument in refutation of Egoism that dates back to G. E. Moore,[8] or perhaps even before, and that attempts to show, in terms of mere logical and linguistic considerations alone, that any Egoism in ethics is necessarily self-refuting.[9] Yes, the contention of the argument seems to run that the Egoist cannot even so much as formulate his position of Egoism without his finding himself committed to an Altruism after all—and that by nothing less than the very terms of his own argument.

What, then, is this argument, and how is the Egoist to respond to it? Admittedly, the underlying principle of the argument is the so-called Principle of Universalizability. And this Principle, as formulated by William Frankena, for example, simply affirms that "moral and value predicates are such that if they belong to any action or object, they also belong to any other action or object that has the same properties."[10] Moreover, what is curiously significant about such a principle is that it seems to point up a quite striking difference between so-called moral or value words on the one hand, and all of the other run-of-the-mill words, on the other hand, that tend to be predicated of actions and objects, so far as such actions and objects reflect but our various needs, desires, likings, preferences, demands, etc. Thus, for instance, consider the difference between saying of a certain object or action (1) that it is good, or that it ought to be done, etc., and saying of the same object or action (2) that it is something that we like or desire, or that it pleases us, or that we want it, etc.

Clearly, so far as (1) is concerned, if I affirm that X is really of value, or that it is something that ought to be done, then clearly I

---

8. See *Principia Ethicia*, ch. III, sec. C (Cambridge, MA: The University Press, 1908).

9. For all that we know, this Moorean refutation of Egoism may have affinities with Kantian arguments to the same effect.

10. V. William K. Frankena, *Ethics* (Englewood Cliffs, NJ: Prentice Hall, second edition, 1973), p. 25.

imply that, X being thus really of value, it must be acknowledged to be of value not just for me, but no less for anyone and everyone else as well. Or likewise, if I say that X ought to be done, then I imply that it is not something that it is merely incumbent upon me to do, but rather that it is equally incumbent upon anyone and everyone to do, given similar circumstances. In other words, moral or value predicates, it would appear, do indeed turn out to be universalizable, just as the Principle states.

But contrast such predicates as are applicable to actions and objects, but that are not value words or moral words—for instance words that are descriptive of such actions and objects as might reflect what Williams calls the several wants, desires, preferences, likings, etc. that we all so continually experience during the course of our lives. Thus if I say that such and such an object is very much a thing that I desire and want, it certainly does not follow that such an object can therefore be declared to be desired and wanted by any and all alike, given similar circumstances. Or again, if I say that I like X, or that I find it pleasing, it certainly does not follow that anyone and everyone else must like it, or find it pleasing, as well. In other words, it is a part of the import of the Principle of Universalizability that moral and value predicates, as it were, just do behave differently from all other predicates that are lacking in the express moral or value import that explicitly moral and value terms have.

All right, given the character of this Principle of Universalizability, and its clear implication of the difference between moral and value terms on the one hand and such terms as are not of this character on the other, then just how is it that this Principle is able to be exploited so as to effect a refutation of Egoism, and, as it were, a refutation that would seem to proceed from out of the very mouth of the Egoist himself? In answer, may we not say of any Egoist that his chief contention is that he means to recognize no other good than simply his own good—which is to say, his own flourishing or his own prosperity or his own well-being, simply as an individual? Applying the Principle, then, will not one be able to say to the Egoist: "No sooner do you contend that you have reason simply to take your own happiness or well-being as being that which is good, and indeed as being the only good or the ultimate good, so far as you are concerned, than you must immediately acknowledge, by virtue of the application of the Universalizability Principle, that the other fellow has no less reason than you do to reckon his happiness and his well-being as being his ultimate good, or as that which is the sole good for him? But then, it would appear that in spite of your professed Egoism, you must now admit that there are other goods in the world besides your own good. Not only that, but if the fact that something is good or of value is precisely that which gives one a warrant or a justification for pursuing or seeking after such a thing, and if your own warrant or justification for pursuing that which you take to be good or of value is no better than the other fellow's warrant or justification for pursuing his good, then there would seem to be no ground on which you can possibly claim that your pursuit of your good should in any way take precedence over his pursuit of his."

But with this, is not the Egoist thereby completely undone, and condemned to a recognition of an Altruism, directly by his own words and out of his own mouth? Not only must he admit that there are other goods besides his own, but also that others have no less reason for pursuing their goods than he has for pursuing his. Worse still, having been brought this far, the Egoist would now seem unable to escape the still further consequence that his very Egoism commits him to nothing less than an Altruism in the end—and that by virtue of the very "logical grammar" of the terms of his own argument. True, he might think that he could just roll with the punch of the Universalizability Principle, and freely admit that there are indeed other goods or values beside his own, and that others are no less justified in pursuing their goods than he his. And so he might then hope to be able to go on to argue that merely because he has to acknowledge that others besides himself have their own goods and values, as well as he his, that in no way means that he is therefore committed to helping them attain their goods, any more than that they are committed to helping him attain his. "Rather," he might say, "it's a case in which each man would be clearly justified—morally justified, that is—in being out for himself alone, and not for anyone else. And why would not the prevalence of such a contention but confirm the contentions of Egoism, and this without the slightest concession being made to any sort of Altruism?"

But no, even such a last stand of the embattled Egoist, it would seem, is one he would not be able to sustain. For consider the following quotation from Sidgwick, which is cited by Williams.

> I obtain the self-evident principle that the good of any one individual is of no more importance, from the point of view (if I may say so) of the Universe, than the good of any other ... and it is evident to me that as a rational being I am bound to aim at good generally—so far as it is attainable by my efforts—not merely at a particular part of it.[11]

---

11. Quoted in Williams, *op. cit.*, p. 105.

With this, however, the very Egoism of the Egoist apparently thus turns out to commit him to just such an inescapable Altruism as by the terms of his own Egoism he particularly wished to avoid: if his own good is no more truly a good than that of any other man, and if a thing's being good is that, and that alone, which can justify or warrant a person's seeking after it, then clearly one has no more ground or warrant for seeking one's own good than he has for seeking the other man's good as well. Worse yet, since the good is no other than that which one ought (*i.e.*, morally ought) to seek after and pursue, then any and every individual is nothing if not morally bound to promote and seek after the good of others no less than his own. In other words, there would seem to be no escaping the fact that there is just no alternative to Altruism for anyone who would give answer to Socrates' question—*i.e.*, to the question Williams simply designates as being the ethical question of how one should live.

Need we say more, then, than that, so far as any contemporary Egoist is concerned, the absolutely inescapable demand or requirement that is placed upon him is that he must find some means of either answering or of obviating the implications of the so-called Principle of Universalizability? For failing this, he has no alternative but to recognize that his Egoism, taken as being a reputable philosophical position, is nothing if not simply dead in the water! Alas, though, so far as our contemporary crop of Egoists are concerned, particularly the recently emergent Libertarian Egoists, they just don't seem able to come up with any very satisfactory response to the challenge of the Principle of Universalizability.

First Attempts at a Response to the Seemingly Altruistic Implications of the Principle of Universalizability

This does not mean, however, that the Libertarian Egoists do not indulge in any amount of kicking and screaming in the face of the Altruistic consequences that appear to be forced upon them by the Universalizability Principle. And yet kicking and screaming would seem scarcely to constitute a proper refutation of what would seem to be a rather tight philosophical argument. Thus for instance, one thing that the Libertarian Egoists like to do is to try to show that however valid the so-called Refutation of Egoism would appear to be, the particular kind of Altruism that tends to be so much touted as being a necessary consequence of the Refutation displays features that quite patently are nothing if not counterintuitive. Thus, for example, it is pointed out that if, by the requirements of the current Altruism, I may never rightfully place my own concerns and those of such others as are near and dear to me ahead of the concerns of anyone else, no matter who she or he may be, then the consequence can only be that it would be nothing less than morally wrong of me were I ever to give the slightest priority to the concerns and interests of members of my own family, say, over those of others utterly remote from me and whom I presumably don't even know at all—say the inhabitants of Outer Mongolia, or of Tierra del Fuego. But is not this just plain counterintuitive?

Or again, the Libertarians like to point out how utterly farfetched it would seem to be that so many of the supposed authorities on moral philosophy in the present day seem ever given to counseling us that what morality requires of us is precisely that we put aside all of our own private and personal concerns and interests and preoccupations—things that we are most passionately and deeply implicated in in our daily lives—and that, instead, we learn to assume what it is now fashionable to call "the moral point of view" (Baier). And what does such a moral point of view demand of us, if not that we henceforth cultivate an attitude of strict and absolute "impartiality" or detachment; or, again, that we become nothing if not mere "ideal observers" (Firth), as the fashionable term now is.[12]

And yet what could be more ridiculous than all of this, just on the face of it? Indeed, imagine how a Kierkegaard, say, might make fun of such recommendations by professorial moralists. For do we not all of us have but one life to lead? And yet what could possibly be of more moment to us than what we ourselves shall make of ourselves, and what we shall thereby be and become? Thus rather than being impartial and detached, is there anything that any man ought to be more passionately concerned with than with his own fate, his own salvation, and what he himself does with himself? Yes, if such be what the so-called moral point of view supposedly requires of us, that we be utterly impartial and mere ideal observers, even with respect to ourselves and our own lives, then it is hard to imagine anything that would seem more farfetched and more absurd.

All the same, telling as such sallies by Libertarians might well seem to be against the consequences of our cultivating an attitude of strict impartiality as being the only appropriate one in the matter of our

---

12. For a very effective marshalling of some of the more egregious examples of the curious and counter-intuitive formulations of their position that present-day Altruists indulged in, see the article by Jon Kekes, entitled "Morality and Impartiality," *American Philosophical Quarterly*, Vol. 18, No. 4, October 1981.

human moral concerns, still it must be acknowledged that this by no means suffices as a proper refutation of that very Refutation of Egoism that seems to be the inescapable logical consequence of the Principle of Universalizability. And so the real question that our Libertarian Egoists must face up to, it would seem, is just the question of what they propose to do about the so-called Principle of Universalizability. And in this matter, present-day Libertarian Egoists are apparently inclined to follow one or the other of two courses. Some try to deny that the Principle of Universalizability needs to be considered as being necessarily applicable to moral or ethical concerns at all. Others among the Libertarians, while not denying the Principle's applicability altogether, would nonetheless want to limit the sphere of its applicability, and to do so in such a way that the Principle can no longer be used as an effective instrument in the refutation of Egoism.

Accordingly, let us consider the latter of these two alternatives first. For it is in this connection that the Libertarians tend to use the tactic of simply asking why any Egoist need worry at all with the question of what the true good of man, or the good of the human individual, may be. For as soon as one asks what the good is for any one individual, then the Principle immediately seems to take over, with the consequence that whatever it may be that is held to be the good of Tom, say, considered simply as a human being, must then be held to be the good of any and every other human individual in similar circumstances—*i.e.*, of Dick and Harry as well. Hence rather than to get caught up in these particular toils of Universalizability, many Libertarians are simply inclined to ask, "Why would it not be better simply to recognize that there just is no such thing as *the* good of man? Instead, there are as many different goods as there are human individuals, such so-called goods being no more than what different individuals regard as being good for them, just in the sense that they are what each of these several different individuals regards as being good for him in the sense of being what he personally happens to like or to enjoy or to cherish or whatever.[13] Accordingly, once 'good' is

---

13. The point that is here being made turns on what has sometimes been called the application of the *Euthyphro* test. Thus in the dialogue of the *Euthyphro*, it will be recalled, Socrates asks whether things are said to be good, only because they are desired; or whether they are desired, precisely because they are good, and are seen to be so. Clearly, in the former sense, "good" is something purely relative, and relative simply to whether such things happen to be liked or desired or sought after by this, that, or the other human being. In the latter sense, on the other hand, "good" is an adjective which is applied to things as they are in themselves, and in this latter sense, on the other hand, "good" is the adjective which is applied to things as they are in themselves, and in this latter and non-relative sense, "good" is clearly universalizable.

taken in this purely relative sense, then the Principle of Universalizability can no longer take over, so to speak, with the unhappy result that the other man's good being recognized as no less good than is mine, I seem to have no alternative but to admit that I am no less bound (morally) to pursue his good than I am to pursue my own—which is just the consequence of the sort of Altruism that as an Egoist I want to avoid.

"Accordingly, to avoid this consequence I have only to put aside all such talk of what *the* good of man may happen to be, and to recognize that there are as many goods as there are human individuals. Moreover, having recognized this much, then, as a Libertarian Egoist, my next concern will naturally be for me somehow to have it guaranteed me that, whatever my own good as I see it may be, I nevertheless be allowed to pursue that good without interference or hindrance from others. To this end, accordingly, I want it recognized that I have a 'right'—yes, no less than a moral right—thus to do my own thing and to seek my own good as I see it. And indeed, is this not just where morals and ethics enter the picture for a Libertarian—not in connection with what we call 'goods,' but rather in connection first of all with what we call 'rights'—individual rights, that is to say."

And with this, may we not all now begin to see just where and how it is that this kind of a stance or position on the part of a Libertarian Egoist can claim to be a proper morals or ethics? For its point of entry into the domain of morals or ethics is not, as we have just seen, at that point at which so-called "goods" make their appearance in the picture, but rather at the point at which "rights" do. That is to say, what the Libertarian is most anxious to have guaranteed for him morally and ethically is that he have the right to do his own thing, or to pursue his own good, whatever he may take that to be. And so it is that morals or ethics for him will turn out to be essentially an affair of individual rights, and thus not at all a matter of determining what the true good or end or goal or, as Aristotle called it, the *telos* of man may be.

Moreover, so far as the Principle of Universalizability is concerned, it should now be clear that with this particular species or brand of Libertarians, the Principle does not have its incidence, so to speak, with respect to human goods at all, but only with respect to human rights. And there it will be applicable indeed. For not only on such a basis will any one individual be able to be said to have the right to seek his own good and pursue his own goals, without interference from others, but so also all other individuals will have no less a right to pursue, each of them, his own good or goods as he sees them. Likewise, to each such right, thus claimed by each individual to do his own thing and to live his own life as he chooses and thinks best, so also will there be an answering duty, incumbent upon each and all other individuals, to respect this right of the first individual. And no less will the first individual in turn have a duty to respect the comparable rights of all others to do each his own thing in turn.[14] And with that, do we not have the basis and ground for an entire moral order of reciprocal rights and duties? Not only that, but such a moral order will be an order that can only be described as that of a thoroughgoing Ethical Egoism or Individualism. And with that, it would seem that our Libertarian Egoist could now properly boast that he has thereby turned the tables on the Altruist, and has done so without really compromising the Principle of Universalizability at all. Instead, he has but shown how the Principle of Universalizability, applicable though it be, is nonetheless applicable in but a very determinate sphere and area, that of rights and duties, and not that of the good.

But for all of his ingenious moves of trying to shift the area of applicability of the Principle from that of goods and values to that of rights, and then, by extension, to duties as well, the Libertarian is still not home free! For the great unanswered question for him now is: On just what basis may it thus be claimed that individuals have such rights, and, more specifically, rights not to be interfered with in their lives, but rather to be able to pursue whatever ends or goals or projects they as individuals may happen to have, or choose to have? For just what is there about mere human "projects," to borrow a felicitous term of Loren Lomasky's[15]—*i.e.*, such projects as those simply of pursuing one's own particular goals or ends or goods as one sees them—what is there about this undeniable fact of human "project-pursuit" that enables one to say that no less than a moral right attaches to such a project-pursuit, a right, namely, that one's projects may not be impeded or interfered with by others?

Be it recalled, after all, how Hume pointed out that it was simply a fallacy for one to try to infer an "ought" from an "is." And now what is it that our Libertarian Egoists are attempting to do, if not something

---

14. The particular line of argument that is used here is not unlike the line of argument that has been devised by Alan Gewirth, and turns on what he, Gewirth, calls the Principle of Generic Consistency. This principle of Gewirth's we have subjected to considerable scrutiny and criticism in various places, but particularly in the foregoing essay, reprinted above in this same section, and entitled, "In Appreciation and In Refutation of Alan Gewirth's Principle of Categorical Consistency."

15. See his excellent book, *Persons, Rights, and the Moral Community* (New York and Oxford: Oxford University Press, 1987). This book would seem to afford a very illuminating discussion of how the Altruistic consequences of the application of the Principle of Universalizability can perhaps best be evaded or avoided.

very much like that? From the mere fact that I have my own projects, and you yours, and the other person his or hers, our Libertarians would like to infer that because we human beings thus do each of us eagerly pursue his or her own projects, we must therefore be adjudged to have a right to such project-pursuit, and a right that everyone else has a duty to respect. But that is simply a *non sequitur*. For however much I may be eager to throw myself into my own projects and give myself over to their pursuit, that in no way proves that I have any moral right to pursue such projects as I have chosen. Nor does anyone else. After all, where does such a right, supposedly on the part of each, just to do his own thing come from? Does it simply descend upon our projects like manna from heaven?

No sooner, though, has the one school of Libertarian Egoists thus found themselves frustrated in their efforts to salvage a proper Libertarian ethics or moral philosophy, by restricting the range of applicability of the Principle of Universalizability to the area of rights and duties alone, than other Libertarians[16] have then come along and suggested that the Principle of Universalizability might perhaps be discarded altogether. For why assume that there is the radical difference between moral words and nonmoral words, such as the Principle would appear to presuppose and to enunciate? Instead, why not consider that such things as our personal interests, our desires, our projects, our satisfactions, while they may not as such be things we may claim to have a moral right to pursue, are nevertheless things that we certainly want to pursue, and thus want to be free to pursue? And why may not this freedom to pursue our projects be something that might well be guaranteed, not by the invocation of any moral rights on our part to pursue our own projects, or of any duty on the part of others to refrain from interfering with our projects, but rather simply by appeals to the self-interest and advantage of all parties concerned in any and all matters concerned with such project-pursuit?[17]

"After all," so we may imagine a Libertarian to argue in this connection, "my neighbor and fellow citizens have no less an interest in their projects, and in their being able to pursue their projects without interference from me, than I do in pursuing my projects without in-

---

16. I am not too sure just which, or even whether any Libertarian thinkers would subscribe, in so many words, to the sort of ethical position that I am about to outline—a position that seeks to dispense with moral words, and hence moral judgments, altogether, relying instead upon counsels of self-interest and personal advantage alone. It is a position of much this sort that would seem to be suggested in the work of Charles King (see note 2 above) and also at times of Loren Lomasky.

17. This is the felicitous term that Professor Lomasky both uses and exploits to the full.

terference from them. Why, then, might it not be possible for us to work out some sort of a deal between us: I won't interfere with you, if you won't interfere with me?" "After all," so one might continue in this line of reasoning, "none of us need be reminded of the lesson that Hobbes managed to impress so indelibly upon our consciousness, as far back as the 17th century, that, barring some sort of compact between individuals, the upshot of a situation in which each individual in society (or, as Hobbes would have it, in a state of nature) would be engaged simply in doing his own thing, or in pursuing his own interests, without regard for anyone else—that kind of a condition of things is bound to lead to a 'war of all against all.' So why not enter into a mutual compact or agreement with one another, in which I agree not to hurt you so long as you agree not to hurt me? It's as simple as that."

"In fact," so our champion of such a Libertarian persuasion might continue, "maybe not even an actual contract or agreement between neighbors or fellow citizens would be necessary. For why need one suppose that life in society must necessarily be an affair of mutual rights and duties at all—even of rights and duties as merely defined, say, by a social contract? Instead, why is it not enough but to recognize that true peace and order in society require no more than an intelligent regard, simply on the part of each and every individual, for nothing more than his own self-interest? For this, and this alone, it would seem, ought to lead an individual to understand, and understand clearly, that the minute he seeks to gain an advantage for himself, however slight, by in some way or other overreaching his neighbor, he is bound to suffer in the long run—and this for no other reason than that if he overreaches his neighbor, that neighbor sooner or later is going to overreach him.[18] Accordingly, rather than any formal contract or compact that would supposedly invest the parties to the contract with mutual rights and obligations, all that might be necessary would be a clear-headed recognition on the part of each and all alike that it is nothing if not contrary to one's own self-interest that one should ever try to profit at another's expense.

"And with that, would it not seem that the need ever to assume anything like a moral point of view, or even to invoke devices like moral words or value words—*e.g.*, 'rights,' 'duties,' 'obligations,' 'responsibilities,' etc.—had simply been eliminated? Oh, it might be true

18. In Professor Lomasky's book (*op. cit.*) he has worked out in his chapter 4 a most intelligent kind of calculus of mutual self-interest, which conceivably ought to work out to a complete social harmony through no special human agency, but only through the operation of a modern equivalent of an "invisible hand."

that, merely as a matter of linguistic convention, if it were generally recognized as agreed between us that my neighbor would not injure me so long as I didn't injure him, I might fall into a certain habit of speaking in which I might talk of my 'rights' as over against my neighbor, or of his 'duties' or 'obligations' as over against me. But notice that the term 'rights,' or the term 'duties,' in such a context would have really no moral import or implication whatever. For suppose that my neighbor did move against me by way of force, fraud, or false witness, I could not properly say that there was anything morally 'wrong' in his so doing, but only that what he was doing was contrary to his own self-interest.

"Accordingly, why worry then about even the apparatus of any so-called social contract or compact? For instead of our having to be concerned either with fancied real rights or wrongs, or even with mere conventional rights and wrongs, is it not sufficient that we all of us try to reconcile ourselves to living under a condition in which all would occupy themselves with no more than a continuing and ongoing reckoning and calculation, each of his own self-interest? What more is needed for ensuring a true peace and order in the social or political community?"

In response, however, to any such Libertarian proposal simply to dispense even with any kind of moral universe of discourse altogether, would not one's initial response be one of deep doubt and unease as to whether we could ever reconcile ourselves to actually living amidst such a radically amoral state of affairs? Would we find it at all tolerable? Just imagine, for example, that, no matter what my neighbor might do to me, I could never say that his action was in any way wrong or unjust. No, at most it would only be contrary to his interest. And while it might be true that what my neighbor might do to me might be to my hurt or injury, there could never be said to be anything actually wrong in his thus injuring me; at most, it could only be said to be something that was to his own disadvantage, and that therefore he would be wise to refrain from doing.

Nor is this the only rejoinder that one might make to any such Libertarian proposal that not only morality but even any moral universe of discourse could be entirely dispensed with. For in addition, what else is it if not actually self-referentially inconsistent for the Libertarian thus to try to dispense with anything like a moral universe altogether? After all, how could our Libertarian Egoist even so much as make a move by way of justifying his own practice of a complete amoralism, without by that very fact appealing to moral or ethical considerations himself? For suppose that his justification should take the form of his arguing that if there be no warranted distinctions, either natural or conventional, between right and wrong, or between "ought" and "ought not," etc., then surely one could hardly require of him that he feel any responsibility or obligation to heed such distinctions in his own conduct and behavior. To which the obvious response would seem to be: "But if you say that you have no responsibility to observe moral distinctions, simply because there are no such things, are you not thereby implying that it is just the absence, or non-existence, of such distinctions that you think provide you with that very justification or warrant that you need for opting out of both the moral universe and moral discourse altogether? And yet by the very fact that you thus hold yourself to be thus warranted and justified in your not having to heed moral or ethical considerations—is not this very claim on your part to be thus warranted and justified in your conduct itself a moral or ethical claim? Not only that, but as a moral or ethical claim, it is necessarily universalizable; and by the very fact of such a universalizability of his own claim to be thus justified, any would-be amoralist would appear to be caught up in a moral universe of discourse after all, and thus, as it were, 'hoist by his own petar.' Q.E.D.!"

In fact, is it not patent that in any such self-referential difficulties as the would-be amoralist must inevitably find himself caught up in, what is really at stake is simply a business of his finding himself having to cite *reasons* for his actions, and not merely *causes*? Thus anyone—the amoralist, no less than the moralist—can perfectly well adduce all sorts of causes for his behaving the way he does, be it selfishly or unselfishly. He can cite evidence of the causal force of his body chemistry, or of his earlier psychological conditioning, or perhaps of the social pressures operating upon him—any or all of which might explain why he acts as he does. And yet so to explain one's own behavior in terms of causes is by no means the same as giving a reason why one's conduct is justified or warranted. However, when the amoralist attempts to justify his purely self-seeking or self-regarding behavior, such a justification has got to be in terms of reasons; and such reasons can only be in terms of moral words to the effect that it is "all right" or "justifiable," or entirely "warranted" that he act out of no regard for so-called moral considerations in the usual sense at all. In other words, even the attempt to justify a supposedly amoral stance or attitude can only be in terms of reasons, and the reasons can only be justifying reasons; nor can a justifying reason be anything other than a morally grounded reason.

"Oh," but one might say in response to all of this, "granted that as soon as the amoralist attempts to give reasons for his position, he is indeed caught in a self-referential inconsistency. For no kind of reason that anyone might give for a deliberately amoral course of action could ever be other than a moral reason. Still," one might continue, "why does the amoralist need to give any reasons in the first place? Why might he not simply refuse to be drawn into any business of trying to justify either what he is, or how he acts? By such means, then, it would seem that he could avoid the trap of a self-referential inconsistency."

True enough, and yet as soon as one comes up against someone who simply refuses on principle to give any reasons for what he does, or even in any way to try to justify his conduct and course of action, such a one must surely remind one of the kind of person of whom Aristotle speaks—who, not wanting to be trapped in an inconsistency by the answer he cannot escape having to give, simply refuses to answer at all. Such a one, Aristotle observes, by his simply refusing to respond, would be no better than a vegetable. And how can one reason with a vegetable?[19]

Could It Be that a More Aristotelian Kind of Egoism Can Deal with the Problem of the Universalizability Principle Better than the Usual Run of Libertarian Egoism?[20]

Does our foregoing section convey any other message than that if any position of Egoism in morals or ethics is ever to sustain or maintain itself, it will have to be by facing directly up to the problem of the so-called Principle of Universalizability, and by showing that such a Principle need in no way necessarily entail an Ethical Altruism at the expense of any sort of defensible Egoism? After all, we have seen how various Libertarian Egoists have sought to obviate the effects of the Principle, either by trying to limit its scope or by trying simply to deny its relevance altogether. But neither way has proved satisfactory.

Why not, then, try turning to Aristotle? For his is an Ethical Egoism that fully accepts the Principle of Universalizability, and yet shows that

19. *Cf. Metaphysics,* Book Γ, ch. 4, 1006 a 13–15. Strictly speaking, it should perhaps be noted that self-referential inconsistency in respect to so-called practical knowledge may be somewhat different from that that holds in the case of theoretical knowledge. *Cf.* my earlier discussion of this in my *Rational Man* (Bloomington, IN: Indiana University Press, 1962), pp. 43–46.

20. The implied contrast suggested in this heading between an Aristotelian and a Libertarian Egoism should not be misinterpreted. There are among the Libertarians not a few who would insist that their Libertarian Egoism is unmistakably of Aristotelian inspiration—*e.g.,* Professor Den Uyl and Professor Rasmussen, to mention but two such.

the supposed Altruistic implications of the Principle are nothing if not largely gratuitous. Oh, it's true that it may not be customary to characterize Aristotelian ethics as being necessarily an Egoism. And yet this is because the contrast between an Ethical Egoism on the one hand and an Ethical Altruism on the other is a contrast that arose originally in the context of discussions of Utilitarian ethics; and Aristotle's ethics can scarcely be fitted into any kind of Utilitarian framework. Instead, it would seem that so far as Aristotle's ethics is concerned, it may properly be interpreted as involving little more than so many counsels of perfection directed to the human individual, and including various instructions and recommendations of how it is that a human individual may go about the business of trying to perfect himself, and to become the sort of person that a human being ought to be. And, as Aristotle sees it, this involves nothing if not the attainment of what he calls happiness or *eudaimonia*. And by happiness Aristotle would understand simply a human being's fulfillment, or perfection, or well-being, or flourishing. Nor can there be any such thing as a proper human flourishing, or a human happiness, just in general. No, for the flourishing and happiness of human beings can only be that of human individuals, and one that is enjoyed by human individuals simply as individuals. Accordingly, it is in this light that one needs to interpret the opening sentences of the *Nicomachean Ethics*:

> Every art or applied science and every systematic investigation, and similarly every action and choice seem to aim at some good; the good therefore has been well defined as that at which all things aim.[21]

Put this way, however, it might at first seem that an Aristotelian Egoism so conceived must surely fall afoul of the Principle of Universalizability, with the result that any professed Aristotelian Egoism must inevitably turn out to be an Altruism after all. For if it be but the individual's own good, or his own perfection, that an Aristotelian ethics prescribes as being the end or goal, and hence the good that is to be sought after by the individual, would it not by the same token have to be acknowledged that the one individual's good is no less a good than the next man's, and so my neighbor's good is no less a good than my own? Accordingly, if the good be that which one ought to seek after and strive for, and if the other man's good be no less a good than my own, then it would seem that by the Principle of Universalizability I could have absolutely no reason or ground for showing even

21. *Nicomachean Ethics*, 1094 a 1–3.

the slightest partiality for my own good, as over against the good of each and everyone else. Accordingly, following out such a line of analysis, would it not seem that Aristotle himself had thereby become entrapped by the implications of the Principle of Universalizability, and would thus have to profess an Altruism in his ethics after all?

Not so fast, though! For in Aristotle's eyes, and in terms of his own explicit exposition, the predicate "good," even in being thus recognized as being universalizable, is not a predicate such as would need to be construed as connoting but a single universal, abstract Form or Idea of Goodness. That would be more Plato than Aristotle. Instead, in expounding his own view of the good,[22] as contrasted with that of Plato, Aristotle insists that for him whatever it is that one may hold the good to be, it must always be reckoned as being the good of him of whom, or of that of which, it is the good. It is in this sense, then, that, as Aristotle insists, the good of a fish is not the good of a human being; nor is the good of a tadpole that of a fir tree, etc.

Not only that, but the good, considered as that which is to be sought after and striven for, and which the individual in turn may be said to be under nothing less than an obligation to seek after and strive for[23]—such a good is never an absolute good, or a good in general, but rather is necessarily and always the individual's own good, or, if you will, his proper and characteristic good. And so it is that without in any way denying the Principle of Universalizability, it would seem that for an Aristotelian there is just no way in which it could ever be claimed that because "the good is that at which all things aim," I, as an individual, am therefore under obligation to aim at my neighbor's good no less than at my own.

This seems not only ridiculous just on its face, but also, once the Principle of Universalizability is rightly interpreted along Aristotelian lines, it can be seen that the Principle just does not have any such implications at all. For the good being always and necessarily the good of X, or the good of Y, etc., what follows in virtue of the Principle of Universalizability would be that the good of X, as universalized, would have to be acknowledged by anyone and everyone to be just that, the good of X, and similarly the good of Y to be the good of Y. But what would not follow would be that the good of X would have to be recognized as being the good of Y as well, or the good of Y as being the good of X, and indeed of anyone and everyone else beside X and Y— and this just in the sense that the Principle of Impartiality would take

---

22. *Cf.* Book I, ch. 9 of the *Nicomachean Ethics*.
23. See my discussion of the so-called *Euthyphro* principle, *infra*, pp. 196ff.

over, as it were, and X would have to recognize that he had no more reason to pursue his own good than to pursue Y's good, or for that matter than any other person's good.

True, there are many interpreters of the Principle of Universalizability who would insist that even the argument of the foregoing paragraph is still not sufficient to undermine the obligation of Altruism, as this would seem to be determined by the Principle of Universalizability, and so by implication of Impartiality as well. No, for however much it might be conceded that that which is said to be good must always be indexed, as it were, as being the good of X, or of Y, or of whomever or whatever, still there is the counter-argument to the effect that, after all, even the good of X, let us say, is nonetheless a good, and if, following the so-called First Principle of Practical Reason, as enunciated by St. Thomas Aquinas[24]—that good is always to be done and pursued, and evil shunned and avoided—the consequence would seem to be that the good of X, for all of its being indexed to X, is nonetheless good. And if, by St. Thomas' principle, good is to be done and to be sought after, and this without qualification, then even the good of X, however much it might be indexed to X, must nonetheless be recognized as good, and hence as that which ought to be done, or ought to be sought after, by Y no less than by X.

But no, this still will not do, as an implication of the Principle of Universalizability, and hence as a way of rehabilitating the Principle of Impartiality and hence of Altruism after all. Moreover, in order to see just how and why it is that the Principle of Universalizability need not be construed as having this seemingly rather odd and curious implication of Altruism, we might do well to invoke a somewhat elaborate apparatus for the explication of the notion of good, which is perhaps rather more Thomistic than it is Aristotelian.[25] Thus "good" having always to be understood as being the good of something, one might therefore quite properly say that the good of a thing stands to that thing of which it is the good, as no less than an end or *telos*, to be achieved by the thing in question. In fact, St. Thomas could even be said in a loose sense to "define" good or *bonum*, as simply being or *ens*, insofar as being or *ens* may be reckoned as an object of desire— which is to say as an end or goal to be attained. Yes, proceeding still further along this same line, the good of anything being no more than

---

24. *Cf. Summa Theologiae* I–II, Qu. 94, Ar. 2.
25. What follows is a highly abbreviated, not to say even somewhat doctrinaire, account of St. Thomas' understanding of good. For a rather fuller treatment, cf. my book *Human Rights* (Baton Rouge: Louisiana State University Press, 1985) ch. II, esp. pp. 67–86.

that which is that thing's end or goal, and hence as being the very perfection or fulfillment of itself which the thing in question is ordered to by its very nature, or that it may thus be said to desire, and to strive to attain, the consequence accordingly would appear to be that any good (or *bonum*) is to that of which it is the good as actuality is to potentiality. Nor do we need to add that in any Aristotelian scheme of things the potency–act distinction pervades the whole of nature, with the consequence that what we might call a thing's good, as compared with that of which it is the good, or a thing's final cause or object of desire, as compared with that whose final cause or object of desire (*appetitus*) it is, may be said to permeate the whole natural order, just as act and potency do.

Surely, though, no sooner is it thus acknowledged that the good of any X is to that X as act is to potency than we can quickly see that the Altruistic construction that has been placed upon the Principle of Universalizability just will not do. For after all, once it is recognized and acknowledged that the actuality of X is but the actuality of X's potentialities, then such a recognition and acknowledgment will entail an unmistakable universalizability: if the good of X is indeed but the actuality of X's potentialities, then this is a fact that not just X needs to recognize, but anyone and everyone else as well. And yet, given the mere fact that a certain good needs to be recognized, and recognized universally, to be the good of X, it by no means follows that X's good must therefore be taken to be Y's good as well, any more than the actuality or perfection or fulfillment of X needs to be recognized as being the actuality or perfection or fulfillment of Y as well. That would be nothing if not downright absurd!

And so with that, have we not at long last succeeded in laying the ghost of that curious notion of so many moral philosophers of the present day that the Principle of Universalizability must somehow entail an Altruism to the exclusion of any and all forms of Egoism?

And now it would seem that there is but one last final loose end that needs tying up before our attempted rehabilitation of a kind of Aristotelian Egoism may be considered complete. For recall how, as we saw, certain of the Libertarian Egoists, determined as they were to uphold their Egoism in the face of the Altruistic exploitation of the Principle of Universalizability, thought that they might do so by simply putting aside any and all concerns as to what the good of the human individual might be. After all, they feared that as soon as they might start talking about what the good of man is—his end, his perfection, his flourishing or whatever—the inevitable result would be that they would find themselves caught in the toils of the Principle of Universalizability, and would find their Egoism refuted in favor of an Altruism. Consequently, as an alternative, they thought that they could simply forget about the question as to what the good of man might be, his true end or goal, and concentrate instead on the matter simply of individual human rights. In other words, let the individual's end be whatever the individual might want it to be, the important thing being rather to insist upon the rights of an individual—his right to project-pursuit, that is to say, whatever his particular project preference might be.

Alas, though, as we had occasion to note earlier, this effort of some Libertarian Egoists to shift the gravamen of ethics from a concern with the good to a concern with rights just did not work. And the reason it did not work was that the Egoists seemed to have nowhere to turn, when it came to the question of what the ground or basis might be for those supposed individual rights, which, most appropriately, the Libertarian Egoist laid such store by. Now, however, in the light of our line of argument in the paragraphs just preceding, it should be clear that a moral-philosophical concern with what the good of man might be—with what his true end or goal simply as a human individual may be taken to be—need in no way lead to any collapse of Egoism in the face of any supposed entanglements with the Principle of Universalizability. Nor is that all that there is to the story either. For just as a concern with what the good of the human individual might be need not implicate one in a refutation of Egoism in favor of Altruism, so also I now propose to show, albeit very briefly, just how, by returning to the question of what the good of man or of what his true end or goal in life might be, it should be possible to provide those very grounds and that very basis for individual rights which, quite rightly, was a matter of such concern to the Libertarian Egoists.[26]

To this end, therefore, let us but remind ourselves again of how it is the very hallmark of an Aristotelian Egoism that the primary concern in ethics should be with the true good of man—that is to say, with what an individual's perfection and flourishing and fulfillment must be, simply in his capacity of being a human being. Nor is that all, for again, proceeding along Aristotelian and even more particularly along Thomistic lines, it needs to be noted that any such good as this perfecting or fulfilling of ourselves is not something that we may either choose to seek after or not, according to whether our tastes

---

26. The line of argument which immediately follows is once more an abbreviated version of the sort of argument that I sought to develop in my book, *Human Rights: Fact or Fancy?* (*op. cit.*), ch. III.

and preferences might so dictate. No, the good in this Aristotelian sense is an objective good, and thus something that each and every human being is under no less than a moral obligation to pursue, for, being no less than man's true end or goal, it represents that which a man—any man—ought to seek after and ought to try to be and become. But again, just as with the Libertarians, it simply would not do for them merely to assert that they had certain rights as individuals; in addition, they needed to show what warrant and justification there might be for such right-claims. And so now with the Aristotelians, it surely is not enough for them just to assert that all human beings are under a certain rudimentary obligation to try to make something of themselves—*i.e.*, to be and become what their nature as men demands of them. No, Aristotelians like anyone else need to show the warrant for such claims, and not just assert them.

Fortunately, however, the Aristotelian, as it would seem, is quite able to display his warrant for these claims of his. For one thing, he can begin by noting that there is an unmistakable ambiguity in the very notion of things that are said to be good or of value. Thus some things are reckoned as good merely because we happen to desire them, or like them, or find ourselves inclined toward them. On the other hand, and as an alternative, we not infrequently recognize and acknowledge that the reason we desire or like or find ourselves inclined toward certain things is because we see them to be good. That is to say, in the latter case, that they are good, not because we like them, but we like them because we see that they are good.

And now let us note still another undeniable feature that pertains to countless varieties of things and substances such as we observe and encounter in the world round about us. For is it not patent and obvious that among such things as we are thus familiar with, some, as it would appear, are healthy and flourishing, whereas others are not so, or at least not so much so? Nor is there any denying that this is as true of human beings as it is of plants and animals. For who is there who cannot appreciate the difference, say, between a tree that is flourishing and one that is sickly and stunted in its growth? And similarly, who has not observed directly among one's friends and acquaintances, some who are just plain foolish and silly, while others are pompous and conceited. Yes, still others and maybe, alas, oneself included, may be seen to have really no control over themselves, and to be at the mercy of their every whim and impulse. And what do such differences as these amount to, if not to differences between what a human being (or a plant or an animal) ought to be and what one ought not to be; or, if you will, in Aristotle's sense, between a good man and one not so good?

Moreover such differences between good and bad, between what one ought to be and ought not to be, etc., are nothing if not discoverable directly in nature and in the world. They are there for all of us to see, if only we have eyes to see. And with that, may we not say that we have therewith uncovered what the proper line of answer is to our earlier question as to just what the warrant or the justification might be for our making judgments as to good and bad, ought and ought not, etc.? Yes, may we not go still further and say that we have here seemingly a true inkling as to how even the question might be answered as to what the basis is for those individual rights claims that the Libertarians are so anxious to press—claims, for example, that we be secure in our persons and our property, that we not be interfered with, or be deprived of "life, liberty, and property without due process of law," etc. For these, as we saw, are the very sorts of things which all too many of the Libertarian thinkers we considered seem not able to give any proper reason for, or justification of. But now consider briefly just how that justification for such right-claims might be worked out on an Aristotelian basis.

Thus to begin with, we have already noticed how the Aristotelian establishes that there is a ground or a justification—yes, even a basis in nature—for our insisting that there is a natural end or good of human life—in other words, a true good which is nothing less than the very *telos* of human life and human existence. Moreover, following the so-called first principle of practical reason which St. Thomas Aquinas lays down, we may properly assert that "good is to be done and to be pursued and evil to be shunned and avoided." In other words, incumbent upon us all, simply as human beings, is no less than a duty or obligation to try to be and become what as human beings we ought to be, and thus to attain to our own true good, so far as we are able.

Surely, though, if all men lie under a natural obligation, as individuals, thus to be and become the human beings they ought to be, and if this is a duty and responsibility that is simply imposed upon all of us by nature, then must it not follow that as human beings we have a right—in this case a natural right—to such things as "life, liberty, and the pursuit of happiness," these being nothing if not the necessary and indispensable means to our achieving that perfection and fulfillment, or that happiness in Aristotle's sense, which we are all under obligation—once again a natural obligation—to try to achieve and to become? Yes, invoking the Kantian principle that "ought" implies "can," then surely if we are under no less than a natural moral obligation to pursue our true ends and goals in life, it would seem that the necessary means to those ends and goals we ought to be able to claim as being ours as well, and that simply as a matter of right. After all, on the principle of "ought" implies "can," if we do not have and cannot procure the requisite means and instruments for doing what it is that it is incumbent upon us to do, or that it is our responsibility to do, then, absent the requisite means to do so and our responsibility and obligation would seem to fall out as well. In other words, our human rights follow upon our human duties and obligations, and this on no other ground than that of "ought" implies "can."

And with that, may we not properly claim to have brought the Libertarian Egoists out of the woods after all and at long last? And how did we do it? Why, simply by making Aristotelians out of them! True, many of them may not like it. And yet what if that be their only salvation!

PART III
A CONCLUDING MISCELLANY, RANGING FROM A DEFENSE OF THE HUMANITIES TO A DEFENSE OF NATURAL LAW

10

THE WHAT AND THE WHY OF THE HUMANITIES[1]

Doubtless, the sentence with which Aristotle begins the Metaphysics, "All men by nature desire to know," has come to be taken as something of a truism by many of us. But what may not be such a truism is the fact that perhaps "knowledge" is not a univocal concept at all, and that our human ways of knowing, as well as the kinds of knowledge that result from them, may be deceptively multiple and various.

Specifically, I should like to raise the question as to whether what is loosely and generally referred to nowadays as "the humanities" may not constitute a way of knowing which is not only distinct from and co-ordinate with but may even be superior and architectonic with respect to that kind of knowledge which today is so often assumed to be no less than the very paradigm of knowledge, science. In short, what I should like to do, if I can, is to bring into focus a type of knowledge that is distinctively and decisively humanistic, as contrasted with the all-too-familiar sort of knowledge associated with modern science and technology.

First, though, just what are the humanities? Rather than deal with this question with the care that is its just due, I shall give no more than a short and arbitrary answer, flatly asserting that what I propose to take the term "humanities" to refer to are three primary disciplines: history, literature, and philosophy. Worse still, I shall immediately follow up this somewhat arbitrary listing with a most unorthodox, and I

---

1. This paper was delivered as an address before the American Catholic Philosophical Association in the spring of 1973, long before there were any storms such as have recently been generated by the publication of Allan Bloom's book, *The Closing of the American Mind*. Nor were there then even many storms, at least not such audible ones, from the opposite camp of the Deconstructionists, the Hermeneuticists, the Critics of the Canon, *et al*. Hence, while I recognize that my own essay, appearing now, will seem to lack polemical pertinence to the current disputes, I nonetheless think that its main theses are still sound and will bear reiteration.

fear very unconvincing, interpretation of the kind of knowledge which at least two, if not all three, of these disciplines tend to give us.

With respect to history I feel tempted to wax pompous and give an answer that may seem as booming, if not as bombastic, as Dr. Johnson's celebrated comment on the occasion of the sale of the Thrale brewery: "Sir, we did not come here to sell a parcel of boilers and vats, but the possibility of getting rich beyond the dreams of avarice." Somewhat analogously, I should be inclined to say that one does not study history to acquire any mere parcel of names and dates, or even of economic forces and cultural changes, but rather, as Sir Henry Savile wrote in the preface to his translation of Tacitus in 1591, because "there is no learning so proper for the direction of the life of man as Historie."[2]

Indeed, there is an interesting passage in an essay by Herbert Davis, entitled "The Augustan Conception of History," where Davis is telling about the conception of history that was held by one of the greatest of English historians—albeit now somewhat neglected and unread—Edward Hyde, Earl of Clarendon and author of the celebrated *History of the Rebellion*. Davis reminds his readers of the somewhat idealized picture with which Clarendon had begun his *History*, a picture in which Clarendon seeks to depict those happy "twelve years of Charles I's reign, before the long Parliament, when"

this Kingdom [*i.e.* England] ... enjoy'd the greatest Calm, and the fullest measure of Felicity, that any People in any Age, for so long time together, have been bless'd with; to the wonder, and envy of all the other parts of *Christendom* ...

In a word, many Wise men thought it a Time, wherein those two Adjuncts which Nerva was Deified for uniting, *Imperium* and *Libertas* were as well reconciled, as is possible.

Davis then continues with this comment regarding Clarendon:

But the real glory of that felicity did not consist for Clarendon in the balancing of any adjuncts such as sovereign rule and freedom, rather in the full flowering of a rich and noble humanity. It is perhaps not too much to say that in this he saw the full tragedy of the Rebellion, that it had destroyed this felicity. He wrote his history to leave for posterity a record of the values that had been lost, and perhaps in the hope of showing the way in which they might be recovered.[3]

In other words, given such an understanding of history, it is little wonder that it should be reckoned among the humanities. It is no less

---

2. Quoted in Herbert Davis, *Jonathan Swift* (New York: Oxford University Press, 1964), p. 281.
3. *Ibid.*, pp. 286–287.

than in and through the study of history that we are able to learn what it is to be human and what the true values in life are, what we are to live for and how we must conduct ourselves if we are to achieve that distinctive excellence that befits us as human beings. In short, what is here being suggested is no less than that the humanistic and, if you will, the humanizing, knowledge that comes from history is precisely a moral or ethical knowledge. As Bolingbroke once remarked—admittedly not an authority distinguished for his own morality, but still one worth listening to—"history is philosophy teaching by examples how to conduct ourselves in all the situations of private and public life."[4]

Nor is that all. What is further implicit in what is here being claimed for that humanistic and moral knowledge that comes from history is that it is indeed a knowledge. Those judgments upon human folly and human wisdom which, as historians or even as mere students of history, we pass on the characters and events of history are not just our own arbitrary personal assessments which we bring to the facts, as it were from the outside, and which are but our way of adorning or dressing up the facts. They are judgments that are determined by the facts themselves.

So much, then, for history; what about literature? Surely, everyone would concede to literature a place, if not actually pride of place, among the humanities. Still, can literature be reckoned among the humanities on anything like the same grounds as history? Can it be said that literature—poetry, the novel, plays, satires, etc.—represent a significant humanistic discipline for the very reason that the study of literature yields not just a knowledge of man and of the human condition and situation, but also a knowledge which, by that very fact, is normative and ethical with respect to human excellence and to what men ought to do and be? Surely the answer must be "Yes." Consider the matter but inductively, albeit by an admittedly crude and unsophisticated induction. Must it not be acknowledged that a novelist such as Kafka is trying in *The Castle* or *The Trial* to bring home to us in no less telling than haunting way just what our human situation is like? Yet, *mutatis mutandis*, is not Jane Austen trying to do much the same thing, to expose through the touch of her irony the pride, for instance, of some and the prejudice of others? In Jane Austen's eyes what is it to be properly human if it is not to be sensitive just to those patent virtues and hidden vices of our fellow men, which are no less virtues and vices for all of their decorous setting in the society of the Regency

---

4. Quoted in Davis, *op. cit.*, p. 291.

and after? Or what about Jonathan Swift? Is it possible to read *Gulliver's Travels* or *A Modest Proposal* without recognizing that what is being laid bare for all to see is nothing less than human folly and human hypocrisy—our own no less than all men's?

While we are about it, let us adduce in evidence a very different example and authority. Consider Sir Maurice Bowra's assessment of Greek poetry and tragedy, particularly the work of Aeschylus and Sophocles. Bowra remarks that

> the Greeks allowed reason a large part in poetry.... Because the Greeks regarded poetry as a rational activity they brought to it a remarkable source of strength. They put into it their own pondered and serious view of life, and they thought it their duty to say what they really meant. For this reason they infuse it with the power which comes from long and intense thought. When Aeschylus constructs a tragedy, he makes his action illustrate the divine laws which operate through human life. His view of these laws is not only original; it has been reached by a deep consideration of human affairs, and his presentation of it comes vastly enriched by all the imaginative and emotional attention which he has given to it. These are no conventional judgments, lightly adopted and hastily presented. They are what experience has forced on him, and in his majestic and searching treatment of them there is an uncommon power because he is desperately concerned with the truth. Unlike him, Sophocles keeps his own views in the background but lets them emerge through the personalities and fortunes of his characters. But the fortunes of these characters present instances of problems which have long troubled his mind—the vast difference between human error and divine knowledge, the conflict between heroic and merely human standards of conduct, the illusions which beset those who are unworthily in power. He sees the issues with extreme clarity and has thought so hard about them that they have become part of his consciousness and, when he puts them into poetry, they are enriched by the associations and the special strength which come from sustained personal familiarity.[5]

In short, what Bowra is here telling us about Aeschylus and Sophocles is no less than what we have found to be true of Swift or Kafka or Jane Austen, and that is that what all of these writers attempt to do is to tell us what is true with respect to human life itself, thus disclosing what it takes for a man to live wisely and intelligently, as against living foolishly or brutishly or even madly.

May we not then conclude from this that literature no less than history places in our hands an instrument and a source and a means of knowledge that is exactly an ethical knowledge of our very conditions as men? Is it not likewise for this same reason that literature and history may both be properly reckoned among the humanities, as being just those elements in the educational curriculum that are pe-

---

5. C. M. Bowra, *The Greek Experience* (New York: Mentor Books, 1959), p. 144.

culiarly and distinctively humanizing, and that are our primary human means of learning how to be human?

Now this is not to say, of course, that, as humanities, history and literature may not be quite distinguishable from one another in both their mode and manner as disciplines. After all, as Aristotle remarked, poetry is more universal than history. By this he presumably meant something to the effect that whereas in history the universally human has to be discerned in the particulars just as they come, with the result that one may all too easily lose sight of the woods for the trees, in contrast, in poetry the particulars are contrived just for the purpose of showing forth the universal more directly and unmistakeably. Yet for all of their differences, history no less than poetry is surely one of the humanities, for no other reason than that, despite all of the ambiguity of its testimony, it still does serve to exhibit what it means to be human and thus, as Sir Henry Savile remarked, to provide a learning that is "proper for the direction of the life of men." Otherwise, what possible point could there be to endless human researches into such things as the foreign policy of Louis XIV, or the struggles between the Empire and the Papacy, or the fanaticism or lack of it of Oliver Cromwell? Save for what such researches can ultimately reveal concerning the ethical import of human affairs and of our human choices and decisions, they have no more business being reckoned among the humanities than have, say, studies on the structure and function of the nerve cells in the human brain, or researches into the causes and cure of rheumatoid arthritis.

While we are about it, let us try to guard against still another misunderstanding that may arise in connection with our thesis that it is for no other reason than because it is an ethical knowledge that is mediated by the study of history and of literature that these disciplines deserve to be reckoned among the humanities—*i.e.* among those pursuits that are aimed precisely at humanizing us and rendering us truly human beings. For surely, you will say, no one any longer believes—if any one ever did believe—that the study of literature is but a way and means of ethical or moral instruction, as if the purpose of all literature were a purely didactic one, and the nature of literary art no more than rhetoric. This seems patently wrong-headed. Besides, literary excellence, you may want to argue, particularly in poetry, is not at all a matter of philosophical or ethical truth, but of aesthetics: a poem, as so many of our lately fashionable critics have been wont to tell us, is something quite autonomous, and estimable solely for the aesthetic pleasure that it gives; it is quite irrelevant what the poem says, or even whether it says anything, not to mention whether what it says is true, and particularly whether what it says is true ethically.

To such criticisms, however, we must give but very short answer. For one thing, merely because the aim of the poet may be to say what is true, it certainly does not follow that the essence of poetry has therefore to be didactic. After all, there is a sense in which the concern of the geometer, for example, might be said to be with truth; and yet no one is tempted to conclude from this that the technique of geometry must be essentially one of pedagogy. As for the view that the aesthetic function of poetry precludes it from ever being properly an affair of statement, I will merely quote the somewhat dogmatic, but eminently forceful, response of the late Yvor Winters:

> I believe that a poem (or other work of artistic literature) is a statement in words about a human experience. I use the term *statement* in a very inclusive sense, and for lack of something better. But it seems to me obvious that *The Iliad, Macbeth,* and *To the Virgins to Make Much of Time* all deal with human experiences. In each work there is a content which is rationally apprehensible, and each work endeavors to communicate the emotion which is appropriate to the rational apprehension of the subject. The work is thus a judgment, rational and emotional, of the experience—that is a complete moral judgment in so far as the work is successful.[6]

Even if one does not wish to go quite so far as Winters would appear to go and to assert that any poem or work of literature is a statement about human experience and a statement that involves a moral judgment upon that experience, still there is no denying that much of literature is of this sort, and that most if not all of literature can be approached and assessed in just such terms. Hence, rather than actually attempting to decide the substantive issue in the present lecture, why not just say that, so far as the humanities are concerned, and in so far as we are seeking a rationale of the humanities that will serve to justify them both educationally and culturally, we will reckon literature to be among the humanistic disciplines only to the extent that it is such literature as does represent a moral judgment upon experience, and quite apart from such other values and character as it may have when considered in abstraction from its moral or ethical import?

No sooner, though, do we say this much, than we would appear to have compounded the oddity and untenability of our thesis still further. Even granting that history and literature are to be regarded as staple articles in the humanities just because of the ethical significance which they have for us as men, unfortunately that significance would seem to be anything but univocal. Rather, it is more like a confusion worse confounded. Clearly, the ethical import of *Macbeth* is radically,

---

6. Yvor Winters, *The Function of Criticism* (Denver: Alan Swallow, 2nd ed., 1957), p. 26.

if not totally, different from that of Joyce's *Ulysses*. As for historians, we need but cite Macaulay as an obvious counter example to the one we appealed to earlier, Clarendon. Surely, Macaulay's—or to make it rather more contemporary, Mr. Trevor-Roper's—testimony as to what would constitute "the full flowering of a rich and noble humanity" would be readily recognizable as being quite other and different from Clarendon's.

To such a criticism, however, is not the obvious answer that for a properly humanistic knowledge of the sort we are contending for, the resources of history and literature are not enough; that philosophy is required as well? Moreover, the peculiar business of philosophy, and more especially of that branch of philosophy known as ethics, is precisely to determine, as over against the seemingly endless variety of conceptions of the good life and of how human beings ought to live, just that conception which is the true one. After all, Aristotle at the very beginning of his *Nichomachean Ethics*, when he is trying to determine just what it is that an investigation of the sort known as "ethics" should concern itself with, remarks:

If therefore among the ends at which our actions aim there be one which we wish for its own sake, while we wish the others only for the sake of this, and if we do not choose everything for the sake of something else (which would obviously result in a process *ad infinitum*, so that all desire would be futile and vain), it is clear that this one ultimate end must be the Good and indeed the Supreme Good. Will not then a knowledge of this Supreme Good be also of great practical importance for the conduct of life? Will it not better enable us to attain what is fitting, like archers having a target to aim at? If this be so, we ought to make an attempt to determine at all events in outline what exactly this Supreme Good is, and of which of the theoretical or practical sciences it is the object.[7]

Moreover, acting almost immediately upon his own declaration of what the business of ethics is, Aristotle, in the pages that follow very shortly thereafter, undertakes to put such a practical or ethical knowledge to work by showing how a knowledge of this kind enables one to assess the respective claims of, and to judge between, the so-called "three lives" which it had been a long tradition in Greek culture to regard as rival conceptions of the good life—namely, the life of mere pleasure or enjoyment, the life of politics and public service, and the life of knowledge and contemplation. Now whether Aristotle was right or not in his final judgment that the Supreme Good for man is to be associated with the life of contemplation, at least his judgment represented no arbitrary choice or decision, but rather a deliberate con-

---

7. Book I, ch. 2, 1094 a 19–28, Loeb Library translation.

clusion arrived at only after the most careful argument and consideration of evidence. Hence, one can reject his conclusion only in the light of still further evidence and argument, thereby confirming the fact that ethics is indeed an affair of knowledge. In this respect at least it is not unlike the sciences, where it is recognized as a matter of course that conclusions can be considered as first established, and then later as having been superseded, on no other basis than that of proper and sufficient evidence.

Moreover, to apply this principle directly to our contemporary situation where our problem may not be exactly that of choosing between "the three lives"—or at least not in so many words—it was but a few months ago that I chanced to come across a leading article in *The Sunday New York Times Book Review,* entitled "Poetry in the Sixties—Long Live Blake! Down with Donne."[8] Now I submit that any such choice as that suggested between Donne and Blake is no mere choice between rival conceptions of prosody and poetic diction, but rather a choice between lives—in this case not three lives but rather two quite radically different life-styles or ways of life. In other words, the choice here is ultimately ethical. Indeed, the reviewer himself in the course of his article makes the point that those earlier poets whose model was Donne were under the spell of the New Critics. But this spell, he says, was thoroughly shattered by Alan Ginsberg. "Ginsberg's original contribution," the reviewer observes,

was a note of hysteria that hit the taste of the young exactly. He spoke for the spiritually disenfranchised members of wretched young people from middle-class homes, who had grown up after World War II—weeds of an affluent society. They flocked to his readings; they had found someone who spoke aloud for them, more than this *someone who gave them a way to live*[9]—ragged and bearded—without feeling ashamed, and even with pride. Hemingway created the life-style of the Lost Generation; Ginsberg created that of the Beat.

Thus, a choice between poets is no less than an ethical choice, a choice between lives, or as the reviewer terms it, between "life-styles." Moreover, if such a choice is not to be something utterly blind and arbitrary, then it had better be made in the light of something like a genuine ethical knowledge and understanding. Nor is it anything other than just such a knowledge that the true humanist ultimately aims at, and that the humanities as a pedagogical and scholarly discipline are intended to convey.

8. December, 1969.
9. My italics.

Once again, though, this entire argument is likely to provoke but the same skepticism and the same criticism all over again: Is there any such knowledge of the sort that we have been claiming for the humanities? Thus one might say it is all very well to talk about a knowledge of our human situation and of what it means to be human—a typically humanistic knowledge that is supposedly mediated by the disciplines of history and of literature, and that is, as it were, assessed and confirmed by philosophy. But what reason is there to think that there really is or could be any such knowledge? More specifically, one might say, it is all very well to invoke philosophy, and more particularly ethics, as the only proper means of adjudicating between the incredibly multifarious and conflicting ways of life that are disclosed in human history and heralded in human poetry and song. But again, what possible reason is there for supposing that philosophy can ever acquit itself of such a function? Is there, or could there ever be, such a thing as a science of ethics that would enable us to make a reasoned and intelligent determination as between ways of life, much as, say, the sciences of medicine and engineering enable us to decide between the right way and the wrong way of treating various diseases, or the right way and the wrong way of building bridges and highways?

Now I would suggest that this most persistent and deep-seated challenge to the very possibility of a humanistic type of knowledge of the kind we have been urging and arguing for derives its force not from any direct critique of such a way of knowledge but rather from an obvious truism that such a humanistic type of knowledge is not at all a scientific knowledge as we understand that term today, plus a not-so-obvious, and indeed very highly suspect, inference therefrom, that if a humanistic knowledge is not scientific it is not a legitimate type of knowledge at all.

To bring out, though, the full import of this contrast between humanistic and scientific knowledge, I wonder if it might not be illuminating for us to consider the two knowledges in action, so to speak, with references to a test case. Not only that, but we would hope that the nature of the illumination might be such as to give us pause with respect to what has heretofore been our inveterate and uncritical tendency simply to write off humanistic knowledge altogether, as if it were not properly a knowledge at all when compared with what one finds in the sciences. At any rate, the test case that I would propose has to do with the common employment in the humanities of so-called philosophical or literary classics. For doubtless, it will hardly be disputed that the traditional and even continuing way, by and large, of studying either literature or philosophy is in terms of what people have generally called classics. Originally perhaps, and particularly from the time of the Renaissance on, the term "classic" has been used to refer specifically to the Greek and Latin classics. Indeed, even today when for the most part we not merely brush Greek and Latin aside as dead languages, but even leave it to the dead to bury their dead, we still consider that research, no less than instruction, in both literature and philosophy, will turn pretty much on a regard for so-called classics, albeit no longer necessarily the classics of Greece and Rome. Thus, it is hard to imagine even the most up-to-the-minute contemporary philosopher who does not spend a great portion of his time and effort poring over the texts of Wittgenstein, say, or of Heidegger or of Merleau-Ponty, or of Bergmann perhaps. Why? The operative consideration in such cases is surely that the philosopher in question is convinced that the text he is studying is in some sense or other a truly classic one, that is, one that stands out from others just in virtue of the decisive excellence that it is presumed to have.

Or again, suppose that in a course in contemporary literature the instructor assigns something of Alan Ginsberg, or Susan Sontag, or Eldridge Cleaver. Of course, it may be that such a course is not really one in literature at all, but rather one in sociology. The motive for studying such writers would be not their excellence either as writers or thinkers, but simply because of their happening to be fashionable, and the motive of the course would be just to study current fashions and trends. Supposing, though, the concern of the course to be primarily with literature and not with sociology, then I submit that the instructor's choice of authors can only be guided by considerations as to the superior excellence of the writers selected—perhaps not excellence absolutely, but excellence of a certain kind and in a certain genre. Under such circumstances it is hard to escape the conclusion that the authors selected, by the very fact that they have been selected, are being treated as classics, whether the actual term be used or no.

Contrast, though, the sciences. Would it be wrong to say that in the sciences there just aren't any classics at all—or at least not any that we might call operative classics? To be sure, it is easy enough to point to any number of great works in science that may truly be said to have been literally epoch-making in the history of science—Newton's *Principia*, Darwin's *Origin of the Species*, Einstein's special and general theory of relativity, etc. Yet, even though such works have been incomparably decisive in the development of science, can it really be said that they have ever been used and studied by scientists in the manner of classics? How many contemporary physicists, for example, have read and proceeded to reread and even to return time and again to the texts of Einstein's papers on relativity in the way in which, say, almost every young philosopher in the present-day analytic tradition finds himself going back again and again to Wittgenstein's *Tractatus* or to his *Investigations*?

Now this is not to say, of course, that we are not all of us familiar with how it has become increasingly fashionable in recent years to take the history of science more seriously. Many scientists—and of these many with the highest reputations—have done a great deal toward making not only scientists themselves, but even the general public, much more conscious of the history of science, and of the startling revolutionary achievements of the great men of science.

All the same, has this new-found interest in the history of science had any very marked effect upon the actual discipline and practice of science itself? Does the ordinary chemist or biologist or geologist or physicist feel that a first-hand acquaintance with the work of Avogadro, or of Mendel, or of Lyell, or of Galileo is absolutely essential to his proficiency and the fruitfulness of his work in his particular scientific discipline? Or is it not rather the case that a knowledge of the history of science, or even if you will of certain of the classics of science, while it may prove most rewarding and even enlightening to the scientist as an educated person and a human being, is really not directly pertinent to his actual work in his particular scientific discipline? In other words, an interest in scientific classics and in the history of science generally is not an interest that is proper and pertinent to science as such, but rather, like any other interest in history, is a humanistic interest. It bears fruit in a deepened and broader understanding of man and of man's characteristic human achievements perhaps; but it contributes nothing, at least not directly, to the advancement of science itself.

Why, though—and here our main question returns to plague us—is there this difference between the sciences and the humanities, in that the pursuit of the one would appear almost invariably to involve a study of classics, whereas to the other, classics are a matter of comparative, if not of complete, indifference? In answer to this question, I would like to hazard an explanation in terms of a contrast between humanistic knowledge and scientific knowledge which, I am afraid, is far from being the currently fashionable one, or even one that many have heard of, and which yet may prove ultimately to be the only sound and defensible one.

First, then, as to humanistic knowledge, we have laid down already as a basic principle that, in literary no less than in philosophical works, the concern of the author is, by and large and in a broad sense, and to express it in the vernacular, simply to "tell it like it is." That is to say, a poet such as Alan Ginsberg, no less than a Dante or a Sophocles, is quite patently a man with something to say, and what he has to say has to do with the truth about ourselves as human beings and our human predicament. Not only that, but the poet, and to a lesser degree perhaps the philosopher too, wishes not merely to tell it as it is, but also to move us to respond to the truth we are being told in a way that is at once proper and appropriate. For instance, the Prophet declares:

> The wolf shall dwell with the lamb,
>   and the leopard shall lie down with the kid,
> and the calf and the lion and the fatling together,
> and a little child shall lead them.
>
> The cow and the bear shall feed:
>   their young shall lie down together; and
> the lion shall eat straw like the ox.
>
> The suckling child shall play over the
>   hole of the asp,
>
> and the weaned child shall put his hand
>   on the adder's den.
>
> They shall not hurt or destroy in all my
>   holy mountain;
> for the earth shall be full of the
>   knowledge of the Lord
> as the waters cover the sea.[10]

Speaking thus as he heralds the Messianic king, the Prophet Isaiah is not merely "telling it like it is" but bringing us to respond in a way that is markedly different from what would be appropriate to the somewhat different truth enunciated in Robert Herrick's poem:

> Gather ye rosebuds while ye may,
> Old time is fast a-flying,
> And that same flower which blooms today,
> Tomorrow may be dying.

Therefore, when, as students of the humanities, we acknowledge ourselves to be but men who want to know and understand what is and what we can expect in the way of a life on earth, as well as how we can make some sense of our lives and avoid making utter fools or knaves of ourselves, then is it not natural that we should turn for instruction to just those works that we have been calling classics—that

---

10. Isaiah XI, 6–9.

is to say to those men who as writers have "told it like it is" and whose words have the ring of truth?

Furthermore, it is but a fact of life that in the day-by-day business of living and earning a living, of activity and idleness, of business and distraction, we tend to forget and lose sight of, or at least to see rather more dimly and to appreciate and respond with ever recurring slackness to, those truths that are central and basic to our proper existence as men. This being true, is it surprising that the classics are just those things to which we must constantly return? By reading and rereading we refresh and reinvigorate that humanistic knowledge which is our true heritage as men, as well as reactivate once more our appreciation of those things that matter most.

Nor is that the whole story. Many might object that even if it be conceded that it is only through classics that we come to know the truth—yes, if you will, the truth that makes us free—still is it not painfully obvious that no set of classics, however chosen, ever speaks with but a single voice or purveys but a single truth? Thus if Blake no less than Donne, or George Herbert no less than Aristotle, are all equally classics, how can one possibly say that through classics, and only through classics, do we come to know the truth? Is it not the case instead that rather than the truth, many truths diametrically opposed and even contradictory to one another—in other words, downright errors no less than truths—are what are mediated by any study of classics, whatever such classics may be and however chosen?

True enough. Yet, is not the answer to this objection that what is at issue is truth that needs to be not merely known but appreciated and responded to, that discloses to us at once the nature of things and of our human situation in the light of the nature of things? This truth can be understood and appreciated only through being sensitive to some of the countless ways that it may be approximated without perhaps ever actually being reached, or the ways it may be missed altogether and never so much as attained at all. Thus professional philosophers are only too familiar with the common phenomenon of how a philosopher of one persuasion—say, an Aristotelian—finds his own insights deepened and the cogency of his arguments reinforced precisely from a continuous and persistent confrontation with a thinker who is almost diametrically opposed to Aristotle, say Immanuel Kant. Nor is this phenomenon confined just to philosophy in the narrower sense. Thus Swift, the Tory High Churchman, considered Lucretius to be almost his favorite writer. Edward Gibbon, whose implacable and mighty disdain for Christianity runs through the entire *Decline and Fall of the Roman Empire*, not only was profoundly influenced in his youth by the satirical pieces of the Non-Juror, William Law, but also in his maturer years was reputed to have reread each year the whole of Pascal's *Lettres Provinciales*. Moreover, what this betokens is surely more than any mere aesthetic sensitivity to stylistic excellence, even that of one's adversaries. It betokens rather that humanistic knowledge simply cannot be attained merely by swallowing key truths in formulas and capsules. Instead, there just is no way of either coming to know or continuing to know what the truth is about reality and about ourselves, without at the same time becoming ever more sensitive to and understanding of the ways of error as well.

Why, though, would there seem to be nothing quite comparable to this in science? Why is it that scientific knowledge is apparently indifferent to such things as might be called classics, whereas humanistic knowledge finds its only proper nourishment and sustenance directly in the classics? To answer these questions let us begin by simply laying aside those stock answers that all of us have grown so accustomed to that we accept them uncritically, but which in the light of everything that we have thus far been saying must indeed be seen to be seriously misleading, if not downright false. Surely we need no longer accept it merely as a truism that the reason science has no truck with classics is because science is concerned only with the facts and with what is objectively the case, whereas the humanities are concerned rather with our subjective human responses to the facts and with the literary and artistic embellishments that these entail. The thesis that I wish to put forward is, if anything, just the opposite: it is precisely because science is not really concerned with knowing the nature of things, or the way things are at all, that it finds itself thus indifferent to anything on the order of classics. The sole justification for being classics is just that they do open our eyes to the truth and to what is our true human predicament, set down as we are in the midst of things and encompassed by a reality that is not of our own making.

Does such a thesis sound utterly paradoxical, perhaps even fantastic? Let us hasten to qualify it a bit by conceding immediately that, no doubt historically, science may not always have been so indifferent to achieving anything on the order of a knowledge of the real, as it would now appear to have become. We may also readily concede that many practicing scientists in the present-day may still not be aware of the radically nonrealistic orientation that their discipline has come to have, and hence may think of themselves in their role as scientists as being concerned simply with trying to observe and to describe the facts as they are. Yet, when one considers the distinctive character of the modern scientific enterprise, as this has come to be recognized and brought into focus by any number of recent philosophers of science, one begins to see that the real thrust of the scientific enterprise is not aimed at anything like a knowledge of reality or the nature of things at all. Oversimplifying somewhat, one might even say that there are at least two dominant features or factors that have been operative in the methodology of science that have made this result inevitable—one is what might be called the nature of scientific data; and the other the nature of scientific hypotheses, theories, and explanations generally.

As to the data, surely all of us know, nonscientists no less than scientists, that although the entire fabric of science is erected on the data of observation and experiment, such data as they function in science are hardly the data of our ordinary experience. Rather they are those bare but presumably public and reproducible data such as pointer-readings, impressions on a photographic plate, etc. In this sense what may be considered to be given to the scientists as data are not at all the things of our everyday experience—tables and chairs, men and mice, night and day, winter and summer, sunlight and clouds. The only properly acceptable data of the scientist are more like those bare sense data which the philosophers of 25 years or so ago were wont to make so much of—momentary patches of color, of sounds, of odors, of tastes, etc.

What is more, these properly scientific data prove to be singularly uninformative, particularly when it comes to anything suggestive of ordered patterns or causal laws in terms of which the things and events in nature could possibly be made intelligible. Thus, ever since Hume it has become something of a truism that no causal connections can ever be observed to hold between the data of sense. As for inductive inferences from such data, these just do not seem to have any properly logical warrant of any kind.

What, then, has been the result of this seeming frustration in any efforts to find meaning or intelligibility in the data of experience, or at least such data of experience as the scientist may properly accept? The answer is to be found in that second factor of the modern scientific situation which I mentioned above, the factor of scientific hypotheses and theories. In effect what the scientists have tended to do is, not being able to find any meaning or intelligibility in the actual facts and data of science, they have fabricated and imposed a kind of intelligibility upon the data from the outside in the form of scientific theories and hypotheses. Thus Sir Karl Popper, the distinguished contemporary philosopher and logician of science, quotes with favor, and even with some furbishing of the text on his own part, a well-known passage from the Preface to the second edition of Kant's *Critique of Pure Reason*:

> When Galileo let his balls run down an inclined plane with a gravity which he had chosen himself; when Toricelli caused the air to sustain a weight which he had calculated beforehand to be equal to that of a column of water of known height; . . . then a light dawned upon all natural philosophers. They learnt that our reason can understand only *what it creates according to its own design: that we must compel Nature to answer our questions,* rather than cling to Nature's apron strings and allow her to guide us. *For purely accidental observations, made without any plan having been thought out in advance, cannot be connected by a . . . law—which is what reason is searching for.*[11]

Moreover, the very logic of this conception of the nature of scientific theories and hypotheses, and of the objectives they serve, tends to have consequences that far outrun anything that either Kant or Popper would seem ever quite to have realized. If a scientific hypothesis be not in any way derived from the facts or data of observation, then even supposing such a hypothesis to have been pretty well corroborated and borne out by empirical test and equipment, it can scarcely be concluded from this that the hypothesis is therefore to be regarded as properly an account or description or reflection of the facts or of the way in which things are. Rather, it would seem that the initial and continuing purpose of a scientific hypothesis so conceived is not at all to disclose or lay bare the nature of things or the order and structure of the real, but simply to provide a convenient and useful ordering device with respect to the manifold sensory data. This ordering device, be it logical or linguistic or mathematical, is devised by the human mind or the mind of the scientist simply for the purpose of helping him to get about, as it were, among the data, associating them one with another, making predictions from certain ones to others, and thus putting them to various calculable uses. Thus as C. I. Lewis, a very perceptive philosopher of a generation ago, very tellingly put it, a scientific hypothesis is really but an intellectual or "conceptual go-cart" that enables the scientist to "get over the intervals" between the sensory data.[12]

If then scientific theories are no longer to be regarded as sources and means through which men can come to a better understanding of the nature of things and of the way things are, if as theories they

---

11. Karl Popper, *Conjectures and Refutations* (New York and London: Basic Books, 1962), p. 189.
12. Clarence Irving Lewis, *Mind and the World Order* (New York: Scribner's, 1929), p. 119.

are not even supposed to disclose the truth about things, but only what might be called the truth of our human predictions, manipulations, and devices for the control of nature, then it is little wonder that scientific treatises in which theories of this sort are presented and expounded can hardly function in the manner of classics. The excellence of theories so conceived is not to be gauged by their approximation to the truth, or by the insights which they offer into the nature of reality, but only by what we might call in the crude sense their pragmatic consequences. Consequently, once a theory comes along that works better than its predecessor, then that predecessor, so far from being able to attain the status of a classic, can hope for no better fate than death and discard. Indeed, if theories or explanations in science are to be respected, not for their being testimonies to human understanding and insight into the nature of the real, but simply for their being testimonies to human inventiveness and ingenuity, then it stands to reason that it will be only the latest and the most ingenious invention that will count, all others being but so many outmoded devices that no longer work. As such, they may be either simply consigned to the dust heap, or else treated as mere museum pieces in the history of science which are now of no further use whatever in science itself.[13]

Returning now to the Aristotelian theme with which we began: "All men by nature desire to know"—may we not add, "Yes, but it makes all the difference just what sorts and varieties of knowledge it is that men desire." If they want to know what the score is, or what their true condition as human beings is, or what they as men can and ought to do about it, then let them turn not to science but to the humanities. If they cannot turn to the humanities as they presently are in their somewhat fallen state, then let them turn to the humanities as they properly ought to be, that is, as those particular disciplines whose responsibility it is to mediate a knowledge of things as they are and that matter most, and, one is tempted to add, a knowledge that is no less than a knowledge of good and evil.

If put in that way, might we perhaps be accused of having suddenly disclosed the knowledge which comes through the humanities as being no less than the very forbidden fruit itself, which, if we eat, will cause us forthwith to be driven from the Garden of Eden? Hardly! Surely

---

13. This anti-realist interpretation of science I have now come to think too extreme. For a rather more temperate account of the limitations of modern natural science as an attempt to provide an account of the nature of things as it really is, see my more recent book, *Human Rights: Fact or Fancy?* (Baton Rouge: Louisiana State University Press, 1985), esp. ch. IV.

any fears we may have about being driven from the Garden are nothing if not gratuitous. For one thing, we are surely all of us only too painfully aware that we are not in the Garden now, and, if we may trust the familiar records, have not been so for some time past. Indeed, our admittedly long-standing condition outside the Garden has now reached such a "parlous state" that perhaps we might be well-advised to try a little humanistic knowledge of good and evil. It might just be that so far from excluding us from the Garden, such knowledge could be the very means that could get us back in! That scientific knowledge cannot do the trick has been palpably borne in upon us, particularly in these very last few years. Why not, then, turn once more to the humanities?

11
WHY NEED A GENERAL BE HUMAN?[1]

Believe me, even as I hear you applaud, I can guess what all of you are saying to yourselves: "Who is this popinjay?" you are asking, "who knows nothing about the military, and yet who presumes to come here into the very sacred precincts of 'the Point,' to tell us—all of us future generals surely—that maybe, as generals, we might cease even to be human! Why, the very impertinence and arrogance of the thing is nothing if not outrageous! Besides, who is this fellow, Veatch, to talk? Not only does he know nothing about the military, but he presumably knows nothing about either 'leader-sleep' or about 'dirt,' but only about 'drugs'![2] And what could be worse, by way of prospects for the talk that we are required to listen to tonight, than knowing that we are going to have to listen to still another lecture on 'drugs'!"

Nor is that all. For already—although doubtless unbeknownst to most of you—I have flunked one test that was earlier set for me by one of your own more eminent authorities on the subject of "drugs," right here at the Point, Major Dixon. As it happens, last summer—apparently on orders from Colonel Hartle—Major Dixon kindly telephoned to me all the way out in Indiana, presumably to arrange some of the details for my projected visit to West Point this fall; but really his purpose, as I believe, was to test me for my suitability to give an address here at all. And, alas, as I say, I promptly proceeded to flunk Major Dixon's test! The trouble was that, being a bit deaf, and none-too-quick-witted besides, I quite failed to catch Major Dixon's name over the telephone. That was bad enough, but there was still more to come!

"What did you say your name was?" I asked. "Dixon, Sir, Major Dixon, just as in the Mason-Dixon Line, Sir. Perhaps you have heard of the Mason-Dixon Line, have you, Sir?" "Indeed I have," I replied,

---
1. This was an address delivered to the cadets at West Point in the fall of 1985.
2. West Point slang for courses in Leadership ("leadersleep"), in Geography ("dirt"), in Ethics ("drugs").

"for I had great-grandparents on both my mother's and my father's sides who were officers in the Union Army." At that, there was a sudden silence at the other end of the line—almost as if the phone had gone dead. Finally, Major Dixon's voice came on again, and in some irritation he remarked, "Well, Sir, I'll have you know that I am from the South, Sir, south of the Mason-Dixon Line, that is, Sir. In other words, Sir, I am a Southerner!" To which I replied, "Yes, Sir."

Accordingly, having thus already struck out with Major Dixon, let me see if I can't compound my offense by telling a story about one of those same great-grandfathers of mine, whom Major Dixon heard about with such dismay over the telephone. For this one ancestor of mine did indeed manage eventually to attain the rank of Major General in the Union Army. And how did he do this? Well, I am afraid that before the War, he could boast of neither military training nor accomplishments. However, at the outbreak of the War in 1861, he organized the 25th Indiana Regiment, and was promptly elected its colonel. (Now at this point I am tempted to add—parenthetically and principally for Colonel Hartle's benefit—that I wonder whether the Colonel might not think my great-grandfather's route to a colonelcy was both rather quicker and easier than his own route of having to go first to the University of Texas, and there to get a Ph.D. in philosophy!)

I return, though, to my story about General Veatch, for it is a story that reflects definitely upon my own fitness, or rather unfitness, to be here this evening. Many years ago, when I was teaching philosophy at Indiana University, and was still on one of the very lower rungs of the academic ladder, a crisis arose one evening in our family household: one of our daughters had come down sick, and I was sent out to get a prescription filled at a local pharmacy that happened to be located just across the street from the Library and the Administration Building of Indiana University. As I was standing at the counter waiting for the prescription, who should walk in but one Professor K. P. Williams. "Old K. P.," as he was called, had been a very crusty professor of mathematics for many years at Indiana University. But also, and as a sort of second career, he had been a high-ranking officer first in the National Guard, and then, for a time, in World War II. Back again in his professor's role, he now, besides mathematics, had decided to devote himself to writing up what had long been a hobby of his—the military history of the Civil War. And sure enough, "K. P." managed to turn out no less than five volumes of a work, entitled *Lincoln Finds a General,* which some of you may doubtless have read. Indeed, the book became a best seller, there being in those years, following World

War II, any number of Civil War buffs abroad in the land, who bought up K. P.'s volumes like hotcakes.

In any case, on the particular evening in question, K. P. Williams had chanced to stop in at the drugstore where I was waiting for my daughter's prescription, it being right on his way home from his office in the library to his house just up the street. Espying me there over at the counter—though I don't believe "K. P." had ever deigned to speak to me before in his life—he suddenly called out, "Veatch!" I said, "Yes, Sir." (No, I don't think I saluted, but it's a wonder that I didn't, given K. P.'s manner and tone of voice.) At any rate, K. P. continued, "Last week I was up in Indianapolis, and I saw a friend of yours, Alan Nolan. Now Nolan said something to me about your being related to that old Civil War general from the little town of Rockport down in the southern part of the state, General James C. Veatch. Is that true?" I replied, "Yes, Sir, that was my great-grandfather." "Well," K. P. growled, "to think that a man like that would have a grandson teaching philosophy!"

And so you see, whatever may be my own opinions about generals not being human, I fear that it would be very hard to find many generals who would ever have a very high opinion of me, be it either for my philosophy or for my humanity! Be that as it may, just what is it that is to be understood by the implied contrast in my title between "being human" and "being a general"? Just think about it for a minute. Isn't it true—sad, but true, no doubt—that someone might indeed be a very good general, and yet not be much of a person? Or vice versa, is it hard to imagine that someone might indeed be the very highest type of person—just, fair-minded, not puffed up, a loyal friend—and yet at the same time be a lousy general?

Let's take some examples—first, suppose we take General Grant, for I don't doubt that there are at least some among you—though I daresay Major Dixon might not be one of them—who would consider Grant to have been a quite remarkable general. And yet what was Grant like as a person, as a human being? Here let me quote a passage written by Henry Adams, the distinguished American historian, intellectual, and man of letters, and a most famous descendant of the renowned Adams family—a family which, as you know, has played a great role in American history.

> Badeau took Adams to the White House one evening and introduced him to President and Mrs. Grant. First and last, he saw a dozen Presidents at the White House, and the most famous were by no means the most agreeable, but he found Grant the most curious subject of study among them all. About no one did opinions differ so widely. Adams had no opinion, or occasion to

make one. A single word with Grant satisfied him that, for his own good, the fewer words he risked the better. Thus far in life he had met with but one man of the same intellectual or unintellectual type—Garibaldi. Of the two, Garibaldi seemed to him a trifle the more intellectual, but, in both, the intellect counted for nothing; only the energy counted. The type was pre-intellectual, archaic, and would have seemed so even to the cave-dwellers. Adam, according to legend, was such a man.

In time one came to recognize the type in other men, with differences and variations, as normal; men whose energies were the greater, the less they wasted on thought; men who sprang from the soil to power; apt to be distrustful of themselves and of others; shy, jealous, sometimes vindictive; more or less dull in outward appearance; always needing stimulants, but for whom action was the highest stimulant—the instinct of fight.[3]

This portrait of Grant by Henry Adams may be anything but a reliable one. For Adams himself, many would say, reflected in his own person that very sort of disparity that I am trying to illustrate—a disparity between a man's excellence in certain skills or in his chosen profession, and his excellence as a person and a human being! Thus it is not uncommon to have the judgment made of Henry Adams that, while certainly remarkable as an American intellectual and man of letters, as an individual he was a far from attractive little man—bitter, pessimistic, acidulous, yes, even downright mean-spirited at times.

But still, let's get on with our story and its illustrations. And this time, rather than give you an illustration of how someone might be reckoned as eminently remarkable as a general, and yet comparatively unremarkable as a person, let me offer now an illustration of someone who was in many ways quite distinguished as to his character, but alas, anything but distinguished in his long and rather unfortunate career as a general. What I will read is the rather deft portrait which the distinguished contemporary English historian, Ms. C. V. Wedgwood, paints of a general, prominent in the English Civil Wars, one James Butler, Earl of Ormonde. Ormonde was an Irish nobleman of the 17th century, who, despite all the trappings of nobility that went with his name and his title and his distinguished family, was nevertheless someone who could be said, in his own person, to have been possessed of a genuine nobility of character. In fact, he was someone of singular balance of mind and possessed of unusual moral courage. For instance, in the character sketch which follows, Ms. Wedgwood recounts how during the Civil Wars, King Charles I had put Ormonde in command of his forces in Ireland. And alas, it needs to be noted that at the time the fighting in Ireland had amounted to a "veritable fury of

---

3. From *The Education of Henry Adams* (Boston: Houghton Mifflin, 1918), pp. 264–265.

destruction and hatred," Irish against English, Catholic against Protestant, and Parliament sympathizers against the forces of the King. This then is the sketch given of Ormonde:

> The Earl of Ormonde, general of the forces of the Dublin Government, refused to lay waste Irish villages or kill civilians. The greater number of his Norman-Irish family were in sympathy with the rebels; his mother was a Roman Catholic, his brother was in arms with the insurgents. ... His competence and popularity with the Government forces made him indispensable, yet there were those on the Council who suspected him of complicity with the rebels. But Ormonde stood with great steadfastness, for law, order, and loyalty to the Crown, and rebutted the whispered slanders: "I will go on constantly," he wrote, "neither sparing the rebel because he is my kinsman, or was my friend, nor yet will I one jot the more sharpen my sword to satisfy anybody but myself in the faithful performance of my charge."
>
> His wife was cut off in Kilkenny Castle with her children and the hundreds of fugitives whom she had received and relieved there. The Irish leaders threatened to destroy them unless Ormonde abandoned his command of the Government forces. The English responded that if the Countess and her children came to harm, no Irish woman or child would be spared. But Ormonde, not slackening his preparation for the spring campaign, proclaimed a different answer. If his wife and children, he wrote, "shall receive injury by men, I shall never revenge it on women and children; which, as it would be base and un-Christian, would be extremely below the price I value my wife and children at."[4]

Alas, though, that same Earl of Ormonde, for all of his nobility of character, found himself repeatedly worsted and beaten in war by the redoubtable Puritan general, Oliver Cromwell. In other words, being a good man was, alas, just no guarantee of being a good general—certainly not of being good enough to stand up to one of Cromwell's formidable cavalry charges!

And now let us ask just who was this Oliver Cromwell, and what sort of a person was he, for all of his greatness as a general? Here judgments do vary. And yet it is hard for many to think of Cromwell as too attractive in a human way—something of a religious bigot he was certainly, and also moody, wrathful, vindictive, utterly ruthless at times; and, much as Henry Adams said of Grant, so also it might be said of Cromwell that he was "more or less dull in outward appearance," a man "for whom action was the highest stimulant—the instinct for fight"—almost as if with him, "the intellect counted for nothing, only the energy counted." As the generally very judicious Earl of Clarendon remarked of him, he was "a brave, bad man."

Enough, though, of illustrations; and now let us try to point the

---

4. From C. V. Wedgewood, *The King's War* (New York: Macmillan, 1959), pp. 79–80.

moral of these illustrations. True, at first glance, the moral might seem scarcely to point beyond what we have already intimated, that there just does not seem to be any necessary correlation between being a good general and being a good man, or vice versa. Nor is it only a matter of one's generalship as over against one's humanity; for whatever your chosen field may be, or whatever your particular profession or area of expertise, there just does not seem to be any necessary correlation between your excellence in your job or in your profession and your excellence simply as a human being. You can be an absolute genius, say, when it comes to modern theoretical physics, and yet be nothing if not a rather paltry sort of person when it comes to being a human being—jealous, petty, disagreeable, and concerned with little else apparently than your own scientific recognition and academic glamour. Or vice versa, you might be a singularly high type of person—hard-working, firm in friendship, a good companion, never pompous or puffed up, unswervingly fair-minded—and yet still be no better than a very mediocre Chaucerian scholar. Yes, it's sad, but true!

O.K., suppose, then, that there so often is this curious-seeming unhappy disparity between a person's excellence in his chosen field or profession, and his excellence in life, or simply as a human being—still just what are we to make of this, and what, if anything, may we do about it? Well, apparently, at least one implication of this contrast and possible disparity between these two quite different kinds of human excellence would seem to be that when it comes to education—yes, even to higher education as it is in America, say—such education would apparently need to be of two concurrent, and yet quite different, kinds. Thus on the one hand, we certainly need to educate for excellence in all of the various arts, sciences, professions, skills, etc.; and on the other hand and at the same time, there would seem to be no less a need to educate for excellence simply in the business of living, or of being human, if you will. For just as one might say that there is no way—or almost no way—that one can be a good engineer or a good accountant or a good army officer or a good doctor without first learning how, so also we might say that there is just no way in which one can very well be much of a human being—*i.e.*, be what one truly ought to be as a human person—without first learning how. Yes, for the matter of that, must it not be acknowledged that there is a veritable art of living that must be learned, if what one wants to be is simply to be a good man or a good person, no less than that there are all of the various arts and skills that need to be learned—such as the art of medicine, or of computer-programming, or of business management, or of military command—if what one wants to be is either a good doctor, or business manager, or army officer, or whatever?

At this point, though, I am sure that there are many of you cadets who would draw back from this last conclusion, if not in some consternation and alarm, then certainly in no little disgust and perplexity. For what must the implication of all of this be with respect to your curriculum right here at West Point? Will it not mean that all of your various courses here in mathematics, in science, in engineering, in computers—you name it—will have to be weighed in the balance on the one side, as being courses that are aimed at making you proficient and expert in your chosen field, say, that of being a good army officer; and over against this entire assemblage and variety of staple West Point courses, there will have to be weighed in the balance on the other side just one single measly, lonely course—or maybe a couple such courses—as being the only one or ones aimed at teaching you how to be a good man (or woman), as over against how to be a good general? And what will that course be? Why, it will be none other than your required course in "drugs," of course!

However, before you let this sudden consequence be for you the veritable *reductio ad absurdum* of my entire line of argument, let me quickly shy away from the narrower question of education just as such, and let me set out, instead, to explore with you just a little further the more substantive implications of this contrast between learning how to be a good man and learning how to be a good general—or how to be a good anything else for that matter. For are there not many of you right now who will be saying to yourselves, "O.K., granted that there is such a contrast between being good at a particular art or skill or profession and being good simply at being human—*i.e.*, being a good man or good person—still," you will say, "who can tell us more exactly what this art of being human—this art of living, if you will—actually amounts to? For while we all know pretty well what it means to be a good doctor or lawyer or engineer or tennis player, who is there who can presume to instruct us in what it means to be a good man? For is this not just the sort of thing that moral philosophers have been arguing about for centuries—Plato, Aristotle, the Stoics, the Epicureans, Kant, the Utilitarians, *et al.*? And yet they never seem to come up with any agreed answer to the question."

Certainly, this is a fair enough challenge. To meet the challenge, however, I propose to proceed in a way that may strike many of you, at least at first, as being little more than a begging of the question. For I will not deny that in matters of moral philosophy, I find myself not a little partial to Aristotle and to an Aristotelian type of ethics. Yes, I would even go so far as to say that Aristotle was indeed one philosopher who did not merely speculate about what it might mean to be a truly good man. No, he actually knew what it was to be human and to attain a properly human type of perfection. Oh, I am not saying necessarily that Aristotle was himself such a good man in the actual living of his life. For nobody really knows much about Aristotle's own personal or public life either one. But what I am saying is that from what Aristotle wrote about ethics, one can certainly see that Aristotle was one who knew what the criteria of human excellence really are, as well as how one must conduct oneself and order one's life, if one is ever to become and be the kind of person that, just as a human being, one ought to be. In other words, in Aristotle's eyes there really does exist no less than an actual art of living, just as in other areas there may be said to be an art of medicine, or of accounting, or of computer-programming, or of military science and tactics, etc. And just as by studying the art of medicine, one should be able to learn how to go about performing an appendectomy, say, or, by studying accounting, one ought to be able to learn how to go about rendering an audit for a business corporation, so also, by studying ethics or the moral art, one ought to be able to learn how to order one's own life in the way in which it should be ordered.

However, before we can actually try to spell out rather more concretely what this moral art, or this art of being human, this art of living, actually amounts to, we must first take just a few minutes to clear away a couple of the roadblocks that certain modern philosophers—the Utilitarians on the one hand and the Kantians on the other, have placed in the way of any understanding of ethics, as being no less than an actual moral art or art of living.

Thus take the Utilitarians, first. For it seems to me that what the Utilitarians do is flatly to deny that ethics has anything really to do with perfecting oneself, with learning how to be accomplished simply as a person and as a human being—as if one could learn this sort of thing much as one can learn how to become accomplished as a musician, or as an engineer, or as a general, say. No, as the Utilitarian sees it, the good man will be one who works not for his own good or his own happiness or accomplishment as an individual but rather for the greatest good or the greatest happiness of the greatest number. And so it is that a properly moral or ethical knowledge for the Utilitarian will be a knowledge not of how to become and be something yourself, of how to perfect yourself, or become truly human; rather it will be a knowledge of how to help others—of how to secure the greatest good or the greatest benefit for the greatest number. As a result, the entire perspective in morals and ethics nowadays, largely as a result of the Utilitarian influence, would seem to me to be a radically distorted one: rather than concentrating on what our proper end should be as human individuals, our entire moral attention is supposed to be directed to a business of trying to figure out how many "goodies," so to speak, we can succeed in procuring for as many of our fellow human beings as possible. Oh, this is not to say, of course, that in the context of an Aristotelian sort of ethics we, as moral individuals, are not ever, or in any way, to concern ourselves with helping others, or with working toward the common good, or with loving our neighbors. Hardly, for be it remembered how, in Christianity, in the so-called Summary of the Law, we are told:

Thou shalt love the Lord thy God with all thy heart and with all thy soul and with all thy mind—this is the first and great commandment.

And the second is like unto it: Thou shalt love thy neighbor as thyself.

On these two commandments hang all the law and the prophets.

Notice, though, more exactly and precisely what it is that this second part of the Summary of the Law commands us to do, for it is something that even Christians nowadays tend to overlook—and this, no doubt, partly because of the influence of a Utilitarian type of morals or ethics. For the Law specifically says: "Thou shalt love thy neighbor *as thyself*." What else, though, does this imply if not that loving thyself is the very standard, and even, as it were, the very source and ground for your love of others? Accordingly, should you not be clear as to what your own perfection and fulfillment as an individual truly consists in, and should you then not love and strive for what is thus best for you yourself, as being your very end and goal and purpose in living, then you will scarcely know how you are to love your neighbor, or what it is that you are either to love in him or to love him for.

Nor can you very well object that, if it is no less than a self-love in this sense that is to have primacy in your life, you will inevitably find yourself committed to an utterly reprehensible selfishness and self-centeredness in your life. For just consider: supposing that someone did work himself into such a condition of utter selfishness—and alas, there are many of us who do this—where he neither loved anyone else, nor was loved by anyone else, would not such a person's utterly self-centered existence be nothing other than a veritable hell on earth for that poor individual? In other words, being that kind of an individual would be the very last thing that anyone would ever really want for himself. And so the Utilitarians must be simply wrong; of course, one must truly love oneself, first, last and always, for only thus will one come truly to see how unlovely it is for a person neither to love nor to be loved by his fellow human beings. Or to put this yet another way, so far from being an affair merely of helping others, morality, it must be said, needs to begin at home; you need first to get your own house in order, before letting yourself be carried away by what may often reduce to little more than so many sentimental concerns with doing good and helping others.

With that, then, let us turn from a consideration of what I have called the Utilitarian roadblock in the way of any proper Aristotelian understanding of ethics as an art of living to what I will call the Kantian roadblock. For just as the Utilitarians would deny that morals and ethics are ever to be conceived as being in any way an art of perfecting yourself, or of getting to know how to make something of yourself as an individual person and human being, so would Kant and his followers, for their part, deny that morals or ethics are ever, or in any way can be, an art or skill at all. No, for as Kant sees it, morals and ethics have absolutely nothing to do with instructing us in how we can best attain our ends in life, of how we can perfect ourselves, or how we may succeed in accomplishing something, or making something of ourselves. Rather for Kant our human moral life is nothing if not strictly an affair of rigidly following certain prescribed moral rules—so many absolute "do's" and "don'ts," if you will, and with respect to which we presumably are never really permitted to inquire why such rules are rules, in the sense of what good it might ever do us to obey such rules. No, we are to devote ourselves exclusively to doing our duty, as this is prescribed by the moral rules, and for no other reason than simply because it is our duty, and regardless of what the consequences for ourselves or for others might be of our thus doing our duty.

But note at once how this Kantian conception of morality as being an affair of one's simply doing one's duty solely for duty's sake quite precludes the possibility of ever regarding morals and ethics as being in any way a kind of art or skill or know-how in the matter of the business of living our lives. For is it not of the very nature of any art or skill that it teaches us how best to attain our ends, or how best to achieve some purpose or goal that we may have set before us—for example health in the case of the art of medicine, or victory in the case of the military art?

Oh, it's true, of course, that in all of the arts, professions and skills, etc., there is never in any one of them any lack of rules—yes, even at times specific "do's" and "don'ts"—regulating how the practitioners of the art or the profession need to go about pursuing the particular business of that art or profession. And in this respect it might seem that art might be rather like morality. Thus suppose we take but a couple of crude examples. Would we not all recognize that in the art of surgery, for example, there are all sorts of rules that a practitioner of the art must observe—*i.e.*, what he must be careful to do, as well as not to do—if he is ever to perform, say, an appendectomy properly? Or to take another example, would not you yourselves be the first to acknowledge that in your studies in military science and tactics you are taught all sorts of rules and guidelines that you had better observe if you are ever to perform, shall we say, a battle maneuver properly and successfully?

At the same time, is it not equally evident that in all such cases—*i.e.*, in cases of the several arts and professions, surgery, military strategy and tactics, electrical engineering, fly-fishing, cost-accounting, or whatever—there either always are, or ought to be, patent and obvious reasons why such rules of the art are rules? For example, why is it that in surgery there is a rule to the effect that one ought never to make an incision in a hemorrhageous tumor? The answer surely is that otherwise the patient is likely to hemorrhage and die. Or why is it a rule in military maneuvers that in launching an attack, one needs to be careful that one's flanks be adequately protected? Is it not because otherwise the enemy will clobber you?

Note, though, how radically different the situation is, in any Kantian type of morality, with respect to such rules as prescribe what our duties are and how we ought to conduct ourselves. For Kant insists that moral rules must never be obeyed for the sake of any ends or purposes to be achieved thereby, or on account of any sorts of benefits to be gained from our thus following such rules. Thus consider how Kant would conceive of his so-called categorical imperative, which for him is the supreme principle of morality. For instance, in the one formulation of his categorical imperative—as many of you will doubtless recall—the imperative reads: "So act that you can always will that the maxim of your action should become a universal law." Or in what Kant thought to be an alternative formulation, the imperative reads, "So act as to treat human nature, whether in your own person or in that of others, always as an end and never merely as a means." Now don't ask me to explicate exactly what these imperatives mean, for I must confess I have never been too clear as to just what the exact sense of them really amounts to myself. Nevertheless, it has sometimes been suggested that in the one formulation of his imperative, Kant's rule comes down to something like the Golden Rule in Christianity: "Do unto others as you would have others do unto you." Likewise, in its second formulation, one might say that Kant's categorical imperative comes down to something very like that part of the Summary of the Law in Christianity that we have already mentioned: "Thou shalt love thy neighbor as thyself." Moreover, from these two supreme principles of morality, the Kantians tend to suppose that they can then derive all sorts of further and more specific moral rules: "Do not lie"; "Do not steal"; "Do not go back on your promises"; "Do not bear false witness," and so on.

But now suppose that you or I or anyone else should simply raise the blunt question: "Why, though, should I obey such rules of morality? What is it that one might expect could be accomplished, or what is it that is to be gained by one's always being scrupulous about never telling a lie, or never bearing false witness, or always keeping your promises, or dutifully loving one's neighbor, etc.?" Notice, again, that when it comes to all of the several arts and skills, no rule may be held to be a valid rule of procedure in the art, unless it can be shown what it is that supposedly may be accomplished or achieved by adhering to such a rule. In contrast, in a Kantian type of ethics, it is just the opposite. Never is it either proper or appropriate to ask the question "why" with respect to any properly moral rules. In fact, the very idea that moral rules might be justified in terms of considerations as to what might be brought about by following such rules—this very idea, Kant would say, is inimical to, and destructive of, the very concept of any properly moral behavior. There one is to do one's duty for no other reason than that it is one's duty, and regardless of any consequences, either to oneself or to others, that such conduct might have.

And so, quite obviously, from a Kantian perspective there is just no way in which morals and ethics may ever be reckoned as structuring no less than a very art of living and thereby come to be likened to the several other arts. With that, though, does it not immediately become evident that, in taking such a curious and uncompromising stance in regard to possible reasons, ends, and purposes of moral behavior, Kantian ethics simply does its own self in? For notice: if the reasons in justification for rules of conduct, be it either in the arts or in our daily lives, can only be in terms of the ends and goals to be achieved by following such rules, then in excluding the very possibility of such reasons in the case of moral rules, the Kantian in effect has to concede that there just are no reasons in justification of moral rules, call them categorical imperatives or whatever. And if it be admitted that moral rules can not be shown to be in any way reasonable or justifiable, then what are they if not, ultimately and radically, entirely arbitrary and unreasonable? And who wants an ethics that is so arbitrary and dogmatic that no rational justification of any kind can be given for it? Yes, what kinder thing can we do at this point, with respect to the now seeming total philosophical embarrassment of a Kantian type of ethics than tactfully to "draw the curtain," as Mark Twain might say!

Very well, then, suppose that we have now removed both the Utilitarian and the Kantian roadblocks to a proper understanding and appreciation of Aristotelian ethics as involving no more and no less than the very art of living—an art which for us to be ignorant of, or to neglect, would leave us little more than mere babes in the woods—or perhaps a better metaphor might be, actual bulls in the china shop—so far as our leading our lives is concerned. "All right, all right," you may now say. "But I still have not told you," you may protest, "just what more specifically this so-called moral art, or art of living, must consist in—what some of its actual rules and precepts are. Besides, if this moral art of living be no other than the very art or skill that all of us need to master if, as human persons, we are ever to attain our true end and goal and purpose in life, then what more precisely is this end or goal? Can I possibly tell you what this is exactly? Or can anyone tell you what it is?"

Turning, then, to this final challenge from you, and attempting to speak to it quite directly, even if briefly, let me begin by suggesting that maybe this supposed difficulty of our ever being able really to know what our true end or goal in life is is surely exaggerated. For have we not all had occasion to observe and thus to come to know, merely from our ordinary everyday experience, "what fools we mortals be"—yes, even we ourselves, you and I and the next one? Indeed, are we not continually being made aware of the sorts of mistakes we all of us make in our lives, as a consequence of which we just don't bring off too well the job of our living our lives? And so, by inference, from those all too obvious mistakes of ours—our own as well as those of others—may we not thereby come to recognize pretty well by contrast what success in life or what truly living well may be seen to amount to?

Thus will you again allow me to read you but a short passage, one that I believe suggests very well by implication what some of the standards are for being a good man, as over against those for being merely a good general, say, or a good lawyer, or a good computer programmer, or whatever. The passage is a brief character sketch which the novelist, Jane Austen, draws of one of her main characters early on in the novel *Persuasion*:

Sir Walter Elliott [of Kellynch Hall in Somersetshire] was a man who, for his own amusement, never took up any book but the Baronetage; there he found occupation for an idle hour and consolation in a distressed one....

Vanity was the beginning and end of Sir Walter Elliott's character: Vanity of person and of situation. He had been remarkably handsome in his youth, and at fifty-four was still a very fine man. Few women could think more of their personal appearance than he did, nor could the valet of any new made lord be more delighted with the place he held in society. He considered the blessings of beauty as inferior only to the blessing of a baronetcy; and the Sir Walter Elliott who united these gifts was the constant object of his warmest respect and devotion.[5]

Surely, one needs to do no more than read or hear such a sketch as this one of Sir Walter Elliott than one immediately recognizes that Sir Walter was hardly the sort of person that as a human being one really ought to be. Not only that, but I am sure that he was hardly the sort of person that either you or I or anyone else would even want to be. For Sir Walter was nothing if not a snob and a pompous ass. True, Sir Walter doubtless never murdered anybody; he never robbed a bank, or bore false witness, or committed adultery, or even, so far as we know, "coveted his neighbor's wife, or his man-servant, or his maid-servant, or his ox, or his ass, or anything that was his neighbor's." And yet, for all of that, he was obviously a pretty poor specimen of human nature, and fell far short of meeting many of even those minimal standards of what we would all recognize that a human being—particularly one of Sir Walter's background and advantages—ought to be.

Very well, then, suppose we come right out and ask what it was that Sir Walter was so sadly lacking in so far as his being anything like what he ought to have been as a human being. May we not say—though it may sound a bit paradoxical at first—that what Sir Walter was most conspicuously lacking in was nothing if not a kind of knowledge? Not scientific or scholarly knowledge, to be sure, for it is not this sort of knowledge that is relevant here. Rather the knowledge that Sir Walter was so obviously lacking in was what Aristotle would have called "a practical knowledge," or what we might call a moral or ethical knowledge. That is to say, Sir Walter just did not know what was good for him; he did not have really any idea of what the true values in life were—as witness his being quite unable to conceive of any greater blessings in life than those of beauty and of a baronetcy! In this sense, we could surely say that Sir Walter scarcely knew what it was to be the sort of human being one ought to be; nor did he really have any idea how one ought to go about accomplishing such an end, supposing him ever to have had the knowledge of man's true end in the first place.

Notice, though—and this might seem to cause a certain complication in our entire line of argument: when we say that's what Sir Walter was lacking in, and why for that reason he failed to be very much in the way of being a truly good man, are we not saying that the art of living is perhaps, after all, very much the same as the other arts? For

5. The first sentence of the quotation is the opening sentence of Chapter I.

what, indeed, is the major factor in anyone's failing to be much of a general, or much of a flyfisherman, or much of a doctor, or much of a cook? Is not the answer simply that the poor fellow just didn't know enough—*i.e.*, he did not know how to conduct the battle, or how to perform the operation, or how to make the desired cast, or how to season the meat? In other words, in life, no less than in all of the other arts, it is lack of knowledge—which is to say, of the relevant know-how—that is the cause of one's failure, that is, of one's not being a good man, or not being a good cook, or not being a good general.

But in saying this, maybe we have still not got it quite right. For surely there is at least one other factor other than that of a mere practical knowledge that accounts, by its presence or absence, for the difference between someone's being a truly good man and one not so good. Thus notice how, by Jane Austen's account, it was not ignorance alone that was the source of Sir Walter Elliott's shortcomings so much as his colossal vanity—"vanity of person and of situation," as Jane Austen puts it. Yes, it was no less than this very vanity of Sir Walter's that was the primary source of his ignorance, just in the sense that it was because he was so stuck on himself that he just could not see himself as others saw him, or could not muster that self-knowledge without which, as Socrates thought, anyone is bound to come off as little better than a fool.

Very well, then, how in more general terms may we best characterize this added factor, besides a mere knowledge or ignorance, that so often turns out to be decisive in the moral choices that we make, and that is repeatedly responsible for those choices being as unwise and ill-advised as they often are? For clearly, it is not always vanity, and vanity alone, that leads us to make choices that we may later come seriously to regret having made. Instead, vanity is but a single instance of all those many and varied sorts of feelings, impulses, desires, inclinations, and emotions that are ever exerting an influence on the day-by-day decisions that we make in life.

In fact, seen against this background, is it not obvious that all of our choices and decisions in daily life are quite inescapably made within a context of what may be loosely designated as the appetitive side of our nature—our desires and aversions, loves and hates, fears and confidences? Accordingly, it is easy to see how, from what I will call this appetitive and emotional side of our nature, we are ever being impelled to do things that are often far from wise, and that our better judgment might surely counsel us against, if only we could bring our rational judgment properly to bear on the situations in which we have to make our choices.

Thus Sir Walter's foolish choices and preferences sprang largely from his vanity. And in my own case—if I may cite my own horrible example—it is only too often sad but true that on many an occasion I could be said to have known perfectly well that I ought not to have that extra drink, but I go ahead and have it anyway. Or I know it unwise, given my tendency to be overweight, to indulge myself in a feast of bacon and eggs and griddle cakes and maple syrup for breakfast, and yet I all too often go right ahead and have them anyway. Or again, how often in political and social situations have I known full well that the time had come for me to stand up and be counted, and yet I didn't do it, either because of fear for my reputation or for my job or for my popularity, or else maybe just because of a sheer laziness and indolence on my part in not wanting to get involved.

Against this background, then, we should now be able to see what is distinctive about the actions and decisions that we need to take in our moral life, as contrasted with such actions and decisions as we make in our particular spheres of competence and expertise. For in our moral life, our knowledge and our judgments as to what needs to be done in particular concrete cases are always such a knowledge, and involve such judgments, as have to be brought to bear in situations that are fraught with all kinds of pressures from our feelings, interests, emotions, etc. Consequently, as Aristotle insists, for our moral decisions we need to cultivate both what he calls the intellectual virtues, or virtues of knowledge, which instruct us (intellectually and cognitively), as to what ought to be done or ought not to be done in the individual situations; and also, and at the same time, and most particularly, the moral virtues, or virtues of choice, through which we come to discipline ourselves to moderate our feelings and passions and emotions in such a way as will enable our better judgment to prevail in the actual choices that we come to make.

Clearly, though, when it comes to the exercise of things like the arts and professional skills, the situation is hardly the same. For there it is only the intellectual virtues, or virtues of knowledge, that come into play, the so-called moral virtues being only indirectly relevant. Thus, for example, the skilled physician or dietician who tells me that it is unwise for me to eat griddle cakes and sausage for breakfast needs to muster no more than his professional knowledge, in order to give me his prescription and recommendation. That is to say, in order simply to deliver his professional judgment—and a true judgment at that—he does not have to overcome necessarily, or fight against, any feelings of rage or lust or revenge that might militate against his making that judgment. In contrast, for me who must choose and act upon the knowledge that the expert has imparted to me, I have to activate such moral virtues as those of temperance and self-control if I am ever to act upon my newly acquired knowledge.

Accordingly, drawing upon no more than these simple and even rather trivial examples, we should now be able to characterize, even if all too briefly, what is the nature of the contrast between ethics on the one hand, as being the art of living, and all of the other arts and skills and professions on the other. In the latter, it is only knowledge that counts. And so it is that the expert proves himself to be a good general, or a good cook, or a good accountant, simply by displaying a knowledge of what needs to be done, or ought to be done, or ought not to be done, in the concrete case. On the other hand, for all of us who, simply as human beings, need to be practitioners of the art of living, it is not enough that we merely know what ought to be done or ought not to be done; in addition, we must actually do it. And for this, moral virtue is needed as well as intellectual virtue.

And here in a nutshell, I suggest, is just where the difference lies between being a good man and being a good general, say. For to be a good general, all that one needs is just such knowledge—difficult and intricate and resourceful as that knowledge must be—of just what needs to be done in this, that, or the other situation such as may arise in the incredibly complex conditions of warfare and of preparation for warfare. In contrast, so far as the good man is concerned, his goal and his objective are not just to have the requisite knowledge and intelligence, but actually to live intelligently, amid those constant conditions of everyday life where we are ever buffeted and pressed by our feelings, impulses, desires, passions and such like. In other words, to live a good life calls for the exercise of both intellectual and moral virtue, whereas to be a good general, or a good anything else, requires the exercise simply of one's professional knowledge, whenever and wherever it may be called for.

And now for one last difficulty, and then I am done! Again, I can imagine any number of you saying, "O.K., that may be all well and good, and that may indeed be what it takes to be a good man as over against being a good general—namely, that one acquire the so-called moral virtues no less than the intellectual virtues." "Still," you will say, "why need anything like this concern me in the least? After all, I am a student at West Point, and all I care about is being a good officer!"

Fine! That may indeed be the way you feel, or at least the way you think you feel, and yet, do you really? For let me conclude with a terse and devastating assessment that K. P. Williams, the military historian whom I mentioned earlier, has made, not just of the military career, but of the personal character as well, of one of West Point's more distinguished graduates—after all, he was second in his class here at the Point! I refer to the one-time famous General George B. McClellan:

> Surely the verdict must be: McClellan was not a real general. McClellan was not even a disciplined and truthful soldier. McClellan was merely a vain and unstable man, with considerable military knowledge, who sat a horse well and wanted to be President.[6]

Now I ask all of you: even if your future careers as generals should turn out to be much more distinguished and brilliant than that of General McClellan's—and I certainly hope they will be, both for your sake and for the sake of the country!—still, would you want your character as a man and as a human being to be known as one who was vain and unstable, and who, even though you may have possessed considerable military knowledge, still as a person had little more going for you than that you sat a horse well and wanted to be President?

Surely, you would not want this. So why not perhaps take the study of ethics a little more seriously!

6. From *Lincoln Finds a General,* by Kenneth P. Williams, Vol. II (New York: Macmillan, 1949), p. 479.

12

THE POOR, HAPLESS HUMANITIES[1]

How better might I begin this talk than by simply commiserating with all of you for having to sit here and listen to it! Moreover, I can say this with some assurance—or perhaps I had better say "with some hope"—that it may not be so much me personally whom you are dispirited at having to listen to, as rather the topic that I propose to treat of. For don't we all know, perfectly well, what the humanities are, as well as that in these days the humanities are really in a bad way, not just academically, but intellectually as well? Thus, for example, if we reckon among the humanities subjects such as literature, be it English literature or American literature or foreign language literature, and history, of course, and philosophy, and perhaps religious studies, and certainly things like music and the arts, and indeed the entire host of so-called cultural subjects—these subjects, we certainly don't need to be told, are limping badly in the curriculum nowadays. Student interest has fallen off, and enrollments have declined, and even the professors who pursue and purvey these so-called disciplines seem not infrequently to have lost their sense of purpose, and hence not to know quite what it is they are about, or why they are about it. And in contrast, the natural and even the social sciences seem to be moving ever from strength to strength; and as for all the burgeoning new technologies and career-oriented subjects, these are continually expanding, thus threatening to trample the old humanistic disciplines under foot, and eventually to drive them out of the regular college and university curriculum altogether. "But don't we all know about this already?" many of you will be saying to yourselves. "So why do we have to hear about it all over again?"

Besides, I can imagine many of you muttering to yourselves something to the effect: "Confound it all," you will say, "once we get through hearing the usual lamentations and jeremiads about the

[1]. Phi Beta Kappa address delivered (in part) at Indiana University in the fall of 1983.

plight of the humanities today—the sorts of things that seem ever to be written on the dour faces and ever to be falling from the dull lips of deans, of college presidents, of commencement-day speakers, of honors-day orators, and other such worthies of the old school, all of them bemoaning how, with the weakening of the humanities, we are fast reaching the point of losing no less than our very cultural birthright, which is to say our precious humanistic tradition which has been ours for so many centuries—hearing all of this, are you not likely simply to rejoin, "Well, so what? For what difference does it make whether in today's academic curriculum one learns about Shakespeare or about philosophy, or about how to read Greek and Latin, or how to appreciate Bach or Haydn? For let's face it, subjects like these bake no bread; they don't help us to get a job, or to keep one once we have got it; they don't enable us to get on in the world any better, or to outdo the Russians, or to solve the problem of the deficits, or to manage the economy, or, for that matter, to do anything else that is of any real importance and concern to us in this day and age at all. So what possible difference does it make whether the humanities be allowed to go by the board or not?"

"True, as a result of the now rapidly changing patterns in the curriculum," you might say, "it may well be the case that we will no longer be able to contemplate a future in which we might spend our leisure hours reading Greek or Latin, say, or, as an alternative, turning to history, or philosophy, or English poetry, or the Pauline Epistles, or whatever, by way of relaxation. No, in this day and age," you will say to yourselves, "it would appear that leisure either spells television or it spells nothing at all! Accordingly, if the humanities seem no longer able to profit us either in our professional pursuits or in our leisure hours, then what good are they? Isn't that just the question?" you will say.

Very well, granted that that is the question, and that you are even now inclined to throw such reproaches as these right in my face, even before I really get started in my purpose to present a kind of defense and apologia for things like philosophy, and the classics, and the humanities generally, a defense and apologia that is aimed at restoring such subjects to what I would insist is their rightful place in the curriculum.

All right, but let me first respond, when you thus chide me with your questions, such as "But why the humanities? What possible good are they? How are they to be regarded as anything but readily dispensable luxuries in these days of ever-increasing academic cut-backs and stringencies?"—when you thus press me with questions like these, as I am sure all of you are doing right now, I assure you that I will respond at first by simply rolling with your punches. For so far from joining the usual chorus of convocation speakers, Phi Beta Kappa orators, establishment-college administrators, *et al.* in their familiar bombast about how we do so sorely need the humanities, I am willing to admit that what you usually hear on this score, even from the most eminent authorities, tends to amount to very little more than just so much stuff and nonsense. Yes, I would go on to say that the trouble seems to be that almost none of the more prominent establishment figures in present-day education and scholarship seem ever able to face up to the really key questions, "But why the humanities? What possible good are they? How can they be justified? And why aren't they simply dispensable in the face of all those newer disciplines such as computer programming, telecommunications, personnel management, psychological counseling, and God knows what else by way of the thousand and one more practical and productive subjects that are so clamoring for attention these days?"

Indeed, are not all of you accustomed to hearing such leading questions in regard to the humanities met with little more than platitudes upon platitudes? "Why the humanities?" the speaker will ask. "Why bother our heads any more with the old pretenses about the need for a liberal education?" And immediately there follow the would-be bold, but usually quite empty, words by way of answer: "Why, a liberal education encourages the development of a tough and disciplined mind." It's an education that serves "a liberating function"; it "engenders in us habits of thought which always ask why, which believe in evidence, which welcome new ideas . . . which accept complexity and grapple with it, which admit error and pursue truth," etc., etc.

All right, all right! I promise you I won't run on any more with truisms like these. And yet would it reassure you, or perhaps still disturb you, to know that the truisms which I have just rattled off are not of my own invention, but rather are just so many direct quotes from a former president of Princeton University? Nor should you be too hard on President Bowen for having used a rather specious eloquence to the effect ultimately of saying practically nothing at all. For suppose you were to listen to almost any other college or university president in today's world; suppose that you were to listen to former Dean Rossovsky of Harvard on the subject of Harvard's new core curriculum of a few years back. Or perhaps you will permit me to cite a somewhat similar example drawn from my own experience. Just a couple of years ago there was a superficially rather stirring address delivered on the campus of Indiana University. (That's where I now live in retirement.) The speaker was the eminent Dr. John William Ward, the prestigious head of the American Council of Learned Societies. He was speaking on the subject of "The Relationship of Scholarship in the Humanities to Society." Nor is there any denying the highly sophisticated performance that Dr. Ward gave on that occasion. For one thing, he did not fail to drop any number of quite important names from among those belonging to the present-day academic and scholarly establishment. And for another thing, he managed to employ in his address an impressive rhetoric, entirely in the best academic style and tradition. The only trouble was that if anyone were to have closely scrutinized the actual argument of that address, which, as I say, was devoted to proving "the relationship of scholarship in the humanities to society," I am afraid that what one would have found would have been not so much an argument as rather a kind of evaporation of any argument. At least, for myself, I quite failed to see what in Dr. Ward's eyes the relevance of humanistic scholarship to society was really supposed to be, or even that there was any relevance at all.

But then, would not much the same story be repeated, if one were to hear or read almost any of the other worthies who today grace the humanistic academic front—the executive secretary of Phi Beta Kappa, say, or any of the sponsors and promoters of the comparatively new Association for the Humanities? Yes, until very recently, I might have added to this list of eminent office-holders the former head of the National Endowment for the Humanities and now the Secretary of Education, Dr. William Bennett. But no, for Secretary Bennett, to the consternation of all and, I am afraid, to the dismay of many, has shown himself to be made of sterner stuff, at least when it comes to anything like an intelligent defense of the humanities. But even allowing that Bennett may be the exception that proves the rule, is not the rule itself that wherever one turns nowadays—be it to a mere hack in the business of convocation speaking like myself, or to those who are among the greatest of the great in our present-day academic and research establishments—one just cannot hope to hear much of substance when it comes to answering the question of what possible justification there might be for the study and pursuit of the humanities, or even of whether there is any justification for them at all any more?

And with this, I can hear all of you muttering to yourselves: "All right, having now heard your hapless speaker running down just about any and everybody else, who may have addressed himself to the hapless task of trying to defend the hapless humanities, what does he think that he can bring off by way of any less hapless a defense and justification, when it comes his turn? Why should he think that he can succeed where so many others, and better than he, have so signally failed?" Well, just let me respond to that one by frankly predicting in advance that no doubt I will fail, just as so many of my more prestigious predecessors have done. And while it might therefore be the part of wisdom for me just to sit down right now, and not bore you any further, let me say that my one excuse for not quitting is that I think you may find that my own fast-approaching failure will be of a new and rather different character from the others. Yes, for rather than simply belaboring you with platitudes, I predict that instead I shall simply offend you with my very wrongheadedness. And don't you think it better to be exasperated by a speaker's wrongheadedness than bored by his platitudes? So it's an ill wind that blows nobody some good, and that, even this very day and on this very occasion!

But to come now directly to some of the respects in which so many authorities in the present-day would seem to have gone astray, in their various attempts to mount a proper defense of the humanities. May we perhaps just analyze some of these to try to see what it is that is amiss about them? And first of all, consider just where and how it was that President Bowen of Princeton may have been led astray in those earlier quoted platitudes of his on the score of the humanities. For when he sought to wax eloquent on how the study of the humanities makes for "a tough and disciplined mind," for modes of thought that "always ask why," "that accept responsibility and grapple with it," I wonder if he might perhaps have been confusing the humanities with the liberal arts.

True, the confusion is not uncommon; and maybe it is a confusion that is even warranted by the current usage of the terms themselves. For doubtless, the two terms "liberal arts" and "humanities" have come to lose their more precise and distinguishable meanings, supposing them ever to have had any. Besides, if we consider the meaning which the term "liberal education" has come to have in recent years, that meaning tends to promote, rather than prevent, a confounding of the humanities with the liberal arts. Still, if one were now to try to distinguish these two sorts of disciplines, the one from the other, would one not need to say that the so-called liberal arts are really in the nature of *formal disciplines*, whereas the humanities are subjects whose *content* is somehow all-important?

For example, suppose we take as the prototype of the liberal arts the old *trivium*, as it was called, that has come down to us from the Middle Ages. The subjects comprised in the *trivium*, as you may recall, were those of grammar, rhetoric, and logic. And is it not true that what we learn from such disciplines are purely formal skills in the sense of word skills, or language skills, or skills in inference and deduction? Moreover, that such are purely formal skills would follow from the fact that they are skills in the use of language or of logic, regardless of what the subject matter might be that the language is used about, or that the logic is used to draw inferences in regard to.

Besides, if we add mathematics and all of the various and sundry computational skills to our list of the liberal arts, then surely it must be recognized that no modern college or university these days is lacking in instruction in such purely formal skills. On the contrary, the curriculum is literally bulging with offerings in things like computer sciences, statistics, applied logic, linguistics, etc., etc. Oh, it's true that, with all of this wealth of offerings in what I am now calling the liberal arts of today's colleges and universities, one still hears complaints on every hand to the effect that students nowadays don't know how to read, professors don't know how to write, and people generally don't know how to think. But, then, that involves a criticism not of any dearth in academic offerings in the formal skills of the liberal arts, but rather of our own aptitudes either as students to absorb such skills or as teachers to communicate them.

And now from these several comments regarding the purely formal skills of the liberal arts, may we not draw a number of conclusions regarding the humanities and the current tendency to confuse them with the liberal arts. (1) The humanities certainly differ from the liberal arts, just in the way in which what we might call content courses differ from courses in purely formal skills; (2) just as humanities courses would appear to be waning in importance in college and university curricula today, so the liberal arts, in the sense in which I would understand these as comprising purely formal skills, are waxing, and waxing mightily; and (3) while it might be tempting, given the flourishing condition of the liberal arts in the present day, to try to rehabilitate the humanities by somehow tying them to the coat-tails of the liberal arts, this, alas, will never do! For the humanities by no stretch of the imagination could ever be said to offer discipline in any of the formal skills such as might be associated with the liberal arts—at least not immediately and directly.

With this, though, is not our problem of trying to find a proper defense and justification for the humanities increased and compounded just that much more? For if the humanities are to be justified only in terms of the content of their offerings, as contrasted with other more formal disciplines, then how, pray tell, can one ever hope to answer such blunt and telling questions as the familiar ones to the effect: But why should so-called scholars in the humanities be devoting their entire lives to finding out about—or, for that matter, why should students, in having to meet requirements for the A.B. degree, be set tasks of having to learn about—such things as, say, Cromwell's defeat of the Scots in 1650, or the use of political and religious themes in the poetry of John Dryden, or the *cogito ergo sum* of Descartes, or the art of the Middle Kingdom in ancient Egypt, or St. Thomas Aquinas' five ways in proof of God's existence? Just what good does knowledge or information of this sort do anybody? Indeed, pose questions like this to today's teachers and students of the humanities and what sort of answers may one expect to get? In fact, isn't that just the question that, in these days of academic stringencies and cut-backs, the humanist scholars and professors have simply got to face up to and try to answer? Yes, is it not almost what one might call their "to-be or not-to-be question"? And yet how many of them can answer it? "Aye, there's the rub!"

To be sure, not infrequently one does hear humanist scholars simply trying to put on a bold front and answering such questions as the above by insisting that the knowledge one gets from studying the facts of history or of literature or of philosophy is a knowledge which is worthwhile just for its own sake. "No," they will say, "one does not have to worry about the import of such facts, or their significance, or of what the point of such a factual knowledge is, or its usefulness." Instead, it is argued, a mere, sheer erudition with respect to any and all facts of literary or political or cultural history is simply its own justification; and the greater one's factual erudition, the greater one's achievement is supposed to be as a humanist scholar.

Yes, I would even venture to say that some such answer as this in defense of the humanities is one that even the eminent Dr. Ward of the ACLS, whom I referred to earlier, rather tended to subscribe to in that address which I earlier mentioned as having been some few years ago at Indiana University. True, he did so somewhat gingerly; and yet he did make it clear that if what any reputed humanist scholar wants is to be a beneficiary of grants from foundations in the humanities, like the American Council of Learned Societies, then he had better be reconciled to abiding by the judgment of what Dr. Ward called the present-day "research university." And clearly for Dr. Ward the term "research university" was but a euphemism for "research establishment." Moreover, what does the standard for such judgments by the research establishment tend to be, if not mere quantity of factual information, unearthed and uncovered, usually in areas that are favored seemingly for their very remoteness, and for their having been comparatively unexplored, and hence almost for their apparent total irrelevance! And so it is that in his talk Dr. Ward admitted—I thought rather sheepishly—that grants from the ACLS are indeed given for research topics of such obvious fascination and pertinence as "Ovid among the Goths," "Motets of Italian Origin in English Sources," "The Qumran Angelic Liturgy," and, as his final example, "The Parable in Midrash."

Really, though, and with all due respect, is it not simply ridiculous to suppose that research into topics such as these, and for no other reason than that of acquiring a knowledge of such facts simply for its own sake, is ever really defensible?

For surely, Dr. Ward must know—and indeed, the entire academic research establishment must know (if they have ever stopped to think about it, as they probably never have)—that while there are kinds of human knowledge that can be said to be justified as being worth having just for their own sake, never does such a knowledge of things, just for its own sake, turn out to be a knowledge of mere facts, facts just in themselves and apart from any significance or import which they may have. No, for it is an elementary truth of philosophy, current ever since the days of Socrates and Plato and Aristotle, that it can only be an account of the so-called universals that are involved in particulars that a knowledge of such particulars is worth having. Hence to suppose it suffices to have a knowledge just of the fact that Ovid was indeed sometimes read by the Goths, but without any concern as to what the import or significance or even reason for such a fact might be; or again, to suppose that it is enough to have discovered that there once was a Qumran angelic liturgy, and that it had such and such features, but without ever bothering one's head with the question, "So what?"—surely, it is a travesty upon true scholarship and learning, as well as a philosophical enormity, to contend that such a knowledge of mere facts, historical or otherwise, is ever justifiable as a knowledge for its own sake.

Indeed, was this not just the point of our original question as to what the point and purpose of a humanistic knowledge might be, considering that it was not a knowledge of mere formal skills, but rather a knowledge with content? For to repeat our questions again, what is the point of knowing items of content such as that Cromwell defeated the Scots in 1650, or that one can actually find in English sources evidence of motets of Italian origin? To attempt to answer such questions by blandly asserting that one need not worry as to what the point is of a knowledge of mere particular facts; that, after all, the knowledge of such facts is something worthwhile just in itself and for its own sake—such an answer simply begs the question it is designed to answer; and not only that, it is a patently sophistic answer as well. That it happens to be the answer that by and large would seem to be relied upon by the present-day research establishment in the humanities, that is just so much the worse for the research establishment!

All right. But we still have our question: why the humanities? and what is the point of the kind of knowledge that we call a humanistic knowledge? For clearly, it is not a scientific knowledge. And we ourselves have noted that it is not such a knowledge as can be justified in terms of being conflated with a knowledge associated with mere formal skills. Likewise, it is not to be justified in the way the present-day humanistic establishment so often tends to justify it—as if it amounted to no more than a knowledge of particular historical or literary or cultural facts simply for their own sake. Very well, but what sort of a reason can be given then for such a humanistic type of knowledge?

Perhaps we might now try to answer by taking an entirely different tack. This time why don't we consider a line of answer—and a most plausible line of answer too—that one is likely to hear from the lips, as contrasted usually with the actual publications, of ever so many scholars and professors in the field of the humanities. Such a line of answer often takes the form of very personal testimonies to the lasting and enduring and unforgettable and even ineffable experiences that one comes to have from the reading of a Dante or a Shakespeare, say, or from hearing a Bach chorale, or listening to a Haydn symphony, or viewing the Rubens paintings on the ceiling of the Banqueting Hall in Whitehall, or taking in that magnificent prospect of the Campidoglio in Rome. It is in terms of experiences such as these that human beings may be said really to live, or to enjoy their finest hours. In other words, it is largely an aesthetic justification that is then given for the pursuit and study of the humanities, as if these somehow bring in their train untold experiences, which for their richness and variety, and for their lastingly satisfying character, are said to be absolutely unrivalled in human existence. And so perhaps they are.

Unhappily, when one points to such experiences by way of offering an *apologia* for the humanities, it seems that such experiences are of a sort that we can far more readily appreciate ourselves than ever manage to tell others about, much less communicate to others who have not experienced them—the peculiar kind of value which such experiences must presumably have. Perhaps that's the very reason that apologias for the humanities are so hard to bring off. And yet it can be done, and even is done, and sometimes with a peculiarly telling rhetorical skill, in contrast to the ordinary banalities that one is accustomed to hear in praise of the humanities. And by way of example, let me cite what I think was a singularly gifted performance in this vein by the president of Georgetown University, Father Healy, at a convocation address just a few years ago. It was an address in which Father Healy recounted his own most recent experience in the matter of teaching the humanities. For it seems that not long after he became President of Georgetown, he had volunteered to offer a very special course in English poetry—Donne, Yeats, Dylan Thomas, and I don't remember who else—that was to be given to just a few select honor students from the Georgetown Medical School. As Father Healy related it, the effect of his course upon those students was—by his own testimony—nothing if not electrifying. Here they were, students who, day in and day out, and doubtless night in and night out as well, were being subjected to a massive and unceasing barrage of scientific facts. For as Father Healy put it, the scientific way is one of the "two major ways in which knowledge impacts the human mind." Now the scientific way consists in "a controlled and logical analysis that adds fact upon fact and ultimately compels assent." Contrast, though, the way of the humanities! "The subjects so included are literature, the fine arts, philosophy, history, theology and probably half a dozen others that I'm missing. Here we see a totally different kind of learning and teaching. We who teach in the humanities are brush-clearers, path-makers, removers of obstacles. We must clear the way, rather like raising the curtain on a play. Ultimately our trade consists in putting the student in touch with the object or process which we are trying to teach. And then as Mark Antony says, 'mischief thou art afoot.' Once I have brought a student face to face with King Lear, so that he reads the play clearly, and with some understanding of the way Shakespeare intended it, I have set up a spiritual chain reaction which is utterly uncontrollable. The explosion which occurs when a young mind meets a great work of art or a great idea is unpredictable, violent and chaotic."

Nor does Father Healy stop there, for the entire world of humanistic scholarship, he says, is "a kind of chaos": it takes the student out of the predictable world where all of us live and into the world of dream.

> "It's a world of gentleness where there is no hurt, where there is much delight, and where we and you are emphatically at our best. After 30 years of coping with this kind of anarchy I have learned not to fear it—and would hope that you won't fear it either."

> "If you let yourself go, you can be drawn out of fatigue and into the wild and daring world of the imagination, where things you never dreamed possible remain impossible, but for brief fleeting moments, moments in and out of

time, let you believe that you can confuse the dancer with the dance and enjoy yourself."

"Come on in, the chaos is fun."

And so drawing to his conclusion, Father Healy notes that "the essential ingredient" in the life of the student is "his capacity to dream. College is ideally a sheltered world where the imagination has free reign and where the most impossible structures can be raised, because they will hurt no one when they fall. Colleges and universities are dream worlds." Moreover, it is toward the engendering of just such dreams that the humanities serve their purpose in a liberal education. And in conclusion, Father Healy quoted that great, fetching speech of Caliban, where he tells how "the isle is full of noises, sounds, and sweet airs," such that, Caliban says, "in dreaming," it was such that "when I waked, I cried to dream again."

Now I ask you, could anything be more persuasive or more eloquent than this? And indeed, do we not have here a line of justification for the humanities that is not just impressive, but practically indisputable? A training in the humanities, it thus may be said, refines our tastes and develops our finer sensibilities, enabling us to have experiences that we should otherwise never have come by, and without which life would become immeasurably more dull and lack-luster and pedestrian. In fact, why not call this simply the aesthetic justification for the study of the humanities? And what's wrong with that?

To which my answer is that there may be nothing wrong with it just as such. And yet if one tries to pass it off as being either the sole, or even an adequate, justification for the humanities, then it seems to me that such a purely aesthetic justification can become dangerous and even downright misleading. Thus as Father Healy would apparently seek to construe such an aesthetic justification of the humanities, it's as if these prized aesthetic experiences served little purpose other than that allowing us to escape from reality and from the real world of human experience in which we live. Indeed, if we heed Father Healy's testimony, aestheticism spells little more than sheer escapism. For it is just such aesthetic experiences which, he says, set off spiritual chain reactions in students and scholars alike—chain reactions which propel us right out of the world of fact and of science and of knowledge, and cause us to lose ourselves in a world of chaos and of anarchy and of dreams.

Yet surely, something is amiss here, for why should it not be precisely the humanities that serve to acquaint us with what it means to be human? In other words, why not consider that the justification for the humanities lies not in the fact that they set off spiritual chain reactions in students, which in turn propel the students right out of the world of fact and of science and of knowledge and into the world of chaos and anarchy and of dreams? Rather why should it not be precisely the humanities that should serve to bring not only students but all of us as well out of the mere dream world of our childish fantasies and into that real world of human fact and human reality—a world, alas, which we all too many of us are ever trying to flee from, and that many of us have scarcely even bothered really to find out about at all. Thus so far from encouraging us to forsake the realm of knowledge for the realm of chaos and imagination and dream, it would rather seem that the very matter of the humanities and of a humanistic education should be no less than the Socratic prescription taken from the oracle of Delphi, "know thyself," which in the present context could be interpreted to mean, "know what it is to be human, and then attempt to put such knowledge into practice."

With this, then, we would seem to have a rather different line of justification for the humanities than the purely aesthetic one that we found Fr. Healy to be proposing. For now the humanities would appear to be justified as offering us precisely a kind of knowledge, and peculiarly valuable type of knowledge at that. Besides, what are we to say that this particular humanistic type of knowledge is, if not a moral or ethical knowledge, or what Aristotle would call a practical knowledge?

Oh, I know that this must all sound dreadfully reactionary, not to say dreary and depressing. For is not morality something that we have all of us in recent years managed to free ourselves from and get shut of in these present palmy days of liberation and enlightenment? Still, for all of that, let me but mention in passing that there are fortunately other and different conceptions of morals and ethics from any that we would appear even to have dreamed of in our present-day philosophy. Thus the Greeks, for example, and notably Aristotle, had a conception of ethics according to which ethics is taken to consist in nothing more nor less than a knowledge of how to live, and of how to become and be truly human. And if you rejoin that this, after all, is something that each of us already knows all about anyway, since who of us does not know perfectly well, each and every one, what his own tastes and preferences are—still, in reply, might we not just ask ourselves whether, in all honesty, we all of us really do know all of the answers when it comes to the living of our lives? Indeed, isn't it obvious that at least some of us, some of the time, have made, shall we say, some mistakes? And certainly, we would none of us have any trouble thinking of any number of friends and acquaintances who we are quite sure have not just made mistakes but even made fools of themselves, and possibly even wrecked their whole lives? Nor can we even be too sure, when we come right down to it, but what we ourselves have perhaps been no less foolish oftentimes than our neighbors. Yes, if only we could see ourselves as others see us, might it not then really be brought home to us that maybe we are not so smart after all but rather are just as much plain damn fools as the next one?

For instance, just by way of illustration, why not recall that passage rather early on in Jane Austen's novel *Persuasion*, where the author, in just a few deft lines, manages to tick off the character of one Sir Walter Elliott:

> Sir Walter Elliott of Kellynch Hall, in Somersetshire, was a man who, for his own amusement, never took up any book but the Baronetage; there he found occupation for an idle hour and consolation in a distressed one. . . .
>
> Vanity was the beginning and end of Sir Walter Elliott's character: vanity of person and of situation. He had been remarkably handsome in his youth, and at fifty-four was still a very fine man. Few women could think more of their personal appearance than he did, nor could the valet of any new made lord be more delighted with the place he held in society. He considered the blessings of beauty as inferior only to the blessing of a baronetcy; and the Sir Walter Elliott, who united these gifts, was the constant object of his warmest respect and devotion.[2]

Now from such a passage, who can fail to recognize that Sir Walter was, indeed, nothing if not a pompous ass? So far from having anything like a proper knowledge of himself, his powers and his responsibilities, he was little better than a fool, not recognizing what the true values in life are, or how someone in his condition and circumstances in life ought to conduct himself.

Oh, it's true that you might say that Sir Walter was not exactly an "immoral man," in the way in which that term tends to be understood nowadays: he never robbed a bank; he was no adulterer; he never cheated on his income tax. (True, there probably was no such thing in England under the Regency, but no matter!) Likewise, so far as we know, he never bore false witness, nor was he known even to have "coveted his neighbor's wife, or his man servant, or his maid servant, or his ox, or his ass, or anything that was his neighbor's." Still, for all of that, there is just no getting around the fact that Sir Walter just did not know what the score was, so far as living his own life was concerned. He simply could not bring the job off any better than to turn out to be but a snob and a stuffed shirt. As Socrates would say,

---

2. The first sentence of the quotation is the opening sentence of Chapter I of the novel.

he just did not have the requisite self-knowledge. Or as St. Paul would say, he thought more of himself than he ought to think.

And right at this point you may say, "Yes, but where are we to turn in order to acquire this kind of self-knowledge, or just how are we to come by this moral or ethical knowledge, in that particular sense of morals and ethics that we have just been suggesting? And indeed, in this very connection it might not be amiss to note that Aristotle conceived a moral or ethical knowledge as being no less than the kind of knowledge that he called a "practical knowledge": it is such knowledge as should make us proficient precisely in the art of living our lives as human beings. In this sense, ethics, or, if we may so term it, the "art of living," might be conceived at least somewhat on the analogy of other arts, skills, crafts, and technologies. For just as when it comes to things like the art of medicine or carpentry or military tactics, or of accounting or bridge-building or whatever, we all acknowledge that one cannot hope to be a good doctor or a good carpenter, or a good field officer or a good accountant, without first learning how, so also, when it comes to that kind of practical knowledge that Aristotle called ethics, there is just no way in which one can ever hope to be a good man—that is to say, one cannot hope to live as a human being ought to live, which is to say, wisely and intelligently—unless, again, one takes the trouble to learn how.

But here again our earlier question presses: just where are we to go, if what we want to learn is not how to practice medicine well, or how to be a good butcher or baker or candlestick maker, but rather how to live our own lives well—*i.e.*, how to be a good man, and not any mere knave or fool? Alas, the answer to this question is not a little complex and difficult. And yet surely, in the light of what we have said thus far, there should be no doubt that one place that one certainly needs to resort to in order to learn about being human is the area of the humanities, and primarily to that subject in the humanities that we call philosophy, and particularly moral philosophy or ethics. For without philosophy, the mere humanities alone, and just as such, will never yield the kind of knowledge that is here needed and wanted. Thus mere study and research in the area of the humanities of the kind advocated by scholars like Dr. Ward tend to yield no more than a purely historical or factual knowledge of a sort we have talked about earlier. Or merely steeping ourselves in the great classics of literature, music, art, poetry *et al.*, while they may indeed pay off in terms of a heightened aesthetic appreciation that we may well derive therefrom—still, all of this cannot as such lead us to that very knowledge of good and evil, and of what it means to be human, and of what we ourselves as human beings ought to do and be if we are ever to attain to being truly human ourselves. No, not even a preoccupation with the humanities in the manner of so-called Great Books courses will necessarily do the trick either. For while such a Great Books approach, when well executed, can lead to no end of student fascination with, and even ongoing vigorous discussions of, what has sometimes been termed, perhaps a bit sentimentally, "the great ideas," that still does not mean that there is any technique provided by such a Great Books procedure that will lead either students or scholars to be able to sort out the true from the false among the so-called "great ideas" and thereby arrive at what can only be designated as a genuine moral or ethical knowledge. For this, it will take philosophy, and philosophy alone—particularly moral philosophy.

True, philosophy alone, or even ethics, divorced from the other areas of the humanities, can hardly lead to anything like a full and proper moral knowledge, if it be completely divorced—as philosophy courses tend nowadays to be, unfortunately—from the other areas of the humanities, history, poetry, art, and so on. And the reason is that it is just those several areas of the humanities, other than philosophy, that one needs to resort to in order to find examples galore of just the sorts of things that one needs to know, when it comes to no less than human wisdom and human folly, human courage and human cowardice, human self-mastery and self-control, as contrasted with self-indulgence.

Oh, this is not to say, of course, that one may not go directly to one's own experience to learn of these things. Besides, hopefully, one may have learned something at least of the differences between right and wrong, or good and bad, simply from one's parents, or from the Church, or from other similar agencies in society. Unfortunately, however, such moral instruction as we may be able to gain from these latter sources is often dogmatic, not to say even arbitrary in some instances. Besides, to suppose that one need not go outside of one's own personal experiences, when it comes to the business of learning how one ought to live—such experience is likely to be far too narrow and provincial. Yes, it would be rather like a physician trying to learn how to practice medicine without much formal instruction in medicine, and really without any wide clinical experience at all, relying instead solely upon cases which he may just happen to have come in contact with within the narrow circle of his own personal friends and acquaintances.

Instead, suppose that what we want and need is a full and proper experience of the human in all of its depth and variety, where else can we go for this sort of thing, if not to the humanities? Already we have seen, just in passing, how one can get at least some sense of what might be called the pathology of human folly in the living of our lives simply by reading Jane Austen. And of course, humanistic learning is happily not limited only to Jane Austen, or even to English literature as a whole, for that matter. No, it is the entire range of human history and literature and art that humanistic learning is, at least in principle, designed to acquaint us with.

And here again, it would seem to me that we can turn to Aristotle for the proper explanation of just why and how it should be precisely the humanities that are the proper sources for us to turn to, when it comes to a business of acquiring a moral experience, to say nothing of that very practical knowledge which each and everyone of us needs if he is ever to live his life well, which is to say wisely and virtuously, and with a proper sense of what the art of living requires of him. Oh, it's true that the particular passage which I am about to read from Aristotle is no longer one that anyone can say is exactly fashionable among today's literary scholars and critics. To which I can only reply that however much what Aristotle here says may now have become unfashionable, it nonetheless has the peculiar distinction of being true! And so let's listen to Aristotle:

> Epic poetry and Tragedy, as also Comedy, Dithyrambic poetry, and most flute-playing and lyre-playing, are all, viewed as a whole, modes of imitation.

(Now, pray, let's not all of us at once get hung up over the meaning of that term "imitation"! For quite patently Aristotle does not mean that art imitates nature or reality in the way a photograph does the scene which it reproduces—if for no other reason than that in Aristotle's eyes there must be a great deal more to reality than any mere photograph could ever represent.) But be that as it may, one thing that Aristotle does intend to suggest here is that, however the notion of "imitation" may be understood, it is just the rhythm or the language or the harmony that in each of the instances cited is the precise means of the imitation. And so Aristotle continues:

> Rhythm alone, without harmony, is the means in the dancer's imitations; for even he, by the rhythms of his attitudes, may represent men's characters, as well as what they do and suffer.

> Likewise, there is the sort of imitation that is brought off by using language alone, be it prose or verse. And as for "the objects the imitator represents," [these]

> are actions, with agents who are necessarily either good men or bad men—the diversities of human character being nearly always derivative from this

primary distinction, since the line between virtue and vice is one dividing the whole of mankind. It follows, therefore, that the agents represented must be either above our own level of goodness, or beneath it, or just such as we are.[3]

Now here we have it, I would say! For if all of the arts—and history, too, as these are comprised within what we call the humanities—if all of these are concerned with but the representation (or as Aristotle says, the "imitation") ultimately of human action and of human character, and if all human action or character must be the actions and characters either of good men or men not so good, then what does a truly humanistic knowledge amount to, if not precisely to that very practical knowledge of what the good is, and what the bad is, in human life and human existence, and of how we human beings need to conduct ourselves and order our lives, if we are not to end up being little more than knaves or fools or even worse? True, this practical knowledge, or humanistic knowledge in the proper sense, is not any kind of knowledge that will bake any bread, or put a man on the moon, or provide us with a nuclear arsenal, or whatever. And yet is it not, for all of that, a knowledge of the things that matter most, and matter most to us precisely as individual human persons, each one of whom must try to lead his own life, as wisely and as well, and with as much insight and knowledge as he can possibly muster?

Now this is not to say that all of the vast number of other subjects in the curriculum, outside the humanities, are of nothing worth. Far from it, and indeed applying the words of Mark Antony, I would be the first to say, "they are all, all honorable men"—physics, computer science, botany, microbiology, urban studies, anthropology, economics, and all of the rest. All of this notwithstanding, what I am saying is that, absent the humanities from the curriculum, and absent a truly philosophical understanding of the very principles of our culture as a whole, and all of the other disciplines will not then be worth a candle!

3. From Chapters 1 and 2 of the *Poetics*, translated by Bywater.

13

NATURAL LAW: DEAD OR ALIVE?

Surely, the ancient and honorable doctrine of natural law is dead, is it not? And many would add, "Long dead and well dead!" What, then, can a bibliographical essay such as this amount to, if not to a kind of funeral oration, or else to a chronicle of "old, forgotten far-off things, and battles long ago"?

Not so, though. For two excellent recent historical studies—the older and shorter one by A. P. D'Entrèves, and the longer and very recent one by M. B. Crowe—both tell a similarly fascinating story of the continual births and rebirths of natural law doctrines in the course of their long history. Professor Crowe has even remarked that "the natural law, as an idea, is almost as old as philosophy itself."[1] He thinks he can find the origins of a natural law doctrine even among the pre-Socratics. Following this, it received at the hands of the Sophists what appeared to be if not a death-blow, then certainly a serious set-back. Plato and Aristotle, however, promptly revived it, if not in name, then certainly in essence. And with the Stoics, it really came into full flower.[2] Proceeding, then, to the Christian thinkers of the Middle Ages, natural law doctrines at first enjoyed a rather more dubious status, only to receive eventually their most definitive formulation and justification at the hands of St. Thomas Aquinas in the thirteenth century.

In the later Middle Ages and the Renaissance, to be sure, there occurred something of an eclipse, only to be followed by the great sunburst of natural law doctrines, albeit in somewhat altered form, in the seventeenth and eighteenth centuries. The great names that always recur are first those of Hugo Grotius and Samuel Pufendorf, and then later and to a somewhat different effect, those of John Locke and Jean-Jacques Rousseau. The story is only too familiar of how their

---

1. Michael B. Crowe, *The Changing Profile*, p. 246 (see Bibliography).
2. For both the fact and the character of natural law doctrines in classical antiquity, Crowe's treatment is excellent. But by far the most discerning and provocative discussion of natural law, as it suffered and flourished at the hands of the Sophists and of Plato and Aristotle, may be found in Leo Strauss *Natural Right and History*, esp. Ch. 3.

influence carried right over into the Age of Reason, when doctrines of natural rights seemed to crop up everywhere, and not least in America with the publication of the Declaration of Independence, followed by the numerous Bills of Rights in the various State and Federal constitutions.

Once again, though, the flourishing of natural law in the eighteenth century was followed by its apparent demise in the nineteenth century. As one contemporary critic has put it, "the philosophers tended to say that the natural law was not natural, and the lawyers said that it was not law."[3] Nevertheless, with the Thomistic revival in the latter part of the nineteenth century, an interest in natural law appeared to be in full swing again by the first quarter of the present century, particularly in Catholic circles. In this country, Catholic institutions of higher learning, especially law schools, pressed for the teaching of so-called natural law along with positive law; and thinkers of the stature of Jacques Maritain enjoyed vogue and influence alike in their efforts to awaken both Europeans and Americans to the pressing demands of human rights, particularly in the light of the ruthless suppression and perversion of those rights at the hands of the Nazis. Then suddenly, in the late 1950s and 1960s, it was almost as if the bottom had dropped out, so far as natural law doctrines were concerned. In academic circles, especially among philosophers and political scientists, no one talked about natural law or natural rights anymore; and if one did, one was promptly relegated to beyond the pale by scornful colleagues.

And now just as suddenly, and seemingly no less unpredictably, there has been a dramatic revival of interest in so-called "rights theories"—and this just in the last ten, perhaps even the last five, years. True, such recent rights theories have not always involved an effort at reinstating anything like "natural" rights, and certainly not "natural law." Yet many of them have. And in any case, they have all had the effect of bringing the issue of whether or not there is a natural law right out into the open again, thus making it not just respectable, but even imperative to discuss it and to take it seriously.

How "Natural Law" Should Be Understood: The Thomistic View of the Objective Grounding of Ethical Standards

What, though, is this doctrine of the so-called "natural law" that has had such a long and checkered career and has even displayed, in

3. Crowe, pp. 246–47.

the words of more than one authority, the happy faculty of repeatedly being able to bury its own undertakers![4] Quite obviously, the doctrine is aimed at affirming that such things as human responsibilities and obligations, as well as human rights and "entitlements,"[5] are more than a mere affair of human convention or human agreement, and this no matter how enthusiastic or how widespread may be the acceptance of those conventions and agreements. Thus whether it be Antigone in Sophocles' drama, Socrates in Plato's *Apology*, or Shcharansky and Ginzburg of today's Soviet Union, the mere fact that a person has been convicted of a crime does not necessarily mean that hers or his was really a crime at all. Likewise, what may be right or just according to the standards of a given community or society may still be radically at variance with the standards of a natural right or a natural justice. Yes, might not one be inclined to say that in the Shcharansky case, for example, it is patent and obvious for all to see the glaring disparity between what the civil or military authorities are agreed in saying is just and right and what is really so? For it is an implication of any doctrine of natural law or natural right that the marks and standards of a natural justice are such as to make it recognizable, even in the face of whatever the prevailing convention or customary justice may affirm to the contrary. Indeed, in this sense natural laws are held to be evidenced by nature itself, and to be there, as it were, right in the facts for all to see, if we have but eyes to see, and are not blinded by habit or by convention or by social conditioning or whatever.

Still, it is one thing to say that in any natural law doctrine, ethical and political standards are objectively grounded, or that they literally have a status as laws of nature, and thus are knowable and rationally determinable. It is yet another thing to understand just how such natural norms and standards may thus come to be known, to say nothing of how they can have an actual ontological status in reality. And it is just such points that we need to be clearer about, if we are ever to find our way around in the contemporary literature, particularly as it surrounds the newly emerging contemporary rights theories.

To this end, we would make reference to an exceedingly illuminating article published in *The Monist* a few years ago by Vernon Bourke, entitled "Is Thomas Aquinas a Natural Law Ethicist?"[6] It is true that Professor Bourke is primarily concerned with medieval versions of the theory of natural law and with the way in which so-called natural laws

---

4. *Cf.* statements by Crowe, p. ix, and by A. P. D'Entrèves, *Natural Law*, p. 13, to this same effect.
5. A term borrowed from Robert Nozick and, admittedly, cited here out of context.
6. "Is Thomas Aquinas a Natural Law Ethicist?" *The Monist* 58 (January 1974). The quoted phrases that follow in the text are from pages 52 and 53 of that article.

were held to be associated with the law of God. In this context "two radically different meanings for natural law" emerged, the one theological in origin, the other naturalistic or secularized, based on the natural light of unaided human reason. According to the one, natural law came to "name a code of moral precepts implanted in man's nature, or mind, and issuing from the legislative Will of God." From such a view, what is good or bad, right or wrong, for man clearly depends on divine fiat. Accordingly, moral and political norms, so far from being in any proper sense "natural" or discoverable by reason in the very nature of things, would appear rather to be but so many "oughts" that are binding for no other reason than that God has decreed them to be so. By contrast, in the other view of natural law, namely, that of Thomas Aquinas, a natural law theory of ethics or politics stresses, as Bourke puts it, "the rational discernment of norms of human conduct, working from man's ordinary experiences in a world environment of many different kinds of things."

Bourke's way of characterizing the Thomistic understanding of natural law may appear to be a bit of a mouthful. But why not consider ethics and politics, as construed in the light of this conception of natural law, as analogous to certain arts, skills, and crafts? Why does the skilled surgeon, for instance, make his incision in one way rather than another? Don't we say that it is because he knows how to do the job? There is presumably some reason—a real reason—for his doing it that way rather than another. In this sense, we should scarcely say that the rules of good surgical practice are mere agreed-upon conventions with no natural basis at all. Or why does the football coach insist that a tackle be made in one way rather than another? Is it just because he happens to like the one way rather than the other; or is it because there are reasons why one way of making the tackle is better than some other? And so also for countless other skills and techniques—bait-casting, accounting, gourmet cooking, pleading a case, teaching a class, building a bridge, or whatever. In all of these cases the expert is said to *know* how to do the job, and his knowledge is but a knowledge of what the *nature* of the case or the situation demands, be it in surgery or fishing or cooking or building a bridge or whatever.

The Art of Living Based on Objective Nature and Reason

Accordingly, in Aquinas' view the living of our lives, be it either as individuals or as political animals, requires certain skills and know-how. That is to say, just as in the various arts the end in view determines the natural ground or reason for the means used—*e.g.*, the health of the patient in the case of medicine, or the instruction of the student in the case of teaching, or victory in the case of strategy, or convincing the court in the case of legal pleading, etc.—so also in the case of living our lives as human beings and attaining such fulfillment and perfection as is appropriate to human nature, this requires that we know what needs to be done and how we need to conduct ourselves to such an end.[7] Just as in making tackles, or preparing meals, or performing surgical operations, or landing a fish, there are right ways of doing the thing as over against wrong ways. And since there are reasons why in the nature of the case such right ways of doing the job are right, so too, by analogy, in the living of our lives, the right way of doing the thing might be said to be that which is naturally right or just. Thus the various moral or ethical rules that need to be followed in the conduct of our lives may be said to be rules that are determined not subjectively by arbitrary whim but rather by "right reason" considering the pertinent facts. In this sense such moral rules may be properly termed "natural laws."[8]

So much, then, for the two rival conceptions of natural law, or rival ways of construing the meaning of that somewhat hackneyed, and now rather ambiguous, term. In the one sense, natural laws are to be understood as scarcely "natural" at all, in as much as they represent no more than certain absolute prescriptions and prohibitions, which, so far from being rationally discoverable by human reason in nature, are simply decreed by God. In the other sense, natural laws are thought of as being none other than such rules of intelligent conduct and behavior as any knowledgeable person ought to be able to see are demanded by the very nature of the case, when it comes to the living of our lives. Unhappily, though, it is just such an ambiguity in the notion of "natural law" that has led to no little confusion and misunderstanding, particularly in current discussions of the topic.

7. This is not to say that, just as there are striking similarities, there are not also just as striking differences between right and wrong behavior in the living of our lives and the right ways and wrong ways of pursuing various arts and skills. For Aquinas these differences would turn on Aristotle's earlier way of distinguishing the so-called moral virtues from the intellectual virtues. For a somewhat simplified contemporary version of such differences, *cf.* Henry B. Veatch, *Rational Man*, Chapters 3 and 4.

8. It perhaps should be explained with some apologies that throughout this essay we have not been at pains to distinguish between what might be called natural laws in the context of ethics and natural laws in the context of what Aristotle would call politics. Suffice it to say that natural laws of the former sort are to be determined in the light of man's natural end, in so far as he is considered just as an individual; those of the latter sort are determined in the light of man's natural end in so far as he is a political animal, *i.e.*, a part of a *polis* or political community.

Grotius and the Secularization of Natural Law

Nevertheless, before we can move to a consideration of what the current climate of opinion is regarding natural law, we need first to consider certain added features of natural law doctrine that are due to the revival of natural law teachings in the seventeenth and eighteenth centuries. Generally, authorities would seem to be agreed[9] that these features amount to two principal ones. For one thing, Grotius in his treatment of natural law was peculiarly insistent that so-called natural laws could, if one so wished, be regarded as literally and exclusively natural, and therefore as not being of divine origin at all. His point was that natural laws, as he conceived them to be, could be seen as binding upon men even if there were no God,[10] and hence eliminates any claim to divine authority for such laws. Naturally enough, such a stand on Grotius' part has been interpreted as heralding that increasing secularization of doctrines of natural law that was so characteristic of the eighteenth century. At the same time, be it noted that if the validity and binding character of so-called natural laws is considered to be in no way dependent upon their being decrees of God, this could not be other than profoundly upsetting to the one view of natural law that based such laws solely on their proceeding from God's will. On the other hand, such a secularization of the doctrine of natural law need not be comparably disturbing to the Thomistic understanding of natural law. Not that in Aquinas' eyes the so-called natural law did not constitute a part of the eternal law of God; and yet as Aquinas saw the matter, the natural laws that are prescriptive of how human beings should conduct themselves are like the how-to-do-it rules in any of the various arts or techniques: there are perfectly good reasons in the nature of the case why such rules are rules; nor are they rules merely because some "ruler" or some authority happened to want things done in that way and decreed that they be done in that way—and this regardless of whether that ruler be man, God, or beast!

---

9. Crowe, *The Changing Profile*, and D'Entrèves, *Natural Law*.
10. Reference should perhaps be made in this connection to the somewhat notorious *etiamsi daremus* clause in Grotius. The full sentence is quoted in translation in Crowe: "What we have been saying (namely, about natural law) would have a degree of validity even if we should concede that which cannot be conceded without the utmost wickedness, that there is no God, or that the affairs of men are of no concern to him." For a full discussion of the exact sense and import of this statement in Grotius, see the illuminating discussion in Crowe, Ch. 9.

From Natural Law to Natural Rights: Is It a Shift in Emphasis or Principle?

But now what of that second feature of natural law doctrine that dates from the eighteenth century? Not only would there seem to be a general secularization of the doctrine, but more importantly, in the eighteenth century, emphasis seemed to shift quite markedly from talk of "natural laws" to talk of "natural rights." Immediately there springs to mind the whole business of "the rights of man"—the right to life, liberty, and the pursuit of happiness; the right to freedom of speech, of religion, of assembly; the rights of property, and the right not to be deprived of "life, liberty, or property without due process of law"; the right of revolution, the right to representation in government, etc.

Superficially, and even to many authorities, it has seemed that such a shift of emphasis from natural law to natural rights was far from being a major shift. For supposing that as in medieval discussions of natural law, the emphasis was upon what might be called the natural duties and obligations and responsibilities of human beings to lead, as the *English Book of Common Prayer* would have it, "a Godly, righteous, and sober life," still there would seem to be a sense in which any and all duties tend to involve rights that are somehow correlative with them. After all, if I have a duty to lead my life and conduct myself in such and such a way, then do I not have a corresponding right not to be interfered with in the performance of those duties, and perhaps even a right to be aided and assisted in such performance?

Nevertheless, the notion that the shift of emphasis from natural law to natural right was but a minor shift, and in no wise a shift in principle, has been effectively challenged by the late Leo Strauss in his monumental work of some years ago, *Natural Right and History* (1953). According to Strauss, the classical natural law tradition, as it stemmed from the Greeks and from Aquinas, while it could hardly be said to have been without concern for so-called human rights, was certainly not concerned about them in the manner of the eighteenth century thinkers, or even in the manner of most contemporary thinkers either. Instead, on the Thomistic theory of natural law—to take this as an example—human duties and rights are both subordinated to, and made intelligible in terms of, the business of human beings attaining their natural end or goal or perfection as human beings.

Suppose that we again recur to our earlier analogy between ethics (and politics) on the one hand and the various arts and skills on the other. For is it not plausible to say that there are right ways and wrong ways for physicians to go about the care and treatment of their patients, and that these ways are determined by the very nature of the case, in the light of the end and purpose of the medical art, which is human health? But analogously, then, when it comes just to the living of our lives, not as butchers or bakers or candlestickmakers, but simply as human beings, may it not be said that our natural end, or what we all naturally seek or aim at as human beings, is nothing if not simply our human well-being or human perfection just as such, and as contrasted with that more restricted sort of mere health or well-being that the physician is concerned with? For would we not all say—perhaps not Nietzsche, to be sure, but then, we scarcely need deal with such an exception in the present context—that someone like Socrates managed to attain an excellence and a perfection, just in the business of being human, that a Hitler or a Stalin, or, in a different way, a Macbeth or a Hamlet, could not be said to have brought off at all? In the light of examples such as these, why would it not be possible to determine what some of those natural laws are—*i.e.*, what are some of the right ways, as over against some of the wrong ways, of our going about the living of our lives? As Richard Hooker in the sixteenth century phrased it—in a rhetoric that may put us off somewhat for being strangely Elizabethan, but which is still effective for all of that:

> All things that are have some operation not violent or casual. Neither doth any thing ever begin to exercise the same without some foreconceived end for which it worketh. And the end which it worketh for is not obtained, unless the work be also fit to obtain it. For unto every end every operation will not serve. That which doth assign unto each thing the kind, that which doth moderate the force and power, that which doth appoint the form and measure of working, the same we term a law.[11]

The Rational Justification of Human Goals: The "Naturally Right" vs. "Natural Rights"

Clearly on this conception, a so-called "natural law" simply determines what our natural obligations and responsibilities are in the living of our lives—how we ought to do it, in other words. And as for "natural right," that term might be taken as but a translation of the medieval expression, *jus naturale*, much as "natural law" is a translation of *lex naturalis*. Indeed, it is in this sense that Strauss takes the term in his title, *Natural Right and History*. Yet note that in this sense of the term a natural right does not so much signify what it is someone's natural right to do, as rather what it is naturally right for someone to

---

11. R. Hooker, *Of the Laws and Ecclesiastical Policy*, Bk. I, Ch. 2, Sec. 1 (A. S. McGrade and B. Vickers, eds. New York: St. Martin's Press, 1975) p. 109.

do. And these senses of "right" are far from being the same. Indeed, in the second and more traditional sense of "right," a right is really equivalent to a duty and obligation, and hence is scarcely "a right" in the current sense of the term at all.

Not only that, but when in the context of classical natural law theory one asks why it is held to be right for someone to act or proceed in a certain way, or why he is obliged to conduct himself in that way, the answer is always to be given in terms of the end to be achieved thereby. That is to say, given a natural or proper end of human life, then it may be determined, both in nature and by reason, what it is that one needs to do, or that one ought to do, or that it is right for one to do, in order to attain that end. But what is this, if not to say that natural rights and natural duties—and hence natural laws as well—are always susceptible of a proper justification? Or in other words, there is always a reason for holding such obligations to be naturally binding upon us: they are so in virtue of the natural end or goal toward which human beings are oriented by their very nature.

Not so, though, "natural rights" in the eighteenth century sense or in the modern sense either. For as Strauss has argued, this newer notion of natural rights was developed in an entirely different philosophical setting from that of the classical or medieval notion. Instead of its being supposed that human beings were naturally oriented toward a proper end or goal of human perfection or achievement, it became fashionable in the seventeenth and eighteenth centuries to consider human beings simply as they are, just naturally and in fact, and quite apart from any fancied notions of what they ought to be, or apart from any supposed natural ends or purposes toward which they might be supposed to be somehow naturally ordered and oriented. In fact, did it really make any sense any more to talk about natural ends or final causes at all? For had not the new science, as it emerged from the hands of the Galileos and the Descartes and the Newtons, simply left final causes out of account altogether? Why, then, continue to talk in the way Hooker had done: "All things that are have some operation not violent or casual. Neither doth any thing ever begin to exercise the same without some foreconceived end for which it worketh"? Surely, such a way of looking at nature and at the changes that take place in nature would now seem to be outmoded.

Revolution in Natural Law: Hobbesian "Natural" Rights as Subjective Desires

Likewise, with respect to human beings, why not follow the lead of a typical modern thinker like Hobbes, and consider human beings simply in their natural state or condition? For considered in that condition, what is a human being if not a creature of countless appetites and desires? And as for there being any natural end or goal or perfection which a human being is under a natural obligation to strive for and try to attain,

> there is no *finis ultimus*, utmost aim, nor *summum bonum*, greatest good, as is spoken of in the books of the old moral philosophers. Nor can a man anymore live whose desires are at an end than he whose senses and imaginations are at a stand. Felicity is a continual progress of the desire from one object to another, the attaining of the former being still but the way to the latter. ... So that, in the first place, I put for a general inclination of mankind a perpetual and restless desire of power after power that ceases only in death.[12]

Here, surely, is a veritable revolution in the understanding of nature and natural law, particularly as it pertains to human nature. For as Strauss remarks, with respect to Machiavelli:

> Classical political philosophy had taken its bearings by how man ought to live; the correct way [now and in the spirit of Machiavelli] of answering the question of the right order of society consists in taking one's bearings by how men actually do live.

> What Hobbes attempted to do [more or less following Machiavelli] was to maintain the idea of natural law, but to divorce it from the idea of man's perfection; only if natural law can be deduced from how men actually live, from the most powerful force that actually determines all men, or most men most of the time, can it be effectual or of practical value. The complete basis of natural law must be sought, not in the end of man, but in his beginnings. ...[13]

And what do these "beginnings" of man, or this natural condition of man, as conceived now in the new sense of "nature," have to teach us regarding man's natural rights? Clearly, any such natural human rights may no longer be understood in the sense of those things which it is right for a human being to do, or which he ought to do, or has a responsibility to do, in the light of his naturally determined human end or perfection. No, for in his natural condition man is no longer to be thought of as having any natural end or perfection at all; instead,

---

12. Thomas Hobbes, *Leviathan*, Part I, Ch. 11, Michael Oakeshott, ed. (Oxford: Basil Blackwell, n.d.), pp. 63–64.
13. Strauss, pp. 178, 180.

he is but a creature of needs, appetites, and desires. And the need or appetite that tops all others is that of self-preservation, and the desire to avoid death. Here, then, is man's basic natural right: it is just his inalienable right to self-preservation; and by derivation his right to gratify his desires and appetites, as far as the power within him lies. And so Strauss thus moves to his conclusion as to this new and radically transformed notion of "natural right," *à la* Hobbes:

> Natural law must [now] be deduced from the desire of self-preservation.... [It is this that] is the sole root of all justice and morality. The fundamental moral fact is not a duty but a right; all duties are derivative from the fundamental and inalienable right of self-preservation.... [D]uties are binding only to the extent to which their performance does not endanger our self-preservation. Only the right of self-preservation is unconditional and absolute. By nature there exists only a perfect right and no perfect duty.... Since the fundamental and absolute moral fact is a right and not a duty, the function as well as the limits of civil society must be defined in terms of man's natural right and not in terms of his natural duty. The state has the function, not of producing or promoting a virtuous life, but of safeguarding the natural right of each. And the power of the state finds its absolute limit in that natural right and in no other moral fact. If we call liberalism that political doctrine which regards as the fundamental political fact the rights, as distinguished from the duties, of man and which identifies the function of the state with the protection or the safeguarding of those rights, we must say that the founder of liberalism was Hobbes.[14]

The Problem with Natural Rights: Are They Natural, and Do They Have Any Foundation at All?

With this mention of liberalism, though, we are getting ahead of our story again. Instead, we need first consider still another point that is relevant to the newly emerging natural rights doctrine of the seventeenth and eighteenth centuries. For so far as these doctrines go, one key question remains: granted that Hobbes may have been right, that on the basis of the new scientific conception of nature in general and of human nature in particular, the natural condition of men is one of ceaseless and ever proliferating appetites and desires; and granted that man's overriding passion is thus one of self-preservation in the gratification of these appetites and desires; still, why should such a natural concern on man's part be considered as being in any way a "right"?

Yes, granted that even among all mankind there is indeed just such "a perpetual and restless desire of power after power that ceases only

14. Strauss, pp. 181–182.

in death," why should the pursuit of such power be regarded as in any wise a right on the part of those impelled toward such a pursuit? After all, on the more traditional and classical view of natural law, the mere fact that human beings, either some of them or all of them, should be naturally endowed with all sorts of limitless and heterogeneous appetites and desires certainly does not make such desires to be right, or their pursuit warranted.

On the contrary, their rightness is entirely dependent upon their conformity with the standards of what a human being ought to do or be, as judged in the light of a man's natural end. Or to put it more bluntly, the mere fact of our having certain desires is of no moral import whatever; rather what is morally relevant is only whether such desires as we have are those we ought to have or not. Nor is that all, for as we were at pains to note in our foregoing discussion, on the basis of the more traditional natural law theory, all human duties and human rights may be reasonably adjudged to be duties and rights only in so far as they can be justified, and thus shown to be duties or rights, in the light of man's natural end and perfection. Take away, then, this notion of a natural end or a natural perfection of human life, and there would no longer appear to be any ground on the basis of which rights or duties of any kind might be rationally justified.

Why Are Natural Inclinations Natural "Rights"?

Yes, suppose we go beyond Hobbes with his basic right of self-preservation, and suppose we open the gates to all of those further and derivative and typical rights so dear to the eighteenth century—and needless to say, to us today as well—the right to life, liberty, and the pursuit of happiness, the right to property, the right to freedom of speech, the right of "one people to dissolve the political bands which have connected them with another," etc. What is the basis of these rights? Why do we hold them to be natural rights? For that matter, what possible ground do we have for taking any supposed right to be a right, much less these particular rights? For on the modern scientific view of nature, as contrasted with the Aristotelian view to which both Aquinas and Hooker adhered, there just does not seem to be any way in which such things as rights can be said to be items in the natural world at all. And granted that we human beings may be naturally inclined to life, liberty, and the pursuit of happiness; that we do have a natural desire to acquire property, or that we naturally cherish certain freedoms; why suppose that our natural inclinations and desires in these regards can in any way constitute a natural right on our part to such things?

Has Hobbes allowed himself to be somehow befuddled on this score, and have the rest of us who are advocates of what Strauss earlier called "liberalism"—have we likewise just followed suit and let ourselves be taken in no less than was Hobbes? For surely, on the new conception of nature and the natural, which Hobbes took over from the newly emerging science, and which presumably none of us in this day and age would be so foolhardy as to question, the mere fact that something occurs naturally, or in accordance with the laws of nature, certainly does not warrant anyone's saying that it was right that it should have occurred, or that it ought to have occurred, etc.

Could it be, then, that our seventeenth- and eighteenth-century predecessors in the natural law tradition have given us a full-fledged doctrine of natural rights, but without providing us with any rational basis or justification for such a doctrine? Indeed, may we even go further and say that theories of natural rights of the kind that emerged in the seventeenth and eighteenth centuries, and that tended to become but so many appendages to the more traditional natural law theories—could it be that by a strange irony such natural rights theories tended almost unwittingly to involve a recurrence to that one meaning or interpretation of natural law theories according to which natural laws, so far from being discernible or discoverable in nature, are rather to be thought of as simply "issuing from the legislative Will of God"? That there should be such an association of "natural rights" with "natural laws" understood as mere divine decrees[15] would surely not be without irony. In fact, the irony becomes apparent the minute we remind ourselves of those two features of natural right theories in terms of which they were originally distinguished from natural law theories of the more traditional sort. The one feature was simply that of the obvious shift of emphasis from so-called "natural laws" to "natural rights"—which thus far has been the feature that we have been discussing at such length.

15. In this connection it is interesting to note that even so eminent and devoted a Thomistic scholar as Professor Vernon Bourke is inclined to give up on the use of the term "natural law" altogether. He feels that its usage has become almost totally infected by that one use of the term which dates back to the Middle Ages and which firmly associates the notion of natural law with "a code of moral precepts divinely implanted in man's nature, or mind, and issuing from the legislative Will of God." Hence he thinks it is hopeless to try to restore to the term the sense which it had in Aquinas, and according to which law is defined as a "rational plan and rule of action." Rather in the article cited above in note 6, Bourke concludes that with respect to Aquinas's teaching the term "theory of right reason" is a better expression to use than "theory of natural law." *Cf.* also Bourke, *Ethics in Crisis.*

But the second feature was what we earlier characterized as being one of the increasing secularization of the notions of both natural laws and natural rights that was so marked a feature of seventeenth- and eighteenth-century theories. How singular it is, then, that a shift of emphasis from natural laws to natural rights should have entailed so radically different a conception of nature and the natural as to make it largely unintelligible how natural rights could have any sort of basis in nature at all. In consequence, the affirmation of natural rights—at least in the seventeenth and eighteenth century context—tended to be just that, namely, a mere affirmation. But to imply that natural rights are really not grounded in nature, but are mere affirmations on the part of those of us who subscribe to them—is this not tantamount to holding that such rights are not rights by nature, but only by decree? Not by divine decree, perhaps, but still by decree.

But by whose decree? Apparently, as it turned out, it might be by decree of just about anybody who might come to feel certain things to be very dear to him or very important, and who would then proclaim them to be his rights, or to be somehow ordained for him by nature. Professor Crowe, in fact, gives some amusing, even if incredible, examples of such appeals to natural rights and natural laws as were not uncommon in the eighteenth century. For instance, it was put forward as a serious contravention of the law of nature "to enter unbidden, or to make journeys troublesome," or to expect soldiers to wear the stiff leather stocks that were then customary. Best of all is an example of a New England delegate to the Constitutional Convention in the U.S. who objected to the proposed two-year term for senators on the ground that a one-year term was "a dictate of the law of nature, [considering that] spring comes once a year, and so should a batch of new senators!"[16]

Theories of Human Rights: Their Decline and Fall in the Nineteenth Century and Their Dramatic Rise and Resurgence Today

In the light of examples such as these, is it any wonder that the popular natural law and natural rights doctrines of the eighteenth century should have tended to be pretty well discredited in the course of the nineteenth century? So patently ridiculous were so many of the claims as to what might be natural rights or natural laws that there came to be an increasing consensus that there just weren't any natural

16. Crowe, p. 233.

rights or natural laws at all. Nor was it merely because individual claims of this sort were so often patently ridiculous that nineteenth century thinkers were inclined to repudiate the doctrine of natural law altogether. In addition, one had only to reflect on the character of the natural world, as this had been disclosed by the scientists, and one could readily see that neither value distinctions nor moral distinctions could possibly have any place in nature. Facts were not values; nor was there any way that values could be said to have a place in the world of facts. And even worse for natural law doctrines was the eventual impact of teachings like those of Hume, who maintained that there is no way in which an "ought" can ever be derived from an "is."

In fact, to revert again to some of our own earlier examples in connection with Hobbes: granted that men actually do work for their own self-preservation, that certainly does not make it right that they should do so. Or granted that men deeply cherish life, liberty, and the pursuit of happiness, or that they will fight to retain their property, or be resentful of any taxation without representation, or whatever, that still does not as such mean that they have any right to these things, or that anyone who interferes with them in this regard is violating a very right or law of nature. Indeed, to think otherwise is to commit the fallacy of trying to infer an "ought" from an "is," or a value from a fact, or, as G. E. Moore was to term it years later, it involves "the naturalistic fallacy." From the point of view then of many thinkers in the nineteenth century and even after, the entire doctrine of natural rights and natural law would appear to rest on nothing less than a patent logical fallacy.

Natural Rights Assaulted: Historicism and Positivism

Of course, this was by no means the only ground on which various nineteenth century thinkers were inclined to challenge natural law theories, be it of law, ethics, or politics—the ground, namely, that all such theories tended to involve a fallacious inference from nature to ethics, from fact to value, or from "is" to "ought." In addition, there was a widespread tendency for thinkers and scholars to fall back, as it were, on history, and to regard the process of historical evolution as somehow ultimate and absolute. Thinkers as different as Edmund Burke in England, or Hegel in Germany, kept insisting that there could not, either in justice or in logic, be any warranted appeal to fancied standards of a natural right or a natural justice over and above those actual standards of justice and norms of political action that had been developed and had evolved in the course of a nation's or a people's history. It is true that this kind of historicism, if we may so term it, with respect to ethics, law, or politics, does tend to end in a position not far removed from a bland acceptance of the principle that "whatever is, is right." But at least the advocates of this kind of historicism[17] could claim that they made no spurious or illogical appeals to any imagined natural norms or natural laws, outside of and beyond the actual historical facts.

Indeed, similar arguments were not uncommon among legal scholars in the nineteenth century as well. For as is clear from our earlier remarks about Grotius and Pufendorf, these men were not so much concerned with a natural law, to the extent that it might have implications for ethics and politics; instead, their preoccupation was primarily with law in the narrower sense and with jurisprudence. Ironically enough, though, just as the natural law thinkers in the seventeenth and eighteenth centuries felt it essential that they be able to appeal to a natural law and justice, over and above the actual laws of a particular country or jurisdiction, or of any particular age or time, by the nineteenth century the pendulum had quite swung in the other direction.

Remember that earlier quip which I quoted to the effect that while the philosophers had come to think that a natural law was not natural, the lawyers had come to think that it was not law. And sure enough, that ancient principle of St. Augustine—and one that was repeated in turn by St. Thomas—to the effect that "an unjust law is no law" became the butt of criticism and attack on the part of both historicists and positivists among the legal theorists of the nineteenth century and after. How could a law be said to be not a law when it is on the statute books and is actually enforceable? And how can positive laws be held to be invalid and of no effect in virtue of mere appeals to a supposed natural law, when such natural laws amount to no more than ideals having no basis in fact at all? Yes, speaking of perhaps the most eminent of the legal positivists of a generation ago, the late Hans Kelsen, D'Entrèves observes that "Kelsen's 'pure theory of law' can be used to show the Achilles heel of positivism." For "Kelsen's refined form of positivism shows its real face [in that it involves] the reduction of law to a mere expression of force."[18]

17. This term is here being used roughly in Karl Popper's sense. *Cf.* esp. his *The Open Society and Its Enemies*. (London: Routledge and Kegan Paul, 1943).
18. D'Entrèves, p. 162.

Consequences of Nineteenth Century Rejection of Natural Law: Utilitarianism

Once more, though, we are getting ahead of ourselves. For before turning our attention to the contemporary reaction against the detractors of natural law and natural right in the nineteenth century and at the beginning of this century, we must first consider what some of the consequences were, philosophically speaking, of that spurning of all appeals to a natural law, which were so characteristic of the nineteenth century thinkers whom we have just been considering. Certainly, so far as ethics and political theory go, it might not be unfair to say that the rejection of natural law led to a triumph of utilitarianism.

Superficially, the essence of utilitarianism can be very tidily summed up in the slogan, "The greatest happiness of the greatest number," or "The greatest good of the greatest number." But going behind the slogan, it is not hard to discern alike the sense and the reason for utilitarianism's great appeal. For suppose one becomes convinced that there really is no rhyme or reason to invoking such things as natural rights or natural laws. For one thing, it would seem that there just aren't any such things. And for another, the very enterprise of a natural law type of ethics or politics, in which one tries to proceed from considerations as to what human beings are by nature, and what their natural ends and goals might happen to be, to some sort of argument about what men ought to be or what it is right for them to be—this enterprise is not just unwarranted; it is fallacious, as involving a patently fallacious process of moving from "is" to "ought."

Or at least, so it would seem. Very well, putting aside all concern with natural ends or goals, to say nothing of the natural obligations and rights that are said to be based upon them, why not just accept the plain facts about ourselves as human beings? For are we not all of us creatures of countless needs, desires, impulses, wants, appetites, and whatever? True, your needs and desires are different from mine; and the other man's from those of either of us. But why get into a tizzy over questions of what our desires ought to be, or of whether we have a right to satisfy some of our interests and desires and not others? Is not the sensible thing for us to do but to settle down to the business of straightforwardly trying to satisfy just as many of our desires—as many of yours and mine and of all mankind's—as is humanly possible?

This is what is meant by the greatest happiness, or the greatest good, of the greatest number; and this is all that it means. And meaning this, doesn't it make eminently good sense? No worries about "oughts" or "rights" in the traditional sense, or about moral values or absolute duties or natural obligations or anything of the sort. Instead, we have only to get on with the business of all of us becoming as happy as possible, and of collectively maximizing our satisfactions in as quick and efficient a way as human calculation may be able to devise.

Rawls, Dworkin, and Nozick: Criticisms of Utilitarianism and Positivism

Alas, though, sensible and even idyllic as this prospect might seem to be that utilitarianism holds out for us, it turns out to have nothing less than a vicious cancer working at its very core—a cancer that suddenly, and seemingly quite unannounced, burst on the consciousness of so many of us a scarce eight years ago with the publication of John Rawls' *A Theory of Justice*. Not that what Rawls had to say was anything very original, and he certainly said it in what many might think to be a somewhat tedious and turgid way. And yet his saying it did somehow manage to capture the imaginations of nearly everyone; and as a result, instead of the plain old diet of ever more and more utilitarianism, we today have set before us a dramatic revival of so-called "rights theories"—not necessarily theories of natural rights, but still rights theories for all of that. For what Rawls succeeded in bringing home to most was the realization that in any utilitarian program of the maximization of the satisfactions of all mankind, there was no reason in principle why such a maximum satisfaction might not be a satisfaction of the majority at the expense of the minority, or else, possibly of the many at the expense of the few.

If the sum total of human satisfactions can be increased, even if it be at the cost of the suffering of some one or of a few or even perhaps of many human beings, then by the utilitarian program it is just that maximum satisfaction that is to be opted for and aimed at. But aren't the implications of this rather damning, so far as utilitarianism is concerned? After all, in the course of the Christian centuries not very many people have been inclined exactly to applaud the judgment of Caiaphas on a certain rather notable occasion, when he said that "it was expedient that one should die for the people" (John 18:14). Yet what could be more in accord with utilitarian sentiments than just such a judgment?

In any case, in opposition to the utilitarians Rawls managed to come right out and say that on any interpretation of justice as fairness, to secure a maximum satisfaction for mankind, and yet to do so at the expense of a few, or even of one, would be unjust. It would violate the rights of those individuals, or of that one individual, whose happiness or satisfaction had had to be sacrificed in order that the total happiness of the rest might thereby be enhanced. True, Rawls did not propound this as a natural right. Instead, in his book he provides for a somewhat elaborate apparatus whereby the rights of individuals, as determined in the light of the principle of justice as fairness, will come to be recognized as a result of a social contract.

Likewise, in the field of law, Ronald Dworkin has come out with a stimulating book, *Taking Rights Seriously* (1977). Dworkin's main opponent in the book is none other than the brilliant and eminent English philosopher of law, H. L. A. Hart. Now, as it happens, the upshot of Hart's work in jurisprudence had been his telling defense of the thesis that in judicial proceedings there cannot properly be any appeals to such principles of right and justice as may transcend and so fall outside of the expressed or implied principles and rules of a given legal system. However, it is just this basic tenet of legal positivism that Dworkin undertakes to challenge. Again, it needs to be said that Dworkin does not base his challenge on any invocation of natural law or natural right. And yet for all of that, in his own enterprise of "taking rights seriously," Dworkin implies that the rights that he would take so seriously and would have others take seriously are precisely such rights as may well not be included within the positive provisions of a given legal system.

But then just where do these extralegal rights come from? Moreover, so long as Dworkin fails to make clear just what their origin and basis is, may he not be criticized for not fully facing up to the question of whether there is a justification, and, if so, what the justification may be, for supposing that there really are such rights in the first place?

Indeed, no less a criticism and in a somewhat similar vein could perhaps be directed at another new and even somewhat electrifying book by one of the new rights theorists, namely, Robert Nozick. That is the book *Anarchy, State, and Utopia* (1974). Nozick's basic conviction seems to be—if we might express it more or less in our own language—that human beings are naturally interested and appetitive animals, each with his own concerns and wishes. Moreover, there is no reason why each should not pursue his own interests—provided always that he recognize that there are certain "side-constraints" on what he does, side-constraints that involve a respect for various rights that others may have. Thus the persons and property of these others, Nozick would say, are things to which they have "entitlements," and these entitlements are such that they may not be violated or interfered with by others. No, they are, as it were, in the nature of absolute rights; and no utilitarian considerations of any kind can ever justify us in any attempt at overriding them.

What if Rights Theories Can Only Draw Sustenance from Natural Law Theories?

Now to all of these newly developing rights theories, which in their different ways might be thought to lead to the establishment of a genuine Libertarian philosophy, one can only say "Bravo!" And yet isn't there one fly in the ointment? For these rights that Rawls, Dworkin, and Nozick have been so vigorous in championing are not held to be natural rights; nor are the various duties and side-constraints, that are correlative with the asserted rights of individuals, to be regarded as having any foundation in nature.

Yet if rights and duties cannot be shown to have any basis in nature or in fact, what reason is there to suppose that they have any basis at all? True, we may feel strongly about them; and nothing is easier than to get human beings to warm to affirmations of their individual rights and freedoms. But mere warmth of feeling can hardly be a substitute for rational justification. And if rights and duties are not held to be natural rights and duties, what is there that is rational about them?

Just recall our own earlier account of the natural law theories in the seventeenth and eighteenth centuries, in which the rights and the laws that were appealed to turned out to be not natural laws or natural rights so much as rights and laws that appeared to rest on nothing more than fiat or decree—in the Middle Ages upon divine decree, and in the later secularized versions of natural law upon no more than man or mankind's decree. But the eighteenth-century experience would surely seem to indicate that rights that turned out to have no more than an asserted, and not a natural, foundation could be only too easily denied and discarded altogether. And might not this be a message that could bode ill for the future of today's newly emerging rights theories?

Indeed, this is a prospective danger that at least some contemporary philosophers have been not a little anxious about, though not necessarily those of a classical liberal persuasion. Two names of authors of two very able books that have appeared just in the last two years might be mentioned in this connection, Alan Donagan and Alan Gewirth. In both cases these writers are concerned to justify human rights and human duties; but they want to do so on some other basis than an appeal to nature and natural law. Instead, they both prefer to follow a more Kantian line of justification.

In general, Kant suspected that egoistic or self-interested motives were nonmoral because they were not so much reasoned to and freely chosen, as given biases or vested interests, caused and determined heteronomously rather than by the autonomous choice of the moral agent. In the hope of making ethical choice more rational and autonomous, Kant turned to a universalizability principle. He reasoned that universalizing one's reasons for action (*i.e.*, by applying those reasons equally to every other agent) would form the decisive criterion for any action that is truly rational and hence a truly moral one. This universalizing approach led Kant to formulate his categorical imperative whose edict applied equally well to all moral agents. Kant was at pains to remove all self-interested goals, ends, or objects of desire as the possible justifying reasons for moral actions. Such self-interested motives seemed to him merely irrational deterministic reflexes of an agent's actions (similar to Hobbes' "passions") rather than authentic, autonomous, and rationally chosen motives.

Thus Donagan wishes to argue that there simply is a basic imperative to which all human beings are subject, and which might be expressed "Humanity is always to be loved and respected for its own sake," or "Every human life is to be respected as an absolute and inviolable good." The only trouble with this is that it would seem only too easy to round on Donagan and say, "But I don't see that this is an imperative incumbent upon me at all. What evidence is there that I am really bound by any such absolute obligation or duty as is here formulated?" Nor does it seem that Donagan has any very good answer to this. True, as far as Kant was concerned, he claimed that such an absolute or categorical imperative as that requiring one to respect humanity or human life as an absolute good was binding on each and all alike—simply for the reason that to deny it was somehow to fall into self-contradiction. However, very few have been convinced that any such self-contradiction could really be shown to be involved in such instances. And in any case, Donagan does not choose to defend his absolute imperative by this means. But what, then, is the warrant for it?

Moving to Gewirth's case, he would, in *Reason and Morality*, appear to want to justify human rights and duties by considering what the implicit assumptions are of any human action whatever. Thus in acting, any human agent cannot but recognize that his action has the characteristics of being purposive as well as being voluntary and free. Moreover, Gewirth feels that to recognize the voluntary and purposive character of our actions is also to recognize the rightness and the desirability of their being so; but to recognize that it is but desirable and right that my own actions be voluntary and purposive is also to acknowledge that it must be no less desirable and right for any and every human being.

In other words, if it is right that my actions be voluntary and purposive, then it is right that everyone's should be so; and just as everyone should recognize my right in this regard, it is no less right and a duty that I recognize the rights of everyone else in this same regard.

Undoubtedly, this is a telling and ingenious argument by way of establishing rights and duties; and yet is it sound? For may not someone make rejoinder by simply saying, "Why, yes, I am glad that I am in a position to act freely and purposefully as a human being. But even though I like this situation of mine and certainly hope that it continues, I do not claim it as a right. Indeed, if I did, it would be an obvious case of the fallacy of trying to infer an 'ought' from an 'is.' Moreover, not claiming the freedom and purposiveness of my actions to be in any way a right, since it is nothing more than a simple fact about my individual situation, albeit a very happy fact, then there is no way in which I can be held to be logically bound to recognize a corresponding right to freedom and purposiveness on the part of other human beings."

How Can We Salvage Contemporary Rights Theory and Rehabilitate Natural Law?

What to do, then, when it comes to trying to save contemporary rights theories from the charge of arbitrariness? If the Kantian moves of Donagan and Gewirth cannot do the trick, what alternative is there by way of justifying rights and duties, save that of showing that such rights and duties are somehow natural rights and duties? And what does this call for, if not for some sort of rehabilitation of the old natural law theory, more or less in its Thomistic form? For on this view, as we saw, the way one justifies rights and duties in the context of ethics and politics is analogous to the way in which one justifies the right ways of doing things, as over against the wrong ways, in the contexts of various arts, skills and techniques. In the latter sorts of cases—*e.g.*, medicine—one justifies a certain care and treatment of patients as being naturally required on the basis of the end of the medical art, which is health. So likewise, given that the natural end of human life is the attainment of one's natural perfection or fulfillment as a human being, then one can come to recognize what it is that is naturally required of one, and what one needs to do or what it is right for one to do, in order to attain such an end.

But if the only way really to restore rights and duties to a proper status once again, either in our individual lives or in society, is to recognize them as having a natural basis and foundation, and a natural basis and foundation such as will enable them to be integrated into an overall scheme of natural law, why has this not been an alternative that has been more readily resorted to by thinkers in the present-day world, particularly by champions of latter-day rights theories? The answer surely is that as nature has come to be conceived and described by modern science there would appear to be just no room and no place in nature for any such things as natural human ends, to say nothing of natural rights or duties. Thus Hooker's unqualified assertion that "all things that are have some operation not violent or casual; nor doth any thing ever begin to exercise the same without some foreconceived end for which it worketh"—this assertion of Hooker's would appear to be directly contravened by the account of nature given by the scientists. Not only that, but the very enterprise of trying to ground moral and ethical and political principles in nature, in addition to being inconsistent with the scientist's account of nature, would also appear to involve the patent fallacy of attempting to reason from fact to value and from "is" to "ought." Little wonder, then, that natural law theories of ethics and politics, in the Thomistic sense, cannot ever seem to get off the ground any more!

Reviving Natural Law: Bridging Facts and Values and Formulating a New View of Nature

Yet that ground is changing, and hopefully changing fast, so that a proper takeoff may become possible after all. The old dogma, for instance, about the absolute and unbridgeable gap between facts and values has recently been subjected to various sorts of devastating analyses and criticisms,[19] and while the dogma still hangs on, even in philosophical circles, hopefully its days are numbered.

The hallmark of a natural law ethics is that the gap between facts and values is indeed bridgeable. Natural law aims at grounding norms and values in fact and nature. Because values are claimed to be natural and factual, and are not mere man-made conventions, it is possible to claim a rational and objective basis for ethics.

---

19. For a fuller discussion of this issue, *cf.* Veatch, *For an Ontology of Morals*, and also, and more especially, *Human Rights: Fact or Fancy?*

In the natural law perspective, however, values are not simple objective properties or facts as we commonly understand these terms. Despite the fact that values are truly objective, they also serve as values for a subject, namely, the human agent. Speaking in terms of their factual status, values resemble goals or perfections which the individual strives to achieve by rational choice. Just as the acorn tends toward the mature oak tree (and never, say, the sycamore), so a young girl tends to actualize her latent potential to blossom into a wise and beautiful woman.

Facts are viewed as values, when we consider them as the mature unfolding or actualizations of human potentials. Human values are also, indeed, facts to the degree that these perfecting actions are worthwhile and obligatory for us humans if we aim to realize our natural potential. For example, such humane values as wisdom or courage are certainly facts; but as facts they are no less developmental achievements which represent the realization of a person's earlier potentialities.

Even more significant for rehabilitating natural law have been the number of recent books and articles which have argued for an out-and-out revisionism, so far as the received scientific account of nature is concerned. On the one hand, there have been studies designed to show that modern natural science is simply not to be interpreted in the Humean and positivistic manner that has been fashionable for so many years.[20] Instead, the ancient Aristotelian causal scheme, including material, formal, efficient, and even final causes, is said to be far more compatible with the actual practices and procedures of scientists than any Humean scepticism, such as has been wont to be predicated upon the usual stereotyped contrast between constant conjunction and necessary connection. Yes, if such a philosophical revisionism with respect to science itself should begin to gain ground, then Hooker's old affirmation about the natural operations of things in the natural world, all of them having foreconceived ends for which they work, will once more gain credence and respectability.

Nor is that all, for just as on the one hand, something rather like the old Aristotelian and medieval view of nature is considered by some contemporary philosophers of science to be the proper framework in

---

20. Three books, all to much this same effect, have appeared just in the last few years: Wallace, *Causality and Scientific Explanation*; Harré, *The Philosophies of Science*; Harré and Madden, *Causal Powers: A Theory of Natural Necessity*. Needless to say, none of these books speaks to the question of natural law in the ethical or political sense. However, their revisionist accounts of both science and the natural world could well prove to be the basis for a revival of natural law theories of ethics and politics.

terms of which the procedures of modern science can best be understood, on the other hand there is another group of philosophers of science who take as their point of departure Sir Karl Popper's celebrated thesis that "the logic of scientific discovery" is to be understood as involving an almost exclusive reliance upon the so-called hypothetic-deductive method.[21] Moreover, if such be the nature of scientific method, then it would seem to follow that science is not really interested in achieving a knowledge of nature and reality at all. Instead, rather than being concerned to know what nature is, or is like, in itself, the modern scientist may be said to be concerned only with nature as it appears to be, depending upon the particular conceptual framework or set of hypotheses in terms of which the scientist happens to be viewing nature at a given time. In other words, the objective of science is to control and manipulate nature, and not necessarily to know it as it is in itself at all.

Notice, though, what the implications of either of these recent revisionist accounts of modern science would be with respect to possible rehabilitation of natural law theories in ethics and politics. For if science is not concerned with nature as it really is in itself, then modern science cannot be said to have undermined that conception of nature in terms of which all operations in nature, and particularly those operations characteristic of human beings, might be said to have their foreconceived natural ends. In other words, there could be no basic incompatibility between what the scientists have to say about nature and the concept of nature that is required by a natural law or natural rights philosophy. Of course, on the other revisionist view of science, there could be no incompatibility between the scientist's view of nature and the natural, and the natural law philosopher's view of them, for the simple reason that the scientist's view of nature ultimately comes down to the same thing as the natural philosopher's view.

"Oh," but you will say, "neither of these revisionist views of science has gained sufficient currency to again render secure the philosophical foundations of natural law theories of the traditional sort." True enough, and yet surely there is enough stirring and going on to admit of a most hopeful answer to the question, "Natural law—is it dead or alive?" The answer is, "It's very much alive!"

---

21. *Cf*. Popper's *The Logic of Scientific Discovery*. It should be noted that rather than Popper himself, it is a number of successor philosophers of science, men like Hanson, Feyerabend, and Kuhn, who have pushed Popper's theories in the somewhat revisionist direction suggested in the text.

14

CAN JOHN FINNIS BRING OFF A REVIVAL OF NATURAL LAW?

In the current flux of books and studies having to do with jurisprudence and legal philosophy, whatever has happened to poor old natural law! Has it somehow just got lost in the shuffle? Or is it rather that, despite no little deference being paid to natural law doctrines as history, nobody nowadays seems to take them very seriously as philosophy? Put a little differently, could not one say that in the current varieties of analytical philosophy, linguistic analysis, *et al.*, that so dominate the scene in present-day Anglo-American thought, there would appear to be almost no way in which natural law doctrines can get even so much as a hearing, much less a firm foothold? That law and legal philosophy might actually have a foundation in nature, rather than in the mere will of the sovereign, or in the pronouncements of judges, or in such logical commitments as are supposedly entailed by our normal and inescapable uses of legal language—this is something that strikes most legal thinkers today as being, if not downright absurd, then certainly no longer tenable!

That's why a book such as this one by John Finnis[1] should come as something of a shocker to the philosophically complacent majority among contemporary legal thinkers, and as no less than an answer to prayer to that now largely silent minority who, notwithstanding their being intellectually cowed, nevertheless do not see why natural law should not be an eminently viable legal-philosophical position, as compared, say, with the various regnant fashions of legal positivism, legal realism, utilitarianism, social-contract deontologism, libertarian entitlement theories, *et al.* Against such a background, it is perhaps not entirely without irony that it should be John Finnis who comes out as a champion of natural law. For Finnis, as it happens, has seemingly impeccable analytic credentials. Indeed, the book itself appears in the

---

1. *Natural Law and Natural Rights*, John Finnis (Oxford: Clarendon Press, 1980).

Clarendon Law Series, edited by H. L. A. Hart; and in the Preface the author acknowledges that his own training and interest in so-called "analytical jurisprudence" "antedates the time when I first began to suspect that there might be more to theories of natural law than superstition and darkness" (p. vi). Besides, whatever may have been Finnis' earlier background and interests, there is no disputing that he has now "put aside childish things," and has succeeded in attaining an impressive mastery and understanding of what he himself calls "classical" or "mainstream" theories of natural law! His grasp of Aquinas, especially the relevant portions of the *Summa Theologiae*, is most impressive. Likewise—at least so far as this reviewer is able to judge, which certainly is not very far!—he has read both widely and perceptively in such seventeenth-century Jesuit writers on natural law as Vasquez and Suarez, and, as he himself acknowledges, he has "referred occasionally to the Roman Catholic Church's pronouncements on natural law." This last is not to imply, of course, that Finnis is not both careful to point out in his Preface, and scrupulous to observe in his practice throughout his book, that appeals to authority have "no place in philosophical argument about the merits of theories or the right response to practical problems" (p. vi). And no less does Finnis make it eminently, even pointedly, clear that he means to present no mere history of natural law theories; rather he is determined to show that human law can and does have a basis in an objective natural law. Thus his purpose is no less than the disclosure of what this natural law is, and hence not to write any mere history of what natural law may have been thought to be by this, that, or the other supposed authority on the subject.[2]

Very well, but just what is it that Finnis must do, if he is ever to succeed in doing what he purposes to do—at least on our interpretation—*viz.* to carry the banner of natural law right into the very citadel of analytical jurisprudence; well, for one thing he needs to expose the obvious misunderstandings and misrepresentations of natural law doctrines that are so prevalent in the present day. And this

---

2. So strongly does Finnis feel about this matter that he gives rather short shrift to a book like that of A. P. D'Entrèves, *Natural Law*. The trouble with D'Entrèves is that he failed to see "the importance of maintaining a distinction between discourse about natural law and discourse about a doctrine or doctrines of natural law" (p. 25). Doubtless, it is for the same reason that Finnis makes no reference to, and may not even know about, the excellent book of M. B. Crowe on *The Changing Profile of Natural Law* (The Hague: Nijhoff, 1977). From the title itself it is clear that Crowe is not above being concerned to discourse about doctrines of natural law; and even where Crowe is given to discoursing rather more substantively about natural law itself, it would appear that his discourse is influenced more by Continental modes of philosophizing than by the modes of Oxford analysis. In any case, Finnis will apparently have none of it.

Finnis does, both deftly and successfully, rather early on in the book. In Part One, Chapter II, he criticizes various judgments of contemporaries like Kelsen, Hart, and Raz to the effect that in the natural law tradition legal validity is simply confounded with moral validity; or that positive law is regarded as being little more than a kind of automatic xerox copy of natural law; or that natural law cannot be thought of as extending beyond those few precepts such as have been recognized by all men, always and everywhere; or that inevitably natural law doctrines involve an illicit inference from what is the case to what ought to be the case.

Nevertheless, disposing of such vulgar errors is but child's play for Finnis, compared with the really difficult tasks that he—or for that matter any other serious defender of natural law in the present day—simply has to address himself to, if he is ever to win a proper recognition of natural law among contemporary thinkers in legal philosophy and in philosophy generally. For one thing, he has got to undertake to rehabilitate ethics, or, if you will, moral philosophy, and to rehabilitate it in such a way as to show how ethics needs to enjoy not just a priority, but rather a presidency, with respect to human law as it exists in various communities and societies. Not that legal obligation is ever to be simply identified with moral obligation; nor is it to be supposed that the former can be merely deduced from the latter, or, as it were, simply transcribed from the latter. Not at all; and yet that moral obligation is somehow a necessary condition of any and all legal obligation, so that there just cannot be any legal obligation without at least some attendant moral obligation—this is a truth which any defender of natural law in the present day has to try to bring home to a generation of lawyers and legal thinkers who have been, both pretty generally and pretty thoroughly, indoctrinated in one or another of the current fashions of legal positivism, legal realism, *et al.* And of this task, be it said that Finnis acquits himself at once thoroughly and tellingly!

Still, that is not the only task that would seem to confront Finnis—or anyone else, for that matter—who would make a case for natural law in the face of the prevailing legal-philosophical convictions of those schooled in contemporary British or American philosophy. For surely, the legal tradition of the likes of Bentham, Austin, and Hart can hardly be said to have been entirely indifferent to ethical and moral considerations.[3] Instead, utilitarianism is found grinning out

---

3. This point is very effectively made in a recent book by Iredell Jenkins, *Social Order and the Limits of Law* (Princeton: Princeton University Press, 1980).

from behind almost every bush throughout the entire history of analytical jurisprudence. And indeed, one could doubtless say that Hart's so-called "secondary rules"—of recognition, of adjudication, and of change—are such rules as may be supposed to have emanated from a solid background of utilitarian concerns that have presumably influenced the legislators, the judges, and the constitution makers, who over the years have been responsible for such rules of law. And more recently, with the likes of Rawls, Nozick, and Dworkin, all sorts of deontological ethical considerations may be said to have obtruded themselves upon current legal and political thought.

Accordingly, for one like Finnis, who would champion a natural law ethic, it is necessary not merely that he rehabilitate ethics, as over against a pervasive moral skepticism and relativism, but also that he show how ethics has its basis in nature itself—*i.e.*, in the very nature of man and the nature of things generally. Yet how can this be? For does not modern science instruct that there just is no teleology in nature, and hence even talking of anything like the natural ends or objectives or purposes, either of human beings or of anything else in nature, is simply ridiculous? And so it is that in current ethical theories, be they of a utilitarian or of a deontological cast, it is usually just taken for granted that, of course, morals and ethics cannot find any warrant for themselves in nature or the natural world: moral laws are in no wise to be regarded as natural laws; nor are human ends and goals ever to be conceived as being in any way determined by nature; nor is there any way in which a scientific knowledge or knowledge of the facts can ever point the way to how we human beings ought to live and to order our lives. Instead, that which men ethically ought to do, or are morally obligated to do, is thought by the utilitarians to be ultimately a matter only of what men want to do, and by the deontologists to be an affair of duties and obligations which we are said somehow to be able directly to intuit, but which are in no way discoverable either in nature or in the facts of our natural human situation at all.

How, then, does Finnis acquit himself of this second task, which it would seem is incumbent upon any philosophically serious defender of natural law in the present day. Alas, I am afraid it must be said that he does much less well at this second task than he does at the first: he is better at showing how law needs to be grounded in ethics than he is at showing how the principles of ethics are discoverable right in the very facts of nature and reality. Of this, though, more later. For the present, let us look briefly at how it is that Finnis does manage to show, and show most successfully, how human law—civil law, positive law, the common law, or whatever—can only draw life and sustenance from ethics, and from a regard for the needs and requirements of man's nature. Indeed, it is just such a concern for what it is that is morally required of us human beings to do and to be that has a direct bearing upon the law and upon the way in which our obligations under the law can be seen to be truly moral obligations.

Here Finnis moves very much along the lines laid down by both Aristotle and Aquinas. It's true that Finnis, to my recollection, nowhere uses terms such as "the natural end" or "the natural perfection" of human life. But he does talk about "the basic values of human existence," and about those things that are undeniably "human goods." For instance, take knowledge. Can anyone deny that knowledge is a value for human beings? Or what about play, or aesthetic experience, or sociability (friendship), or religion, or practical reasonableness? Likewise, there is life itself, where "life" signifies "every aspect of the vitality (*vita*, life) which puts a human being in good shape for self-determination" (p. 86). None of these things, Finnis suggests, are things which this, that, or the other of us may just happen to have a liking for or not, as the case may be; nor are they goods or values whose value is derived merely from the fact that all men, or at least most men, happen to like them or go for them. No, they are "really desirable," or "objectively good," in the sense of being determined to be so for human beings by man's very nature or essence—and so much so, indeed, that were any human beings to deny such things to be of any particular value for them, they would simply be mistaken, that's all! They wouldn't know what was good for them!

Of course, that an individual should come to see that such things are things that are really and naturally of value for a human being—this would still be a far cry from that person's actually being a good man, or himself actually leading a moral life. No, for this, it is not enough that one should know such goods to be goods; in addition, one has to bring oneself actually to cultivate them, and to pursue them, and to order them, the one with respect to the other in the serious business of living and of actually leading one's life. Indeed, right here is where the virtue of what Finnis calls practical reasonableness (cf. Aristotle's *phronesis* and Aquinas' *prudentia*) comes into play, a virtue which is the source of one's being able to work out a rational and coherent plan of life. Although Finnis, so far as I know, does not employ the analogy, one might draw an analogy here between the person who is thus intelligent and reasonable in the decisions that he makes in his day-to-day choices and decisions and the person of skill and know-how in various arts like medicine, engineering, cooking, accounting, or whatever. In the one case, as in the other, it cannot be denied that there is a real knowledge that is involved: the one person knows how to live, or to practice medicine, or to cook, or whatever, whereas the other doesn't, or at least not so well—he just hasn't mastered the art, in other words. Moreover, just as in medicine, the skilled practitioner needs more than just an extensive knowledge of chemistry, anatomy, biology, etc.; he also needs to know how to put such knowledge to use. And likewise, the good man or the man of practical reasonableness will know more than just what the goods of life are; he will also know how to put them into practice.

At this point, though, one might well ask, "But just what do all such ethical considerations regarding the natural ends and goods of life, or regarding that practical reasonableness that is necessary both for the recognition and the attainment of such human ends and goods— just what does all this have to do with law in the usual sense?" True, there may be a sense in which what Finnis calls practical reasonableness, to the extent to which we possess it, may involve us in laying down rules and even laws for ourselves, that we realize we ought to follow if we are ever to attain that fullness and perfection of human existence that is somehow incumbent upon us and is morally required of us as human beings. Such rules and laws might thus be said to be analogous to the rules and laws that might be said to govern good practice in medicine, or in accounting, or in automotive engineering, or in military strategy, or whatever. But still, one can hardly call rules or laws of this sort "law" in any very proper sense—*i.e.* in the sense of positive law. Indeed, one would need in this connection only to cite Aquinas, who in his so-called definition of law cites no less than four notes or criteria of "law" in the proper sense: (1) it must be ordinance or a rule of reason; (2) directed toward the common good; (3) laid down by such a proper authority, or authorities, as have the care of the community; and (4) promulgated (*Summa Theologiae*, I–II, 90, 4). Clearly, of these four criteria, the so-called rules of skill in the various arts and crafts, as well as such rules of practical reasonableness as an individual needs to follow if he is ever to lead his life in a truly human way—it is only the first of these four criteria that such rules of art or skill might be said to meet, and not the last three at all. And yet is not Finnis' book supposed to be about law in the proper sense, and not about any mere requirements of practical reasonableness as there may be in morals and ethics?

To such a challenge Finnis' response is properly to point out that human beings in their pursuit of the human good are no mere atoms, utterly independent of one another. "No man is an island." Instead, as Aristotle would say, man is by nature a political animal, and as a political animal he cannot but be implicated in a common enterprise with others, and a common enterprise that is directed toward the realizing of a common good of a community of human beings. Yes, it should be noted that right at this point in his book, Finnis manages skillfully to steer clear of those numerous shoals with which contemporary ethics is so much fraught, and in which the supposed claims of an egoism in matters of ethics are forever being pitted against the supposed claims of a countervailing altruism, and vice versa. Instead, as Finnis points out, that very perfection or fulfillment of himself which each individual needs to recognize as being a moral responsibility of his own to achieve, he also must recognize as pointing to a like and comparable responsibility resting upon each and every other individual, as being something that that individual in turn is obligated to try to achieve for himself as well. Moreover, no man being an island, there can be no living well, or no attainment of one's own good simply by oneself alone, and apart from the achievement of a common standard of living, involving, as it does, a participation in a common enterprise and aimed at no less than the attainment by all of what each and everyone individually is somehow capable of being and thus ought to be, but which no one can ever manage to be, just by himself alone.

And so it is that human beings, being political animals by nature, as Aristotle would say, the very living of their lives as men requires their deliberate implication in a common good. Here it is, then, that law in the most proper sense emerges for the first time. Moreover, considering that in any natural law context, politics is nothing more than an extension of ethics, so also law, in the sense of the civil or common law of the community, is but the extension of those ethical and moral obligations that are incumbent upon all individuals as individuals. In other words, the very rules of practical reasonableness in our personal lives require supplementation through so-called laws of the community, which in turn will be such as to meet all four of the criteria of law according to Aquinas' definition.

Indeed, it is in these reaches of his book that Finnis would seem to be really at his best, and his performance truly *non pareil*, where he seeks to show, not just the consonance and compatibility of law with ethics in and through law. True, both his argument and his information in these chapters VI–XII of Part II are very densely packed— so much so that it is sometimes hard not to miss the woods for the trees. And yet what Finnis is trying to show is how any common enterprise of human beings aims at achieving a common good, and hence demands something which can only be called political or governmental authority. Nor is the function of such authority to be understood exclusively, or even primarily, in terms of any mere exercise of coercive force. No, it is rather for the necessary and indispensable coordination of the efforts of the different agents of the community that the authority is instituted in the first place; and it is only through the exercise of such a directing and coordinating authority that the common good of the community can even be concretely determined, much less achieved. And as for law—human law or positive law—it is nothing if not the indispensable instrument of such a public or governmental authority, aimed at the attainment of the good of the community. Moreover, since the good of the community is not any literally collective good, or even an additive good, but simply the well-being of each and all of the members of the community individually, the law needs to be so constituted as to respect the rights of the individual members of the community. And here again, in his discussion of the rights, *i.e.* the natural rights, of citizens, Finnis is very careful to construe such rights—*e.g.* common law rights, such as the right to property, to a fair trial, to protection against self-incrimination, to safeguards against violence—not as absolute rights, in the way in which this term is so often understood nowadays, but rather as rights that are justified in terms of the natural needs and requirements of the individual, if he is ever to be able to live the life of a truly moral and autonomous human person.

Of course, one question in connection with all of this that is likely to be disturbing particularly to lawyers and legal scholars is a question that perhaps could be put in some such way as this. Isn't such an account of law in terms of natural law and ethics likely to be profoundly disconcerting to, and even subversive of, such established systems as exist in various communities? And who is the lawyer who does not need to be concerned with the preservation of the constituted legal system of his community? Not only is such a thing his very bread and butter, but also the preservation and the smooth functioning of the legal system would seem to constitute the very service and function that a lawyer as lawyer owes to his community. And yet what would become of that needed stability and predictability of systems of law and justice if moral and ethical considerations were always being brought to bear upon the law, as it were from the outside, and therefore as having the ever renewed effect of upsetting existing judicial decisions and even actual legislation? After all, is it not a veritable principle of all natural law legal thinking, and one that is constantly being cited and repeated by natural law thinkers throughout the ages, that "an unjust law is no law"? And yet what could be more upsetting, so far as any legal system is concerned, if all that one needs to do is to show on ethical grounds alone that a law is unjust; and presto, that law just ceases to be law forthwith!

To all such considerations, Finnis' responses are at once careful and decisive. For one thing, in his effort to indicate what law is, he largely repudiates the standard logical practice of so many legal scholars and philosophers of supposing that there is but a single set of proper criteria for law, such that whenever any presumed legal system does not meet those particular standards, it is to be pronounced not really a legal system at all. No, says Finnis, a far better logical practice is to invoke certain features of the older doctrines of analogy. Thus in his own case, rather than use a cumbersome term such as "the analogy of attribution," or "*pros hen* equivocation," or whatever, Finnis speaks of what he calls the "focal meaning" of a term like that of "law." What such a focal meaning serves to do is to point up those features that pertain to law, considered in the fullest and most developed sense. Keeping such a focal meaning in mind, then, one would not need to deny that less perfect legal systems—*i.e.* those which lack, say, secondary rules, or those which make no provision for the rights of the accused, or whatever—were systems of law at all. No, they would need only to be adjudged less perfect legal systems, but legal systems nonetheless. Moreover, it would be the focal meaning of the notion of law that would enable one to specify just how and in what respects such less-than-perfect systems would fall short.

Thus, for example, with respect to the principle of *lex injusta non est lex*, Finnis is able to offer an altogether nuanced and convincing discussion. For one thing, he points out how Aquinas, although he subscribed to the principle, still was careful to explain how even laws that are "more outrages than laws," or "are not law but a corruption of law," are not for that reason to be supposed not to be legally binding in any sense. Rather such laws or "such a law is not a law *simpliciter* [*i.e.* straightforwardly, or in the focal sense], but rather a sort of perversion of law'" (p. 363). Indeed, Finnis goes further and points out how even admittedly corrupt and perverse laws can nevertheless be held to be binding, not just legally, but even morally. Accordingly, one can say that there are gradations in the injustice of unjust laws, such that at one end of the scale their injustice may not be so great as to render them no longer morally binding in any sense, and at the other end of the scale the moral agent could rightly decide that he was in conscience obligated to refuse obedience, even though such refusal might be fraught with the gravest consequences to himself.

This much, then, must suffice by way of discussion and illustration of Finnis' unflagging skill in handling an incredible range of questions and difficulties that are bound to arise in the minds of people today, the minute any defender of natural law seeks to show the dependence of law upon morals and ethics, as well as the continuity of law with morals and ethics. Still, it remains for us to enter that final criticism—yes, even a downright complaint—against Finnis, that we earlier hinted at in respect to that second task which we mentioned as being incumbent upon any defender of natural law in the present day, but which Finnis, so far from taking up, seems rather to renege on. This is simply the task of offering a convincing demonstration of how our moral and legal obligations under so-called natural law are indeed "natural"—*i.e.* that they are a matter of *physis*, rather than *nomos*. Of course, it goes without saying that this is a task that anyone might well wish to avoid if he could. For it would seem to be a thing as impossible of accomplishment as it is inescapable for any would-be defender of natural law. That it is presumably a well-nigh impossible task, who can deny? For has it not been borne in upon us throughout the whole history of modern culture that it is modern natural science, and only modern science, that can either credibly or creditably inform us as to what the facts of nature are, to say nothing of the laws of nature? Yet no scientific investigation has ever been able to uncover any such things as objective moral values, or real moral obligations anywhere in the so-called facts of nature. And no less than the scientists, modern philosophers have repeatedly made much of the fact that it is nothing if not a logical fallacy to suppose that values can never be gleaned from facts, or a moral "ought" derived from an "is." Is it any wonder, then, that modern moral and legal philosophers have come to be singularly united in their repudiation of anything like natural law as being the sort of thing that could ever provide a basis either for moral or legal obligation?

However, if morals and ethics are not to find their basis and foundation in the facts of nature or in discoverable laws of nature, then where and how are they to find a basis or foundation? This is not to say that we are not all familiar with how the many varieties of contemporary utilitarians and deontologists have struggled, if not mightily, then at least desperately, to substitute for nature, as a basis for ethics, something like a social contract, or a general will, or a supposed inescapable linguistic universalizability of human value judgments, or even a pretended logical implication to the effect that any repudiation of ethical principles must somehow involve one in inconsistency and contradiction. But such heroic efforts notwithstanding, let's face it: for all of the philosophical sophistication and ingenuity of modern ethical writers, this effort to find a basis for ethics elsewhere than in nature would seem to be little more than just so many efforts to pull rabbits out of hats!

Why not then say that contemporary natural law ethicists and legal philosophers have but little choice: either they have got to show that the basis of both law and ethics is one of *physis* and not mere *nomos*; or there is just no sense to be made of their own claim of being natural law philosophers? Accordingly, it is for this reason that we would say that the task confronting any modern natural law philosopher is nothing if not one that would appear to be unavoidable and impossible. Not so, however, Finnis! For when in his role as a defender of natural law he comes up against this formidable task, he seems to feel that rather than having to try to make a hit, he can perhaps just try to get a base on balls. And instead, what does he do but strike out? Even more incredible, though, is that rather than being embarrassed or apologetic over his failure to demonstrate that natural law is indeed natural, he would appear rather to want to make a virtue out of his very necessity. For it really isn't necessary, he seems to say, that so-called natural laws in law and in ethics should be laws of nature at all, or in any sense discoverable in nature. No, and as if to puzzle and perplex his readers even more, Finnis apparently wants to claim no less a one than St. Thomas Aquinas as being on his side in this regard. For St. Thomas, Finnis suggests, was one who was never taken in by any such notion as that one might be able to derive ethical principles from nature, or that one would ever need to suppose that ethics had to be based on metaphysics. Yes, it is almost as if Finnis would go so far as to say that St. Thomas never even thought that *bonum* was to be understood in terms of *ens*.

To all of this, one might at first be tempted to make the somewhat captious reply that despite Finnis' impressive mastery of the *Summa Theologiae*, it is odd that he nowhere makes reference to the *De Veritate*, and particularly to Question I, art. 1, and to the several articles of Question XXI, where St. Thomas specifically addresses himself to the matter of *bonum* as being inseparable from, and intelligible only in terms of, *ens*. Not only that, but it is in these same questions in the *De Veritate* that St. Thomas seems to give the unmistakable impression that ethics must discover its own principles directly in being and in the context of the discipline of metaphysics (*Bonum est in rebus, ut Philosophus dicit*). Yes, there are a number of discussions in the contemporary literature bearing on these very points in St. Thomas. True, they are not too numerous, and they may be almost exclusively by American writers, rather than English. Still, they do exist, and yet

Finnis takes no note of them. Indeed, the only contemporary writer of a more or less Thomistic persuasion whom Finnis not only cites, but relies upon very heavily, is Germain Grisez. Yet again it is significant that Grisez's otherwise excellent study on "The First Principle of Practical Reason"[4] is not concerned to take particular account of the *De Veritate*.

For all of this, though, our concern in this review is not so much to question Finnis' understanding of Aquinas as rather to assess the adequacy of his treatment of natural law. And here, so far as that second task of the contemporary natural law philosopher is concerned, Finnis would seem to have been somewhat misled into thinking that, such a task being impossible to accomplish, it is therefore a task that the natural law philosopher would do well to find excuses for avoiding. But is the task so impossible to accomplish? True, in a review such as this it is scarcely our business to demonstrate that the thing may be possible after all, and this despite Finnis' seeming conviction as to its impossibility. Nevertheless, it is surely no more than fitting that we indicate just briefly how and why we feel that Finnis' conviction on this score may have been both exaggerated and somewhat misconceived. Thus for one thing, like so many English philosophers of recent years, he would seem to be inordinately concerned over the impossibility of ever deriving an "ought" from an "is." To which the obvious reply is, "True enough, no 'ought' can ever be derived from an 'is,' or no value from facts." And yet this surely does not mean that facts may not be so read and construed that values will be recognized as being no less than an integral part of them. Likewise, that man's very nature can be seen and understood to involve certain inescapable and undeniable obligations that are integral to such a nature—this in no way entails any unwarranted inference from "is" to "ought."

Indeed, if we might ourselves cite Aquinas in this connection, it can hardly be denied that goodness or value are ever understood by Aquinas—yes, even "defined" by him[5]—as being simply the actual as over against the potential, or as that very actuality toward which any given potentiality is, as it were, but naturally ordered. Accordingly, just as the actual is that which, in Aristotelian metaphysics, the potential

---

4. Germain Grisez, "The First Principle of Practical Reason: A Commentary on the *Summa Theologiae*, 1–2, Qu. 94, Art. 2," originally published in *Natural Law Forum*, Vol. 10, 1965, pp. 168–196, and then reprinted in *Aquinas: A Collection of Critical Essays*, ed. by Anthony Kenny (Garden City, N.Y.: Anchor Books, 1969), pp. 340–382.

5. *Bonum* being a transcendental, it is, of course, impossible that it should ever be defined *per genus et differentiam*. On the other hand, even though in *De Veritate* XXI, 1, Aquinas does not in this sense define *bonum*, he does show how it is to be understood in terms of *ens*.

might be or could be, and hence, in an extended sense, ought to be, so also it may be said that, likewise in an extended sense, such actuality is just that which is desired by, or is aimed at, or is perfective of,[6] that which is still but potential. It is thus that toward which any potentiality may be said to be ordered, as fulfilling it or perfecting it, and thus as realizing what it has a natural capacity for being. Consequently, transferred to the context of human nature and human life, what this means is that the good for a human being is none other than that actuality of fulfillment or perfection for which a human being has a potentiality, and which is thus rather different from the worth of a thing that a toad or a tree or an amoeba has a potentiality for. Yes, as Finnis himself has argued so well, the characteristic goods or values of human life toward which men are ordered, as constituting their natural perfection or their fulfillment, and which men may thus be said naturally to desire, are such things as knowledge, society and friendship, practical reasonableness, aesthetic enjoyment, and, indeed, life itself.

And with this, are we not brought back, as it were, almost full circle,

6. It perhaps should be remarked that in that same article of Grisez's cited above (note 4, above), one of the things that Grisez and, following him, Finnis as well, are so concerned about is that practical reason in a thinker like Aquinas (and hence in the natural law tradition as well) not be regarded as simply reducible to theoretical reason and theoretical knowledge. Instead, practical reason always presupposes that a thing be desired by an agent, and only then can so-called practical reason be brought into play, as being that which devises ways and means of attaining that which men desire. All well and good! And yet it would seem important that the fact of something's being desired, or being an object of interest, and hence being the starting point of a practical reasoning—it is important that such a desired object or object of interest be not construed in the manner of the utilitarian, or of the partisans of any kind of interest theory of value. Instead, in an Aristotelian or Thomistic context, either one, it surely needs to be borne in mind that that which is desired, and thus is held to be good, must also be recognized as being that which is desirable, and hence as not merely desired. That is to say, a good in this connection is that which is truly perfective of that of which it is the good, and hence is something that ought to be desired or really is desirable, whether it happens actually to be desired or not.

In fact, it might be remarked in this connection that in a review of Finnis' book by Ted Honderich, appearing in the *Times Literary Supplement* for September 12, 1980, not only does Honderich seem strangely insensitive to the import of Finnis' book as being a defense of natural law, but he even complains of his not being convinced that Finnis' basic position and argument need be regarded as being so different from an ordinary consequentialist view of ethics! One cannot down the suspicion that the reason for Honderich's insensitivity to the nonconsequentialist implications of a natural law position in law and ethics is that Finnis himself in his book has so thoroughly downplayed the objective basis, and basis in nature and reality, of a natural law type of ethics. Had Finnis made it clear that our human obligations are toward those things that are truly perfective of our human nature, whether we happen to desire them or not, then Honderich would doubtless have realized that natural law ethics involves obligations of a very different sort from those that are supposedly calculated solely on the basis of the maximizing of men's any and every object of interest and of desire.

and can we not see that Finnis must acknowledge, almost in spite of himself, that the good life for a human being and for human existence is determined by man's very nature? And does this not mean that the norms of human existence are based on the facts of human nature, and yet without there being any illicit inference from the one to the other? And no less can we understand, and Finnis should be able to understand, how *bonum* in the case of human beings has its basis and ground in the very *ens* that a human being is. Nor surely does this involve any "deduction" of ethical principles from metaphysical principles, or any blurring of the distinction between practical reason and theoretical reason, as Finnis (and perhaps Grisez) would seem so inordinately to fear.

What, then, could have possessed Finnis to have thus rather uncritically endangered the entire argument of his otherwise brilliant book, a book that bids fair to being the one really definitive treatment of natural law in the present day? Could it be that he was somehow tempted by the devil, so as to seem to say that natural law doctrines are not really based on a knowledge of nature after all! Or was he somehow just dazzled and blinded by the brilliance of a Grisez? Or was it that despite his penetrating reading of St. Thomas he just didn't read far enough? Or maybe one has to explain it by the fact that, being a citizen of the United Kingdom, Finnis somehow could not shake himself loose from the veritable *mortmain* of contemporary English philosophy, as a result of which one cannot even begin to philosophize about ethics without suddenly finding oneself paralyzed by a rigor mortis that seems ever to be brought on by the mere mention of such things as the naturalistic fallacy, or the impossibility of deriving an "ought" from an "is," *et al.*

Such speculations, however, scarcely befit a mere reviewer. Instead, let us just say that the reviewer's business is not so much to diagnose as merely to lament that, in even so thorough and powerful an exposition and defense of natural law as this present one, the author should have allowed a needless canker to slip into his account, and to threaten to eat away the very vitals and inwards of his otherwise excellent argument!

15

NATURAL LAW AND THE "IS"–"OUGHT" QUESTION: QUERIES TO FINNIS AND GRISEZ

John Finnis' achievement in his book, *Natural Law and Natural Rights*,[1] is nothing if not truly remarkable! Only yesterday it would have been no exaggeration to say that one would have had to beat the bushes to find even a single legal philosopher, or political philosopher, to say nothing of any ethicist or moral philosopher of note or standing, who would not have dismissed natural law doctrines out of hand as being utterly discredited philosophically and as entitled to survival only as historical curiosities. But not so today, especially since the publication of Finnis' book. And indeed, this sea-change in philosophical opinion is something that Finnis would appear to have wrought almost single-handedly.[2] To which one can only say, "Bravo!" and again "Bravo!"

Is it not, then, rather captious and in bad grace that I should now be taking it upon myself to come at Finnis with some rather sharp questions? Worse yet, my questions could seem almost irrelevant in that they are aimed largely at but a single section of what is otherwise a very substantial book, namely, section 4 of Chapter II, entitled "The illicit inference from facts to norms." Still, that section is rather fundamental, so far as the very theory and understanding of natural law is concerned; and what Finnis says there is so puzzling as to cause one almost to wonder whether he could have quite meant what he says, or

---

1. John Finnis, *Natural Law and Natural Rights* (Oxford: Clarendon Press, 1980). References in the text will be to pages of this edition.
2. No doubt, Finnis would be the first to deny that his achievement is in any way single-handed. For he most generously gives credit to Germain Grisez for practically all of the specific philosophical formulations of natural law doctrines, particularly with reference to the current philosophical situation, that Finnis himself has availed himself of. But although the formulations may be due to Grisez, I wonder if the actual turning of the tide of prejudice against natural law may not be due to Finnis himself and his excellent book.

293

said what he meant. Thus from the very title of the section one gets the impression that any inference from facts to norms must be illicit. And yet just how can the enterprise of a natural law ethics be anything other than an effort to find some sort of a basis for morals and ethics in nature itself, and thus in the facts of nature?

Still, let us hear Finnis out, and in his own very words:

(1) "It is simply not true that 'any form of a natural-law theory of morals entails the belief that propositions about man's duties and obligations can be inferred from propositions about his nature'" (p. 33).

(2) Speaking of the view of St. Thomas Aquinas in regard to natural law, Finnis notes that Aquinas "asserts as plainly as possible that the first principles of natural law, which specify the basic forms of good and evil . . . are not inferred from the speculative principles. They are not inferred from facts. They are not inferred from metaphysical propositions about human nature, or about the nature of good and evil, or about 'the function of a human being,' nor are they inferred from a teleological conception of nature or any other conception of nature" (pp. 34–35).

(3) Finally, in seeking to explain why it should ever have come to be so generally supposed that defenders of natural law do indeed fall into fallacies such as that of trying to make "an illicit inference from 'is' to 'ought'" (p. 34), Finnis suggests that one reason for so widespread a misapprehension is that "the very phrase 'natural law' can lead one to suppose that the norms referred to, in any theory of natural law, are based on judgments about nature (human and/or otherwise)."

What is one to make of assertions such as these? Were it not known that Finnis' whole book was devoted to a sustained and brilliant defense of natural law, one might suppose that anybody who insisted that "the norms referred to in any theory of natural law" must not be taken to be "based on judgments about nature (human and/or otherwise)"—that such a one must surely be an opponent of natural law doctrines in ethics, not their defender! Surely, though, our reaction must be over-hasty. For suppose that we put ourselves in Finnis' shoes for the moment. No one could have been more aware than he that so far as traditional defenders of natural law doctrines are concerned, they have ever been wont to affirm (1) that, in any natural law ethics, moral laws and moral norms have an existence right in nature itself; and (2) that it should be possible to discover such natural moral laws somehow from an examination of the facts of nature themselves. But remember, Finnis is an Oxford don; and in Oxford, no doubt, if anyone who would so much as dare to say that maybe moral norms do have a basis in fact, or that perhaps an "ought" can be derived from an "is"—of such a one, not just the Oxonians but doubtless the entire English philosophical establishment would exclaim, "Let him be anathema!" Clearly, then, if Finnis would wish to defend natural law in Oxford and at the same time avoid a total Oxbridge ostracism, he would have little choice but to do a Falstaff (Falstaff being never out of place in Oxford!) and acknowledge discretion to be the better part of valor.

All the same, while it is easy to understand why Finnis would not want to commit what is surely a capital philosophical offense in England today, namely, that of trying to extract norms from facts, or duties from nature, or an "ought" from an "is," still why would he continue to want to have himself regarded as a natural law philosopher? Could it be that the word "natural law" has an unsuspected aura of respectability about it, and that, unlike the proverbial rose, "natural law" is not a thing that by any other name would smell as sweet? And so the game would have to be one of seeking to enjoy all the sweet perfumes of the word "natural law" at the same time that one is careful to clear one's name of any possible taint that might come from putting it about that the thing itself was in any way a thing to be taken seriously!

Enough of such teasing, though. And why not instead come right out and unmask the battery from which I am choosing to bombard the position which Finnis has apparently taken up in that one section of his book? For I believe that in that section Finnis has somewhat inadvertently, and seemingly almost unwittingly, stumbled into a very curious dilemma. The dilemma is simply this: either figure out a way to get from facts to norms, or just give up trying to be a natural law philosopher altogether. But, of course, Finnis is quite insensitive to any such dilemma. Instead, he seems to see no reason why he should not simply disclaim all attempts at finding a basis for moral laws in nature, and at the same time insist that his ethics is nothing if not an ethics of natural law. Accordingly, I propose to mount my criticisms of Finnis on two fronts. First, let me try to give a brief and somewhat fanciful account of some of the major stages in the history of Western moral philosophy, just to show that the dilemma I have proposed is a real one and that, for that very reason, Finnis will have to make up his mind: either he is going to be a natural law philosopher and discard his Oxbridge superstitions about the wall of separation dividing "is" from "ought," and facts from values, etc.; or he will have to break with Oxbridge entirely (and, for that matter, with most of our latter-day establishment ethics) and then he can, in both good conscience and good grace, declare himself to be a natural law philosopher after the mind of St. Thomas Aquinas himself.

And what about my second front? Well, it will consist in a series of challenges that I would like to direct at the specific reasons Finnis gives by way of showing why he thinks it to be both bad logic and bad philosophy ever to make inferences from "is" to "ought," or ever to try to find a basis for morals and ethics directly in nature and in reality.

First, then, as to my somewhat off-the-cuff reading of the history of Western moral philosophy. Consider again Finnis' pronouncements to the effect that it is at once futile and illogical to suppose that propositions about man's duties and obligations can be derived from propositions about his nature, or that moral norms and moral standards can ever be based on considerations as to the nature of man, or the nature of things, either one. But must it not occur to one that for someone to take a line such as this in matters of morals and ethics is but to hark back to those ancient disputes between the Sophists on the one hand and Socrates on the other (and indirectly Plato and Aristotle as well)? For what was the position of a Sophist like Callicles in the *Gorgias,* if not that morals and ethics, as ordinarily understood,[3] are simply matters of νόμος, and not of φύσις? And in opposition to the Sophists, what was it that Socrates was contending for, if not that morals and ethics are not mere matters of human choice or convention, as rather that they are and ought to be grounded in nature—in the nature of man primarily, but also and more fundamentally in the nature of things generally?

Nor does such a line of argument in repudiation of natural law stop there. For coming down to the present day and to the contemporary scene in ethics, must not one say that contemporary moralists, be they utilitarians or deontologists, if the question were put to them directly, would find themselves to a man (or woman) having to agree with the Sophists, as opposed to Socrates, that there is just no way in which morals and ethics can be viewed as a matter of φύσις, rather than νόμος? True, the utilitarians would insist that in holding that morality is a matter of social convention, and not of nature, they do not want to think of themselves as being committed to the moral relativism and even scepticism of the ancient Sophists. Instead, present-day utilitarians think that they can combine a pure conventionalism in ethics with

---

3. This qualification is important, since, of course, the morals of might-makes-right that Callicles himself would advocate he would take to be a morals of φύσις and not of νόμος, whereas with the more standard views of right and justice it is just the other way around—at least so Callicles would say.

a nonrelativism, presumably by involving certain linguistic or logical considerations like that of universalizability. And for their part, even the deontologists, while they would doubtless not mean to say that morality is no more than a matter of νόμος, in the sense of mere social convention, would still deny that it could in any sense be considered an affair of nature or φύσις. No, our duties and obligations are recognized to be such, not in virtue of any investigation of nature, but rather in virtue either of a direct intuition of such obligations or else of a recognition of a supposed inevitable logical inconsistency that will manifest itself whenever one tries to deny such a thing as the categorical imperative.

Nor is it to be wondered at that contemporary moralists of whatever school would be so unanimous in repudiating anything like nature—the nature of man, the nature of things, or whatever—as a possible basis for morality. For given the almost unquestioned recognition in the modern world of modern natural science as being alone qualified to give an account of nature, be it either of the natures of things or of the nature of man, the evidence, in consequence, seems overwhelming: no so-called scientific study or investigation of nature is ever going to be able to turn up evidence of the existence of real norms or values right within the facts of nature. For the matter of that, was not Thomas Hobbes in the early days, alike of modern philosophy and of modern science, entirely correct in his insight that a scientific knowledge of the laws of nature can never give one instruction as to what is really right or wrong in terms of nature itself, but only of what is right and wrong in terms of the self-interest of human beings and of their need to preserve themselves in the face of what might be called man's natural situation, in which the life of man would be no better than "poor, nasty, brutish and short"?

Very well, if such a reading of the history of moral philosophy and of the contemporary lay of the land in establishment ethics be anything like a correct and accurate one, then anyone who would seek to rehabilitate a natural law ethics in the present day simply cannot hope to follow a course like that of John Finnis. To think that one could champion natural law, and yet at the same time insist that ethical principles can have no grounding in fact and in nature—no way! That would be like trying to run with the hare and ride with the hounds. No, for one to uphold natural law doctrines on the current philosophical scene must mean that one must be prepared to break not only with ancient sophistry, but with Hobbesian contractarianism, with Kantian deontologism, with the so-called naturalism of modern science, and, last but not least, with everything that is up to date in

Oxbridge philosophy! And who would dare to do this, save only a fool, and John Finnis is no fool. True enough; and yet the question I want to raise is not so much one as to whether John Finnis is, or meant to be, a fool; but rather whether, being so particular about not being a fool, he can any longer be a natural law philosopher, and if so, how!

And now to come to the second front on which I would mount my attack. For granting that I may have raised at least some doubts about whether John Finnis can very well claim to be a natural law moralist, if he is not willing to be written off as a fool by the majority of contemporary philosophers, still whatever his concerns may be not to be cast into outer darkness by his contemporary analytical philosophical colleagues in Oxford, Finnis is not behindhand in giving reasons to show just how and why it is impossible, alike in logic and in nature, ever to extract moral principles from considerations of reality and of the way things are. It's like trying to get blood out of a turnip, or possibly a rabbit out of a hat. Not only that, but in his arguments Finnis is ably seconded by the more than formidable Germain Grisez![4] Accordingly, my task now becomes one of trying to defuse these Finnis–Grisez arguments, which are designed to show that appeals to nature can never provide proper support for ethics and morality.

These arguments I shall classify under roughly three main headings, and the first such heading is that of the supposed logical "deducibility" or "inferrability" of a science such as ethics from either metaphysics or philosophical anthropology. Nor is it to be denied that the Finnis-Grisez position here is one that is exceedingly well-chosen. For certainly anyone will want to recognize that ethics has a characteristic autonomy of its own, with its own first principles; and hence there is no way in which ethical principles can be shown to be not so much principles at all as mere deductions from metaphysical principles, after the manner, say, of a Spinoza.

In response to this first argument, let me respond by conceding that of course there can be no *deduction* of ethics from metaphysics, or no simple *inference* of "propositions about man's duties and obligations" simply from "propositions about his nature." Yet is not the soundness of such contentions due to one's taking the terms "deduction" and "inference" in a somewhat straitened and overly technical sense? And

---

4. My references to Grisez will be confined simply to his brilliant and influential essay entitled "The First Principle of Practical Reason: A Commentary on the *Summa Theologiae*, 1–2, Qu. 94, Art. 2." This originally appeared in *Natural Law Forum*, Vol. 10, 1965; however, the references to this essay that I shall make will be to the abridged version that was published in the volume of essays on *Aquinas* edited by Anthony Kenny (Garden City, NY: Anchor Books, 1969), pp. 340–382.

can one legitimately extend such a point about the noninferrability of ethics from metaphysics to what might seem to be the somewhat overdrawn conclusion of Finnis that ethics may not be considered to be even based on metaphysics in any way, or that metaphysical considerations need be regarded as largely irrelevant even to rendering ethical principles intelligible?

It is true that we have all become accustomed to that sense of "deduction" that has sometimes been associated with modern logic, especially the older *P.M.* logic (*i.e.,* the logic of *Principia Mathematica*). And indeed, in that sense of deduction, we all know what it means to say that the principles of arithmetic are simply deducible from those of logic. Yes, it is not uncommon to hear the still further construction put upon this sense of deduction according to which any relation of premises to conclusions in a deductive argument never amounts to anything more than a mere tautology. Very well, let us say straight-off that, taking a natural law philosopher like St. Thomas Aquinas as our example, he would surely never say that ethics was simply deducible from metaphysics, or morals from anthropology, in this sense of deduction.

Of course, this is not the place for, nor do I have the competence to enter into any criticisms of the possible narrowness and even arbitrariness of this sense of deduction as it functions in modern logic. On the other hand, I don't see why I could not cite a perfectly plausible and familiar example of how one science or discipline might be said to be radically dependent upon another for the very intelligibility of its first principles, and yet without the one being considered to be in any sense merely "deducible" from that other in any *P.M.* sense of deduction. For take the case of Aristotelian physics in its dependence upon so-called metaphysics or first philosophy in Aristotle. Surely Aristotle would hold that physics has its own first principles, and that as first principles, the principles of physics are not simply inferrable from those of metaphysics, as if the former amounted to no more than a restatement of the latter, in the manner of mere tautologies. For instance, consider the famed three principles of change in Aristotelian physics—matter, form, and privation. Now these can of course be set out as if they comprised but a single first principle of change in the physical world: any change must be the change of something (the material principle) *from* something (the principle of privation) *to* something else (the formal principle). As a first principle, this could surely be considered as self-evident—at least in the traditional sense of that term, as signifying something *per se notum,* and therefore as something that may not be thought to be merely deduced or inferred from anything else. Yet for all of its self-evidence, is not such a principle regarding *ens mobile* entirely dependent for its proper intelligibility upon various prior principles of *ens*? For example, in his metaphysics, Aristotle would hold that to be a being, a being must be a substance (or at least ordered to substance). Likewise, to be a being, a being must be determinate—*i.e.* it must have an essence, or proper formal determination. And finally, if chapters 3–10 of Book A of the *Metaphysics* are properly a part of the Aristotelian metaphysics, then there is the further principle of metaphysics that for any being to come into being, it must be possessed of a principle of matter or of potentiality.

Very well, given such principles in metaphysics, may it not be said that the first principles of Aristotle's physics are indeed based upon, and even in a sense derived from, his metaphysics, and that while it certainly does not suffice for a knowledge of *ens mobile* to know only about *ens*, or about being *qua* being, it is no less true that there can never be a proper understanding of *ens mobile* for one who does not have a prior understanding of *ens*?

Very well, given such principles in metaphysics, there is certainly a sense in which the first principles of Aristotle's physics are based upon and even derived from his metaphysics. Yet this surely may not be taken to mean that one has only to know about *ens*, or the principles of being *qua* being, and these will tell you, at least by implication, all that you need to know or can know about *ens mobile*. Of course not! Accordingly, *mutatis mutandis,* why could not one say that for Aristotle—and certainly for Aquinas—while ethics is indeed an autonomous discipline with respect to metaphysics (or philosophical anthropology), and hence possessed of its own first principles, it by no means follows that the moral philosopher in his concern with *ens*, considered as *bonum*, need take no account whatever of the principles of *ens* just as such. And with this, have we not pretty well drawn the teeth of what we have labelled the first of the Finnis–Grisez arguments regarding the supposed absolute independence of ethics as over against metaphysics, or of morals with respect to a knowledge of nature? True, there is a sense in which our human moral obligations can scarcely be said to be simply "inferrable" from a knowledge of human nature. And yet Finnis is surely going too far when he would apparently conclude from this that "the norms referred to in any theory of natural law" are not to be regarded as being even "based upon judgments about nature (human and/or otherwise)" (p. 35).[5]

---

5. Be it noted that Finnis and Grisez would not argue that ethics is independent of metaphysics merely in the way in which, say, physics is independent of metaphysics. For

And now to come to the second line of argument which Finnis and Grisez would appear to use in order to show that even in a natural law ethics, the principles of morals and ethics are really not to be thought as being in any sense principles of being or of nature at all. This time, as it would seem to me, the Finnis-Grisez argument turns on a certain understanding, or perhaps misunderstanding, of what may be supposed to be meant by "nature" in expressions like "the nature of man" or "the nature of things." Moreover, the argument is presumably designed to show that any effort to derive one's morals or ethics from nature must inevitably involve the fallacy of trying to get from "is" to "ought." Nor is there any denying that the kind of example which Finnis and Grisez choose by way of fleshing out their argument is an eminently telling and well-chosen one. Let me, then, try to put this argument and this way of illustrating it first in my own words. In effect, what Finnis and Grisez would charge traditional, professed natural law moralists with doing is conceiving nature, and more specifically human nature, purely statically. In fact, though Finnis and Grisez do not say so in so many words, I would say that many of those natural law moralists, whom they are criticizing, doubtless have tended to conceive human nature and the nature of man largely on the model of the nature of purely geometrical figures. After all, recall that it was Aristotle who insisted that it is only proper to conceive of the natures of mathematical objects—squares, circles, triangles, etc.—as if they were purely static and allowed of no change or development of any kind. Thus the nature of a square or a circle is such that it neither comes into being nor passes away; it is not susceptible to any growth or development, or even to locomotion or change of quality: instead, it simply is what it is, and that's that! As a result, as Aristotle sees the matter, the so-called causes of being in the case of a triangle are reducible to the formal cause alone. Certainly, there can be no efficient cause or causes of a triangle just as such, since it neither comes into being nor passes away. And if no efficient cause, then no final cause or end or goal of any kind, in the case of a triangle. No, there is not even any material cause either, there being no potentiality for change in the case of a triangle.[6] And so it is that a triangle is, and can only be, just what it is, it having developed neither from nor out of anything else, nor is it the kind of being that may be considered to be aimed or directed toward becoming anything.

---

in addition, ethics is to be distinguished from metaphysics, they would say, in the way in which a practical science is different from, and hence independent of, any theoretical science. This further mode of differentiation, however, we shall consider later on.

6. True, there is so-called "intelligible matter" involved in Aristotle's account of mathematical objects; but that's a different story.

Very well, suppose now that we conceive of the nature of man, after the model of a triangle or a square. Clearly, so far as a square is concerned, we might say that it is contrary to the nature of a square that its size could ever be doubled by doubling the length of its sides. Correspondingly, then, if we were to conceive of the nature of man on such a model, one might say that it was contrary to the nature of a human being that he should not be characterized by upright posture, or that he not be either unequivocally male or unequivocally female, or that certain human organs should be put to a use other than their natural use. And so proceeding along these lines, one might be tempted to argue that, it being contrary to nature for a human being, say, to walk on all fours, it is therefore wrong for a human being to do so; or that certain sexual practices being deviant or perverse, when judged by the standard of a given, static human nature, such practices must therefore be wrong. Quite patently, though, inferences of this sort would be clear cases of an illicit process from "is" to "ought," or from the natural or the unnatural to the right or the wrong. Moreover, it I have understood them aright, this is just the criticism that both Grisez and Finnis would level against any number of natural law thinkers. Nor can it be denied that such criticism in such instances would seem to be entirely warranted and right on the mark: these are clear cases of illicit processes from "is" to "ought," or from facts of nature to alleged norms of nature.

Nevertheless, however justified Grisez and Finnis may be in leveling these criticisms at least at certain so-called natural law thinkers, it needs to be recognized that such criticisms are not necessarily warranted with respect to any and every seeming inference from nature to norms—and this for the very reason that there are other ways of understanding the natures of things than simply on the model of geometrical figures. Indeed, if it be human beings that one is concerned with, then it is nothing if not an errant mistake to try to conceive of their natures as if they were like the natures of squares or rectangles or circles. Moreover, the difference lies precisely in the fact that change is relevant to the nature of a being such as a human being, whereas it is not at all relevant to that of circle or a square. For what is a man, or a human being, if not a creature who, by his very nature and in his very nature, is a creature subject to development, a creature of potentialities, in other words, and therefore a creature who is not all that he might be or could be, and whose present or actual condition needs always to be compared with what, as such a person, he might be or could be? Nor may one stop there. For a human being is not merely a being who by nature is subject to change and development, but also a being of such a nature as to be in large part responsible for his either being or not being all that he or she might be or could be. In consequence, it needs to be added as a further characterization of human beings that they are seldom all that they should be or ought to be, and hence that they are usually not what they are morally responsible for being or what it is morally incumbent upon them that they be.

With this, then, is it not clear that an "ought" has been directly introduced into our very account of man and of human nature? Nor on this occasion can analytical philosophers—or Finnis and Grisez either—any longer say that the introduction has been made through a kind of illicit process from "is" to "ought. On the contrary, the very "is" of human nature has been shown to have an "ought" built right into it. That is to say, just as it is impossible to determine what a human being, just as a human being, really is in fact, without determining what he might be or could be—*i.e.* without taking account of a man's potentialities and the actualities toward which those potencies are oriented—so also it is no less impossible to determine, or really even adequately to state, what a human being is, without making reference to what he ought to be—*i.e.* without making reference to that natural end or fulfillment or good which it is incumbent upon any human being (by nature) to try to be or become. Here, clearly, there is no dubious inference from "is" to "ought"—as if somehow from out of an "is" that was exclusive of any "ought" one could somehow manage to conjure up an "ought," much as one might pull a rabbit out of a hat! No, for as our foregoing account should have now made clear, the very "is" of human nature already has its "ought" contained within it. Indeed, if it comes to a question of inference, it is now possible to say that the so-called inferences from "is" to "ought," or from nature to norms, are nothing if not inferences from an "is" that already involves an "ought" to the "ought" that is there already implicit in that "is." Or if one should prefer to use the language of "nature" and of "norms," one could say that the nature of man, when rightly understood, and not understood on any misleading geometrical model, is a nature that is inescapably ordered to certain norms or standards of its own perfection. Nor need we be fearful at this point of being open to any stern reprimands about how we need to go to school again to David Hume, and to listen once more to his complacent censures of supposed inferences from "is" to "ought." On the contrary, may we suggest instead that it is not the natural law moralist, but rather Hume, who now needs to be taught a lesson. For while there is no denying that there are ways of construing natures and the facts of nature such that inferences from what things are by nature to what they ought to be would be illicit, still those inferences which Hume thought he was confident of having disposed of as being fallacious were not so at all. Rather those were inferences that proceeded from a far richer and more versatile conception of the "is" of human nature than poor David "ever dreamed of in his philosophy"!

But where does all of this leave us with respect to Finnis and Grisez? Well, it leaves us at the point where we would readily concede to them that if human nature be conceived on what we have been designating as the geometrical model, then there can indeed be no proper inferences from "is" to "ought," or from natures to norms. Not only that, but we may also concede to Finnis and Grisez that no doubt many so-called natural law moralists, particularly in recent years, have, either consciously or unconsciously, fallen into the very bad habit of uncritically construing human nature simply on what we have called the false geometrical model; and to the extent to which these natural law thinkers did lapse into bad habits of construing human nature in this unfortunate way, then their would-be inferences from "is" to "ought," or from the natural to the normative, would need to be pronounced to be fallacious. Besides, come to think about it, it really is not so surprising that many such latter-day advocates of natural law should have thus carelessly come to construe "nature" in this misleading way, for it is, after all, the way in which nearly all modern philosophers from Descartes and Hobbes on have tended to understand a notion like that of the "natures" of things; and, of course, modern natural scientists have merely followed suit upon the philosophers in this regard.

But having made these concessions to Finnis and Grisez, we feel we must now round on them, and ask them how they would construe the notion of "nature" in those contexts in which, in a natural law ethic rightly conceived, one has occasion to use notions such as "human nature" or "the nature of man." Surely, they themselves would repudiate construing nature on what we have called the geometrical model. Instead, professing themselves to be Thomists of the true persuasion, one would imagine that they would be the first to acknowledge, with both Aristotle and Aquinas,[7] the geometrical model for

---

7. On the matter of Finnis' and Grisez's reliability in their interpretations of St. Thomas Aquinas on the subject of natural law, I have largely refrained from commenting in this paper—and with very good reason, considering my own limitations, when it comes to a knowledge of the texts of St. Thomas. Besides, a most illuminating article that is critical of many of Finnis' and Grisez's interpretations of St. Thomas has already been published by Ralph McInerney in *The American Journal of Jurisprudence*, 1980, Vol. 25, pp. 1–15.

natures is by no means to be carried over uncritically from the domain of mathematics to that of physics and metaphysics, and hence of anthropology and of ethics as well. No! But supposing that Finnis and Grisez would go along with us this far, our question then becomes one as to what all of the shouting is about, so far as either Finnis or Grisez is concerned. For the problem would now seem to be simply dissolved as to any possible illicit inferences from "is" to "ought," or from facts to norms. Not only that, but for all of Finnis' rather anguished formulations about how "the very phrase 'natural law' [must be so construed as never to] lead one to suppose that the norms referred to, in any theory of natural law, are based on judgments about nature (human and/or otherwise)," we may now calmly defuse and correct the greater number of the proposed Finnis–Grisez remedies and formulations. One has only to recognize the Aristotelian account of natures and essences and there is no longer any problem of how "the norms that are referred to in theories of natural law [can be] based on judgments about nature." On the contrary, that's what they are based on precisely. And what's wrong with that!

And now for a final line of argument which, as it would seem, Finnis and Grisez are inclined to resort to by way of maintaining their would-be wall of separation between nature and norms, or "is" and "ought," or ethics and metaphysics. This is an argument based on the old Aristotelian distinction between practical sciences and theoretical sciences. An entirely legitimate distinction surely! And not only is the distinction legitimate, but also the resulting relative autonomy and independence of a practical science such as ethics *vis-à-vis* a theoretical science like metaphysics. But still, it will be our contention that in exploiting this particular distinction, Finnis and Grisez would appear to push their argument rather too far.

Nevertheless, let us let Grisez articulate just how he would understand the distinction between practical and theoretical reason, and what he would make of the resulting autonomy of ethics with respect to metaphysics. First, he makes the entirely legitimate point that ethics being a practical science, it follows that our direct concern in ethics is with determining which actions we need to perform, and which we must not perform, if we are ever to attain our natural human end or goal—or, as Grisez might prefer to put it, the basic goods of human existence. And here Grisez adds, by way of a further specification, that "because good has the intelligibility of an end, and evil the intelligibility of contrary to end, it follows that reason naturally grasps as goods . . . all of the objects of man's natural inclinations" (p. 345).

And what, then, is practical reason for Grisez? He answers that it is just what it is for Aquinas. For according to Aquinas, Grisez states, practical reason is "the mind functioning in a certain capacity, the capacity in which it is 'directed to a work.' . . . Practical reason is [thus] the mind working as a principle of action, not simply as a recipient of objective reality. It is the mind declaring what is to be, not merely recording what already is. In theory, the world calls the turn, the mind must conform to the facts; in practice, the mind calls the turn . . ." (pp. 350–351).

And so Grisez continues: "Now if practical reason is the mind functioning as a principle of action, it is subject to all the conditions necessary for a very active principle. One of these is that every active principle acts on account of an end. An active principle is going to bring about something or other, or else it would not be an active principle at all. It is necessary for the active principle to be oriented toward that something or other, whatever it is, if it is going to be brought about" (p. 351). Moreover, against the background of statements like these it should be possible to understand the first principle of practical reason as enunciated by St. Thomas: *Bonum est faciendum et prosequendum, et malum vitandum*, which Grisez is careful to translate as "Good is to be done and pursued, and evil is to be avoided" (p. 341).

Directly at this point, however, it would seem not altogether out of place to ask the question as to just how this first principle of practical reason is to be understood. True, it is a first principle, and as such is self-evident, and in this sense indemonstrable. Nevertheless, we are not asking for a demonstration of the principle, "Good is to be done and pursued, and evil is to be avoided," but only for a clarification and explication of the principle. Remember, as St. Thomas was careful to point out, and Grisez repeats the point (p. 344), a principle may be evident in itself, and yet not be evident to us. And so I will particularize this lack of self-evidence with respect to myself, and say that I am in this case "the rustic" who doesn't quite see the self-evidence of this first principle of practical reason. Clearly, though, it being a self-evident principle, the only way it can be made evident to a rustic like me, or to anyone else for that matter, is through a further clarification of the subject term "good" (or "evil"). Just how is the notion of good to be understood here?

And by way of anticipation of my own answer to this question, I would suggest that the only way such a question in this context can be answered is by invoking certain principles from metaphysics. Moreover, this explication will turn out to be such that if I can really make good on it, then it should serve effectively to breach that wall of separation between ethics and metaphysics that Grisez would appear to think he has erected. But this is to anticipate. For the present let us just continue to follow Grisez's lead. In response to the question of how the notion of good needs to be understood in the first principle of practical reason, Grisez's move is to say that the notion of good is to be understood in terms of the notion of end. "Good," he says, "has the intelligibility of end" (p. 345), good being simply "what each thing tends towards."[8] Moreover, if one needs to have light shed on how such a notion of "tending towards" is here to be construed, Grisez invokes the notion of "inclination," and more specifically that of "man's natural inclinations" (p. 345). That is to say, to requote the already quoted passage from Grisez, "reason naturally grasps as goods ... all of the objects of man's natural inclinations."

Nor can one possibly take exception to anything said thus far. No, for Grisez in large measure is simply following and paraphrasing Aquinas, and correctly so. Still, having got to the point of understanding good as being the object of inclination, Grisez cannot very well stop there. Nor does it seem to me that Aquinas stops there. Yet oddly enough, it is just there that Grisez would appear to insist on stopping, and to insist that Aquinas stops as well. And yet how so? For if good is to be construed simply as end, or as object of inclination or desire, a dangerous ambiguity immediately suggests itself—an ambiguity which I believe can be best brought out by what I like to call "the *Euthyphro* test." Thus it may be recalled how in the *Euthyphro* Socrates voices the question of whether a thing is said to be good (or an end) because it is beloved of the gods; or is it rather that it is beloved of the gods because it is good?

That the consequences for ethics can be of the utmost import, depending upon how one resolves this ambiguity, can be readily seen if we but try opting for the former, as opposed to the latter alternative: things are good for no other reason than that men happen to desire them, or go for them, or be inclined towards them. Immediately, the consequence follows that nothing is really good, but desiring (or interest, or inclination, or a tending toward) makes it so. And what does this do but completely shatter that first principle of practical reason that Grisez, following Aquinas, is so insistent upon? For if goodness and value be entirely relative to tastes and inclinations, then there is not the slightest ground for holding that good is anything *to be* done and or *to be* pursued (or evil *to be* avoided). No, for in the Latin of Aquinas' formula, *Bonum est faciendum et prosequendum*, the verbs have

---

8. This, of course, is a rendering of the opening sentence of the *Nicomachean Ethics*. See Grisez, *op. cit.*, p. 353.

a gerundive force, so that the force of the formula in English is that good is necessarily or self-evidently that which ought to be done and should be done. And yet clearly, if good be no more than "any object of any interest,"[9] then goodness will have not the slightest obligatory, or morally compelling, force at all. Nor, with respect to the supposed logically self-evident character of the first principle of practical reason, will it be in the least evident why that which we merely like or desire or are inclined towards should be the sort of thing that we ought to do, or to pursue, or to go for.

In fact, is not this last the nerve of the general Kantian line of criticism that is directed against all hedonistic theories, or interest theories, or supposedly teleological theories of ethics? Just because someone is naturally disposed or inclined toward something, or likes it, or wants it, or finds it a source of satisfaction, or even of happiness or contentment, all of this, Kant in effect says, has no bearing at all on the question of whether such a thing ought to be pursued or cherished or liked, or of whether it is right that it be pursued or done or sought after. To try to perpetrate such an inference would be to commit the "is"–"ought" fallacy surely—at least such would be the contention of any Kantian; and in this Kant would surely be right!

But what now of Grisez? Surely, he would be the last to want to opt for this first alternative, when called upon to apply the *Euthyphro* test. Instead, he has got to go beyond his own way of stating what is to be understood by a good or an end: goods in the proposed sense may well be said to be objects of inclinations; and yet this must immediately be construed to mean that they are objects of inclination in the sense of being things that we ought to be inclined towards, or should be inclined towards, whether we actually are or not. And this in turn means that goods in this sense are goods that are objectively so, or really so, or goods in themselves, and not merely goods relative to their being desired, or to how men happen to feel about them. What, though, does this mean but that goods must be understood as beings? Or to invoke Aquinas' formula, which he uses in order to contrast what might be called the ontological status of *bonum* as contrasted with that of *verum: Bonum enim est in rebus, ut Philosophus dicit in VI Metaphys.* (*De Veritate,* Qu. XXI, art. 1.)

Very well, having thus located good in being, Aquinas insists that good needs to be understood as being, and as a being. In other words, it is precisely metaphysics that here takes over, in order to clarify and

---

9. Those of us whose philosophical education dates back to ancient times will recall that this was the late R. B. Perry's key formulation of his so-called interest theory of value.

render intelligible that first principle of ethics or of practical reason, the principle, namely, that good is to be done and to be pursued. And indeed, it is precisely in his metaphysical treatment of the transcendentals, particularly in the *De Veritate,* Qu. I, art. 1, and Qu. XXI, art. 1 and 2,[10] that Aquinas addresses himself to the question of what *bonum,* or good, really is, as opposed to what some Tom, Dick or Harry may happen to think it is. *Bonum,* he there says, is nothing but *ens,* considered as an object of desire, or *appetitus.* Moreover, all of these terms—*bonum, ens,* and *appetitus*—need to be understood each in its fully analogous sense, as is proper to all notions in metaphysics. For as Aquinas here expounds *bonum* and *ens,* considered as so-called transcendentals,[11] he avails himself of the distinction between potency and act, which, taken as a metaphysical distinction, may be said to pervade the whole range of being or reality. How, then, is *bonum* to be understood in this fully analogous or transcendental sense, if not simply as *ens* or being, considered as just the actuality toward which a given potentiality is ordered, as to its proper fulfillment or completion or actuality? Or put a little differently, any potentiality is ordered to its proper actuality as being just that which such a potentiality may be said to lack and to need and to have an *appetitus*[12] with respect to. Or again, since the proper actuality of any potency is that to which the latter is objectively ordered as being what naturally fulfills or completes it, one may say that such an actuality, as the *bonum* of the relevant potency, is just that which such a potentiality "ought to" desire. In other words, with reference to the *Euthyphro* test, one may now say that good or *bonum* is defined[13] and determined by St. Thomas as nothing but being or *ens,* considered not as that which simply is desired, but rather as that which is *desirable,* or ought to be desired.

Moreover, if at this point one should feel inclined to protest that what we have just been discoursing about is what might be called the metaphysical good, whereas Grisez is concerned only with the ethical good, I am afraid that such an escape route is not here open to Grisez. For granted that he is concerned with the good, or the end, in ethics,

10. It is interesting that, so far as I know, Finnis, no less than Grisez, seems scarcely even to advert to these passages, much less weigh them carefully.

11. By a "transcendental" here, we mean, of course, that which is not classifiable under any one category alone, but rather which runs through them all, and thus transcends them all.

12. Again, be it noted that Aquinas is quite patently taking *appetitus* in a fully analogous sense, considering that he is maintaining that any and every potency may be said to be ordered its proper actuality in sense of having a "desire" for it, or being "inclined" towards it.

13. Need I add that *bonum* being a transcendental, it cannot be defined in any strict sense of *per genus et differentiam.*

and not in metaphysics, there just is no way in which the former can ever be determined without having recourse to the latter. For if it is Grisez's proposal simply to consider the human good as being such an end or ends as human beings have an inclination towards, then that ambiguity which, as we saw, the *Euthyphro* test is so aptly designed to expose, immediately comes to the fore. Nor can this ambiguity be successfully obviated without one's recognizing that the good or end that is here in question cannot be any mere good that is such only relative to the chance interests or desires of a human being, but rather a good that is so objectively, and in being, and in just the sense that it is something that ought to be desired, whether it actually is so or not. And to understand what good or the good is, considered simply as *ens* or being, it is necessary to have recourse to metaphysics, and to St. Thomas' "definition" of good as simply the actual as over against the potential.

Then retracing one's steps from metaphysics to ethics, one finds that to determine what the human good is, or the end or goal of a properly human existence, one needs but to specify the metaphysical good, or the good in general, in terms of the specifically[14] human good. Moreover, if good simply as *ens*, or the good in general, is but the actual as over against the potential, then obviously the human good specifically has to be understood as simply that full actuality or perfection, or flourishing or fulfillment, to which our specifically human potentialities are ordered, and without the attainment of which we human beings can scarcely be anything other than incompletely or imperfectly human.

Of course, it is not our place in this paper to spell out what our human good must thus consist in more concretely. After all, we are all familiar with how Aristotle attempts to spell this out in the *Ethics,* or Aquinas in the two *Summas,* or Grisez and Finnis themselves in the respective accounts which they give of what they call the basic goods of human life. But for present purposes, it is not what the end or the basic goods of human life are that is of concern, but rather how they are determined, and what the line of argument is by which one is able to show that such goods are truly human goods, and do not only seem to be so. This line of argument, we would insist, can only be in terms of what Grisez calls speculative or theoretical reason, and not practical reason. No, for even by Grisez's account, practical reason but serves to tell us how the good may best be attained once it has been deter-

---

14. In this rather loose use of terms like "in general" or "specifically," we trust that the qualification noted in note 13 above will not go unregarded.

mined. However, thus to determine what that good is can only be the work of theoretical reason, proceeding from the determination of what the good is metaphysically, and simply as being, to its determination in terms of the actuality or perfection of human life in its specificity as being human, rather than simply as being *qua* being. To paraphrase Grisez, but in a sense somewhat contrary to his, the mind is indeed in such a context concerned to declare "what is to be." But so far from this being in contrast to its "recording what already is," it is only in so far as it makes such a recording in metaphysics that it is ever able to make a properly warranted declaration of what is to be in ethics. Likewise, it is this same domain that is the domain of theory, where, as Grisez says, it is "the world that calls the turn," the mind having to "conform to the facts." In other words, it is definitely not the domain of what Grisez calls "practice," where in a formulation rather frighteningly suggestive of idealism, Grisez says "the mind calls the turn." And yet, clearly, there can be no such domain of practice or of practical reason, unless it be in terms of metaphysics and of theoretical reason, through which it gets its proper determinations.

With this, then, need one say more by way of breaching that wall of separation that both Grisez and Finnis would seem to want to maintain between practical reason and theoretical reason, between ethics and metaphysics, between nature and morals, between "is" and "ought"? Nor would it seem to be unimportant that we should have been able to effect such a breach, for without it, one wonders if both Finnis and Grisez would not have to be viewed as being on the slippery slope down into an ethics merely of νόμος rather than φύσις, which is everywhere so prevalent today, and which would seem radically irreconcilable with anything like an ethics of natural law. Instead, let me just conclude in the face of both Finnis' and Grisez's seeming equivocations, "Long live natural law!"

16

A POOR BENIGHTED PHILOSOPHER LOOKS AT THE ISSUE OF JUDICIAL ACTIVISM[1]

Why did I ever undertake to consider the issue of judicial activism? After all, I am not trained as a lawyer or legal scholar, and I do not have any proper knowledge, much less any facility, when it comes to the key notions of contemporary jurisprudence and legal philosophy. Why, then, am I attempting to do what I have just confessed I am quite incompetent to do? The answer, alas, is none other than that "fools rush in where angels fear to tread."

Accordingly, in my very folly, let me begin by saying straight off that for some reason I find I have considerable difficulty even in getting the hang of just what judicial activism, as well as its presumed contrary—call it judicial passivism or restraint—really are. Besides, just what is it that is supposed to be so wrong with such an activism on the part of judges, or right with the opposed attitude of judicial passivism or restraint? After all, if one chanced to read, as I am sure all of us did, various of the newspaper accounts of a few months ago of the considerable flurry caused by some of the pronouncements of Attorney General Meese, and the irritated responses of Justices Brennan and Stevens, one may still find oneself puzzled to know quite what all of the shouting is about.

Superficially, of course, the issue sounds simple enough—so simple, in fact, that even the usually gravel-voiced columnist, James J. Kilpatrick, could manage to put the matter almost matter-of-factly, and with scarcely a trace of the normal rasp in his voice:

In deciding constitutional questions, should the court abide by the intentions of the framers and the ratifying states, as best these intentions can be deter-

---

1. This was an address delivered on the occasion of the annual meeting of the Natural Law Institute at the Notre Dame Law School, April 16, 1986.

mined, or should the court apply contemporary social and moral values instead?[2]

Clearly, though, one ought not to be beguiled by any such statement as would thus seem to leave the issue comparatively uncomplicated. For if the issue be of the sort that Kilpatrick and others would appear to represent it as being, then unhappily it is not an issue that can possibly be resolved—at least not if one hopes to rely for its resolution on the resources of anything like reason, evidence, and argument. For if the question be simply one of whether today's judges should be guided in their decisions by the social and moral values of our Founding Fathers in the eighteenth century, or whether they should look rather to contemporary social and moral values and try to apply these instead, then what does that do if not turn the whole issue into one of mere rival ideologies? And as between rival ideologies, one can only say that, by the very definition of the term "ideology," the ultimate arbiter can never be anything like reason and argument but only force, and force alone—"whoever gits to the Supreme Court first with the mostest men," one might say.

But this will never do, surely. And yet is there any way in which this issue of judicial activism can ever be got out of what would seem to amount to little more than its present quagmire of rival ideologies and onto the high ground once again of truly proper legal and judicial principles? For once on this ground, then the issue should be able to be resolved in terms of principle, and not as a result of mere political power-plays. Not only that, but no sooner is it even so much as suggested that the issue of judicial activism might be considered an issue of principle after all, than immediately there arises before us on the current legal-philosophical scene that gleaming white knight of principle in the law, offering to do battle with the dark, intrusive forces of mere political power! I refer, of course, to the distinguished Ronald Dworkin.

For as I interpret Dworkin, what he basically intends to say is that the trouble that is caused by the practice and example of activist judges in recent years is just that such judges have tended to go quite beyond their properly judicial functions and to arrogate to themselves what amount to no less than administrative and even legislative functions. Put a stop to this, Dworkin insists, and as Brian Barry has remarked in a review of Dworkin's latest book,[3] it is one of Dworkin's

---

2. Quoted from "Commentary by James J. Kilpatrick," Autumn, 1985.
3. The following quotations are all taken from a review of Ronald Dworkin's *A Matter of Principle* (Harvard University Press), by Brian Barry, *Times Literary Supplement*, October 25, 1985, p. 1195.

main contentions that "judicial review insures [or should insure] that the most fundamental issues of political morality will finally be set out and debated as issues of principle and not political power alone." And how may one recognize such issues of principle as are properly (in Dworkin's eyes) the business of courts to decide? Again, Barry's answer on Dworkin's behalf is that "an argument of principle is [an argument] to the effect that some individual has a right to something; it is contrasted with an argument of policy, which appeals to the public benefit of doing one thing rather than another." Accordingly, Dworkin's contention thus appears to turn out to be one to the effect that the business of the courts is with what may be called "rights," and in this sense it is not with matters of public policy in the usual sense at all. Moreover, the virtue of this kind of division of labor, as between the judicial and the legislative, might be summed up in the "proposition that courts should always reach their decisions on the basis of principle rather than policy." For after all, "courts are not well adapted to reaching judgments based on probable consequences." Indeed, it is just "this that makes them unfit to intervene in matters that by the universal consent of [almost] every country [in the world] except [possibly] the United States are the appropriate province of legislation and administration." This is again, much of it, quoted from Barry as summing up Dworkin's views.

Fine, then! Bravo! May we not accordingly say that Dworkin is just the one to point the way to how we can get out of that quagmire of rival ideologies in the matter of judicial activism, and onto that high ground of legal and judicial principle that we spoke about earlier. But not so—at least not so just yet, for let us give brief consideration to the views of a legal philosopher who might be taken to be almost diametrically opposed to Dworkin. I refer to Iredell Jenkins, of the University of Alabama, who, I venture to say, has been a close friend and associate of nearly every one of us here in this room. For Jenkins, if I mistake not, was one of the Founding Fathers, not of the Federal Union, to be sure, but of the Natural Law Institute! Yes, in previous years, he has been a frequent attender and participant in these very meetings here at Notre Dame.

Now in Jenkins' eyes—if I understand him—Dworkin, so far from being one who has succeeded in pointing to the cure for the enormities of present-day judicial activism, is really one who has only aggravated the disease. For the sources of judicial activism are by no means traceable to any failure on the part of the courts to confine themselves to questions of human rights, as distinguished from matters of public policy, as Dworkin supposedly holds. True, Jenkins is most emphatic—

and in this he presumably would agree with Dworkin—that the courts ought not to allow themselves to be drawn into the business of determining public policy. At the same time, Jenkins would insist, it is not by confining themselves to considerations of human rights that courts will ever be able to avoid being drawn into such policy issues. No, it is rather precisely because of their seeming preoccupation with rights issues in recent years that the courts have been led right down the garden path into their present unfortunate habits of judicial activism. And here Jenkins would insist that we need to draw an important distinction with regard to the very notion of human rights. This is the distinction between what have sometimes been called "negative rights" on the one hand and "positive rights," or "welfare rights," on the other.[4] True, the terms "negative" and "positive" here are perhaps not as illuminating as they might be; nor is the distinction that the terms are designed to point up always as reliably determinable as one might wish. Still, as a rough and ready distinction, it is readily recognizable the sort of thing that Jenkins here means.

Thus as for "negative rights," why not say that these amount to such rights as we human beings might be said to have, simply *not* to be interfered with in, say, our lives, our liberties and our properties? Moreover, such an entitlement to noninterference is clearly to be construed as a noninterference by others, be these others either private persons or the public authorities. Hence, the term "negative" rights.

In contrast, when it comes to positive rights, these may be construed as being rights, not merely not to be deprived of what is already ours (like our lives, our liberties, and our property), but rather as being rights actually to have certain things bestowed upon us, such things as we presumably neither now have nor are likely ever to come to have, unless perchance or by good luck they should come to be bestowed upon us by others—that is to say by our fellow citizens, or by the public authorities, or by whoever may have such goods either at their disposition or in their disposal. For example, such goods and services as might be the objects of positive rights could clearly be any of the so-called welfare rights—such things as old-age benefits, health care, facilities for education, a living wage, etc., etc.

But now, it is at this very point, and with respect to just such supposed positive rights, that Jenkins, as I understand him, would wish to enter an emphatic demurrer to Dworkin's major thesis that the business of the courts is with adjudicating matters of principle—which

---

4. *Cf.* Iredell Jenkins, *Social Order and the Limits of Law* (Princeton: Princeton University Press, 1980), Chapter XIV, *passim.*

is to say, in Dworkin's view, with matters involving human rights, especially positive rights. Thus as Jenkins sees it, it is no less than as a direct consequence of judges allowing themselves to be drawn into this very area of positive rights that judges have become guilty of the most flagrant examples of judicial activism. Yes, Jenkins would insist, it is precisely because of their having allowed themselves thus to become preoccupied with what Dworkin would call issues of principle—which is to say with rights issues—that the courts have now got themselves so hopelessly bogged down in problems involving the determinations of public policy—matters which by Dworkin's own insistence are clearly beyond the competence of courts to decide.

Moreover, by way of illustration and substantiation of such a line of criticism, one has only to recall Jenkins' telling analysis and criticism of Federal Judge Johnson's decision in *Wyatt v. Stickney*.[5] For it was in this case that the judge held that patients in the mental hospitals of the State of Alabama were entitled to certain minimum standards of care and supervision during the periods of their confinement in the state mental institutions—a clear case, in other words, of a claim to certain positive rights or welfare rights. Moreover, in order that such minimum standards be met and maintained, the judge in effect ordered the State of Alabama to expend large sums of money, as well as drastically to shake up the administrative staffs of the hospitals—actions which, it would seem, were clearly within the jurisdiction of the executive branch of the government—and all of this in order that the state hospitals be brought up to snap—*i.e.,* up to Judge Johnson's snap!

Nor is it hard to see why, for Jenkins, *Wyatt v. Stickney* is to be regarded as exhibiting the classic pattern of judicial activism. First off, the judge presupposes that he needs to base his decisions on what Dworkin would call "principle"—*i.e.,* upon what are supposedly recognized as being undeniable social and political principles of right and justice. Then, guided by these principles, the judge finds himself led to acknowledge that such principles open for litigants all sorts of hitherto unsuspected right-claims. And with that, the entire legal system finds itself beginning to be flooded with an incredible, seemingly almost incalculable, wave of new rights—a phenomenon which all of us have been witnessing in the last several years as a consequence of activist judges rendering their decisions on grounds of what Dworkin would call a "principle."

Clearly, though, such an emergence of new rights betokens nothing

5. *Ibid.,* pp. 135–150, 282–83.

quite so much as an actual "creation of new law." And what would seem more amiss than that judges, who presumably are sworn to uphold the law, should now be allowing themselves to be drawn into a business of making new law? Nor is that all. For each such change in established law, as this comes to be effected by an activist judge, must surely constitute no less than a grave offense against that fundamental constitutional principle in this country of the careful separation of powers, as between the judiciary and the legislature. Is it any wonder, then, that Jenkins and other like-minded legal philosophers might be imagined to have come increasingly to adopt almost as their particular slogan, not the liberal-sounding slogan associated with Dworkin, "Principle, not Policy," but rather a slogan that has an obviously more conservative ring to it, "Precedent, not Principle." Only under such a slogan would it seem that one might put a stop to the seeming hemorrhaging, in the matter of human rights, that our activist judges have unhappily started.

Moreover, what is of particular interest and significance for us at this present juncture in our argument is how such developments in legal thought, as are typified by Jenkins and others like him, really give the lie to Dworkin's rather dramatic earlier proposals for curing judicial activism. For remember it was Dworkin's basic contention that, by confining their judicial review to what Dworkin called issues of principle, and therefore to rights-issues, the courts could avoid being drawn into the business of having to make decisions and pronouncements about matters of public policy. Unhappily, though, in the light of an analysis like that of Jenkins of Judge Johnson's decision in *Wyatt v. Stickney*, it turns out that, so far from its being the case that, by sticking strictly to rights-issues, considered as issues of principle, the courts can avoid being drawn into trying to decide issues of public-policy, it is rather just the opposite. Precisely because the courts have taken to occupying themselves with rights-issues and thus, supposedly, with issues of principle, the courts have become hopelessly involved in just those issues that do involve public policy. In short, the irony of Dworkin's position is that when it comes to his own proposals for remedying judicial activism, the poor man would seem to be "hoist by his own petar!" as Shakespeare might say.

Perhaps, though, Dworkin is not one to be dismissed quite so fast or so easily. True, on the surface it certainly does look as if the Dworkin proposals for remedying judicial activism tended not to cure the disease, but only to aggravate it. All the same, let us not forget what there was about Dworkin's position that originally commended it to our attention. Thus he wanted the courts to confine their attention, as he said, to questions of principle, and not of public policy. And yet the reason behind Dworkin's insistence upon this point was that if the decisions of judges failed to be principled ones, it could only mean that such decisions could be based on little more than purely ideological considerations. And how then could it be said that such justice as might be dispensed by our courts could ever claim to be a proper right and justice at all?

Besides, how might Jenkins and other conservative-minded critics of Dworkin respond to this kind of challenge? After all, they want to fault Dworkin for saying that judges should base their decisions on considerations of moral and social principle. For this, they say, leads only to a ceaseless proliferation of human rights, as well as to an ever-increasing arrogation to itself by the judiciary of functions that belong properly to the executive and legislative branches. Nor, apparently, do they see any other cure for the disease than a return to a condition of things where judges would come to rely once again upon precedent, rather than upon principle, in rendering their decisions. *Stare decisis* would thus be the rule; and not anything like moral or political principle!

Surely, though, such a prescription for curing the disease of judicial activism, while it might well cure the disease, would at the same time seem possibly to kill the patient in the process. For no sooner are precedents made to replace principles, as a basis for judicial decisions, than we would seem to be thrown right back into that old quagmire of ideology all over again, which is just what, at the very outset of our discussion, we sought to find some way out of. For just recall that earlier quote from James J. Kilpatrick on the view of Attorney General Meese: in Meese's eyes, apparently, it is far better that in matters of adjudication the courts be guided by the precedents laid down by our Founding Fathers, rather than by any "contemporary moral and social values."

Nevertheless, if the rationale here for relying upon precedents rather than principles consists solely of formal or institutional considerations, and not a reliance upon substantive considerations as to the intrinsic superiority of the precedents involved, then this would in no wise provide any solution to the problem of allowing mere ideology to become the ultimate determinant of judicial decision-making. Indeed, to recur to our earlier example of Attorney General Meese: if the ideals of right and justice of the Founding Fathers are not considered to be inherently or intrinsically superior to the ideals of the present-day, then to rely upon such ideals, merely because they are precedents, would be to admit that one has no reason to consider such ideals as being anything more than purely ideological in character. And would not this land us right back where we started from?

On the other hand, if, as would seem more likely, those conservative-minded legal scholars for whom the proposals of Dworkin would seem to be anathema—if these same conservatives were actually to argue that it is not just because they are precedents that they would have judges abide by traditional principles of right and justice, but rather because, as principles, they think the principles, say, of the Founding Fathers, to be inherently superior to such moral and social values as are current today, then that would render the whole question an issue of principle after all. In fact, I doubt not that something like this is really Jenkins' position, although he seems hardly to acknowledge as much. For upon reflection, it does seem that Jenkins' basic objection to Dworkin is that he, Jenkins, just does not think that there are any such things as "positive rights." Negative rights, yes; but positive rights, no—or at least not in the same sense in which there are negative rights.

And likewise, even Meese—although I daresay it may be a mistake to probe too deeply into the mind of Meese: for instead of depths, one's probes might reveal nothing but shallows! Still, for all of that, and recurring to the quotation from Kilpatrick, would it not seem that when Meese holds that "in deciding constitutional questions, the court should abide by the intentions of the framers [of the Constitution] and the ratifying states, rather than try to apply contemporary social and moral values instead"—surely, if such be Meese's conviction, he is thus not arguing that we should stick by the precedents set by our Founding Fathers, merely because they are precedents, but rather because they are superior as social and moral principles to the social and moral values that have come to be fashionable more lately. In other words, it would seem that in this connection Meese clearly implies that the issue involved is an issue of principle, and not one of either policy or mere precedent.

Very well, then, if Jenkins, and Meese, and presumably other like-minded conservatives in matters of jurisprudence, are really at one with a liberal like Dworkin when he (Dworkin) says that what the courts need always and ultimately to concern themselves with are issues of principle—*i.e.*, issues of whether human individuals actually have certain rights or not, then just where and how does the conservative differ from the liberal? Clearly, it seems to me, in the light of our immediately foregoing discussions, we might now hazard the guess that the issue rather precisely concerns the distinction between negative and positive rights—the conservatives being convinced that there are only negative rights, whereas the liberals are the obvious champions of positive rights as well. In fact, it is precisely here, it seems to me, that the really significant issue of principle lies, when it comes to the right-claims of individuals as these come to be processed through the courts.

Yes, I wonder if one might not go even further and show that perhaps Dworkin was not wrong after all when he enunciated his general formula to the effect that, by confining their attention to issues of principle in matters of adjudication, judges should thereby be able to avoid being drawn into dealing with questions of public policy, which after all are none of their business. Instead, why might not Dworkin be correct in his general formula, but mistaken in his failing to see that it is not as a result of their occupying themselves with questions of rights as such that activist judges become involved in questions of public policy, but rather because of their failing to draw the distinction between negative and positive rights? So long as they confine themselves to adjudicating questions of negative rights, there need be no implications here with respect to public policy. But let them entertain questions about the positive right-claims of individuals, and immediately they will find themselves implicated in just such questions of public policy as we have found Jenkins exposing so skillfully and tellingly in his analysis of *Wyatt v. Stickney*.

Unfortunately, though, all of these last several random suggestions as to where the precise problems of judicial activism may be seen to lie, as well as to how that problem may best be resolved—these suggestions, I fear, not only will not carry conviction, but will not even be too intelligible, considering the sorry confusions and blindnesses that would seem nowadays to prevail almost everywhere with respect to nearly all the basic notions, alike of legal and moral philosophy— notions such as rights, duties, obligations, yes, even the notion of law itself. Moreover, I am afraid that such confusions and blindnesses afflict present-day liberals and conservatives alike—the Jenkins, the Meeses, the Nozicks, *et al.* on the one hand, and the Dworkins, the Rawls, the Ackermans *et al.* on the other.

Accordingly, in the short time that still remains to me in this address, let's see if it may not be possible at least to make something of a beginning at clarifying and straightening out some of these basic legal-philosophical notions. And first of all, let us have a closer look, not just at the general issue of human rights, and whether there really are such things, but also at the more specific and tricky issue of negative rights vs. positive rights. For no sooner does one raise the question of whether and what might be the basic justification for supposing that there are negative rights as over against positive rights, or vice versa, than we shall see that we are confronted with a fundamental issue of principle, and an issue of principle that neither conservatives nor liberals can afford to overlook. Not only that, but it should also prove instructive, if we can show how such an issue of principle is susceptible of a genuine legal-philosophical resolution, and not merely something to be written off as a mere difference of ideologies.

Suppose, then, I simply start out by suggesting that this issue of positive rights vs. negative rights is nothing if not the very issue that divides a thinker like Rawls, say, from someone like Nozick. For example, what might one say is the fundamental conviction that underlies Rawls' two principles of justice? Is it not very largely a radical and fundamental conviction to the effect that, so far as we human beings are concerned, all of a person's individual gifts either of nature or of fortune—*e.g.*, the gifts of our lives, of our abilities, of our talents, of our properties and possessions, so long as all of these are due simply to what might be called our own good fortune—all of these goods, it would seem, are hardly such that we can very well say that we have earned them or therefore that we could even say that we have deserved them. But if we have not earned them or deserved them, then how can we consider that they are simply ours to dispose of in whatever way we see fit or may happen to choose? And if they are not ours to dispose of, then why not say that it is presumably up to the community, or to the society, or to the *polis,* to make a distribution of such goods to meet the needs and requirements of those others of our fellow citizens, who, being less fortunate than ourselves, are consequently entitled to an equalization with those more fortunate?

With this, though, the relevance of Rawls' second principle of justice, as it is called, immediately becomes evident. This is the principle that summons us to acquiesce in what Nozick invidiously calls a "patterned" distribution of goods according to the needs and requirements of each and all within the community. "But why," Nozick would rejoin at this point, "is it claimed that 'justice' calls for this sort of patterned distribution; and on what grounds can it be claimed that it is our duty to accede to such a distribution?" And of course, Nozick's reply to his own question is that there are no grounds of justification here. Rather, as Nozick sees things, instead of there being any such preconceived pattern or blueprint for the just distribution of goods within a community or society, there is no more than the purely "historical" distribution of goods that takes place in the course of a society's historical evolution; and it is this that may be said to give rise to such just entitlements as individuals may be said to have to the full posssession and enjoyment of their goods, be they goods of nature or of fortune—provided always, of course, that such goods have come into their owners' hands either through the owners' good fortune or through their labor and enterprise, but not through anything like either force or fraud.

And what then do we have here, if not two radically conflicting theories or principles of right and justice, which certainly cry out to be decided surely on principle, and not simply as one might decide between two rival ideologies? Yes, if you will, the root issue between Rawls and Nozick is none other than the perennial issue of liberty vs. equality: is it the function of the state or the community to try to secure the liberty of its citizens, or rather their equality? Nor is that all, for the historical antecedents of this conflict between these two basic and seemingly irreconcilable principles of justice in society are only too familiar to all of us. Thus on the one hand, there are the likes of a Sir William Blackstone, who, as we know, maintained stoutly that an individual has no less than "an absolute right" to his life, his liberty, and his property. In contrast, we need scarcely be reminded of the almost diametrically opposed principle of justice as enunciated by Marx: "To each according to his needs, and from each according to his abilities."

And with that we are brought face to face with what in our own terms is the basic issue: do we, as human individuals, possess only negative rights, as libertarians like Nozick or Blackstone, for example, would appear to insist; or do we have positive rights as well, such as more equalitarian thinkers like Rawls or Marx would appear to contend for? In other words, how may human rights, be they either of the negative or the positive sort, ever be justified? Or still more generally, if law—civil law, that is to say—is to be reckoned as specifying what the rights and duties of citizens are, how is it possible to show that such rights and duties are warranted on the basis of principle, and not just of precedent?

With this, however, we are brought face to face with one of those singularly lamentable lacunae in nearly the whole of contemporary moral and political philosophy: there just does not seem to be any reasoned accounting for why and on what grounds we human beings can properly be said to have rights or duties either one.[6] Oh, it's true that a Nozick, for example, can insist that human individuals in their basic entrepreneurial activities are inescapably subject to certain "side

---

6. For a fuller treatment of the several issues which follow, I refer to my own book, *Human Rights: Fact or Fancy?* (Baton Rouge: Louisiana State University Press, 1985), esp. Chapter III.

constraints." But why and on what grounds may it be affirmed that there are rights of this sort, that individuals may be said to have, and that impose side constraints on the activities of their fellows? True, given that individuals do have such negative rights, then one can infer the existence of such duties or side constraints as correspond to those prior rights. Or supposing with Rawls that, given the condition of their being behind the veil of ignorance, individuals will be acknowledged to have certain positive rights, and given the rights, then one, of course, can infer the corresponding duties, such as were specified under the two principles of justice, for example. But what is the basis or ground of justification for the assertion of the rights in the first place, to which there are such answering duties? Or if one reckons duties as prior, then one can infer certain corresponding rights, be they either negative or positive, depending upon the character of the duties. But again, why the duties in the first place? In other words, rights can always be derived from duties, or duties from rights, but who is to say that there are either duties or rights in the first place?

To generalize, therefore, it is simply a fact that neither men's duties nor their rights can ever be reckoned as being self-evident. Instead, for any assertion of either a duty or a right, the question "Why?" is always relevant and demands an answer: "Why am I obligated to do thus and so?" or "On what grounds am I able to claim this, that, or the other thing, as being a right?" Responding to such questions, I would make bold to say that even though it is no longer fashionable in contemporary philosophy to think or to speak in this way, it is nevertheless perfectly possible to determine, and to find evidence for one's determination of, a certain order of dependence in respect to our rights and duties. In fact, I would even say that rights by their very nature are always dependent upon certain prior duties, and yet upon duties of a rather particular and even peculiar kind. Not only that, but I would also suggest that our duties, in turn, are always and ultimately dependent upon prior ends or purposes or goals, which we human beings come to have.

How do I, though, propose to make out my case for all of this? To begin with, let me but suggest that with respect to laws—moral laws and civil laws both—they always, in some sense or other, specify certain rules for us that need to be observed, things that ought to be done or ought not to be done. Yes, even in the various arts and skills, and techniques, it would surely seem to be true that the laws, or better the rules of the art, specify how the practitioner of the art ought to proceed or ought not to proceed. Thus as we say, the skilled craftsman is just the one who knows how to do this, or how to do that—which is to say, he has mastered the rules as to how one ought to proceed, or ought not to proceed, in going about the kind of undertaking that is governed by the particular art in question. And if one asks, "What determines the several different varieties of rules of skill that go with each of the different arts or skills?" is not the answer that the rules as to what one ought to do, or ought not to do, in pursuing a particular art, are determined by the end in view—by health, say, in the case of medicine, or victory in the case of the military art, or by profits in the case of the arts and techniques of business enterprise? In other words, in the various arts, the reason the rules of the art are as they are, and the reason the practitioner of the art ought to follow such rules, is in order to attain the end or goal of the particular art in question.

Accordingly, if we understand rules as being simply specifications of the "oughts" that need to be observed in the pursuit of any particular art, then clearly such "oughts" derive all their force and authority simply from the end or goal that is proper to the particular art in question. Proceeding, then, from the example of the various arts or techniques in the usual sense, may we not say that the situation is altogether analogous in the case of what I will now call the moral art, or art of living, if you will? Here the end in view is simply man's natural end or *telos*, what a human being, simply as a human person, ought to be and become. This is the end that Aristotle specified as being the end simply of living wisely and intelligently, of being guided by one's better judgment amidst all of the pressures of feelings, appetites, desires, impulses, emotions, etc., with which human life is so continually fraught. It is just such a life, Aristotle insisted, that it behooves man as a rational animal to live. And so it is that, just as in the other arts, so in the art of living as well, it is the end to be achieved, that determines what the rules of practice, or if you will, the "oughts" of the particular art are to be. Accordingly, when it comes to the moral art, it will be man's natural end or goal of simply living intelligently, of leading the good life, that will determine what the moral rules and the moral "oughts" are that a human being will need to observe if he is ever to become the kind of being that, as a human being, he ought to be. In short, in morality, the rules are no less how-to-do-it rules than are the rules in all of the several other arts as well.

Here, then, we can begin to see what the ground or basis of justification is for all of those countless moral rules, or moral "oughts," or moral imperatives, that pervade the life of man and his existence in the world. To put it bluntly, "oughts" or duties are determined entirely on the basis of ends—specifically of man's natural end or *telos* simply as a human being. But now you will ask, "What about rights?" If our duties are determined in the light of what our ends are, what is it that determines what our rights are? Again, be it remembered that rights are not things that we have merely on the ground that we make a claim to them. No, a right-claim is a valid claim only if it can be shown that the right in question is justified as a claim. But now, given the sorts of human duties that we have just been talking about—call them duties to oneself, if you will, or duties that are determined in the light of our human end or ends—we ought to be able to see how such duties-to-self necessarily determine certain rights that we can be said to have simply by nature, or simply in virtue of our being human.

Thus, to take a somewhat trivial example, is it not simply evident that if one is under obligation to do a certain job, or to perform a certain task, then there is an obvious sense in which that person may claim a right not to be interfered with, or impeded, in the exercise of that task which it is properly his to perform? Thus if my boss gives me a job to do, and I recognize that it is my job, and thus my duty and responsibility to do it, then surely it would be unfair and a violation of what is only right, if my boss, having assigned me the task, then did everything he could to hinder me, or interfere with my doing what I am supposed to do. Building on this analogy, why may we not now say that if as a human individual I am under a basic and continuing obligation in life to make something of myself, to try to be and to become the sort of person that as a human individual I ought to be, then may I not claim it is my right not to be interfered with in the pursuit of my basic responsibilities in life, and not to be deprived of those natural means—my life, my liberty, my property, say—that are necessary means to my acquitting myself of my natural human responsibilities? But with this, what do we have, if not a proper justification for those fundamental human rights—the so-called negative rights to things like life, liberty, and property, without which we would scarcely be able to be the human beings that we ought to be, or to acquit ourselves of our obligations as human individuals?

So much, then, for negative rights. But what now of positive rights? Likewise, and in the same vein, it must occur to one that if duties-to-oneself, as we have called them, are to be accounted for in terms of an individual's due and proper end or goal in life, what about duties to others? Usually, nowadays it is supposed that all duties must, in the nature of the case, be duties to others. And yet if that is all that there is to it, it would seem that there is just no way in which any duties that an individual may have toward others can ever be grounded or justified. For why, following Dworkin, for example, should I hold that I am under obligation to treat my fellow human beings all of them with an equal concern and respect? Who is to say that I am under any such obligation? And why should it not be quite all right for me simply not to have either compunction or concern regarding the well-being of my fellows, much less to feel that I should treat each and every one with an equal concern or respect?

Such questions, it seems to me, are simply not susceptible of any proper answer, unless we first recognize that our duties to self take precedence over any duties that we might be supposed to have toward others. For given our duties-to-self, construed as being simply the necessary means that we must follow if ever we are as individuals to attain to our proper ends as persons, there follow from such duties-to-self, as we have already noted, various so-called negative rights. And attendant upon such rights as I may have, as being consequent upon my having the duties-to-self that I do, then it follows that my rights, being real rights, as it were, or natural rights, my fellow citizens and fellow human beings have a duty to respect such rights in me. Also, and by parity of reasoning, if I have certain rights based upon my duty to myself, then others will have comparable rights for their part, based on their respective duties to themselves; accordingly, I will be no less obligated to respect their rights than they to respect mine. And does this not simply confirm that seemingly rather paradoxical contention that I have already touched upon in this very paragraph, namely that there are no duties or obligations which we owe toward others, unless and until such duties toward others can be grounded and justified in terms of prior duties to self—my own to myself, and yours to yourself? Yes, this may sound paradoxical, and yet I believe that it is true for all of that: all duties toward others are ultimately based on duties toward self.

Still, what about positive rights? Is it possible to find any ground and basis for these, now that we have seen how so-called negative rights can be justified, no less than duties-to-others, and both of them in terms of duties-to-self? As a first reply, I am inclined but to repeat what I have already intimated: there just is no warrant for supposing that as human beings we have any positive rights at all! After all, on what grounds may I claim that, just as a human being, I am entitled to adequate food, clothing, and shelter, to education, to health care, *et al.*? True, it might be very nice if I had such things, but how may I claim them as being mine by right? True, if my fellow human beings, either all of them or some of them, could be shown to have a duty to provide me with such things, then I could doubtless claim that I had a right to such things on the basis of these others' duty. And yet such an argument would surely only beg the question. For on what other grounds could it be claimed that my fellowman has a duty to relieve my necessities, unless it could be shown that I might claim as a right such relief of my own needs and necessities? And yet that was just what needed to be proved.

Of course, one might try to argue along the lines that were suggested earlier—that if I had the good fortune to possess more than a sufficiency of goods, then such goods being, as it were, mine by luck would hardly be mine through any desert on my part, or through my having in any way earned them. Hence one might contend that, their being mine largely by good fortune, they are hardly mine to dispose of simply at will. Yet even conceding the justice of this argument, it can hardly be concluded from it that therefore society or the governing powers have a right, for their part, to move in and dispose of my possessions as they, rather than I, see fit. And even if either I or others should choose to dispose of my goods to others, and supposing there to be warrant in either my or their so doing, it still does not follow from this that whoever is the recipient of such benefactions must have had a prior right to what he thus received. Rather than consider the benefaction to be a right under such circumstances, why would it not be no more than reasonable to consider that it is precisely what it is called, a benefaction, and not a right?

Nevertheless, even supposing there to be no proper ground in justification of positive right-claims, is it not necessary, in our consideration of human rights and duties generally, and as they may come to be specified by both moral law on the one hand and civil law on the other, that we take further cognizance, beyond what we have so far done, of what might be called the fact that man is not merely an individual animal but also a political animal and a member of society? Moreover, considered as a member of society, will not any and every individual come to have certain social duties, other than mere duties just to himself, and other than such duties as are derivative from the individuals within a community possessing what we have called negative rights? Of course, the answer to such a question is, "Yes"; and yet adequately to develop such an answer is quite a large order.

Still, let us let just a few brief observations suffice. For one thing, being a political or social animal by nature means that no human being can have a properly human existence outside of the *polis*: he and everyone like him can scarcely even live, much less live well, without being able to enjoy such fruits as only a proper division of labor within a society would be able to afford him. As a result, it pertains to the very perfection and flourishing of any individual—and hence needs to be reckoned as an integral part of the individual's own natural end—that he be a citizen and a member of the *polis*, so to speak. Moreover, inasmuch as we have already seen how our duties and obligations as individual persons are determined in the light of our ends, it naturally follows that, as members of a *polis*, individuals will have duties as citizens to promote not just their own private good, but the common good of the community as well.

Likewise, in the very nature of the case, it would seem that there could be no way that an individual could ever acquit himself of such public duties as he might have, save by contributing of his own resources in time, in money, in energy, *et al.* Clearly, though, in view of any individual's possession of a natural and negative right to what is his own—his life, his liberty, and his property—it follows that any enforcement of public duties by the community can never be such as to deprive the individual totally of his negative rights. For these rights, being natural rights, are clearly inalienable, even if they be not necessarily either illimitable or unregulable.

And with this, we can now return in our conclusion to our original issue as to what the proper business of the law courts is in a well-ordered *polis* or political society. Clearly, it would be the business of courts to adjudicate the right-claims of individuals within a political community, even when such rights should come to be threatened or actually invaded by the public authorities no less than when they are threatened by private citizens. But what about claims to positive rights? If courts assume jurisdiction over these, will the courts not be drawn into just such matters of public policy as we found Dworkin insisting that it was no business of courts to be drawn into, and yet which, on Jenkins' showing, Dworkin's own theory of rights would make it inevitable that the courts should be drawn into? To which the answer is: Of course, this is just what would happen if courts let themselves in for trying to adjudicate positive right-claims. But on our analysis, the whole problem may be simply obviated by recognizing that there are no such things as positive rights; and that hence, claims to such rights need have and should have no standing in the courts at all.

This is not to say, of course, that in a given political community, it could not be the policy of the public authorities to try to promote the public welfare by instituting systems of health care benefits, of old age benefits, of aid to education, of encouragement to business enterprise, or to whatever it might seem wise and advisable to the authorities to give aid and encouragement to by way of furthering the common good. The only thing is that such public policies of seeking to benefit citizens within the community ought now, in the light of these present discussions, to be understood as policies designed not to meet right-claims but rather to extend benefits—yes, maybe at times, even out and out charity—to such as might be deemed to need it. Still, considered as matters of policy, such matters would not belong in the courts at all, there being no rights in the proper sense involved. Once this is recognized, then Dworkin's distinction between matters of principle, as being of relevance for courts of law, and matters of policy, which belong in the hands of the legislative and administrative authorities—this distinction not only emerges intact, but also turns out to be a distinction that would seem eminently viable and yet free from the embarrassing consequences that attended the distinction as it was originally drawn by Dworkin.

"Still," you may object by way of a final and once more recurrent objection, "will not judicial activism still be a danger, if judges are encouraged to decide cases on the basis of principle, rather than of precedent? For what is to prevent judges, when guided by supposed principles, from coming up with all sorts of new and wacky ideas of their own about what our human rights and duties are?" To which the reply is, "But how so, for have we not just seen how when the determination of what our rights and duties are is based on a regard for genuine principles of right and justice, that themselves are determined by nature and not merely by habit, there could scarcely be much chance of any proliferation of either rights or duties based only on the chance whims of judges?" For that is just the point of our having insisted that judicial decisions are to be based on a knowledge and understanding of recognized and established legal principles, and therefore not upon the mere "bright ideas" that may happen to pop into some judge's head.

Nor is that all. For as we noted earlier, albeit only in passing, the rules of right and justice in the law are like the rules of practice in any established art or skill. And so it is in medicine, for instance, that the rules of sound medical practice are based on nothing short of demonstrated scientific principles. And for that reason it is that they have come to be firmly established in the art. Accordingly, what physician who really knows what he is about would ever feel free to disregard the recognized rules of sound medical practice simply at will? Yes, even if he should in his own practice choose to depart sometimes from the established precedents of the medical profession, it may be supposed that he would do so only for good reason, and only if he could justify his departure in terms of the very principles of medical science itself.

Why, then, is it not in a like case with the law, particularly the civil or common law? For embedded in the law are surely long-tested principles of what we can only call a natural right and justice. Hence it is on the basis of these that judicial precedents have come to be established, much as in medicine it is on the basis of scientifically determined principles of anatomy and physiology, *et al.*, that the precedents of sound medical practice have come to be established. In other words, why assume that there is likely to be any conflict between principles and precedents in law, any more than in medicine? Is it not rather the case that the precedents have come to be determined in the light of properly intelligible and justifiable legal principles? And this being the case, judicial precedents, if they are worth their salt, will be informed ones, rather than merely traditional ones or merely mechanical ones. Why assume, then, that in such a context judicial activism in the bad sense need be a problem at all?

Select Bibliography

The following is a list of various books, all contemporary, or at least modern, which have had a bearing on the four divisions of this book. First, though, let me list those of my own books which bear most particularly on the several ensuing topics.

Veatch, Henry. *Human Rights: Fact or Fancy.* Baton Rouge: Louisiana State University Press, 1985.
———. *For an Ontology of Morals.* Evanston, IL: Northwestern University Press, 1971.
———. *Rational Man: A Modern Interpretation of Aristotelian Ethics.* Bloomington: Indiana University Press, 1962.
———. *Aristotle: A Contemporary Appreciation.* Bloomington: Indiana University Press, 1974.

Part I. Quieting Various of the Alarms and Excursions in Recent Philosophy

Bernstein, Richard J. *Beyond Objectivism and Relativism: Science, Hermeneutics, and Praxis.* Philadelphia: University of Pennsylvania Press, 1983.
Connell, Richard J. *Substance and Modern Science.* Notre Dame, IN: University of Notre Dame Press, 1988.
Danto, Arthur C. *Nietzsche as Philosopher.* New York: Columbia University Press, 1980.
Gilson, Etienne. *The Unity of Philosophical Experience.* New York: Charles Scribner's Sons, 1937.
Hanson, N. R. *Patterns of Discovery.* Cambridge: Cambridge University Press, 1958.
Harré, Rom and Edward H. Madden. *Causal Powers: A Theory of Natural Necessity.* Oxford: Basil Blackwell, 1975.
Hesse, Mary. *Revolutions and Reconstructions in the Philosophy of Science.* Bloomington and London: Indiana University Press, 1980.
Kuhn, Thomas. *The Structure of Scientific Revolutions,* 2nd ed. Chicago: University of Chicago Press, 1970.
Popper, Karl R. *Conjectures and Refutations: The Growth of Scientific Knowledge.* New York: Basic Books, 1962.
———. *The Logic of Scientific Discovery.* New York: Science Editions, 1961.
Quine, Willard Van Orman. *From a Logical Point of View: Logico-Philosophical Essays.* Cambridge, MA: Harvard University Press, 1953.
———. *Word and Object.* New York: MIT Press, and John Wiley & Sons, 1960.

———. *Ontological Relativity and Other Essays*. New York and London: Columbia University Press, 1969.
Rajchman, John and Cornell West, eds. *Post-Analytic Philosophy*. New York: Columbia University Press, 1985.
Rorty, Richard. *Philosophy and the Mirror of Nature*. Princeton: Princeton University Press, 1979.
Russell, Bertrand. *The Problems of Philosophy*. London: Oxford University Press, 1912.
———. *Logic and Knowledge*. Edited by Robert Marsh. New York: Macmillan, 1956.
Russman, Thomas A. *A Prospectus for the Triumph of Realism*. Macon, GA: Mercer University Press, 1987.
Wallace, William A. *Causality and Scientific Explanation*, 2 vols. Ann Arbor: University of Michigan Press, 1972–74.
———. *From a Realist Point of View: Essays on the Philosophy of Science*. Lanham, MD: University Press of America, 1979.

Part II. What Price Ethics in the Eyes of Modern Moral Philosophers?

Baier, Kurt. *The Moral Point of View*. Ithaca, NY: Cornell University Press, 1953.
Cooper, John. *Reason and Human Good in Aristotle*. Cambridge, MA: Harvard University Press, 1975.
Den Uyl, Douglas, and Douglas B. Rasmussen. *The Philosophic Thought of Ayn Rand*. Champaign, IL: University of Illinois Press, 1984.
Donagan, Alan. *The Theory of Morality*. Chicago and London: University of Chicago Press, 1977.
Finnis, John. *Fundamentals of Ethics*. Washington, DC: Georgetown University Press, 1983.
Frankena, W. K. *Ethics*. Englewood Cliffs, NJ: Prentice-Hall, 1973.
Gauthier, R. A. *La Morale d'Aristote*. Paris: Presses Universitaire de France, 1958.
Gewirth, Alan. *Reason and Morality*. Chicago: University of Chicago Press, 1978.
Hare, R. M. *The Language of Morals*. Oxford: Oxford University Press, 1952.
———. *Freedom and Reason*. New York: Oxford University Press, 1965.
Lomasky, Loren. *Persons, Rights, and the Moral Community*. New York and Oxford: Oxford University Press, 1987.
Machan, Tibor R., ed. *The Libertarian Reader*. Totowa, NJ: Rowman & Littlefield, 1982.
MacIntyre, Alasdair. *After Virtue: A Study of Moral Theory*. Notre Dame, IN: University of Notre Dame Press, 1981.
Mackie, J. L. *Ethics: Inventing Right and Wrong*. New York: Penguin Books, 1972.
McInerny, Ralph. *Ethica Thomistica: The Moral Philosophy of St. Thomas Aquinas*. Washington, DC: The Catholic University of America Press, 1982.
Moore, G. E. *Principia Ethica*. Cambridge: Cambridge University Press, 1908.
Norton, David. *Personal Destinies*. Princeton: Princeton University Press, 1976.
Perry, R. B. *General Theory of Value*. New York: Longman's, Green & Co., 1926.

Porreco, Rocco E., ed. *The Georgetown Symposium on Ethics: Essays in honor of Henry Babcock Veatch.* Lanham, MD: University Press of America, 1984.
Robins, Michael H. *Promising, Intending, and Moral Autonomy.* Cambridge: Cambridge University Press, 1984.
Rothbard, Murray. *The Ethics of Liberty.* New York: Humanities Press, 1982.
Searle, John R. *Speech Acts.* Cambridge: Cambridge University Press, 1969.
Stevenson, Charles L. *Ethics and Language.* New Haven, CT: Yale University Press, 1944.
Toulmin, Stephen. *An Examination of the Place of Reason in Ethics.* Cambridge: Cambridge University Press, 1953.
Williams, Bernard. *Morality: An Introduction to Ethics.* New York: Harper & Row, 1972.
———. *Ethics and the Limits of Philosophy.* Cambridge, MA: Harvard University Press, 1985.
Wolff, R. P. *The Autonomy of Reason:* A Commentary on Kant's *Groundwork of the Metaphysics of Morals.* New York: Harper Torchbooks, 1973.

Part III. A Concluding Miscellany, Ranging from a Defense of the Humanities to a Defense of Natural Law

Re the Humanities

Abrams, M. H. *The Mirror and the Lamp: Romantic Theory and the Critical Tradition.* New York: W. W. Norton & Company, 1953.
Alquié, Ferdinand. *The Philosophy of Surrealism.* Translated by Bernard Waldrop. Ann Arbor: The University of Michigan Press, 1965.
Babbitt, Irving. *Rousseau and Romanticism.* Boston: Houghton Mifflin, 1919.
———. *Literature and the American College.* Boston and New York: Houghton Mifflin, 1908.
Bird, Otto A. *Culture in Conflict: An Essay in the Philosophy of the Humanities.* Notre Dame and London: University of Notre Dame Press, 1976.
Bloom, Allan. *The Closing of the American Mind.* New York: Simon and Schuster, 1983.
Bowra, C. M. *The Greek Experience.* New York: Mentor Books, 1957.
Crane, R. S. *The Idea of the Humanities.* Vols. 1 and 2. Chicago and London: University of Chicago Press, 1967.
Eagleton, Terry. *Literary Theory: An Introduction.* Minneapolis: University of Minnesota Press, 1983.
Graff, Gerald. *Literature Against Itself: Literary Ideas in Modern Society.* Chicago and London: University of Chicago Press, 1979.
Hutchins, Robert. *The Higher Learning in America.* New Haven, CT: Yale University Press, 1936.
Lilge, Frederic. *The Abuse of Learning: The Failure of the German University.* New York: Macmillan, 1948.
Maritain, Jacques. *Education at the Crossroads.* New Haven, CT: Yale University Press, 1943.
Palmer, Richard E. *Hermeneutics: Interpretation Theory in Schleiermacher, Dilthey, Heidegger, and Gadamer.* Evanston, IL: Northwestern University Press, 1969.
Steiner, George. *In Bluebeard's Castle: Some Notes Towards the Re-definition of Culture.* London: Faber and Faber, 1976.
Wind, Edgar. *Art and Anarchy.* New York: Vintage Books, 1969.

Winters, Yvor. *In Defense of Reason*. Denver: Alan Swallow, 1947.
——. *The Function of Criticism*. Denver: Alan Swallow, 1957.

Re Natural Law

Ackerman, Bruce A. *Social Justice and the Liberal State*. New Haven, CT: Yale University Press, 1980.
Crowe, Michael B. *The Changing Profile of Natural Law*. The Hague: Martinus Nijhoff, 1977.
D'Entrèves, A. P. *Natural Law: An Introduction to Legal Philosophy*, 2nd ed. London: Hutchinson University Library, 1970.
Dworkin, Ronald. *Taking Rights Seriously*. Cambridge, MA: Harvard University Press, 1977.
Finnis, John. *Natural Law and Natural Rights*. Oxford: Clarendon Press, 1980.
Fuller, Lon L. *The Morality of Law*. New Haven and London: Yale University Press, 1964.
Grisez, Germain. *The Way of the Lord Jesus*. Vol. 1, *Christian Moral Principles*. Chicago: Franciscan Herald Press, 1983.
Hart, H. L. A. *The Concept of Law*. Oxford: Clarendon Press, 1961.
Hittinger, Russell. *A Critique of the New Natural Law Theory*. Notre Dame, IN: University of Notre Dame Press, 1988.
Jenkins, Iredell. *Social Order and the Limits of Law*. Princeton: Princeton University Press, 1980.
Macedo, Stephen. *The New Right vs. the Constitution*. Washington, DC: Cato Institute, 1986.
Machan, Tibor. *Human Rights and Human Liberties*. Chicago: Nelson Hall, 1975.
Nozick, Robert. *Anarchy, State, and Utopia*. New York: Basic Books, 1970.
Rawls, John. *A Theory of Justice*. Cambridge, MA: Harvard University Press, 1971.
Schall, James V. *Reason, Revelation, and the Foundation of Political Philosophy*. Baton Rouge and London: Louisiana State University Press, 1987.
Simon, Yves. *Philosophy of Democratic Government*. Chicago: University of Chicago Press, 1951.
Strauss, Leo. *Natural Right and History*. Chicago: University of Chicago Press, 1953.
Wild, John. *Plato's Modern Enemies and the Theory of Natural Law*. Chicago: University of Chicago Press, 1953.

Index

Ackerman, Bruce A., 320
Ackrill, J. L., 2
Adams, Henry, 221–222, 223
Aeschylus, 204
Anscome, Elizabeth, 2
Aquinas, St. Thomas, 1, 2, 3–4, 7, 9, 10, 13, 27, 30–31, 41, 118, 119, 132, 135–136, 139, 171, 193, 197, 243, 254, 256–258, 259, 260, 265, 266n, 269, 280, 283, 284, 285, 287, 289–290, 291n, 292, 294, 296, 299, 300, 304, 306, 307–310
Aristotle, 1, 2–11, 12–13n, 13, 27, 28, 30–31, 37, 41–42, 54, 57, 58, 72–73, 84n.11, 91, 92, 99–103, 104, 106–110, 113, 116, 118, 130, 132, 135, 137–138, 162, 171, 184, 190–198, 201, 205, 207–208, 213, 225–226, 232, 234, 244, 248, 250, 252–253, 254, 258nn.7,8, 283, 285, 296, 299–300, 301, 304, 310, 324
Arnold, Matthew, 41
Augustine, St., 269
Austen, Jane, 203–204, 231–234, 249–250, 252
Austin, John, 2, 47, 281
Avogadro, Amedeo, 211

Bach, Johann Sebastian, 238, 245
Badeau, Adam, 221
Baier, Kurt, 161, 182
Barker, Sir Ernest, 142
Barry, Brian, 313–314
Bennett, William, 240
Bentham, Jeremy, 281
Bergmann, Gustav, 3, 57, 210
Bernstein, Richard, 81
Blackstone, Sir William, 322
Blake, William, 208, 213
Bolingbroke, Henry St. John, 203
Bosanquet, Bernard, 142
Bourke, Vernon, 256–257, 266n
Bowen, William Gordon, 239, 241
Bowra, Sir Maurice, 204
Bradley, Francis Herbert, 38, 142

Brahe, Tycho, 65
Brandt, Richard, 46, 167
Brennan, William J., 312
Burke, Edmund, 268
Burns, Robert, 52
Butler, James, Earl of Ormonde, 222–223

Caiaphas, 271
Callicles, 296
Cartwright, Richard, 76–77
Charles I (King of England), 202, 222
Churchill, Winston, 49
Clark, Sr. Mary, 55
Clarke, Fr. Norris, 55
Cleaver, Eldridge, 210
Cooper, John, 2, 99n, 100
Cromwell, Oliver, 49, 205, 223, 243, 244
Crowe, M. B., 254, 267, 280n

Dante, 212, 245
Danto, Arthur, 81–82, 83, 85, 87, 88
Darwin, Charles, 210
Davidson, Donald, 2, 47
Davis, Fr. Royden, 25
Davis, Herbert, 202
D'Entrèves, A. P., 254, 269, 280n
Derrida, Jacques, 80–81, 82, 83–84
Descartes, René, 13, 26, 36–38, 57, 243, 262, 304
Dewey, John, 38, 79, 83
Dixon, Maj., 219–220, 221
Donagan, Alan, 26, 46, 117–123, 125–126, 133, 138, 139, 164, 167, 273–274
Donne, John, 208, 213, 246
Dryden, John, 243
Duhem, Pierre, 64–65
Dworkin, Ronald, 272, 273, 313–320, 325, 328, 329

Einstein, Albert, 33, 50, 210–211
Esau, 52

Feyerabend, Paul, 50, 278n
Finnis, John, 279–305, 310, 311

335

336 INDEX

Firth, Roderick, 182
Foot, Philippa, 144, 146–147, 151
Frankena, William, 117n.2, 131, 132, 133, 151–152, 159, 167, 178
Furth, Montgomery, 2

Galileo, 211, 216, 262
Garibaldi, Menotti, 222
Gauthier, R. A., 101–102, 103, 108, 110
Geach, Peter, 2
Gewirth, Alan, 26, 46, 158–172, 185n.14, 273–275
Gibbon, Edward, 213–214
Gilson, Etienne, 2, 28
Ginsberg, Alan, 208, 210, 212
Gracia, Jorge, 2n
Grant, Ulysses S., 24, 221–222, 223
Grisez, Germain, 140n, 290, 291n, 292, 293n.2, 298–311
Grotius, Hugo, 254, 259, 269

Hanson, N. R., 50, 278n
Hardie, W. F. R., 100
Hare, R. M., 46, 102, 143, 144, 146, 162, 167
Harman, Gilbert, 60, 76
Hart, H. L. A., 272, 280, 281, 282
Hartle, Col., 219, 220
Hartman, Edwin, 2
Haydn, Joseph, 238, 245
Healy, Fr. Timothy, 246–247, 248
Hegel, Georg Wilhelm Friedrich, 4, 26, 54, 152–153, 160, 268
Heidegger, Martin, 26, 48, 77, 83, 210
Heisenberg, Werner, 50, 142
Hemingway, Ernest, 208
Henle, Fr. Robert J., 25
Herbert, George, 213
Herrick, Robert, 212
Hitler, Adolf, 49, 261
Hobbes, Thomas, 103, 104, 107, 108, 187, 263–264, 265, 266, 268, 274, 297, 304
Homer, 68, 87
Honderich, Ted, 291n
Hooker, Richard, 171, 261, 262, 265, 276, 277
Hume, David, 13, 161, 168, 185, 215, 268, 303–304
Hyde, Edward, Earl of Clarendon, 202, 207, 223

Irwin, Terence, 2
Isaiah, 34, 212

Jaspers, Karl, 26

Jenkins, Iredell, 314–317, 318, 319, 320, 328
Johnson, Judge Fred M., 316, 317
Johnson, Samuel, 20, 202
Joyce, James, 207

Kafka, Franz, 203, 204
Kant, Immanuel, 13, 14, 38–39, 53, 54, 58, 61n, 66–74 passim, 76, 92, 93–94, 99n, 101, 118–125 passim, 132, 133, 134, 143, 146, 148, 149, 150–151, 153, 159, 160, 161, 164–165, 167, 169n, 173, 174, 213, 216, 225, 228, 229–230, 274, 308
Kelsen, Hans, 269, 281
Kepler, Johannes, 50, 62, 65
Khomeini, Ayatollah Ruhollah, 49
Kierkegaard, Søren, 182
Kilpatrick, James J., 312–313, 318, 319
King, Charles, 186n.16
Kripke, Saul A., 47
Kuhn, Thomas, 50, 86, 154, 278n

Law, William, 214
Lear, Jonathan, 2
Leibniz, Gottfried Wilhelm von, 26
Lewis, C. I., 26, 71, 216
Lincoln, Abraham, 41, 42
Locke, John, 254
Lomasky, Loren, 185, 186nn.16,17, 187n
Louis XIV (King of France), 205
Lovejoy, A. O., 26
Lucretius, 44, 213
Lyell, Sir Charles, 211

Macaulay, Thomas Babington, 207
McClellan, Gen. George B., 236
McFeely, William S., 24
Machiavelli, 263
Machina, Kenton F., 61n
MacIntyre, Alasdair, 2, 81, 152–153
McKeon, Richard, 169n
McLean, Fr. George, 55
Mahommet, 49
Mao Tse-tung, 49
Maritain, Jacques, 255
Marx, Karl, 4, 38, 49, 322
Meese, Edwin M., III, 312, 318, 319, 320
Melissus, 4
Mendel, Gregor Johann, 211
Merleau-Ponty, Maurice, 210
Mill, John Stuart, 161
Moore, G. E., 3, 13, 46, 142, 144, 145, 178, 268

Napoleon, 49
Neurath, Otto, 70, 73, 75
Newton, Sir Isaac, 12–13n, 50, 62, 210, 262
Nietzsche, Friedrich Wilhelm, 26, 40, 81–82, 83, 85, 86, 88, 91, 261
Nozick, Robert, 46, 102, 159, 272–273, 282, 320, 321–323

Ovid, 244
Owens, Father Joseph, 2–3, 6, 7, 19, 25, 55, 132n.20, 135–136n.27

Parmenides, 4–5, 8, 9, 10, 12
Pascal, Blaise, 214
Paul, St., 27, 34–35, 250
Perry, R. B., 26, 46
Pilon, Roger, 166n.2
Plato, 4, 5, 57, 103, 106, 132, 171, 192, 225, 244, 254, 256, 296
Popper, Sir Karl, 48, 50, 61–64, 86, 215–216, 278
Porreco, Rocco, 24–25
Prichard, H. A., 100, 167
Pufendorf, Samuel, 254, 269

Quine, W. V., 3, 13, 38, 47, 48, 51, 53, 57–59, 83, 87

Rand, Ayn, 175
Rawls, John, 46, 100, 102, 159, 167, 271–272, 273, 282, 320, 321, 322, 323
Raz, J., 281
Rochester, Earl of, 122
Rorty, Richard, 3, 13, 40, 81, 82–86, 88–91, 93–95
Ross, W. D., 27, 100, 167
Rossovsky, Henry, 239
Rousseau, Jean-Jacques, 254
Rubens, Peter Paul, 245
Russell, Bertrand, 3, 13, 38, 45–46, 47, 142
Ryle, Gilbert, 2, 47

Sartre, Jean-Paul, 38, 48, 77
Savile, Sir Henry, 202, 205
Searle, John, 143, 144, 154–155
Sellars, Wilfrid, 3, 38, 48

Shakespeare, William, 206–207, 238, 245, 246, 247, 317
Shcharansky, Anatoly, 256
Sheffer, Henry M., 26
Sidgwick, Henry, 180
Smart, J. J. C., 68n
Socrates, 4, 33, 100, 132, 176, 177, 181, 183n, 233, 244, 249–250, 254, 256, 261, 296, 307
Sontag, Susan, 210
Sophocles, 204, 212, 256
Spinoza, Baruch, 26, 57, 298
Stalin, Josef, 261
Stevens, John Paul, 312
Stevenson, Charles, 46
Strauss, Leo, 103, 104, 106, 107, 108, 109, 111, 260, 261, 262, 263, 264, 266
Strawson, Peter, 2, 48, 70, 77
Suarez, Francisco, 280
Sweeney, Fr. Leo, 55
Swift, Jonathan, 204, 213

Thomas, Dylan, 246
Toricelli, Evangelista, 216
Toulmin, Stephen, 46, 143, 144
Trevor-Roper, Hugh, 207
Turnbull, Robert, 2n
Twain, Mark, 230

Vazquez, Gabriel, 280
Veatch, Gen. James C., 220, 221
Veatch, Janie, 25
Ver Eecke, Wilfried, 23

Ward, John William, 240, 243–244, 250
Wedgwood, C. V., 222–223
Whitehead, Alfred North, 26, 57
Wild, John, 27
Williams, Bernard, 100, 176–177, 178, 179, 181
Williams, K. P., 220–221, 235–236
Winters, Yvor, 206
Wisdom, John, 141–142, 156–157
Wittgenstein, Ludwig, 3, 26, 47, 48, 77, 83, 149, 210, 211
Wolff, Robert Paul, 69, 101, 109, 124–125, 132, 134, 135

Yeats, William Butler, 246

www.ingramcontent.com/pod-product-compliance
Lightning Source LLC
Chambersburg PA
CBHW031405290426
44110CB00011B/267